First Comes Love

First Comes Love

Power Couples, Celebrity Kinship and Cultural Politics

Edited by
Shelley Cobb and Neil Ewen

Bloomsbury Academic
An imprint of Bloomsbury Publishing Inc

B L O O M S B U R Y
NEW YORK • LONDON • NEW DELHI • SYDNEY

Bloomsbury Academic
An imprint of Bloomsbury Publishing Inc

1385 Broadway	50 Bedford Square
New York	London
NY 10018	WC1B 3DP
USA	UK

www.bloomsbury.com

BLOOMSBURY and the Diana logo are trademarks of Bloomsbury Publishing Plc

First published 2015

© Shelley Cobb, Neil Ewen, and Contributors, 2015

Library of Congress Cataloging-in-Publication Data
First comes love: power couples, celebrity kinship and cultural
politics/edited by Shelley Cobb, Neil Ewen.
pages cm
Includes bibliographical references and index.
ISBN 978-1-62892-121-2 (hardback) – ISBN 978-1-62892-122-9 (paperback)
1. Celebrities--Social aspects. 2. Unmarried couples. 3. Married people. 4. Popular
culture–United States. 5. Fame–Social aspects. I. Cobb, Shelley, editor.
II. Ewen, Neil, editor.
CT105.F46 2015
305.5'20973–dc23
2015003281

ISBN: HB: 978-1-6289-2121-2
PB: 978-1-6289-2122-9
ePub: 978-1-6289-2120-5
ePDF: 978-1-6289-2119-9

Typeset by Deanta Global Publishing Services, Chennai, India
Printed and bound in the United States of America

For Susan and Jason

Contents

List of Illustrations

Acknowledgements

Sincere thanks to the contributors, who worked diligently and enthusiastically, and who made compiling the volume a real pleasure. Hannah Hamad, who stepped in at short notice, deserves special gratitude. Vanessa Díaz put us in contact with Eduardo Pimentel and Galo Ramírez, who kindly gave permission to publish their original photography. Katie Gallof and Mary Al-Sayed at Bloomsbury have been generous and helpful throughout. We are grateful, too, for the comments of the reviewers who appraised the proposal: Christine Becker, Jennifer Clark, Sean Redmond and another anonymous reader.

Thanks to Diane Negra, who has been a mentor to us both for over a decade, and whose invitation in 2011 to present a co-authored paper (on *The Beckhams*) at UCD set in motion a series of events culminating in the publication of this volume. One of those, the 'Celebrity Couples' conference at the University of Southampton in November 2012, saw more than thirty scholars from around the world present original and stimulating research, some of which has been reworked and appears herein. We should like to thank everyone who attended the conference, as well as those sponsors who provided financial support: the English discipline and The Centre for Modern and Contemporary Writing at the University of Southampton; and Routledge Journals. We are also very grateful to Sarah Churchwell, Diane Negra and Linda Ruth Williams for their keynote addresses, for contributing to this volume, and for their ongoing support to our work.

We appreciate greatly the constant backing provided by our families and friends. Thanks to our clans in Scotland (Dave, Brenda, Graham, Shaheen and grandparents) and California (Ty, Rosie, Tyson, Lauren, Rebecca, Hugh, and all our nieces and nephews: Joy, Tristan, Kennedy, Ellis, Walker, McKenzie and Evan). Thanks to our folk in England, too (Nicky Marsh, Liam Connell and Malachy and Jonah; Mary Hammond and Mike Hammond; and Yvonne Tasker and Rachel Hall). Cheers to Mindi Combs, Stephen Harper, Holly Shepherd Edmonds and Rick Edmonds.

This book is dedicated to Susan and Jason Starr: our family, best friends and favourite couple.

Contributors

Sarah Churchwell is professor of American literature and public understanding of the humanities at the University of East Anglia, UK. She is the author of *Careless People: Murder, Mayhem and The Invention of The Great Gatsby*, *The Many Lives of Marilyn Monroe*, and co-editor of *Must Read: Rediscovering the Bestseller*, as well as many scholarly articles and book chapters. Her literary journalism has appeared internationally, including in the *New York Times Book Review*, *Guardian*, *TLS* and *New Statesman*, among many others, and she is the Eccles Writer in Residence at the British Library for 2015. She comments regularly on arts, culture and politics for UK television and radio, and has judged many literary prizes, including the Bailey's (Orange) Prize for Fiction and the Man Booker Prize for Fiction in 2014.

Shelley Cobb is associate professor in Film and English at the University of Southampton, UK. Her research interests centre on women and contemporary media culture. She is the author of *Adaptation, Authorship and Contemporary Women Filmmakers* (Palgrave Macmillan, 2014) and has published on women directors, celebrity culture, chick flicks, film adaptation and breast cancer culture. She is the principal investigator of the AHRC-funded research project 'Calling the Shots: Women and Contemporary UK Film Culture, 2000–2015'.

Beccy Collings teaches in the Interdisciplinary Institute for the Humanities at the University of East Anglia, UK. She has recently conducted research on the relationship between humour and aesthetics in British dark comedy television, and her ongoing research interests include the body in performance, and celebrity studies, particularly in relation to Action and Adult films.

Vanessa Díaz is a journalist, filmmaker and PhD candidate in Anthropology at the University of Michigan. A Ford Foundation and Smithsonian Institute Fellow, she is currently completing her dissertation, 'Manufacturing Celebrity, Marketing Fame: An Ethnographic Study of Celebrity Media Production'; she also wrote and produced the independent feature-length documentary *Cuban HipHop: Desde el Principio* (2006).

Rachel Dwyer is professor of Indian cultures and cinema at SOAS, University of London. Her main research interest is in Hindi cinema. Among her many books is one in the British Film Institute's 'World Directors' series about one of the great figures of the Hindi film industry, Yash Chopra, with whom she worked for several years. She later wrote the BFI's guide to '100 Bollywood films'. Her most recent book is *Bollywood's India: Hindi cinema as a guide to modern India* (London: Reaktion; Chicago: University of Chicago Press)/*Picture abhi baaki hai: Bollywood as a guide to modern India* (New Delhi: Hachette). Her forthcoming books are *Bollywood* (Critical concepts in media and cultural studies), 4 edited volumes (London: Routledge) and *Key concepts in modern Indian studies* (New Delhi: Oxford University Press/New York: New York University Press), co-edited with Gita Dharampal-Frick, Monika Kirloskar and Jahnavi Phalke.

Neil Ewen is a lecturer in Film and Media Studies at the University of Winchester, UK. His research concerns cultural politics, particularly in the realms of sport and celebrity. His writing has appeared in various academic publications, and he is currently preparing a monograph on soccer, affect, and national identity in England.

Hannah Hamad is a lecturer in Film Studies at King's College London. She joined the department in January 2013, where she teaches in the areas of film history, the cultural politics of contemporary Hollywood cinema, fathers in film, and research and scholarship in Film Studies. Previously she worked as a lecturer in Media Studies at Massey University in New Zealand from 2009 to 2012, where she taught in the areas of gender and race in the media, popular culture, and stardom and celebrity. She is the author of *Postfeminism and Paternity in Contemporary US Film: Framing Fatherhood* (London and New York: Routledge, 2013) as well as numerous articles on postfeminist cultures of popular film and television, Hollywood stardom, contemporary celebrity culture, and UK cultures of reality TV. And she is a member of the editorial board of the journal *Celebrity Studies*.

Michael Hammond is associate professor in Film at the University of Southampton, UK. He is the author of *The Big Show: British Cinema Culture in the Great War (1914-1918)* (2006) and many scholarly articles on silent cinema, film history and stardom. He is also the co-editor of *The Contemporary Television Series* (2005), *Contemporary American Cinema* (2006) and *British Silent Cinema and the Great War* (2011).

Suzanne Leonard is associate professor of English at Simmons College, and the author of *Fatal Attraction* (Wiley-Blackwell, 2009) and co-editor of *Fifty Hollywood Directors* (Routledge, 2014). Her specialties include feminist media studies, American film and television studies, and contemporary women's literature, and her articles have appeared in *Signs, Feminist Media Studies, Genders*, and *Women's Studies Quarterly*, as well as in various anthologies.

Alice Leppert is assistant professor of media and communication studies and film studies at Ursinus College. Her work has appeared in *Cinema Journal, Celebrity Studies, Genders, In Media Res, In the Limelight and Under the Microscope* (Continuum, 2011) and in the forthcoming *Cupcakes, Pinterest, Ladyporn* (University of Illinois Press, 2015).

Diane Negra is professor of film studies and screen culture and head of film studies at University College Dublin. She is the author, editor or co-editor of nine books, the most recent of which are *Gendering the Recession: Media and Culture in an Age of Austerity* (with Yvonne Tasker, Duke, 2014) and *Extreme Weather and Global Media* (with Julia Leyda, Routledge, 2015). She is co-editor of *Television and New Media*.

Maria Pramaggiore is professor and head of media studies at Maynooth University in Kildare, Ireland. She is the co-author of *Film: A Critical Introduction* (2011) with Tom Wallis and has published widely on cinema and television. Her most recent book is *Making Time in Stanley Kubrick's* Barry Lyndon (2014). She is currently co-editing *Vocal Projections: The Voice in Documentary* with Bella Honess Roe and writing a monograph on horses, cinema and modernity.

Margaret Schwartz is assistant professor of communication and media studies at Fordham University. Her work has appeared in *Genders, Communication Plus One* and *Framework*. Her book *Dead Matter: The Meaning of Iconic Corpses* is forthcoming from the University of Minnesota Press in Fall 2015.

Anthea Taylor is a lecturer in the Department of Gender and Cultural Studies at the University of Sydney, Australia. She is the author of *Mediating Australian Feminism* (Peter Lang, 2008), *Single Women in Popular Culture: The Limits of Postfeminism* (Palgrave Macmillan, 2012), and *Celebrity and the Feminist Blockbuster* (Palgrave Macmillan, forthcoming).

Linda Ruth Williams is professor of film in the English Department at the University of Southampton, UK. She is author of four books including *The Erotic Thriller in Contemporary Cinema* (2005) and editor of others including *Contemporary American Cinema* (with Michael Hammond, 2006), as well as author of numerous articles on gender, sexuality and censorship in US and UK cinema and culture. She is now writing a book on childhood and child performers in Spielberg's films (*Steven Spielberg's Children*, Rutgers University Press, forthcoming), and, with Shelley Cobb, is developing a large-scale project on contemporary British women filmmakers.

Michael Williams is associate professor in Film at the University of Southampton, UK. His monograph *Film Stardom, Myth and Classicism: The Rise of the Hollywood Gods*, exploring the use of antiquity in the creation of Hollywood stardom, was published by Palgrave Macmillan in 2012. He is also author of *Ivor Novello: Screen Idol*, a contextual study of arguably British cinema's first major film star (BFI, 2003), co-editor of the collection *British Silent Cinema and the Great War* (Palgrave Macmillan, 2011), as well as various articles and chapters on stardom, heritage cinema and British film. He is currently writing on a book for Palgrave Macmillan that examines stardom and the ancient past from 1930 to the present.

David Zeglen is a PhD student in Cultural Studies at George Mason University. He is also a lecturer in GMU's Department of Global Affairs. His research focuses on the cultural politics of post-Cold War dictatorships, on globalization and critical theory, and on North Korea's official culture and ideology.

Introduction

Shelley Cobb and Neil Ewen

We all know that in celeb land, two big names – think Victoria and David, Beyoncé and Jay-Z – equals more than twice the influence.

Clare Geraghty[1]

Power couples and other kinds of celebrity relationships are extremely visible in the everyday circulation of celebrity identity in today's western media, yet up to this point they have received very little sustained scholarly attention. One key signifier of the attraction, ubiquity, power and cultural value of celebrity relationships is the recent rise of what is referred to as the portmanteau, but is also known as the uni-name/blended name/combined name/composite/name-mesh/bundled celebrity couple.[2] Among the most recognizable names in this trend are *Brangelina* (Brad Pitt and Angelina Jolie), *Tomkat* (Tom Cruise and Katie Holmes), *Bennifer* (Ben Affleck and Jennifer Lopez/Ben Affleck and Jennifer Garner), *Kimye* (Kim Kardashian and Kanye West) and *Billary* (Bill Clinton and Hillary Clinton). Further down the celebrity hierarchy we find such names as reality TV couple *Speidi* (Spencer Pratt and Heidi Montag) and the former Disney Channel alumni *Zanessa* (Zac Efron and Vanessa Hudgens). The portmanteau phenomenon arises in a number of chapters in this volume and is interrogated in different ways. While it is well known that Douglas Fairbanks and Mary Pickford's four-storey, twenty-five room Beverly Hills mansion was named 'Pickfair' by the press way back in 1919, the film historian Michael Williams, in his chapter here, has uncovered what might be the first instance of a celebrity couple portmanteau in his original archival research on Greta Garbo and John Gilbert: a fan letter from 1928 that pronounces the couple *Gilbo*, a name that stuck with the pair.

The portmanteau couple appeared in various forms sporadically throughout the twentieth century. Examples mentioned in this volume include various business ventures, such as Desilu, the production company of the married couple Desi Arnaz and Lucille Ball who shot to fame in the 1950s' hit television show *I Love Lucy* (CBS, 1951–7), and Lenono Music, the name of John Lennon and Yoko Ono's publishing company established in 1980. As the academic and celebrity reporter Vanessa Díaz shows in her chapter, however, the portmanteau couple accelerated as a phenomenon in the mid-2000s when *People* magazine's New York bureau (where Díaz worked) conjured the juggernaut term *Brangelina*. As Díaz writes, although *Bennifer*'s first iteration (comprising Affleck and Lopez) had at that point enjoyed a modest degree of cultural currency for a couple of years, the advent of *Brangelina* in 2005 saw a 'snowball' effect on the use of portmanteaus. Díaz's chapter stands out in this volume for its inside perspective of the celebrity media industry, explaining the processes behind the use of the term, before going on to examine what she calls its 'social meanings'.

While the rise of the portmanteau is indicative of the ubiquity of celebrity couple in contemporary western media culture, 'the blending of celebrity couples' names', as Díaz argues, is also 'an exclusionary practice that predominantly promotes white heteronormativity': as of yet, no gay or lesbian celebrity couples have been given a portmanteau, and *Kimye* is the only portmanteau couple that includes a person of colour. In her chapter here, Maria Pramaggiore suggests that the portmanteau 'thoroughly endorses heterosexual hegemony'. The fact that there are other white, heterosexual couples that do not have celebrity portmanteaus does not discount either of their arguments, but goes to show that the power and reach of the celebrity power couple is not easily quantified. *The Beckhams* are a couple that, as Neil Ewen points to in his chapter, have had a name change – from *Posh n' Becks* to *The Beckhams* – that appears to signal both their movement across class boundaries and their current identity as a famous family whose children are part of their group identity (see Figure 0.1). They are not the only famous family with celebrity currency in the media, of course – Brad Pitt and Angelina Jolie, Beyonce and Jay-Z, Will Smith and Jada Pinkett Smith – are all high-profile examples of celebrity couples with children who, to varying degrees, are recognized as celebrities themselves, but whose famous families add exponential value to their commercial and cultural appeal.

The public fascination with these celebrity relationships is evinced in many ways: from the space they are given in celebrity magazines to the airtime on entertainment shows and to the words written about them on celebrity gossip

Figure 0.1 *The Beckhams* out and about in Los Angeles, 19 April 2008.
Photo: Galo Ramírez

websites. They also circulate beyond the celebrity gossip sphere. The celebrity 'listicle' (a short form of writing made popular by bloggers that uses lists to structure the content) often goes viral on social media and there are many variations on the celebrity couple or family given prominence and cultural capital by mainstream publications: *Forbes* has one list for the 'highest earning celebrity couples' and another for the 'world's most powerful couples', *US Weekly* lists 'Hollywood's gay power couples', *The Guardian* lists the ten best power couples, and *Men's Health* details the 'hottest' celebrity couples. Families appear in *Glamour*'s list of 'acting dynasties', the *Huffington Post*'s 'seventeen gorgeous celebrity families', and *Marie Claire*'s 'famous Hollywood families'. The chapters that make up this volume respond in various ways to this expanding celebrity couple universe.

* * *

Of course, the present volume is not only concerned with portmanteau celebrity couples, but a wide variety of celebrity relationships, and the politics that inform their identities. *First Comes Love* therefore intervenes into star and celebrity studies by placing front and centre different types of celebrity relationships, focusing on their production and reception and the multiple meanings they generate. It challenges the now established critical position that individualism is at the heart of stardom and celebrity. As Martin Barker[3] and P. David Marshall[4] have shown, interest in fame has a long history, however it is now generally accepted that it was not until the institutionalization of film studies in the university during the 1970s and 1980s that academic studies of stardom blossomed as an area of scholarship. Film studies provided the foundation from where this focus on the individual performer arose, rising particularly out of the seminal work of heavyweight scholars such as Richard DeCordova,[5] who investigated the 'picture personalities' of the early twentieth century, and Richard Dyer,[6] who paid close attention to the film star as a cultural text and highlighted that stars should be acknowledged as ideological 'signs' whose power said something profound about their socio-historical contexts. In his *Heavenly Bodies*, first published in 1986, Dyer writes: 'Stars articulate … ideas of personhood, in large measure shoring up the notion of the individual but also at times registering the doubts and anxieties attendant on it.'[7]

This focus on the individual continued as the study of celebrity emerged and expanded from its star studies origins, with many of its now canonical texts emphasizing and reproducing the power and importance of the single celebrity. P. David Marshall's *Celebrity and Power: Fame in Contemporary Culture* (1997), for example, 'addresses the way the celebrity has been represented, critiqued, and celebrated, in order to clarify the articulation of power that the celebrity embodies as an individual'.[8] Meanwhile, Chris Rojek's foundational taxonomy, elaborated in *Celebrity* (2001), configures 'ascribed' celebrity – whereby fame follows from bloodline – as a remnant of the past, which serves to emphasize that 'achieved' celebrity – which comes as a result of talent and/or labour – as being particular to the contemporary, relatively democratized world. Rojek notes that 'celebrity divides *the individual* from ordinary social life', and suggests that 'to be a celebrity is to be recognized as different'.[9] As Graeme Turner notes in the second edition of *Understanding Celebrity* (2014) – an updated version of another highly influential text – 'Most accounts of the history of celebrity relate it to, among other things, the pairing of the growth of individualism with the rise of democracy.'[10] Turner himself flirts with critiquing the power of collective celebrity in a discussion about 'brand-bands' in general, and the Spice Girls in particular, arguing that their girl-band celebrity power was always more than the sum of its parts; however, this assessment is fairly brief and it remains underexploited as a point of inquiry.[11] Moreover, Su Holmes and Sean Redmond's influential collection of essays, *Framing Celebrity: New Directions in Celebrity Culture* (2006),[12] begins by elaborating the desires for fame embodied by Redmond's fictional creation 'Leif Memphis', in an entertaining and ironic commentary of the narcissistic individualism associated with contemporary celebrity culture: 'I want to be a star. I want to be adored. I want to see and hear the screams of *my* fans and the roar of an ecstatic applause.'[13] The importance and the power of the individual celebrity are therefore indisputable. In many cases, however, the construction of even the single celebrity is bound up in discourses of companionship that have yet to be taken into account by academic celebrity studies.

* * *

This volume is split into four sections – *Golden Couples, Kinship, Marriage* and *Love* – which were dictated by the process of its production. As editors, we were not prescriptive in terms of content, or of interpretations of central concepts such as 'cultural politics', and we gave our contributors relatively free reign to approach their subjects in any manner they so chose. Beyond making key decisions, such as limiting the historical scope of the book so that it reached only so far back as the early twentieth century (something we elaborate upon below), the volume was shaped by our contributors' imaginations and intellectual interests. There are obvious risks to this approach, such as the potential for a lack of cohesion that may manifest politically or thematically. As it turned out, however, the quality of the chapters we received more than assuaged our anxieties. While there is no 'party line' on methodological or ideological approach, the diversity of the individual threads has, we think, created a rich and complex tapestry that we hope will be of interest to many readers. In the process of production, key themes and concerns quickly began to emerge and the sections that structure the final draft began to make themselves clear. Each section has its own short introduction (which includes summaries of the individual chapters), but we should note here that we began with a section on the early Hollywood period because of its centrality to the historiography of stardom and celebrity that we outline above. We should also note that the volume is weighted towards the present, with the scholarship in the opening section providing historical context for later chapters that engage with, and critique, the ways celebrity relationships dramatize companionship in a contemporary world in which neoliberal policies have increasingly compromised the pursuit of togetherness and community. The sections are not hermeneutically sealed: so, for example, themes of marriage, or (especially) love, bleed out of their respective sections and can be found colouring chapters located elsewhere; although it is true to say that, by and large, each section theme is a particular focus of the chapters within it. The astute reader will identify other motifs not granted their own sections – such as the importance of weddings, sex and branding, to name but three – and will likely find other connections not highlighted here.

Readers will also note many celebrity examples that this book does not cover, as well as limitations of historical, geographical and theoretical scope. We have already noted the issue of history, and are aware that the history of celebrity couples and relationships could be extended much further into the past. Indeed, this volume grew out of an academic conference that showcased presentations of original research on celebrity relationships that went back as far as the French Revolution in 1789. Due to restrictions of length, and our desire for the volume to have a clear(ish) underlying chronological trajectory, we made the decision before commissioning the chapters to impose this historical boundary. In terms of geography, we acknowledge from the outset that the volume is considerably western centric. Partly this is due to our own locations and limitations as scholars, but is also a reflection of the ways that Hollywood has dominated studies of stars and celebrities thus far. While the volume does include excellent contributions on non-western subjects (see, for example, the chapters by Zeglen and Dwyer), there is clearly much more theoretical and critical work to be done in terms of charting and examining celebrity relationships from outside our limited geographical context.

In terms of practical and theoretical methodology, there is also much more room for expanding the study of celebrity relationships in the future. As the title suggests, the focus of this volume falls particularly on cultural aspects and textual functions of celebrity couples and kinship relations. While each chapter is aware of its own peculiar socio-historical and cultural context, and many attend to issues of production, few of the chapters here (with perhaps the exception of Díaz and Leppert) anatomize the conditions of production to the extent of, say, a book like Turner, Bonner and Marshall's *Fame Games: The Production of Celebrity in Australia* (2000).[14] As such, we would welcome future interventions into this area that explore in more detail the celebrity production industries, taking into account such aspects as publicity, management and the work of agents. We would also encourage a wider diversity of theoretical approaches. This volume does not include, for example, sociological work on reception that details and scrutinizes gossip sites and other forms of celebrity fan culture, such as fan fiction, in terms of the ways these areas interact with celebrity relationships. Furthermore, we would like to see emerge a more widespread coverage of the different industries in which celebrity relationships are produced and reproduced. Future research might take into account couples from the realms of sport, literature, politics, business, royal families other than the British monarchy, music and fashion, to name but a few: and, of course, more relationships that straddle industries and cross disciplinary and national boundaries.

Finally, we are also very aware that many readers will be disappointed that their favourite celebrity couple or family does not feature in this volume. One of the peer reviewers of the proposal for *First Comes Love* commented that to satisfy every expectation the anthology would need to run to fifty volumes. We thought it rude to ask for that many from Bloomsbury. But we do hope this is a beginning to work in this area and not an end.

Notes

1 Clare Geraghty, 'Perfect Pairs: The New Power of Two', *Mail Online*, 15 April 2012, http://www.dailymail.co.uk/home/you/article-2128307/Carey-Mulligan-Marcus-Mumford-The-new-British-power-couples-.html.

2 Linda Ruth Williams is one of the few writers to have previously interrogated this phenomenon. See 'Brangelina: Celebrity, Credibility, and the Composite Überstar', in *Shining In Shadows: Movie Stars of the 2000s* (London: Rutgers University Press, 2012), 200–19. See also Erin Clements, 'Kimye, Brangelina, Bennifer: The Evolution Of Celebrity Couple Nicknames', *Huffpost Celebrity*, 18 April 2012.

3 Martin Barker, 'Introduction', in *Contemporary Hollywood Stardom*, ed. Thomas Austin and Martin Barker (London: Arnold, 2003), 1–24.

4 P. David Marshall, *Celebrity and Power: Fame in Contemporary Culture*, new ed. (Minneapolis: Minnesota University, 2014), xi–xlvi.

5 Richard DeCordova, *Picture Personalities: The Emergence of the Star System in America* (Urbana and Chicago: University of Illinois Press, 1990).

6 Richard Dyer, *Stars* (London: BFI, 1998); Richard Dyer, *Heavenly Bodies: Film Stars and Society*, 2nd ed. (Abingdon: Routledge, 2004).

7   Richard Dyer, *Heavenly Bodies*, 9.

8   Marshall, *Celebrity and Power*, 4.

9   Chris Rojek, *Celebrity* (London: Reaktion, 2001), 177, our emphasis.

10 Graeme Turner, *Understanding Celebrity*, 2nd ed. (London: SAGE, 2014), 27.

11 Ibid., 62.

12 Su Holmes and Sean Redmond, *Framing Celebrity: New Directions in Celebrity Culture* (Abingdon: Routledge, 2006).

13 Ibid., 1.

14 Graeme Turner, Frances Bonner and P. David Marshall, *Fame Games: The Production of Celebrity in Australia* (Cambridge: Cambridge University Press, 2000).

Part One

Golden Couples

Shelley Cobb and Neil Ewen

In *The Classical Hollywood Cinema: Film Style and Mode of Production to 1960*, David Bordwell, Janet Staiger and Kristin Thompson estimate that 85–95 per cent of mass culture movies before 1960 contained a significant romance element.[1] As the dominant form of mass entertainment in the first half of the twentieth century, Classical Hollywood clearly had the power to shape hegemonic western notions of romance and intimacy. In her analysis of screen couples like Fred Astaire and Ginger Rogers and Katherine Hepburn and Spencer Tracy, Martha Nochimson is more interested in how the couples' on-screen performances

> articulated a multifaceted fantasy universe in which the various couples they played ... create a nuanced portrait of passionate connection. ... The screen couple in its most significant form has a significance beyond business and basic narrative issues. It is about the way we process information about eroticism and intimacy.[2]

The chapters by Michael Williams and Michael Hammond in this section show how issues of fantasy, business, eroticism and intimacy – which Nochimson identifies as central to the analysis of the screen couple – also structure the representation of Golden-era couples' off-screen celebrity lives. In fact, their investigations of fan magazines of the 1920s and 1930s suggest that these issues are even more explicitly at play in the discursive negotiation of stardom between the stars, the studios, and the fans.

Of one of the few real-life couples in her book, Hepburn and Tracy, Nochimson says, "'belief" in the characters they played, and thus in the ideological positions they espoused, depended upon what the public believed about Hepburn and Tracy as private persons'.[3] Williams and Hammond take this idea further by showing how what the public believed about the couples and the ideological positions of the roles they played were more complicated than Nochimson's statement allows; partly because of the ways the studios had a hand in managing the image of the stars both on screen and off, and partly because of the agency of individual fans who may not have 'believed' certain narratives of the star couples so easily. Importantly, both chapters consider how the polysemic formation of the star couple, as an entity that is interconnected with the individual stars' identities but also distinct from them at the same time, is 'related to contradictions in ideology – whether within the dominant ideology, or between it and other subordinated/revolutionary ideologies'.[4] By situating the celebrity lives of their star couples in their socio-historical context, Williams and Hammond articulate a foundation for understanding the ways public discourses of love, sexual attraction and marriage (key themes running through the present volume as a whole) not only constructed the image of the celebrity couples' lives but also how they contributed to public perceptions of these discursive signifiers of coupledom.

Though much of the historiography of stardom and celebrity focuses on Hollywood and its stars in the 1920s and 1930s, during this period new forms of celebrity came into existence outside the Hollywood sphere. As Sarah Churchwell shows in her chapter here, 'The symbiotic relationship between celebrity and American aristocracy began to flourish in the early 1920s.' In his history of the gossip columnist Walter Winchell, Neal Gabler shows how publicity came to be the source of social power over wealth, breeding, or talent, and he says that 'social authority in the early thirties had been turned on its head: it is now derived from the media'.[5] Churchwell's close analysis of the celebrity coupledom of Scott and Zelda Fitzgerald demonstrates how contemporary concepts of celebrity should not be seen as just developments of star theory and analysis, but that celebrity has been an important sign of status in American culture since the earliest decades of the twentieth century.

Like Williams and Hammond, Churchwell's analysis is based on original archival research. This methodology allows all three chapters in this section to shed new light on this early period of stardom and celebrity in two important ways. First, all three chapters chart an unwritten history of early-twentieth-century stardom and celebrity by showing how important couples were to the fan magazines and gossip columns of the time. Second, they not only challenge Barry King's assertion that 'from the perspective of the audience … stars appear as finished products of semiotic labor',[6] but also illustrate that the contemporary obsession with the production of celebrity has long historical roots. Taken together, these chapters demonstrate that the semiotic labour of stardom has always been a process of change and maintenance; furthermore, they show that the changing private lives of these stars always seeped through and informed the ways they appeared in the imaginations of the public.

In his chapter, '"Gilbo-Garbage" or "The Champion Lovemakers of Two Nations": Uncoupling Greta Garbo and John Gilbert', Michael Williams' excavation of the history of early celebrity coupledom reveals possibly the first celebrity portmanteau of two Hollywood stars – *Gilbo*. He shows how the couples' 'on-screen romance slipped to off-screen passion' and how the off-screen passion seemed to inform their on-screen liaison in a way that troubled some fans. He argues that *Gilbo* – a term created by a fan – 'was a term that granted [fans] agency to express their views not only about the couple but about what a star should be and how they should behave'. He considers this particular form of fan agency as emblematic of the final years of the silent era when the phenomenon of the individual star as a remote and divinized being, of which Garbo is the exemplar, reached 'such mythic heights that the pedestal was bound to wobble'.

Sarah Churchwell picks up the theme of the changing status of fame in the 1920s, and in her chapter, '"The Most Envied Couple in America in 1921": Making the Social Register in the Scrapbooks of F. Scott and Zelda Fitzgerald', she shows how 'the Fitzgeralds understood the capacity of envy to operate as itself a status symbol, one that they catalogued and commodified in [their] scrapbooks.' That the Fitzgeralds loved fame and glamour is widely agreed among scholars. However, Churchwell uses their scrapbooks of various news and gossip items about them (both individually and as a couple) and a close reading of Scott Fitzgerald's long out-of-print essay 'Rolling Junk', to suggest that 'the tendency has been for the Fitzgeralds' audience to psychologize this value system [of acclaim and envy] as a symptom of the couple's pathologies', when rather, as she argues, it is 'symptomatic more generally of the era they are widely held to have epitomized'.

After Williams' focus on the agency of fans in the production of celebrity and Churchwell's focus on the self-production of celebrity, Michael Hammond turns to the Hollywood studios' management and re-production of Clark Gable's and

Carole Lombard's star coupledom. In his chapter, '"Good Fellowship": Carole Lombard and Clark Gable', Hammond argues that though Gable was still married and Lombard was recently divorced when they first became a public couple in 1935, 'their respective studios (Paramount and MGM) worked to "normalize" their relationship as pragmatic and in touch with changing attitudes toward marriage as the Great Depression wore on'. As he notes, the economic crash of 1929 and its aftereffects meant that 'marriage was simply too expensive for many young couples', and he suggests that as a celebrity couple, Gable and Lombard 'offered a model for childless working couples … that chimed with broader attitudes toward coupling that the times demanded'.

Notes

1 David Bordwell, Janet Staiger and Kristin Thompson, *The Classical Hollywood Cinema: Film Style and Mode of Production to 1960* (New York: Columbia University Press, 1985), 16.

2 Martha Nochimson, *Screen Couple Chemistry: The Power of 2* (Austin: University of Texas Press, 2002), 6–7.

3 Ibid., 189.

4 Richard Dyer, *Stars* (London: BFI, 2002), 26.

5 Cited in Graeme Turner, *Understanding Celebrity*, 2nd ed. (London: SAGE Publications, 2014), 24.

6 Barry King, 'Stardom and symbolic degeneracy: Television and the transformation of the stars as public symbols', *Semiotica* 92, no. 1–2 (1992): 3.

1

'Gilbo-Garbage' or 'The Champion Lovemakers of Two Nations': Uncoupling Greta Garbo and John Gilbert

Michael Williams

In the summer of 1928, in the golden age of the picture palace, a self-confessed 'flapper' wrote to *Picture-Play* magazine in exasperation at ubiquitous coverage of the celebrity coupling of silent stars Greta Garbo and John Gilbert, since they had set screens ablaze in *Flesh and the Devil* (Clarence Brown, 1926).[1] In describing this coverage as 'Gilbo-Garbage', nearly a century before the ubiquitous *Bennifers* and *Brangelinas* of the contemporary celebrity age discussed by others in this volume, we find a fan apparently coining their own portmanteau term for the star coupling, as on-screen romance shifted to off-screen passion. *Gilbo*, an inharmonious phrase designed to mock the vacuous nature of celebrity, while evidencing its power, is evoked as a sign of resistance to the rising public fascination with star culture and particularly the private lives of the stars. In the final years of the silent era, the phenomenon of the star as a remote and somewhat divinized being – of which Garbo is the exemplar – reached such mythic heights that the pedestal was bound to wobble.

As the fan letter above testifies, ever since the release of Brown's film, few fans across the USA and Europe were unaware of Garbo and Gilbert's romance, both on and off the screen. Perhaps precisely because the exact nature of their relationship was shrouded in mystery and intrigue and so fuelled speculation then as now, it was a gift to studio publicists and gossip columns alike and their screen coupling would be repeated in a further three films. This ostensibly unlikely combination of Garbo, the 'Stockholm Venus',[2] and the dashing American idol, was central to Metro-Goldwyn-Mayer's publicity campaign for the film, and would consolidate Garbo's stardom in this, her third Hollywood feature. The stars obligingly arrived arm-in-arm at *Flesh and the Devil*'s Hollywood premiere, with the *Los Angeles Times* noting their screen roles 'may or may not account for the appearance of the two arm in arm at the premiere', alluding to a blurring of on- and off-screen worlds. The paper added that the stars 'were supposed to have been engaged at one time and who have since, according to report, broken that engagement'.[3] In this way, fans were invited to participate in a guessing game with the press and, by proxy, the stars and sometimes, as we shall see, arguments with other fans. The contrasts between the couple and the uncertainty about what actually happened between them is as much a part of *Gilbo* as the seemingly genuine affection shared by two high-powered and talented stars. The pairing also deepened the mythology of Garbo as the siren who lures but who must always be alone, and Gilbert as a full-hearted but troubled romantic, whose career was faltering before his untimely death of a suspected heart attack in 1936 (linked to his problems with alcohol). If Garbo (with Stiller's assistance), as Betsy Erkilla has noted,[4] authored herself in choosing the name 'Garbo' over her original Greta Lovisa Gustafsson, then *Gilbo* is a name authored by fans in resistance to studio promotion and press fascination with the couple. Whether they were for or against the stars, it was a term that granted them agency to express their views not only about the couple, but about what a star should be and how they should behave.

While the *Gilbo* timeline is uncertain, the story goes that the couple fell in love during the shooting of *Flesh and the Devil* in the late summer of 1926, with Garbo soon moving into Gilbert's Los Angeles home. There are different accounts of a marriage being arranged for 8 September that year, with some contemporary reports stating that Garbo jilted Gilbert at the altar at a planned double wedding (with actress Eleanor Boardman and King Vidor), or that she had never actually intended to marry him in the first place. Another attempted marriage was reported in April 1927, along with the story of Gilbert's short spell in jail after brandishing a revolver following a disagreement with Garbo's close friend, director Mauritz Stiller.[5] Indeed, Stiller was described as 'Garbo's first and greatest love' in the press with, needless to say, no mention of Stiller's homosexuality.[6] Coincidentally, or not, *Flesh and the Devil* continued to break records at the box office while this intrigue was running. By 1928, Garbo's biographers tell us that she had moved out of Gilbert's home, with Gilbert hastily, and briefly, forming another celebrity couple by marrying actress Ina Claire in May 1929. Garbo stayed loyal to Gilbert, however, respecting the professional support he had given her in the past and insisting that he co-star with her in their final film together in 1933, *Queen Christina* (Rouben Mamoulian). All this time, Garbo's famously taciturn and media-shy personality contrasted with the garrulous Gilbert, whose later seemingly unguarded outpourings to the press when the relationship did not lead to the marriage he desired would not have endeared him to Garbo. It perhaps also challenged Gilbert's 'great lover' image, already affected by other troubled couplings, as we shall see.

This chapter will focus on the earlier period of Garbo and Gilbert's association, from late 1926 leading up to the release of *Flesh and the Devil* until around 1930, when the debates around *Gilbo* were still raging in the letters pages of *Picture-Play* magazine in particular. I examine how the Garbo–Gilbert romance, 'real' or 'fictional', impacted on the stars' reception and had lasting implications for the images of both stars and particularly Garbo, who has become synonymous with Hollywood stardom at its most heightened. This chapter thus reads the promotion and fan reception of *Gilbo*, as being as much about the changing nature of stardom as the Garbo–Gilbert relationship itself. I first turn to the film that launched the couple onto the public, *Flesh and the Devil*.

Venus meets the Doughboy

Flesh and the Devil is an adaptation of the 1894 German novel by Herman Sudermann, and stars Gilbert as Leo, and Lars Hanson as Ulrich; two military men who have shared a close friendship since childhood. Upsetting the symmetry of their relationship is Garbo's Felicitas, a married woman with whom Leo has an affair. The discovery of this illicit romance results in a duel, in which Felicitas' husband is killed by Leo, who is then sent into temporary exile at a military outpost in Africa. Ulrich marries Felicitas in Leo's absence, not knowing of her past with Leo, and tensions develop when Leo returns and proves unequal to the task of resisting Felicitas as she attempts to rekindle their relationship, once more illicit, upon his return (see Figure 1.1).

Felicitas is one of many 'vamp' figures to cause Garbo to complain of typecasting, the star having just appeared in *The Temptress* (Fred Niblo, 1926). Garbo's success as Felicitas would only reinforce that type, with her reported real-life temptation of Gilbert meaning that the vamp persona would inevitably inform the reception of their relationship; the *Los Angeles Times* would call her 'the luring Garbo' while *Flesh and the Devil* was in production.[7] The image of the alluring and yet distant siren is typical of the way Garbo's Hollywood image had evolved since the early awkward publicity pictures circulated by MGM of

Figure 1.1 Illicit embrace: Felicitas (Greta Garbo) and Leo (John Gilbert) surrender to passion in *Flesh and the Devil* (Brown, 1926).

Garbo posing at the USC athletics track, and shows how the studio struggled to locate, and then dis-locate, the actress in space and time. She thus becomes the 'statuesque blonde' from 'the Land of the Vikings', as one *Picture-Play* feature put it in 1925.[8] Continuing the elemental theme, the *Los Angeles Times* described a maelstrom of emotional peril gathering around the star at MGM, adding that few are truly able to understand her. The star, columnist Katherine Lipke opined, gave meaning to the phrase "there were drowned men in her eyes", describing her as the 'eternal siren' and 'a woman of fatal fascination' (a type later becoming the femme fatale), who had directors clamouring to star the actress in their films. Garbo comes across as powerful and potentially destructive, but is credited as innovative and intense in her performance, even as she struggles to resist typecasting. Her new co-star, Gilbert, however, is described as 'almost beyond the reach of helping hands', and 'does not spare himself in talking of her, and is seen constantly in her presence.'[9] In the same year that European émigré, Rudolph Valentino, was being attacked on a sexist and homophobic basis for being an effeminate or a woman-kept man, there is a hint here that while Gilbert may be unambiguously heterosexual, and certainly passionate, he is somehow 'unmanned' by Garbo, and becomes driftwood caught up in her wake. Although their relationship is not directly mentioned here, a quote from Garbo – unlike Gilbert, words are evidently forced from her – hints at trouble ahead: "'I do not want to get married!" This much she does say, over and over like a well-learned lesson.' The actress then expresses her desire for seclusion away from Hollywood parties and particularly the public gaze, asserting: 'I have not energy enough. People take energy from me and I need it for pictures.' This is revealing, indicating Garbo's resistance to a model of stardom that demands the sharing of one's personal life, and her associated rejection of the institutions of Hollywood society and heterosexual romance alike. By the mid-1920s, Garbo's press already foreshadowed her 'I want to be alone' persona, which a future line from *Grand Hotel* (Edmund Goulding, 1932) would immortalize.

If Garbo was a creature of singular, divinized abstraction, John Gilbert was a man of a more earthly realm. Indeed, despite being one of the silent era's greatest matinee idols, it was Gilbert's particular strength that he made good-looks and romantic sensuality a tangible thing. As Jeanine Basinger puts it, for fans, 'meeting John Gilbert might be a stretch, but it seemed possible'.[10] He is the gregarious Everyman exemplified by his best-known role, an American soldier in *The Big Parade*, MGM's most profitable film of the silent era,[11] released the year before *Flesh and the Devil*. He is affable, gregarious, romantic and American and, unlike Garbo, was seemingly more willing to speak to the press about his own worldly flaws and anxieties, including his troubled marriage to actress Leatrice Joy, which ended in divorce in 1924. Of his star image, Gilbert is quoted as saying in 1927 that he didn't stand a chance until the screen stopped being dominated by 'Greek profiles' and began 'to reflect some of that earthiness which is akin to real life … [so that] my bottle nose and scraggy neck didn't matter'.[12] The contrast between Gilbert and 'the divine' Garbo is striking, making him appear an unlucky hero of Greek myth who meets one of the gods passing their time slumming-it on earth. Gilbert's mannerisms are familiar to the repertoire of screen acting, while Garbo moves with a diffuse and otherworldly gravity. Where the 'divine' Garbo is unknowable, Gilbert is familiar.

This dynamic is evident in Brown's film, as I've explored elsewhere.[13] While Leo and Ulrich possess a shared history whose memory can be recaptured and spaces physically revisited, Felicitas seems to just materialize at a railway station from another realm, her past actively obscured at every turn. I've previously written about the development of the film, and how successive scripts foregrounded a military atmosphere to appeal to Gilbert's persona. The link is underlined when the film's pressbook refers to Gilbert as 'the famous doughboy of "The Big Parade". Railway stations are associated with couples parting and meeting in wartime, and later in the film, as Leo travels home from 'exile', we witness an extraordinary montage sequence where pictures of Felicitas are superimposed in thought bubbles that echo imagery of wartime postcards. Awareness of Gilbert and Garbo's extra-textual romance would have given the film's love triangle an extra frisson. Where the real-world romance of *Gilbo* was fragmented and contested, the screen affair of Felicitas and Leo lent it tangibility through its imagery, fuelling the popular imagination.

'The champion lovemakers of two nations'

Inevitably, most stars' reception involves some slippage between character and performer. In terms of the first screen pairing of Garbo and Gilbert, Felicitas has few redeeming features beyond her glamour and the passionate (and often deceitful) affair she initiates with Leo. Beyond his passion, Leo's finest quality, his rarefied 'bromance' with Ulrich, is only fully realized with the demise of Felicitas, and it is this relationship that the film ultimately privileges and is what lifts it from routine melodrama. When fans choose to attack stars, the easiest weapon is the very discourse that has been fed to them by studios and critics. Thus Garbo is sometimes identified with the worst aspects of Felicitas, and the vamp more widely (as emphasized by the title of her previous film, *The Temptress*), as an avaricious, foreign ice queen, who tricks, breaks hearts and then vanishes. While Garbo's European credentials, and exoticism, were her key features, this was also a target for a wave of xenophobia rippling through American fan magazines in the mid-late 1920s.

MGM's pressbook for *Flesh and the Devil* opportunistically heralded its stars as 'the champion lovemakers of two nations'; a tag line primed for any columnist seeking to blur the lines of on- and off-screen romance. This was also something of a risk. While star romance may fascinate, and offer another level of extra-textual engagement with fans, it is equally likely to irritate and create an air of exclusivity. Even Edwin Schallert's glowing review of the film worried about the 'vulgarity' of a couple of scenes that might cause audiences to titter due to the way it 'over emphasises its love making'.[14] Indeed, a fan from London wrote to *Picture-Play* suggesting that watching Garbo and Gilbert's love scenes was akin to eating too much sticky chocolate cake, and mentions that he has heard that the love scenes had been cut down for London showings:

For this I would pass a vote of thanks to whoever is responsible, because the 'sexy' scenes were the flaws of the picture. Garbo and Gilbert both went at them with a serious savageness that gave me the impression that they were saying to themselves: 'Now, for a treat, we'll give them five minutes' love-making. I'm sure they'll like it. Let's do our best.'[15]

Regardless of the ratio between genuine artistic motivation and exploitation opportunity (it's fair to say there's a bit of both), the love scenes continue to be read, problematically, as evidence of genuine passion between its stars, rather than its characters. Irrespective of the authenticity of the stars' ardour, these differing readings are evidence of fans interpreting star images in different ways, and seizing the polysemic possibilities freely offered to them by film publicity, with the fan magazine acting as their ideal organ for expression. *Picture-Play*'s 'What the Fans Think' letters columns between 1928 and 1930, as we'll see below, saw fans enter the heated 'Gilbo-Garbage' debate.

Many fans saw the publicity around *Gilbo* as a means of entering into dialogue into the nature of stardom itself, and its central fascination with the private life of screen personalities. Biographies have highlighted an unusually hostile article towards Gilbert published by *Vanity Fair* in May 1928 that pulled few punches in its depiction of the star's apparently bad behaviour towards his family, and his alleged abandonment of his wife, actress Leatrice Joy, and their child to pursue his affairs.[16] However, the fan magazines had already been full of veiled, and not-so-veiled, references to the affair over the preceding months. One fan letter that initiated a key thread in this debate was sent in by Irene Hart of Cincinnati, who branded Gilbert a 'woman chaser' and 'egotist', who 'deserted a lovely wife and child', declaring that 'that affair with Greta Garbo finished him for me'. Criticizing his 'nerve' for trying to appeal for public sympathy, Hart points again to the excess of the Garbo–Gilbert relationship – 'It seems he has so much love to waste where it is not wanted' – before concluding, with another xenophobic touch: 'He was once my idol, now he is just another sap to me. Trying to help Greta Garbo live her roles! All this crazy stuff is going to hurt Gilbert more than he thinks. Give me Leatrice Joy any day, and send all the eve-rolling Gretas back to Sweden.' To this fan, the affair seems to have grounded her idol into the sordid everyday realm, tainted by Garbo's representation of 'all' the heightened stardom that seems to come from Europe.[17] The letter is perhaps inflecting the wider reception context in the mid-1920s, with American fan-magazine letters pages printing sometimes xenophobic letters about the presence of foreign stars in Hollywood. Garbo was one of the stars most cited, perhaps adding to some fans' hostility towards her later pairing with the all-American John Gilbert. 'Down with foreigners' railed one Detroit moviegoer, pointedly named 'U.S.A.': 'I am in favor of letting "Getta Cargo," the sensational "find" from Vulgaria, start at the bottom, *with a beginner's salary*, and *work* her way up and *earn* her stardom, if any, before she gets her *cargo* of good American dollars.'[18] The implication being that Garbo's crime was not only in failing to be American but in bypassing the *work* that qualifies the actor to become a star, rather than a puffed-up celebrity.

Among other letters sent to *Picture-Play*, one fan in October 1927 declares that of Garbo's reported behaviour in the studio, but particularly 'her affair' with Gilbert, 'I have long since drawn the conclusion that she is not all there', again returning to the theme of Garbo as a disturbing force.[19] In November, one of two letters on this issue saw a British fan reply to Hart, arguing that 'instead of considering a star as either an "idol" or a "sap," let us think of him as a hard-working individual, a human being with feelings like our own.'[20] The Garbo–Gilbert relationship in this way found fans question what a star should be. It is notable that letters in late 1927 were particularly concerned with the aftermath of the death of Rudolph Valentino in August 1926, which brought focus onto the question of what a star should be, how much their legacy should be idealized, and in what ways their nationality and romantic affairs should be remembered. There is a certain shift in the late 1920s in the public attitudes to stars and a questioning of the pedestals onto which they were placed, and Valentino's death, and the debates around *Gilbo* both fuelled this discussion.

By December 1927, with Garbo–Gilbert's second feature, *Love*, on release, *Picture-Play* was full of such letters, with fans on either side of the debate responding to earlier correspondents (the average three-month publication cycle in this era tends to draw out cycles of discussion). In a letter headed 'In Defense of Mr. Gilbert's Private Life', a Santa Monica fan also takes to task Irene Hart's view of Gilbert:

> For some time I have felt that the practice of revealing the private life of a star to the public, through interviews and various other forms of publicity, is all wrong. … Mr. Gilbert did not "desert his lovely wife and child," as Miss Hart contended, and most likely it is the press agents and interviewers who are "playing on the sympathy of the public," and not Mr. Gilbert.[21]

A female Canadian fan joins in, arguing that no one could blame Gilbert for admiring a 'glorious creature' like Garbo.[22] A male fan, Elmer Walkenhorst, contributes to the same issue, and while accepting the truth of the story, thinks it no concern of the fans so long as stars provide 'good, wholesome pictures': 'Let Jack Gilbert have his own affairs without criticisms from us fans, for if Jack wishes to desert Leatrice, that's his business, and not ours. If he wants to fall in love with Greta Garbo, that his business, not ours.' Finally that month, declaring 'The Battle is Still On!', 'A Southern Fan', declares 'This is in answer to Irene Hart. You poor thing!', before turning to Gilbert: 'Of course, he is not a saint! We grant you that. But when viewing perfect acting, do we need to go into the private affairs of a perfect actor to appreciate art? … We are holding our breath to see how badly hurt Mr. Gilbert is by "all this crazy stuff."'[23] Conceding that Gilbert's 'finest work was not done with Miss Garbo', it seems that it is the Garbo–Gilbert combination that provides the constant thread here.

After the coverage above, it is not surprising that *Picture-Play*'s rival *Photoplay* responded with a weary rhyme for its readers on a February 1928 editorial page:

> Off again, on again, Greta and John again,
> How they have stirred up the news for a while.
> Making the critics first sigh with them, die with them,
> Making the cynical smile
> Off again – on again – Greta
> and John again,
> They say it's over now – let
> that be true!
> Let's hear some other, more
> staple love stories.
> At least they'll be new![24]

Many readers would have agreed. Indeed, *Photoplay* seemed to making the case more strongly in Gilbert's favour, and editor James Quirk, having already backed Gilbert by giving him magazine space to present his own story after the *Vanity Fair* attack, picks up the theme of those letters, and used the occasion of continuing rumours around Garbo and Gilbert to pronounce, somewhat disingenuously (it was still promoting stars as idols as much as it ever was, although perhaps with added tongue-in-cheek disclaimers), upon its position in the construction of stars in its November issue:

> PHOTOPLAY's circulation is increasing because this magazine is not trying to create gods and goddesses; it is concerned with the men and women of the screen and their pictures.

Clara Bow and Greta Garbo are not saints in the eyes of the public, nor are they trying to pass themselves off as criterions of manners and morals. They are popular because they are interesting and because their names carry the guarantee of pictures worth seeing.

John Gilbert and Emil Jannings can draw huge audiences in any theater in this country or in Europe. There are no wings sprouting on Gilbert. But he can act.[25]

The argument that stars should not be divinized, nor held up as ideals, did little to silence the critics, of course, and the Garbo–Gilbert coverage continued through the Spring, with the issue of privacy a key focus. In May 1928, a male fan warned *Picture-Play* readers of the dangers of wanting to know of Garbo and Gilbert's relationship: 'As to their private business – well, you all knew that "curiosity killed the cat."'[26] Another fan extended the lesson:

'I do not attempt to judge the real Greta Garbo by her pictures. I do not take it for granted that Greta Garbo and John Gilbert are having an affair just because they are such perfect lovers on the screen. ... I do not know them personally and have no right to criticize their characters or praise them for being *noble*. I know only their screen personalities. ... For Heaven's sake, let them be responsible for their own characters – let them at least have one thing into which the public cannot pry.'[27]

It was at this point in the summer of 1928, after a year of gossip and argument, and as the release of *A Woman of Affairs* (Clarence Brown, 1928) approached at the end of the year, that a 'flapper' from Montana intervenes and apparently coins the term *Gilbo* in dismay at the celebrity couple's 'contortionist' screen lovemaking:

My gosh! I'm writing to throw a particularly large and heavy brickbat at Greta Garbo. The person who said Garbo is 'a perfectly inane-looking little idiot' is right.

I'm a flapper, and I don't mind telling people so; but whoever said flappers like these hectic love scenes, that Garbo always plays, is all wet! We don't mind petting, but when they start showing that kind of loving, good Lord! ... Can you imagine a normal boy and girl doing the contortionist stunts that Garbo and Gilbert do in the name of love? I can't. Nobody ever sees that except in the movies. That isn't love; it's plain bunk! We call it "Gilbo-Garbage" out here, and the name fits it to a 'T.'

A Flapper Who Is Not a Garbo Fan.
Kalispell, Montana.[28]

The deployment of a hybrid noun for the couple is a somewhat backhanded compliment to their high profile at this juncture. Writing on the *Brangelina* phenomenon of the early twenty-first century, a composite term for the coupling of Brad Pitt and Angelina Jolie, Linda Ruth Williams observes how there 'is a stratum of stardom so elevated that it needs only the simplicity of the given name'. This term becomes a brand name and a shorthand reference for their romance.[29] In the case of *Brangelina*, the portmanteau alludes to figures who are seen to 'exemplify contemporary hyperfemininity and hypermasculinity' and their associated ideals of beauty and social aspiration, and the perennial star tensions between the ordinary and deified image.[30] Unlike *Brangelina* or *Bennifer*, however, *Gilbo* uses the family, rather than given name. This signatory aspect emphasizes formality and distance, and perhaps artistry; especially for Garbo, who, like Chaplin, or Valentino, really doesn't need any more names. Yet as I have already suggested, *Gilbo* is an inelegant term that does little credit to the 'divine' Garbo – the ultimate singularity – while Gilbert is reduced to the 'Gil', which unfortunately reminds one of the way fish breathe (or, indeed, drink) more than anything. It reduces them to the mundane in affecting a flippant and mocking intimacy, and reminds fans of the kind of fallibility Gilbert had recently become associated with. *Brangelina*, too, may be redolent of celebrity magazine fodder, but it has a ring to it, and is more playful than reproving. Brad Pitt and Angelina Jolie were somewhat complicit in the production of their image as a savvy power couple, courting some of the highest fees in magazine publishing history for coverage.[31] However, as Vanessa Díaz indicates in this volume, the stars also resisted the *Brangelina* moniker through Jolie's threat to withdraw cooperation with *People* magazine if they did not refrain from using it. For Garbo, a star famous for avoiding all acts of publicity wherever possible (perversely becoming more lastingly famous *because* of this reclusiveness), the fan production of the pejorative celebrity term *Gilbo*, evidencing the degree to which she had transitioned beyond acting to become a Hollywood celebrity, might have seemed the perfect insult.

The fan from Montana clearly associated 'Gilbo-Garbage' with a form of on-screen sexual excess they viewed as abnormal. Indeed, one can see how a protesting-too-much form of heterosexuality here might be seen to add a Queer dimension to the stars' clearly dysfunctional and increasingly one-sided relationship, with Garbo's homoeroticism becoming magnified into the 1930s, and most famously in her final film with Gilbert, *Queen Christina*. Indeed, from the outset of the Garbo–Gilbert pairing in *Flesh and the Devil*, it is the relationship of Leo and Ulrich that triumphs[32] – described in the press as 'peculiarly forceful'[33] – while heterosexuality is curiously decentred. Arguably, Garbo's presence doesn't un-queer the waters here, and Garbo was a star building a lesbian appeal,[34] who was likely at least bisexual herself and was evidently not inclined to marry. In any case, as the Montana fan implies, it would be the heterosexual pairing of *Gilbo* that would cause most squirms. Garbo is picked out by the fan for attack with the repetition of casual sexism, but in the context of 'What the Fans Think', this is also a perspective informed by publicity focusing on the couple's on and off relationship. In due course, another fan, W. A. Burford, probably male, criticized the 'girl who originated the term "Gilbo-garbage"' for being, as some other fans, 'vindictive in true feminine fashion' in denouncing Garbo's appearance and talent. He then embarks on an extraordinary assertion of the star's mythic appeal, arguing that 'she deserves no ordinary appraisal, yet all I can say is that she is medieval, modern, and futuristic. ... Garbo's beauty lived before the golden age.'[35] Significantly, Burford effectively uncouples *Gilbo* and neglects to mention Gilbert at all. While he mentions other stars, it is Garbo that he seeks to place back on the pedestal as an idol. Another fan in the July 1929 issue uses the 'too-forward love-making' of 'Gilbo-Garbage' (praising the 'flapper fan' who coined it) to praise John Barrymore and Camilla Horn's love scenes by contrast.[36] Even the major columnists started using the term. In the same issue, Norman Lusk's review of Garbo's *Wild Orchids* (Sidney Franklin, 1929), which did not co-star Gilbert, remarked that 'the complete absence of that commodity a fan rather cruelly termed "Gilbo-Garbage" adds to the dignity and credibility of the picture'.[37]

The final reference I have found to 'Gilbo-Garbage', to date, came in March 1930, from a British fan praising Garbo's unique quality, and arguing that she needs better material to escape the trappings of the past:

> Greta has such unique individuality and fascination that she might well be content merely to exploit them, but she doesn't. I believe she could be one of the very greatest actresses the world has known, if she were given stories worthy of her. ... Unfortunately, she has become associated with what has been pithily termed 'Gilbo-Garbage.' John Gilbert is a great actor, but not a great lover.[38]

This and the previous issue contained letters attacking Gilbert's performance in *His Glorious Night* (Lionel Barrymore, 1929), a feature failing to live up to its title and which suffered from infamously poor sound recording and/or direction. It wasn't all Gilbert's fault, but it was a terrible debut in talking pictures. Some fans supported Gilbert, but many voiced the following sentiments: 'Without Greta Garbo there is no such thing as John Gilbert, after seeing him in *His Glorious Night*, and hearing the burst of laughter during his love scenes, when the audience should have been held at the highest pitch of emotion. ... We would rather have silent pictures with Greta Garbo than all the talkies without her.'[39] Thus successfully uncoupled in discourse, *Gilbo* was no more, and Gilbert was no longer romantically associated with Garbo. He remarried in 1929 to actress Ina Claire, before another divorce in 1931, and a final, fourth, marriage in 1932 to another actress, Virginia Bruce. When he starred with Garbo again, she was the major star, with her regal character resolutely steering a path to her own destiny. 'Gilbo-Garbage' was left far behind in her wake.

While not constituting the trend-setting impact of *People* magazine's *Brangelina* spread seventy-seven years later, as discussed by Vanessa Díaz, the fact that *Gilbo* was coined into existence in 1927 indicates a pressure point in the development of screen celebrity; a moment when off-screen gossip threatened to supersede screen performance, though neither could be divorced from the other.

Mythic zenith

Thus one thing that the partnership with Gilbert did do for Garbo was consolidate her persona as one who remains apart from the world, and who bears witness to it with almost sculptural aloofness rather than through the impassioned embraces associated with *Gilbo*. This is a sense conveyed by an interview with Gilbert in between the two reported marriage 'attempts', charitably titled, 'Up Speaks A Gallant Loser', where he is quoted as explaining his fascination with Garbo with the words: 'She is like a statue. There is something eternal about her.' He then relates that Garbo baffled him, but that she was 'dangerous, too. When she comes into a room, every man stops to look at her. And every woman. ... She is capable of doing a lot of damage – unconsciously, of course. Upsetting thrones, breaking up friendships, wrecking homes – that sort of thing.'[40] These words, printed beneath an atypical image of Garbo who appears to be saying 'oops!', seem to describe the melodramatic plot of *Flesh and the Devil* as much as the appeal of Garbo herself, and were indeed printed as that film was on release, their romance seemingly almost over before it has begun. The final line of the piece says much about the value of the stars' relationship: 'Surely Greta Garbo is the luckiest actress in pictures to find, in her rejected suitor, her most ardent press agent.' A very similar spread in *Picture-Play* followed in the summer, titled 'Is the Gilbert–Garbo Match Really off?' and opening with another association with Garbo and the ancient world – 'She is a thousand years old' – their respective captions beneath ever-further separated portraits note her 'calm', and his sadness. Their personae are quite separate and distinct, however, their relationship labelled as 'merely very good pals'; he is described as 'a fighter', 'impassioned', boyish, gallant, but also vain and fitful, and linked here to 'Latin temperament'; she is 'the Scandinavian, confined within its hereditary reserve of the frozen North, moves fatalistically, stoically, heavily'. The more she thought of love as a 'everyday, concrete thing', it opines, the further away she removed herself from it.[41] There were hints in the press that year that Gilbert had lost some of his prestige since the release of *The Big Parade*, and that the pairing with Garbo had served to boost his image through association with her.[42]

Edgar Morin rightly described the celebrity coupling of Garbo and Gilbert as 'the mythic zenith of the star system'.[43] It was a meeting of screen romance with apparent real-world passion, and of the ordinary with the extraordinary star binary described by Richard Dyer; the more present and known Gilbert, with the distant and ever-elusive Garbo. When the film first opened at the Capitol Theatre in New York, the press were incredulous that it hadn't been granted a bigger opening or had not been more widely advertised. The reason why it managed to gain an audience was eagerly pointed to by the *Los Angeles Times*:

> I lay it entirely to the potent appeal of Greta Garbo's name and to some extent the combination of Garbo and Gilbert … [the film] has captivated the highbrow critic who professes to see in it all he wants of rhythm, nuance, tempo and color, and all the way down the line to the tabloid critic who plays up the love scenes for all they are worth, which is a great deal.[44]

Flesh and the Devil would make Garbo MGM's most lucrative female star of the silent era, particularly so for her three films with John Gilbert, but her solo films did particularly well in foreign markets, perhaps indicating the commercial basis to their pairing for MGM's strategy.[45] Garbo, likely, would have developed a similar image without Gilbert, but the flickering light of their binary star is irresistible, and this juxtaposition of 'Venus' and the 'Doughboy' no doubt help crystallize the intangible nature of her appeal. The *Gilbo* affair also functioned, for a brief while, as a microcosm for the mechanisms of stardom. It was fuelled by the tensions between public and private, European artistry and American populism, elusive, sometimes mythologized attraction, plus plenty of sexual intrigue. *Gilbo* – without the 'garbage' – was a marriage worthy of broadsheet *and* tabloid; a commercially expedient, if not entirely civil, partnership.

Notes

I would like to thank the staff of the Cinema-Television Library at USC, and the Margaret Herrick Library (AMPAS), Los Angeles, as well as the BFI Library, London, for their assistance with research contributing to this essay. Thanks also to Shelley Cobb and Neil Ewen for their valuable feedback during the editing process.

1 A Flapper Who Is Not a Garbo Fan. Kalispell, Montana, 'What is "Gilbo-Garbage?"', *Picture-Play*, August 1928, 9.
2 Myrtle West, 'That Stockholm Venus', *Photoplay*, May 1926, 36.
3 'Garbo and Jack Attend', *Los Angeles Times*, 4 February 1927, A8.
4 Gilbert also changed his surname from Pringle.
5 Barry Paris, *Garbo: A Biography* (London and Basingstoke: Sidgwick and Jackson, 1995), 125, 137.
6 'Garbo's First Love', unidentified clipping, folder 251, Greta Garbo—Scrapbook Leaves from a scrapbook entitled: 'Garbo: Her First Thirty Years, September 18—1905—1935', Vertical File Collection, Margaret Herrick Library, Los Angeles.
7 'Claimants to Celebrity', *Los Angeles Times*, 12 September 1926.
8 'From the Land of the Vikings', *Picture-Play*, December 1925, 82.
9 *Los Angeles Times*, 17 October 1926.
10 Jeanine Basinger, *Silent Stars* (Hanover, NH: University Press of New England, 2000), 372.
11 H. Mark Glancy, 'MGM Film Grosses, 1924-1948: The Eddie Mannix Ledger', *Historical Journal of Film, Radio and Television* 12, no. 2 (1992): 127–44 (131).
12 March 1927: 'Manhattan Medley', Aileen St. John-Brenon, 59.
13 See Michael Williams, ch. 5 'The Undying Past: *Flesh and the Devil*', in *Film Stardom, Myth and Classicism: The Rise of Hollywood's Gods* (Basingstoke: Palgrave Macmillan, 2012), 145–73.
14 Edwin Schallert, 'Jannings on First Venture', *Los Angeles Times*, 2 June 1927, 48.
15 G. Pentways, London, 'What the Fans Think', *Picture-Play*, May 1928, 119.
16 See Barry Paris, 172–73; Eve Golden, 164, Golden calls the article 'one of the most jaw-dropping attack pieces ever written about a Hollywood celebrity, before or since'.
17 Irene Hart, Cincinnati, 'She's through With John Gilbert', Ohio, *Picture-Play*, June 1927, 8.
18 'U.S.A', 'Down With Foreigners!', *Picture-Play*, September 1926, 8 [original emphasis].
19 Dorothy Kendall, Milwaukee, Wisconsin, 'What the Fans Think', *Picture-Play*, October 1928, 10.
20 'Dorothy Grace Shore, London, What the Fans Think', *Picture-Play*, November 1927, 12.
21 Virginia Hope Jeffery, Santa Monica, 'In Defense of Mr. Gilbert's Private Life', 'What the Fans Think', *Picture-Play*, December 1927, 10.

22 Hazel Weatherston, Hamilton, Ontario, 'What the Fans Think', *Picture-Play*, December 1927, 10.

23 'The Battle is Still On!' 'A Southern Fan', 'What the Fans Think', *Picture-Play*, December 1927, 114.

24 'Greta Garbo and John Gilbert' in 'Our News Reel in Rhyme' Paris, 125 (from Fountain, 132), I've added text, *Photoplay*, February 1928, 63.

25 James L. Quirk, 'Close-Ups and Long-Shots', *Photoplay*, November 1928, 29.

26 Clayton Lott, Lawrence, Kansas, 'Why Criticize?', 'What the Fans Think', *Picture-Play*, May 1928, 12.

27 Harriette Eikel, 'An Open Letter to Fans', 'What the Fans Think', *Picture-Play*, April 1928, 10.

28 A Flapper Who Is Not a Garbo Fan. Kalispell, Montana, 'What is "Gilbo-Garbage?"', *Picture-Play*, August 1928, 9.

29 Linda Ruth Williams, 'Brangelina: Celebrity, Credibility, and the Composite Überstar', in *Shining in Shadows: Movie Stars of the 2000s*, ed. Murray Pomerance (New Brunswick, NJ: Rutgers University Press, 2012), 200–19 (200).

30 Linda Ruth Williams, 207–08.

31 Linda Ruth Williams, 202.

32 See Michael Williams, op. cit.

33 Edwin Schallert, 'Story Triumph at the Forum', *Los Angeles Times*, 5 February 1927, 7.

34 Andrea Weiss, 'A Queer Feeling When I Look at You: Hollywood Stars and Lesbian Spectatorship In the 1930s', in *Stardom: Industry of Desire*, ed. Christine Gledhill (London: Routledge 1991), 283–98.

35 W. A. Burford, Waukomis, Oklahoma, 'Rudeness Out of Place, But—', 'What the Fan's Think', *Picture-Play*, April 1929, 11–12.

36 Florence F. Dostal, Mercer Island, Washington, 'A Rose for Camilla', 'What the Fan's Think', *Picture-Play*, July 1929, 11–12.

37 Norbert Lusk, 'The Screen in Review', 'The Eternal Triangle' (review of *Wild Orchids*), *Picture-Play*, July 1929, 104.

38 Marguerite Edgelow, Gerrard's Cross, England, 'Upholding Fellow Fans', 'What the Fan's Think', *Picture-Play*, March 1930, 11.

39 'The Accused Please Rise', 'What the Fan's Think', *Picture-Play*, February 1930, 10.

40 Agnes Smith, 'Up Speaks a Gallant Loser', *Photoplay*, February 1927, 32–33, 120.

41 'Is the Gilbert-Garbo Match Really off?', *Picture-Play*, March 1927, 24–25, 98.

42 Edwin Schallert, 'Story Triumph at the Forum', *Los Angeles Times*, 5 February 1927, 7.

43 Richard Dyer, *Stars* (London: BFI, 1997); Edgar Morin, *The Stars* (Minneapolis: University of Minnesota, 2005) [originally published 1957], 52.

44 Norbert Lusk, 'Long Lines at Garbo Picture', *Los Angeles Times*, 16 January 1927, C25.

45 Glancy, 132.

2

'The Most Envied Couple in America in 1921': Making the Social Register in the Scrapbooks of F. Scott and Zelda Fitzgerald

Sarah Churchwell

He has distorted the anecdotes that people have told him in such a way as to put Scott and Zelda in the worst possible light, and he has sometimes taken literally the jokes and nonsense that Scott was always giving off in letters and conversation and representing them as sinister realities. On the other hand, he gives no sense at all of the Fitzgeralds in the days when they were soaring.

Edmund Wilson, 1950 letter concerning Arthur
Mizener's biography of F. Scott Fitzgerald, *The Far Side of Paradise*[1]

'Superior People – Who Aren't'

In her 1932 autobiographical novel *Save Me the Waltz*, Zelda Fitzgerald famously offers a quasi-fictionalized account of her marriage to Scott Fitzgerald, in which a Southern belle marries a brilliant artist whose sudden fame catapults the couple into wealth and the highest social circles. They paste all the newspaper clippings that mention them into 'four bulging scrapbooks full of all the things people envied them for.'[2] Like their fictional counterparts, the Fitzgeralds also kept scrapbooks that registered, and measured, the assumed envy of others; by the end of their lives they had accumulated five, one that was labelled with Zelda's name, and the other four with Scott's. The clippings across all five scrapbooks frequently mention them in tandem, however, which is fitting for a couple whose celebrity had always been at least partly symbiotic.

A month after *Save Me the Waltz* came out, Fitzgerald wrote a story in which he makes a similar observation about a celebrated young couple who 'thought of themselves as a team, and it was often remarked how well mated they were. A chorus of pleasant envy followed in the wake of their effortless glamour.'[3] By the early 1930s, such recollections were wistful: few people were envying Scott and Zelda as they struggled with the consequences of Zelda's mental breakdown, Scott's escalating alcoholism, and the collapse of Wall Street. In 1933, the Fitzgeralds met with Zelda's doctor to discuss their struggles; Zelda said their marriage had been a battle for as long as she could remember, and Scott replied, according to the doctor's notes, 'I don't know about that. We were about the most envied couple in about 1921 in America.' Zelda responded, 'I guess so. We were awfully good showmen.'[4]

The idea that the Fitzgeralds were awfully good showmen has become a truism in the writing about them. Their self-consciousness was part of a burgeoning culture of emulation, in which status envy emerges as a key gauge for assigning a value to fame, and measuring achieved celebrity.[5] In particular, I will argue, the Fitzgeralds understood the capacity of envy to operate as itself a status symbol, one that they catalogued and commodified in the scrapbooks. Their mutual recognition of the constitutive force of status envy marks an early intuitive registering of the basic Foucauldian insight that modern power is often productive, and not merely coercive. After Scott's death, Zelda wrote their daughter: 'Daddy loved glamour & I also had a great respect for popular acclaim.'[6] The conflation of glamour with acclaim is telling: glamour, acclaim and envy are all functions of the audience, dependent upon that audience for ratification. But the tendency has been for the Fitzgeralds' audience to psychologize this value system as a symptom of the couple's pathologies, rather than as symptomatic more generally of the era they are widely held to have epitomized. If it is true, as Edmund Wilson observed, that 'if ever there was a pair whose fantasies matched it was Zelda Sayre and Scott Fitzgerald', it is equally true that those fantasies matched those of their society, and continue to do so.

By no coincidence the two pairs most frequently cited as America's 'first celebrity couple' are Scott and Zelda Fitzgerald, and Mary Pickford and Douglas Fairbanks, the era's most famous movie stars.[7] The two couples were married within less than a week of each other, in the spring of 1920. *This Side of Paradise*, which catapulted Fitzgerald into fame, was published on 26 March; Pickford and Fairbanks were married on 28 March, while Scott and Zelda married on 3 April 1920. If the marriage of Pickford and Fairbanks might fairly be viewed as a merger, a joint investment of two individuals' celebrity stock, both Scott and Zelda were unknown until the success of his book combined with their mutual physical attractiveness, outrageous behaviour and instinct for self-promotion to win over audiences across the country. They quickly began to deploy their own publicity as a status symbol, simultaneously emulating the markers of upper-class distinction and ironizing them.

The fact that art was said to be imitating life had contributed greatly to the initial success of *This Side of Paradise*, which was viewed as a scandalous exposé of the lives and loves of America's privileged youth. Ruth Prigozy offers a usefully representative summary of the received wisdom regarding the Fitzgeralds' enthusiasm for self-promotion, and its relation to self-authorship, what she calls 'the couple's public role-playing, as fabricated as everything else they concocted for public consumption in those days', a mythology that she rightly deems 'suspect'. Nonetheless, much of their behaviour was 'aimed at keeping their image alive for the public and further enhancing their legend'.[8] This sense that their behaviour was a calculated performance was never distinct from their celebrity; many years later, John Dos Passos remembered disapprovingly, 'They were celebrities in the Sunday supplement sense of the word – they were celebrities, and they loved it'.[9]

The Fitzgeralds' scrapbooks, registering that celebrity, have been variously ignored or dismissed as a symptom of their vanity: in the early 1920s their friends Edmund Wilson and John Peale Bishop created a burlesque 'exhibit of Fitzgeraldiana for Chas. Scribner's Son's', which sarcastically comprehended his 'entire seven-book library', including a notebook and two scrapbooks.[10] Keeping a scrapbook was considered prima facie a dubious enterprise, an ersatz substitute for proper aesthetic dedication as symbolized by a personal library. Biographer Jeffrey Meyers adds that this mocking catalogue reflected, for Wilson and Bishop, 'Fitzgerald's immaturity, vanity, shallowness, narcissism'.[11] But the Fitzgeralds' scrapbooks are not mere registers of self-regard: they also constitute a reception history, one that returns consistently to tropes of class and status, often in ironic ways.[12] Restrictions of space mean I can only read the scrapbooks gesturally here, but a few representative pages will, I hope, suggest some of the ways in which we might usefully complicate the simplistic, and moralistic, charges of 'narcissism' and 'exhibitionism' that continue to trail the Fitzgeralds, occluding our reading of the complexities of their mutual construction of celebrity.[13]

Far from being chronicles of self-absorption, the scrapbooks demonstrate that the Fitzgeralds were profoundly attuned to, and always registering, the social; and they were liable to lampoon status-consciousness, as well as seeking ratification from it. We might bear in mind that such a burlesque is, in one sense, the entire thrust of *The Great Gatsby,* which *The New Yorker* described upon its publication in 1925 as 'a most brilliant satirical story' about a bootlegger who proves a 'pearl of chivalry' but is 'cast before swine on Long Island', the supposedly 'superior people – who aren't'.[14] The Fitzgeralds' scrapbooks can be read, in this context, as a highly provisional inventory of what might – and might not – constitute social superiority in their era. At a time when the Social Register remained the arbiter of so-called superior people in high society,[15] the Fitzgeralds' scrapbooks were making the social register in every sense: they were registering the social, making it count, and validating their aspirational social status, all at once.

The Fitzgeralds were joined in a mutual desire for the high life, loosely defined, and they were members of a society that was increasingly shaped by aspirational emulation, a normative value they eagerly embraced in their early years. The role of self-promotion in the development of modernist art has been much discussed over the last few decades.[16] The publicity the Fitzgeralds generated, however, continually threatened to backfire when they were viewed as stepping across the boundaries of taste and discretion, into unacceptably obvious self-promotion, which was read as 'egotism'. Zelda saved one clipping that referred to her facetious review of *The Beautiful and Damned,* which the New York *Tribune* commissioned from her in the belief that she would add some celebrity 'sparkle' to their review pages (a letter that Zelda also pasted into her scrapbook).[17] The piece ended: 'From the things one has read about Fitzgerald the impression was that he is an abnormal young man with a supreme ego, but with such a sensible wife with such ready wit and fine differentiation of thought, it does not seem possible that his ego will ever get a chance to be too obstreperous'.[18] Similarly Zelda saved another clipping that claimed:

> Fitzgerald is not nearly so black as he has been painted. His bad reputation has been fostered by publicity sleuths who always try to give the public what it wants. ... We are accustomed to this kind of rumour in regard to stage stars, but it is fairly new in relation to authors. The great drinking bouts, the petting, may be what the public expects of Fitzgerald, whose books told so much of this kind of life. However, if there is so much smoke, some of it must be of Fitzgerald manufacture. ...[19]

It was the age of 'ballyhoo', the increasing recognition that audiences were being sold excitement itself, and the manufactured was seen as suspiciously inauthentic, even pathological ('abnormal').

At the same time, 'high art' remained defined by the Kantian tradition of an aristocracy of taste marked by its disinterest. As Terry Eagleton famously observed, such a system creates a paradox in which 'the commodity as fetish [is] resisting the commodity as exchange'.[20] Artistic self-promotion signalled self-interest, and thus pre-emptively degraded any aesthetic associated with it: the difference between artistry and a vulgar 'careerism' was troped as the difference between reticence and self-advertisement, the cultured and the philistine, art and commodity, as Fitzgerald himself made clear in 1934 when he wrote to H. L. Mencken that he had eventually made the decision 'that I would rather be an artist than a careerist'.[21]

In the 1920s, professional authorship was in a transitional stage, its symbolic capital still under dispute; so was celebrity, which has worked over the last century to disrupt and to a large extent overturn older intersections of caste and wealth in American society. The symbiotic relationship between celebrity and American aristocracy began to flourish in the early 1920s, and the Fitzgeralds emblematized this fluid process, as celebrity destabilized and altered their class positions, which had already been transformed by Fitzgerald's artistic status. Fitzgerald's negotiations of the troubled relationship between self-marketing and a definition of literary artistry marked by its disinterest in the market have increasingly garnered critical attention: as Timothy Galow notes, literary celebrity for writers like Fitzgerald became 'a complex recursive process that involves authorial actions, the production of specific works, the promotion of texts and their authors, and audience reception'.[22] Amid the Fitzgeralds' documentation of their own celebrity by means of the scrapbooks they compiled, and the self-mythologization that these scrapbooks catalogue, the scrapbooks also register the moment of America's transfer of social power from traditional 'high society' to emergent celebrity culture.

The moment the Fitzgeralds exemplify is by no coincidence the very moment when the iconography of American class aspiration shifted from a glamorized ideal of the patrician life to an ideal of the famous one. As scholars such as Robert Van Krieken have suggested, aristocracy gradually became democratized in two crucial ways: 'Increasing numbers and categories of people gain the capacity to become celebrities, and the power-balance in the relationship between celebrities and their audience shifts increasingly towards the latter, so that celebrity is to a large extent controlled by the audience. ... Celebrities are in many respects *democratized aristocrats*, both the subjects and the objects of power relations.'[23] But this democratization comes at the cost of charges of vulgarization. If Van Krieken is surely right that celebrity gossip 'establish[es] and reproduce[es] a particular moral grammar of recognition and esteem,'[24] any such moral grammar also includes censure and disapprobation. Envy both registers and sustains the democratization of achieved celebrity, constituting a barometer of the pressure of social desire. Fitzgerald grasped this clearly enough that by 1924 he was writing of the 'satisfaction' Jay Gatsby derived from the interest of reporters in his factitious biography. It was a satisfaction that Fitzgerald and his society understood: in *American* magazine in September 1922, Fitzgerald published an article headlined, 'What I Think and Feel at 25', a simple exercise in self-promotion (and income generation). Turning the page he would have seen another headline: 'People Do Love to See Their Names in the Paper.'[25] In fact, the Fitzgeralds' so-called 'exhibitionism' was that of the individual constructing an identity in a mass age, in which celebrity affirms individuation, an idea that is one of the fundamental tenets of celebrity studies.[26]

In Scott and Zelda's case, their enthusiasm for self-promotion rapidly elicited a moralizing strain that persists to this day, a judgementalism that inflects readings of them along axes of both aesthetics and class. Before long the phrase 'the beautiful and damned' would become determinative of our concept of celebrity itself, especially as epitomized by Scott and Zelda Fitzgerald. It is celebrity *per se* that both celebrates their beauty and damns them: the discourse would eventually shift to suggest that the process of modern celebrity itself is destructive – that the very self-consciousness of the celebrity's self-presentation does damage, that the external performance is at odds with the internal 'authentic' identity and that this disjunction creates a gap into which the celebrity plummets (a story that would reach its apotheosis with Marilyn Monroe). As the question of self-consciousness seeps into public awareness, it brings metonymically charged questions of fraudulence and therefore of spiritual or psychological corruption, as well as financial corruption *qua* 'selling out'. As Simone Weil Davis has argued, 'Self-promotion, consumption, assemblage, and display – these became the means whereby many people organized their thinking about selfhood, gender and the fashioning and expression of an identity.'[27] And celebrity was increasingly seen as the ideal validation of such an identity, with envy its ultimate tribute.

"Look me up in the Social Register" (Scott Fitzgerald's Notebooks)

Like most writers of the day, Fitzgerald subscribed to a cutting service to track reviews across local papers around the world. But cuttings also registered mentions of the Fitzgeralds' social achievements, as well as their artistic and professional ones. The conflation of the social and the aesthetic was instant and constant, and if not unique to the Fitzgeralds, it was by no means universal. (Joseph Conrad, for example, whom Fitzgerald greatly admired, employed a cutting service to act as a research assistant and news filter, not to assess his own publicity. Clippings were 'delivered to him in the mails each morning; and he doesn't have to bother to go through the papers reading interminable columns of stuff for something that awakes his interest; but gives him the news, in which he might reasonably be interested, in convenient form'.[28]) But bourgeoning forms of mass media also ensured that clippings provided an easy way to measure a person's status among mass audiences. This is why, for example, Jay Gatsby keeps his own clippings about Daisy, and shows them to her as validation of his fidelity – and, not incidentally, of his status envy ('"Look at this," said Gatsby quickly. "Here's a lot of clippings – about you"'). The Fitzgeralds' scrapbooks are primarily filled with newspaper cuttings about them: stories, news items, reviews, advertisements, gossip columns, photographs and illustrations, which combine to validate the fact of their celebrity while simultaneously offering interpretations and value judgements about it.

Zelda also used her scrapbook to compile more conventional keepsakes and memorabilia, including photographs, programmes, tickets and passports, billets-doux and dancing cards, all blended in among the cuttings. In one sense, these various items might seem to suggest the movement between subject and object, as mementoes of subjective experience are juxtaposed with documents registering objective, or at least externalized, social approbation. But in fact the apparently personal items also serve to register social status. Read together, these mementoes often suggest the triangulation among celebrity, aristocracy and gossip, each presumed to register status. The anonymity of gossip, as embodied by these cuttings, works to reinforce the self-authorized aspect of contemporary celebrity; self-promotion becomes a kind of self-fashioning, the creation of a modern notion of the representative, or idealized, individual. Older models of aristocratic privilege were in the process of giving way to the status of self-fashioned modern celebrity, a contingent transformation that in some sense is registered on the very pages of the Fitzgeralds' scrapbooks.

For example, on one page in Zelda's scrapbook, she pasted four items from 1923 and 1924: an engraved invitation from the film star Gloria Swanson for Mr and Mrs F. Scott Fitzgerald to join her for 'supper & dancing' at the Ritz-Carlton New York at 10 pm on Thursday 27 March; a ticket for game four of the 1923 World Championship polo match; and two photographs clipped from Scott Fitzgerald's nearly forgotten essay 'The Cruise of the Rolling Junk', posed photos of Scott and Zelda that had been used to illustrate the essay in *Motor* magazine when it was published in early 1924.[29] 'The Cruise of the Rolling Junk' was an account of a road trip the Fitzgeralds had made in 1920, in a broken-down second-hand car that they dubbed 'the Rolling Junk'. The car they drove was a Marmon, a prestigious make on a par with a Pierce Arrow or a Packard; in the essay, Fitzgerald calls it an 'Expenso', and much of the comedy of the piece derives from the Fitzgeralds' inability to pay for the upkeep of the 'Expenso', even as they strategically deploy the status that accrues from driving it to negotiate the difficulties they encounter.

I'll say more about 'Rolling Junk' and its posed photos later, but for now suffice it to note the complicated, not to say labile, implications about class and fame from this scrapbook page, which preserves engraved invitations from movie stars to fêtes at the most exclusive (and expensive) of hotels; a ticket to the world championship match of the sport most associated with plutocratic wealth and aristocracy (hence Fitzgerald's decision to make Tom Buchanan a polo player); and the Fitzgeralds' own inclusion in a magazine, complete with accompanying photographs of the famous author and his wife as characters in their own story. That story, however, hinges on their lack of funds to maintain the status symbol in which they are journeying – an image which, in a nutshell, might seem proleptically to sum up the careers of the Fitzgeralds to come, their aspirations to the high life and their inabilities to pay for it. But it also suggests the complexity of their relationships to social hierarchies, the ways in which their experiences veered dizzyingly between emulation of and inclusion within a certain version of high society.

I say a certain version of high society, for it's also worth noting that celebrity winds through all the versions of the high life on offer on this scrapbook page: film stars, famous authors, sporting champions. All are achieved celebrities based (at least in part) on talent or skill, rather than aristocrats defined by inherited privilege. Inherited aristocracy remained marked by a disinterest that was meant to apply to the entirety of economics and the marketplace, so that it was deemed common even to mention money, as when in Fitzgerald's 1924 story 'Love in the Night' an American heiress who has married a Russian prince tells her son, in all seriousness: 'Don't touch me. You've been handling money.' Through at least the mid-1920s, American aristocracy continued to view those in 'the show business' with variations of the suspicion, hostility and contempt reserved for anyone actively engaged in any kind of business. Again, this is the tension Fitzgerald documents in *Gatsby* between the show-business world of West Egg and the disavow-business world of East Egg. Fitzgerald was well aware that old money rejected self-promotion and ostentation as crass: this is why Tom Buchanan drives a plain blue coupé and asks Jay Gatsby not to describe him to party-goers as 'the polo player'. The Social Register remained the manifest of aristocracy in the 1920s, but the older model of heritable privilege was being challenged by achieved celebrity. The two value systems existed simultaneously, and began to intermingle. The Fitzgeralds were not in the Social Register, but their mode of celebrity meant that they rubbed shoulders with the *haut monde*, both in life and in print, as they moved, often uneasily, between the two worlds.

For example, the Fitzgeralds quickly found their way into the New York gossip magazine *Town Topics*, which billed itself 'The Journal of Society' – but for the most part the Fitzgeralds were not described in flattering terms. Because Fitzgerald would burlesque *Town Topics* as 'Town Tattle' in *The Great Gatsby*, the magazine is of particular interest, and the Fitzgeralds appeared in it many times, mostly in items that are censorious, spiteful, or both.[30] Each weekly issue of *Town Topics* opened with a gossip department called 'Saunterings', which was known for its malicious tone and its own close brushes with libel and blackmail[31]; 'Saunterings' focused on the 'fashionable worlds' of the major North American cities, extending even to provincial St. Paul, Minnesota, Fitzgerald's hometown. Most of the names in 'Saunterings' were socially registered, but occasionally the merely famous would slip in, so that the Fitzgeralds appeared alongside the actual aristocrats upon whom Fitzgerald would model the Buchanans' world. For example, Fitzgerald later wrote in a note that the first chapter of *Gatsby* was based on his memories of encountering the 'glamour of the Rumseys and the Hitchcocks' on Long Island; in the pages of *Town Topics* he found his own exploits chronicled among the same polo-playing Charles Cary Rumsey and Tommy Hitchcock. Fitzgerald also saved clippings from the magazine mentioning Mrs. William H. Mitchell III, the married name of Ginevra King, the Lake Forest debutante who had been his first love and was one of the models for Daisy Buchanan.

But *Town Topics* was also notorious for heaping scorn upon social climbers, and the Fitzgeralds soon came under fire. Zelda saved an early clipping from March 1921, pasting above it the masthead *Town Topics*, which suggests that she took pride – or found humor – in the mention. It is a blind item, describing recent press mentions of 'a rising young author in New York who had married a timid and unsophisticated little Southern girl and had introduced her to the gayest of the gay on Broadway'. But 'to those who know the bride before she married the young writer, who has recently sprung into prominence, this "stunt" is by no means evidence of the groom's teaching. In fact, it is generally thought that neither the groom nor any other young Broadwayite could teach this demure-looking Southern girl anything....'[32] Other names mentioned alongside this item include the Astors, Morgans, Vanderbilts and other well-known patrician families. Zelda would doubtless have been gratified not only by the company she was keeping in print, but also by the recognition that she had cut a swathe before Scott Fitzgerald ever crossed her path.

Before long, 'Saunterings' turned decidedly against both Fitzgeralds, on the tide of self-promotion. In 1921, they moved to St. Paul for the birth of their daughter, and lived there until September 1922, when they returned to New York to begin the adventures that would inspire *Gatsby*. In December 1921, *Town Topics* wrote that the citizens of St. Paul, having expected Zelda to be 'a young woman of great beauty and charm, have decided that the young author has indubitable gifts of imagination. He is engaged in imitating his *tour de force* and he has not outgrown his custom of peddling his writings around to his friends.'[33] In August 1922, 'Saunterings' became more hostile:

> Neither Francis Scott Key Fitzgerald ... nor Zelda makes much of a hit. The women are jealous of Zelda's looks and of her soft voice ... and both men and women fear lest Francis should lampoon them in some *a clef* novel. ... Francis behaves in a patronizing way to people who have known him all his young life, and that does not add to his social popularity. To justify his airs his literary baggage should be far less frothy than it is.[34]

By 1923, *Town Topics* was chastising Fitzgerald for 'selling his opinion for many shekels', the anti-Semitic slur implying that self-promotion is an unsavoury usury, an insult that constitutes an implicit policing of Anglo-Saxon ruling-class mores of discretion and disdain for any kind of paid labour.[35] Fitzgerald saved the cutting, unattributed, in his scrapbooks; it is perhaps unsurprising that he decided to pay back *Town Topics* in its own coin, high-hatting it in turn as a jumped-up gossip rag, and burlesquing it as the preferred reading matter of the social-climbing and tasteless Myrtle Wilson.

Self-promotion was part of the age of advertising and publicity that boomed during the 1920s. With the publication of influential books such as Walter Lippmann's 1922 *Public Opinion* and Edward Bernays' 1923 *Crystallizing Public Opinion*, a new field known as public relations emerged along with a language of publicity in the early decades of the twentieth century. In 1904, the word 'publicist' was first recorded; in 1908, 'publicity stunt', then 'publicity value' (1910), and 'publicity monger' (1915). In 1919, a magazine wrote of a society woman who 'did not shun publicity', where previously that would have been what defined her social status. By the early 1920s, as 'mass market' (1922) and 'mass media' (1923) were coined, so were 'publicity hound' (1920), 'publicity release' (1923), 'publicity campaign' (1923), 'publicity person' (1924), 'publicity-shy' (1924), 'publicity driven' (1925), 'publicity-minded' (1929) and 'publicity shot' (1929).[36] Publicity could commodify anything, even entire regions: the 1920s also embraced so-called 'civic boosterism', as citizens were encouraged to be overtly chauvinistic in championing their local businesses and services. On one of Zelda's scrapbook pages, a clipping says that Fitzgerald was 'illustrating his own title', *This Side of Paradise*, as he and Zelda were photographed summering in Westport in 1920. Modern 'paradise' is an image of privileged leisure, ratified by the gossip pages and circulated as an aspirational ideal. Zelda pasted this clipping above an item headlined 'Montgomery Boosted' by the Fitzgeralds' sojourn in Zelda's hometown: their attendant publicity meant that the town benefitted by association – and advertised that fact to compound the publicity.[37] The Fitzgeralds were not just 'boosting' themselves, they were 'boosting' everyone with whom they were associated.

This is the logic of celebrity endorsement, which by no coincidence emerged for the first time in its modern form in the 1920s, thanks to changes in mass media (radio, film, advertisement) and their distribution. By the end of the 1920s, Americans were very clear that endorsement was linked to a culture of emulation. In 1929 American advertisers were informing executives that advertising 'testimonials' (endorsements) worked by arousing the 'spirit of emulation', which derived from consumers' readiness 'to copy those whom we deem superior in taste or knowledge or experience', in a desire for self-improvement.[38] By no coincidence, throughout the 1920s endorsement also registered a shift from socialites to celebrities. As Pamela Church Gibson has noted: 'The cosmetics company Ponds used "Society Ladies" to advertise its products until they were gradually displaced and finally banished by the dominance and the ubiquity of screen actresses in the 1920s and 1930s.' Gibson further argues, however, that 'the bright young things' of the Roaring Twenties, most of them aristocratic, rich or both, and their American counterparts, the flappers, were baptized as such and then closely followed in the press'.[39] Although Gibson's assessment of the British bright young things is indubitably correct, American flappers were not really their 'counterparts', as they were a considerably less aristocratic, and less wealthy, group; conflating the two collapses important differences between them. American flappers, like film stars, were identified with populist and demotic tastes, not aristocratic ones. Indeed, flappers were often associated in American popular culture with working-class girls: as Marjorie Rosen noted, 'flappers were always shopgirls and blue collar workers on screen' in the 1920s,[40] while a 1935 article summed up the attitudes to the American flapper when she emerged in the early 1920s:

> The reading public soon became inured to flappers who revelled in rouge, danced cheek-to-cheek, smoked cigarettes and drank gin, sat in parked cars without chaperones, engaged frankly in petting and 'necking', and talked Freud and sex appeal. These were the younger girls in the stories of Hergesheimer, Lewis, Dell, Atherton, Fitzgerald, and Marks. Their elders looked on, shocked but not greatly alarmed. After all the War had unsettled things. Even grave Victorian gentlemen begrudgingly admitted that these vulgar creatures were an offense more against manners than morals. Certainly the flapper did not regard herself as vicious.[41]

But equally certainly they were regarded by mainstream American society at the beginning as 'vulgar creatures', if harmless ones. Thus Fitzgerald's newspaper-anointed status as America's 'flapper king' was to many a decidedly backhanded compliment, while Zelda's equally prominent role as the 'original flapper' was as likely to elicit censure as envy, and not merely from reactionary circles (see Figure 2.1).[42]

But Zelda herself was helping the flapper secure her social position. In her scrapbook Zelda saved a cartoon with the headline 'Junior League Rehearsal', at the centre of which was a drawing of Zelda, smoking a cigarette with a cluster of cocktails at her feet; it was captioned 'Mrs. F. Scott Fitzgerald tries to exemplify one of hubby's flappers'. She and the other women in the cartoon were described

Figure 2.1 A 1923 article in which Scott interviews Zelda offers an 'insider's view' of the famous couple, *Courier-Journal*, Louisville, 20 September 1928.

as 'society girls in their final dress rehearsal for the junior league annual frolic'. The junior league, a high society women's charity, was founded by Mary Harriman Rumsey, one of the Long Island millionaires upon whom Fitzgerald would base East Egg society in *Gatsby*. Mrs Rumsey was the daughter of the magnate E. H. Harriman; she epitomized the rapidly cycling American class system, in which a single generation sufficed to get the family of self-made industrialists into the Social Register. A few pages later, Zelda saved a clipping of her 1922 essay 'Eulogy on the Flapper', in which she explained that 'the first Flappers are so secure in their positions' that 'they have won their case. They are blasé.'[43] When the flapper made her way into the junior league with Mary Harriman Rumsey, she had arrived.

'The Rolling Junk'

As noted above, Zelda preserved several images from 'The Cruise of the Rolling Junk', alongside mementoes of the Fitzgeralds' encounters with high society during their sojourn in Great Neck from 1922 through early 1924. The 'Rolling Junk' essay described the Fitzgeralds' picaresque misadventures on the American road before there were American roads – among the many problems they encounter on their trip to Alabama are unpaved roads and constantly running out of gasoline in their highly unreliable 'Expenso'. Over the course of their journey the Fitzgeralds are stymied by confusing guidebooks, inaccurate signposts, bad weather, contemptuous locals, scornful car mechanics, and even a highwayman, experiencing one automobile catastrophe after another. As backdrop to all these misadventures is the comic bickering of the young couple: Zelda the bad navigator and Scott the bad driver.

The images Zelda saved were the photographs that had been used to illustrate the essay, in which the Fitzgeralds are posed in scenarios of exaggeratedly comic mishap. In one, they sit together on the car's running board, as Scott looks ruefully into an empty wallet and Zelda, in stylish cloche hat and pleated skirt, stares at him worriedly. In another, she is behind the wheel craning her head out the window as her husband, at the engine of the stalled car, clasps his head, his mouth wide open in comic horror at holding some (presumably indispensable) mechanical object in his hand. They are, as Matthew J. Bruccoli noted dismissively, 'gag photos', but the gags are worth considering more closely. The photographs, posed for *Motor* magazine, were taken more than three years after the trip; even the car they used was a prop, as the actual 'Rolling Junk' had been sold off after their calamitous journey. As Janet Lewis observes, in this 'fictionalized autobiography' all the characters are 'caricatures as much as portraits'.[44] Much of the comedy depends upon stock situations that were already clichés, as when the Fitzgeralds struggle with maps and directions. In April 1923, a *Harper's* magazine article titled 'The Get-There Sex' commented on the well-known phenomenon of the husband who refuses to ask for directions and the wife who can't read maps. In that sense, 'Rolling Junk' offers a very early version of the road trip as an allegory for the difficulties of navigating the modern world, while also suggesting that the ways we interpret that world are always already mediated by the mechanics of publicity and celebrity.

But 'Rolling Junk' is also disparaged, even in its own marketing paratexts, for being too 'egotistical' a text, a presumptive narcissism that means Fitzgerald is faulted for failing to register the social in his writing. The essay was virtually forgotten until 2011, when it was reissued by Hesperus Press with a new foreword and introduction, and a subsequent review from Fitzgerald scholar Kirk Curnutt. Paul Theroux's foreword opens the volume, arguing that 'Rolling

Junk' describes (in a realistic register, Theroux implies) 'the excursion of two reckless, posturing, and self-conscious people'.[45] 'Epitomising the egotism of the age', Theroux adds, 'Fitzgerald saw himself and his own exploits as central to his trip. He was not travelling to listen but rather in the thrust of exhibitionism. This is the chief weakness of "The Cruise."'[46] In his review of the reissue, Curnutt concurs: 'It is a fair and accurate point … the exhibitionistic instinct the Fitzgeralds revelled in during this heady period of young fame marks a major difference in the emotional tenor of their road trip. Whereas other writers set out seeking other people's stories, the Fitzgeralds are interested only in their own.'[47] The idea that Fitzgerald's egotism risks spoiling his art stretches right back to the beginning of his reception: in his first scrapbook, he saved an early review of *This Side of Paradise*, in which the influential critic Heywood Broun wrote, 'The self-consciousness of Fitzgerald is a barrier which we are never able to pierce. He sees himself constantly not as a human being, but as a man in a novel or in a play. Every move is a picture and there is a camera man behind each tree.'[48]

Later in his essay, Theroux discloses another, equally telling, judgement: 'Fitzgerald was himself déclassé and socially insecure.'[49] It is difficult to know whether Theroux is using 'déclassé' in a strictly orthodox sense, to denote one who has come down in the world, or more loosely to damn the merely uncouth, but either way as an assessment of Fitzgerald's class status it is inaccurate. Fitzgerald's mother's family was Irish working-class; his father's family was merchant-class, but of old Maryland stock; Fitzgerald himself was educated in elite institutions thanks to a wealthy aunt. His own prosperity and tastes fixed him pretty firmly in the ranks of the haute bourgeoisie, while his education, and then his celebrity, meant that he socialized almost exclusively with patricians, artists or other celebrities. His behaviour was only 'déclassé' in any meaningful sense when he was drunk. The error is significant, for it is metonymically associated with Theroux's expressed distaste for the couple's 'exhibitionism', a vulgar self-display at odds with aristocratic mores of refinement: author, subjects and work are declared mutually, and objectionably, egotistical. It is only in such classed terms that 'exhibitionism' could ever be understood to damage the aesthetics of Fitzgerald's essay: there is, after all, no rule enjoining that art must register the social rather than the self, or that it must be self-effacing to be good (indeed, such a rule would exclude a great many literary masterpieces).

As early as 1951 an academic review of *The Far Side of Paradise*, the first serious Fitzgerald biography, was equating Fitzgerald's 'penchant for buying expensive but second-hand automobiles, his exhibitionism in hotels and restaurants,' with 'his temperamental restlessness and instability.'[50] By 2011, this presumption that exhibitionism relates to an appetite for conspicuous consumption is framing Fitzgerald's essay as an exercise in self-regard, when in fact 'Rolling Junk' is a comedy of status manqué, of failing to make the grade. The humour of the essay derives from Fitzgerald's ironized pretensions to power – both as man and as quasi-celebrity driving a status-symbol car that is actually a lemon ('to offset these weaknesses, which amounted to general debility, it *was* an 'Expenso', with the name on a little plate in front, and this was a proud business').[51] The tale's farce is driven by Fitzgerald's failures to live up to gendered and classed expectations throughout the journey.

Even the essay's casual racism, which Theroux, Evans and Curnutt all carefully (and understandably) deplore, works in part as a marker of the couple's failures on their road trip: Fitzgerald's incompetence, and their haplessness, mean that the Fitzgeralds' misadventures thrust them among the 'lowly', even being forced to encounter the 'miasmatic atmosphere' of a country store peopled by 'Negroes', and by a dubious counterman whose racial indeterminacy is meant to contribute to the comedy of the mighty fallen. My point is not to defend the passages' racism as aesthetically justifiable (it's not), but rather to say that such racism should be read as part of the essay's comedy of self-deprecation: Fitzgerald is using race as a social marker, a classed category, to mock his own fall in status. By no coincidence he is equally affronted by the 'poor white' they later encounter, who insults Zelda, resplendent in daring white knickerbockers, twice over by telling her, 'It's a pity that a nice girl like you should be let to wear those clothes.' The 'poor white' is marked as a yokel not merely by his retrograde sartorial tastes, but by his reactionary gender politics, his assumption that the way Fitzgerald 'let' Zelda dress lowered her class status. 'It was fifty years of provincialism speaking,' Fitzgerald concludes: 'it was the negative morality of the poor white.'[52] Zelda's outrageous dress puts the 'poor white' in the false position of believing he has a 'moral advantage' over Fitzgerald, but it is not Fitzgerald who defends his wife's honour: instead, the insult fills him 'with helpless and inarticulate rage.' It is Zelda who masters the situation, her 'coolness in the face of such a charge' rendering her accuser – and by extension her husband – socially impotent. All of this, even the racism, constitutes a social comedy, which is just what Fitzgerald is being censured for failing to provide.

The critics' overdetermined fear of 'exhibitionism' flattens out the Fitzgeralds' performance of comic exuberance and playfulness in the essay: the assumption that the Fitzgeralds' egotism was always already 'morbid', in the language of their day, elides its role in the construction of a successful social personality.

Knowledge of the Fitzgeralds' later disintegration is read retrospectively back into their social personas to conclude that they were always pathological. For example, in his introduction to 'Rolling Junk', Julian Evans, who also calls Fitzgerald an 'exhibitionist', goes on to argue that Fitzgerald frames his marriage to Zelda from the outset of the essay as a competitive relationship, but this is to misread the facetiousness of Fitzgerald's tone: he and Zelda are more like a vaudeville act, hamming it up, clowning around, pretending to upstage each other but also relying upon each other to solve the problems they encounter. If Fitzgerald were really 'competing' with Zelda on the page, he would not present her as besting everyone they encountered, including himself. She is equal to everything; he is the one who comically fails.

Evans also reads in *ad hominem* terms – again along the axis of a presumptive 'egotism' – another gag that is surely a social one. At one point, Fitzgerald says they stopped at a garage and 'were filled with the usual liquids, gasoline, water and oil of juniper – or no! I was thinking of something else.' Evans glosses this joke, humourlessly, as a 'hint at Fitzgerald's alcoholism', but in 1920, at the age of just twenty-four, Fitzgerald was no more an alcoholic than anyone else he knew. More important, this is a joke not about alcoholism but about prohibition. Oil of juniper was the essential ingredient for bathtub gin, and everyone in 1920s America knew the recipe. It is a cultural gag, but assumptions about Fitzgerald's pathological 'egotism' are being conflated with his other presumed pathology (alcoholism) to foreclose precisely the social perspective that he is being faulted for not offering: the charge becomes circular and question-begging.

The illustrations of 'Rolling Junk' make clear, if it were in doubt, that the tone of the piece is farce, as they patently quote the visual style of silent screen comedy. Silent comedy was populated by emasculated husbands, whose hand-cranked flivvers kept breaking down while bemused, disappointed or vindicated wives looked on in disgust or dismay. A flivver was a slang term for 'failure', originally denoting cheap or flimsy cars (a 'lemon'),[53] and then by extension denoting a man who was a failure, before becoming a verb for falling short of success. Buying an 'Expenso' and finding himself stuck with a flivver, the Fitzgerald persona is further mocked through the illustrations replicating these stock gags of emasculation. In one image, Zelda plugs both ears with her fingers as Scott gingerly, arm extended from a distance, tries to make electrical contact. In another, he is scratching his head at a gas pump as more money is extracted from his wallet. Many of the jokes with the 'Expenso' echo other contemporary cinematic jokes: for example, in 1920, Harold Lloyd made a popular comic short called *Get Out and Get Under*, about a young man whose flivver keeps breaking down. At one point he injects it with liquid cocaine, which jump-starts the engine and makes the car drive off without him. Fitzgerald's jest of putting juniper oil in the engine is a similar kind of joke about Chaplinesque modern times, the mechanics of modern life and the ineptitude of the modern man.

If the comedy is playing off of generalized cultural anxieties about new technology, however, 'The Cruise of the Rolling Junk' is also satirizing the new power of publicity. The photographs are staged, but they purport to reveal the couple 'caught out' in a series of embarrassing scenarios. The emasculation of the comedy is partly contained by the focus in the frame upon Fitzgerald's dominant poses – Zelda is increasingly marginalized visually. But the implicit prosopopeic invocation of the paparazzo, the idea that this famous author has been discovered in moments of humiliation, is at the heart of the comedy – the publicity that affects not to be publicity while broadly giving the game away. Meanwhile, behind all of the comedy is the implicit understanding that the entire mechanism will contribute to and reinforce the same celebrity that is being satirized. The posed photos of 'Rolling Junk' implicitly mock the idea of cameras ready to capture the Fitzgeralds' every move, Heywood Broun's photographers actually waiting behind every tree.

Even the joke of naming the car the 'Expenso' is self-satirizing as much as it is self-promoting, for the true aristocrat does not confuse expense with quality. Believing that wealth equates to aristocracy is the hallmark of the upstart, as Fitzgerald well knew: this is the entire import of Jay Gatsby's mistake, his misplaced faith that money will buy him an entrée into the Buchanans' socially registered world. Fitzgerald was drafting *Gatsby* even as the 'Rolling Junk' essay was revised in 1923 and published in early 1924: he was not very likely to replicate the precise social errors that he was satirizing his deluded protagonist for making. The Fitzgerald persona's errors in judgement about the power that will be conferred upon him by the 'Expenso' status symbol comprise a joke at his own expense; they are part of the comical self-caricature he is drawing.

As I mentioned at the beginning of this chapter, Zelda pasted these illustrations from 'Rolling Junk' alongside their invitation from Gloria Swanson, who had come to New York to work on Long Island with director Allan Dwan, whose magnificent parties would be one of the inspirations that Fitzgerald named for Jay Gatsby's parties. Celebrity becomes self-ratifying and autotelic: invitations from other celebrities validate the Fitzgeralds' celebrity, but they also provide the genesis of the next installation of Fitzgerald's satirical art. At Jay

Gatsby's final party, Fitzgerald famously describes a tableau of a movie star and her director, sitting frozen at the edge of the gathering's frame. In the early drafts of the novel, Fitzgerald provides a telling encounter in which Daisy rejects the movie star's request to share her hairdresser. Gatsby 'proudly' informs Daisy, 'here's a chance to become famous – she wants to know where you got your hair cut.' Daisy has no interest in becoming famous, however; when Gatsby presses her, she explains, 'Do you think I want that person to go around with her hair cut exactly like mine? It'd spoil it for me.' Aristocracy viewed itself as vulgarized by celebrity; its value was precisely in its exclusivity, as Fitzgerald perfectly understood. Composing *Gatsby* in 1924, he wrote of a milieu in which old money would still describe a movie star as 'that person'. But by the time of the novel's publication in April 1925 Fitzgerald had decided to cut that scene, to leave even Daisy Buchanan bewitched by the movie star, as Fitzgerald captures like a snapshot, more indelible than any scrapbook cutting, the precise moment when aristocracy cedes its power to American celebrity, which becomes the only social register that matters.

In the end, the Fitzgeralds' scrapbooks register many moments of resistance to, or vexing of, uncomplicated or naïve notions of celebrity endorsement as a measure of status envy. Zelda saved one cutting that appears at first to be a straightforward advertisement relying on celebrity endorsement for something called 'Pigman's Portable Eyelashes'. They 'go on easily', the ad quotes Zelda as saying, 'and a pair of pliers will remove them with success.'[54] Neither Zelda nor Scott would have been oblivious to the comedy of false eyelashes with the unfortunate name 'Pigman's', and Zelda's diction gives further reason to construe her comment as facetious: the word 'tweezers' dates back to 1654, so her invocation of pliers as necessary for the lashes' removal suggests that she was mocking Pigman's lashes. If the company missed her joke and reprinted her satirical comment as a recommendation, then the comedies inherent in the process of celebrity are what Zelda was documenting, as much as the status of cultural reference. Nearly a century later, Scott's equally facetious 'Rolling Junk' essay would be read as a similarly straightforward endorsement of himself, instead of a self-mocking comedy of status *manqué*. The Fitzgeralds' scrapbooks don't merely record the early workings of celebrity society and status envy; they show, if we read in ways that are alert to the Fitzgeralds' sense of comedy, that our presumptions of the couple's narcissism continue to preclude our own ability to register the full complexity of both Fitzgeralds' understanding of celebrity, which has no meaning unless the social registers.

Notes

1 Edmund Wilson, *Letters on Literature and Politics, 1912-1972*, ed. Elena Wilson (New York: Farrar Straus Giroux, 1977), 475.

2 Zelda Fitzgerald, *Save Me the Waltz*, in *The Collected Writings*, ed. Matthew J. Bruccoli (Reprint London: Abacus, 1993), 58.

3 F. Scott Fitzgerald, 'What a Handsome Pair!' in *Bits of Paradise: Twenty-One Uncollected Stories*, ed. Matthew J. Bruccoli and Scottie Fitzgerald Smith (1973. Reprint Harmondsworth, UK: Penguin Books, 1982), 311.

4 Quoted in Nancy Milford, *Zelda Fitzgerald* (1970. Reprint Harmondsworth, UK: Penguin Books, 1974), 304.

5 As Warren Susman influentially argued, a nineteenth-century 'culture of character,' in which character was measured by internal merit and external self-control, was steadily replaced in the first decades of the twentieth century by a 'culture of personality,' which emphasized external performance. Thus, for example, Nick Carraway's conceit that what made Jay Gatsby 'gorgeous' was the idea that 'personality is an unbroken series of successful gestures.' The American ethos of heroic individualism fused in the early twentieth century with emergent notions of celebrity and consumer self-fashioning. See Warren I. Susman, *Culture as History: The Transformation of American Society in the Twentieth Century* (New York: Pantheon, 1984).

6 Quoted in James R. Mellow, *Invented Lives: F. Scott and Zelda Fitzgerald* (New York: Houghton Mifflin, 1984), 491.

7 For the Fitzgeralds, see for example Penelope Green, 'Beautiful and Damned,' Review of *Z: A Novel of Zelda Fitzgerald*, by Therese Anne Fowler, in *The New York Times Book Review* (19 April 2013), BR16. For Pickford and Fairbanks see, for example, Scott Curtis, 'Douglas Fairbanks: King of Hollywood,' in *Idols of Modernity: Movie Stars of the 1920s*, ed. Patrice Pentro (New Brunswick, NJ: Rutgers University Press, 2010), 21.

8 Ruth Prigozy, 'Introduction: Scott, Zelda, and the Culture of Celebrity,' in *The Cambridge Companion to F. Scott Fitzgerald*, ed. Ruth Prigozy (Cambridge: Cambridge University Press, 2001), 4, 8.

9 John Dos Passos, *The Best Times* (New York: New American Library, 1966), 130.

10 Jeffrey Meyers, *Edmund Wilson: A Biography* (New York: Houghton Mifflin, 1995), 55.

11 Jeffrey Meyers, 'Scott Fitzgerald and Edmund Wilson: A Troubled Friendship,' *The American Scholar* 61, no. 3 (Summer 1992): 380.

12 In 1974, Matthew J. Bruccoli edited some excerpts from the scrapbooks in a collection he called *Romantic Egoists*. The title reworks Fitzgerald's original title for *This Side of Paradise*, but it also reinforces the notion that the scrapbooks were exercises in self-regard, and Bruccoli's selection is somewhat idiosyncratic. I have relied throughout this chapter upon the original scrapbooks in the Princeton archives. See Scottie Fitzgerald Smith, Matthew J. Bruccoli and Joan P. Kerr, eds, *The Romantic Egoists: A Pictorial Autobiography from the Scrapbooks and Albums of F. Scott and Zelda Fitzgerald* (New York: Charles Scribner's Sons, 1974).

13 Both Fitzgeralds are regularly termed 'exhibitionists' and 'narcissists' across academic, biographical and popular culture. A general introductory volume like Edward J. Rielly's 2005, *F. Scott Fitzgerald: A Biography* casually remarks, 'Fitzgerald and Zelda's antics tended to cross the line from spirited good times to exhibitionism' Edward J. Rielly, *F. Scott Fitzgerald: A Biography* (Westport, CT: Greenwood Press, 2005), 39; while John T. Irwin writes: 'Fitzgerald's statement that he and Zelda "could be twins" evokes the narcissistic component' of their mythic self-construction. John T. Irwin, *F. Scott Fitzgerald's Fiction: 'An Almost Theatrical Innocence'* (Baltimore: Johns Hopkins University Press, 2014), 204–05. Further examples are discussed in the essay below.

14 *The New Yorker* ran weekly segment titled 'Tell Me A Book to Read,' which offered a different précis of recommended books each week. These phrases come from a series of synopses of *Gatsby* from the summer of 1925: 'satirical story': *The New Yorker* (15 August 1925); 'pearl of chivalry': *The New Yorker* (8 August 1925); 'cast before swine': *The New Yorker* (20 June 1925); 'superior people': *The New Yorker* (27 June 1925).

15 A directory of high society families in America, the Social Register first appeared in 1886, as America's expanding industrial wealth in the Gilded Age meant that personal acquaintance could no longer be relied upon to place a family's position in polite society. Beginning with catalogues of aristocratic families in Newport, Rhode Island and then in New York City in 1887, the Social Register has remained in print ever since.

16 See, for example, Detmarr and Watts' *Marketing Modernisms: Self-Promotion, Canonization and Rereading;* its first section is titled 'Modernist Self-Promotion.' Kevin J. H. Dettmar and Stephen Watts, eds, *Marketing Modernisms: Self-Promotion, Canonization and Rereading* (Ann Arbor, MI: University of Michigan Press, 1996).

17 Zelda Fitzgerald Scrapbook, Princeton University Archives, F. Scott Fitzgerald Collection.

18 Ibid.

19 Ibid.

20 Terry Eagleton, *Against the Grain: Essays, 1975–1985* (London: Verso, 1986), 140.

21 F. Scott Fitzgerald, *A Life in Letters*, ed. Matthew J. Bruccoli (New York: Scribner, 1994), 256.

22 Timothy W. Galow, *Writing Celebrity: Stein, Fitzgerald and the Modern(ist) Art of Self-Fashioning* (New York: Palgrave Macmillan, 2011).

23 Robert Van Krieken, *Celebrity Society* (London: Routledge, 2012), 8, original emphasis.

24 Van Krieken, 8.

25 *American Magazine*, September 1922.

26 See for example Graeme Turner, 'Approaching Celebrity Studies', *Celebrity Studies* 1, no. 1 (2010): 11–20.

27 Simone Weil Davis, *Living Up to the Ads: Gender Fictions of the 1920s* (Raleigh, NC: Duke University Press, 2000), 4.

28 Burton Rascoe, *A Bookman's Daybook* (New York: Horace Liveright, 1929), 118.

29 Zelda Fitzgerald Scrapbook, Princeton University Archives, F. Scott Fitzgerald Collection.

30 In a 2010 article for *The F. Scott Fitzgerald Review*, Sharon Hamilton argued that *Gatsby's* 'passing allusions' to *Town Topics* 'show that [Fitzgerald] noticed the conversations around him that first spring he and Zelda spent in New York, and understood their importance.' Hamilton then adds: '(I have not yet found any gossip on Scott and Zelda in the magazine). It seems more likely that … Fitzgerald was referring generally to the gossip business, of which *Town Topics* was a part.' In their scrapbooks the Fitzgeralds saved several clippings from *Town Topics* that mention them, from 1921 through 1923, and there are several more articles naming them that the Fitzgeralds didn't save. I have identified eleven named mentions thus far, and one 'blind' or anonymous but pointedly targeted item; there are almost certainly more blind items to be located. See Sharon Hamilton, 'The New York Gossip Magazine in *The Great Gatsby*', *The F. Scott Fitzgerald Review* 8 (2010): 45. For more quotations from *Town Topics* mentioning the Fitzgeralds, see Sarah Churchwell, *Careless People: Murder, Mayhem and the Invention of The Great Gatsby* (New York: Penguin Press, 2014).

31 See Hamilton 2010; Andy Logan, 'That was New York: *Town Topics*', *The New Yorker* (14 August 1965), 37–91 and *The New Yorker* (21 August 1965), 41–98.

32 *Town Topics* (24 February 1921, vol. 85, no. 8), 7–8. Also in Zelda Fitzgerald Scrapbook, Princeton University Archives, F. Scott Fitzgerald Collection.

33 *Town Topics* (1 December 1921, vol. 86, no. 22), 10.

34 *Town Topics* (17 August 1922, vol. 88, no. 7), 9–10.

35 *Town Topics* (22 March 1923, vol. 89, no. 12), 8.

36 Each of these dates comes from the digital version of the OED.

37 Zelda Fitzgerald Scrapbook, Princeton University Archives, F. Scott Fitzgerald Collection.

38 Quoted in Marina Moskowitz and Marlis Schweitzer, eds, *Testimonial Advertising in the American Marketplace: Emulation, Identity, Community* (New York: Palgrave Macmillan, 2009), 2.

39 Pamela Church Gibson, *Fashion and Celebrity Culture* (London: Bloomsbury, 2012), 49.

40 Marjorie Rosen, 'How The Movies Have Made Women Smaller Than Life', *Journal of the University Film Association* 26, no. 1/2, Women In Film (1974): 6.

41 Alexander Cowie, 'The New Heroine's Code for Virtue', *The American Scholar* 4, no. 2 (Spring 1935): 193.

42 'To Scott Fitzgerald, flapper king / A flappy new year do I sing' read one newspaper clipping, probably from 1922, the he kept in his scrapbook. Zelda was repeatedly called the 'original flapper', and saved in her scrapbook a widely syndicated 1923 interview that asked 'Is She His Model?' and called her 'the living prototype … of the American flapper'. See F. Scott Fitzgerald Scrapbook, vol. II, Princeton University Archives, F. Scott Fitzgerald Collection, and Zelda Fitzgerald Scrapbook, Princeton University Archives, F. Scott Fitzgerald Collection.

43 Zelda Fitzgerald Scrapbook, Princeton University Archives, F. Scott Fitzgerald Collection.

44 Janet Lewis, '"The Cruise of The Rolling Junk": The Fictionalized Joys of Motoring', *Fitzgerald/ Hemingway Annual* 10 (1978): 69–81.

45 Paul Theroux, Foreword to 'F. Scott Fitzgerald's The Cruise of the Rolling Junk' (London: Hesperus, 2011), 7.

46 Theroux, 10.

47 Kirk Curnutt, 'Junk Bonds In A Jerrybuilt America', *The F. Scott Fitzgerald Review* 10 (2012): 159.

48 Heywood Broun, Review of *This Side of Paradise*. New York *Tribune* (14 April 1920), 14, and Scott Fitzgerald Scrapbook, vol. I, Princeton University Archives, F. Scott Fitzgerald Collection.

49 Theroux, 11.

50 John T. Flanagan, Review of Arthur Mizener, *The Far Side of Paradise: A Biography of F. Scott Fitzgerald*. *Minnesota History* 32, no. 2 (June 1951): 116.

51 F. Scott Fitzgerald, *The Cruise of the Rolling Junk* (London: Hesperus, 2011), 31, original italics.

52 Fitzgerald, 'Rolling Junk', 69.

53 A 1930 scholarly essay on the new American vernacular inspired by the Ford
    'Lizzie' suggested that owners of the so-called Tin Lizzie made defensive jokes about
    the car, because it competed in 'a world of cars with more distinguished pedigrees
    and more money in the bank. ... Half-contemptuously, half-affectionately, he dubs
    his car a flivver (failure).' See B. A. Botkin, 'The Lore of the Lizzie Label', *American
    Speech* 6, no. 2 (December 1930): 85–86.

54 Zelda Fitzgerald Scrapbook, Princeton University Archives, F. Scott Fitzgerald
    Collection.

3

'Good Fellowship':
Carole Lombard and Clark Gable

Michael Hammond

It is almost as if the people of the United States had walked backwards into the Depression, holding for dear life to the customs and ideals and assumptions of the time that was gone, even while these were one by one slipping out of reach; and then in 1933, had given up their vain effort, turned about, and walked face-forward into the new world of the nineteen thirties.

Frederick Lewis Allen[1]

The woman who earns her own living has a definite set of problems.

Carole Lombard[2]

Carole Lombard and Clark Gable's romance was a persistent news item in fan magazines from 1936 to Lombard's death in January 1942. When their relationship began Lombard had been divorced from leading man William Powell for two years. Gable was separated from his second wife socialite Rhea Langham. Star couples who were not married were a source of concern for studio publicity departments and once Lombard and Gable began appearing in public together in 1935 their respective studios (Paramount and MGM) worked to 'normalize' their relationship as pragmatic and in touch with changing attitudes towards marriage as the Great Depression wore on. Their strategy played out across the tensions between contemporary and traditional conceptions of extra marital sexual relationships and had the effect of building on the fact that the financial pressures and high unemployment brought about by the Crash had resulted in falling marriage rates. Marriage was simply too expensive for many young couples. Lombard and Gable's high-profile divorces, their association with 'screwball' comic roles, the combination of Lombard as independent career woman with Gable's 'man's man' persona offered a solution in the form of practical coupledom that spoke directly to these shifting attitudes. Their relationship, as presented in the fan press, offered a model for childless working couples that combined the 'fun' of their screen roles with a utilitarian nature that chimed with broader attitudes towards coupling that the times demanded. Rather than suppress past relationships, these strategies worked to emphasize their dilemma and their choice to work against convention out of necessity. As early as 1936, Adele Whitely Fletcher labelled it a 'good fellowship'.[3] Considered in retrospect, the narrative of the Lombard–Gable couple resonated with the shifting concepts of relationships in and out of marriage during the Depression.

Lightening the taboo for the 'Hinterland'

In the February 1939 issue of *Motion Picture Magazine*, columnist Ford Black wrote a feature entitled 'Will Clark Gable Ever Marry Carole Lombard?' (see Figure 3.1) His article brought into high relief the tensions between tradition and utility that had characterized fan magazine discourse concerning their relationship

Figure 3.1 Ford Black's feature 'Will Clark Gable Ever Marry Carole Lombard?' in *Motion Picture Magazine*, 1939.

for the previous three years. He mapped these contrasting positions through the kind of metaphorical geography employed by the fan press that implicitly othered rural areas and small towns as the 'hinterland' in favour of a modern sensibility. The piece presaged their marriage by a month and was a three-page layout that outlined the star persona of each and trumpeted their modern lifestyle. Lombard is depicted as a savvy business woman under an exterior of the carefree 'screwball' who can match Gable in his rough and tumble humour, and parodies his 'uber-masculine' persona through direct jabs at his pretentious masculinity. Black begins by confronting the 'technicality' that Gable is still married to Rhea Langham. Rather than speculate on whether a divorce is imminent he describes the couple as more unconcerned about conventions than rebellious, and notes that Hollywood insiders think the couple happy with their arrangement and that there will never be a divorce. Such an attitude cut against the prevailing Hollywood wisdom about the way that ostensibly immoral behaviour played in 'the hinterland':

> Hollywood has its own table of ethics about things like this – a set of rules and taboos that are governed to a large extent by such things as publicity and the so-called 'hinterland reaction'. Hollywood fears, above all else, the wrath of millions of moviegoers whose moral sensibilities are assumed to be as fragile as a gold leaf, and as pure, [and that] the box office status of both Gable and Lombard would suffer a deep pain in the (box-office) intake. And what Hollywood can't stand at all is a drop in the box-office rating.[4]

Black equates box office success with public approval, while at the same time wryly reinforcing assumptions about the primacy of profit margins among the studios. Hence the rationale for the out-of-wedlock romance is twofold: Gable is in a loveless marriage with Langham, and the box office has not suffered.

In fact, Black admits 'There has, in the past, been terrific pressure to "kill" all publicity linking the Gable and Lombard names … [and it] … was a policy in line with the fear of that hinterland reaction.' He and other journalists in Hollywood have noticed that both MGM and Paramount have demonstrated a 'gradual but definite lightening of the taboo.'[5] Black shies away from giving reasons, or even evidence for this, and engages in the type of star construction that would seem more or less dictated by the publicity departments from both studios. While no doubt true of Gable, whose career was carefully managed by MGM publicists Howard Strickling and Eddie Mannix, Lombard had, by this time, taken a much more active role in managing all aspects of her career. Emily Carman's study of female stars and freelance labour in the Hollywood industry has shown that by 1935 Lombard's image in the fan press had transformed from an 'image as fashion icon' to independent and talented actress.[6] The transformation was enabled primarily through her hit with John Barrymore in the Howard Hawks comedy *Twentieth Century* (1934). Thereafter she was able to exercise her choice over the roles she played and took part in creative decisions in her productions and in her own publicity. Three years later, in 1937, Lombard did not renew her contract with Paramount but instead negotiated single picture deals with Paramount and with Selznick studios at $150,000 per picture.[7] Yet Carman argues that even before the new contract the fan press had been connecting this professional independence explicitly to her personal life, and her recent divorce from William Powell: '... her divorce worked to rejuvenate her career and established her independent image as a sophisticated comedienne ...'[8] Her divorce was also rationalized in the fan press as being the result of professional pressure. In the May 1934 issue of *Motion Picture Magazine* Lombard told journalist Sonia Lee there was a need for a new type of marriage for working women who did not want to 'sacrifice personal development to a code ... Professional women must be free, not to be outlaws, but to be themselves, to realize themselves as individuals.'[9] Such an apparently transgressive statement was qualified by her recognition that actresses 'lived a totally different life than the automatic program that the majority of women follow.'[10] Yet her celebrity enables the statement to stand. As a star she is simultaneously extraordinary and ordinary and hence her appeal for professional women's independence can be read to extend beyond her own experience to that of fan magazine readers.

Black's construction of her relationship with Gable as carefree and connected to her 'screwball' image was built upon the convergence between professional and personal independence that was predicated by her divorce. His article brought to light the discursive ingredients of marriage and divorce that came into play in fan magazine discussions of their out-of-wedlock relationship and was unique in that it brought together the narrative of their relationship under a headline that ostensibly addressed the concerns of the hinterland directly in order to play them down. The article appeared a month before the divorce from Rhea Langham was finalized in March 1939. Moreover the divorce was followed a few weeks later by Gable and Lombard's marriage.

Viewed in retrospect the article culminates a three-year period of negotiating their out-of-wedlock relationship through the fan press. Articles about the couple had begun to surface in 1936 and though many of these were simply mentions in gossip columns the central themes in the reportage were marriage and divorce and their apparent decision to be together regardless. As with virtually all fan-magazine gossip involving relationships, matrimonial status was a centre-piece of both stars from the outset. As early as 1931, when Gable's star was rising, Dorothy Calhoun's article 'How Many Marriages for Clark Gable?' appeared in *Movie Classic Magazine* focusing on his first divorce from Josephine Dillon and his second marriage to Ria Langham.[11] In 1934, a year after her divorce from William Powell, Carol Lombard wrote 'I'm a Gay Divorceé' for *Hollywood* magazine which lamented the life of divorcee closing with '... there's no such thing as a perfect state for a woman with a Hollywood career! For the great god Studio is the most jealous lover of all!'[12]

Black followed the publicity trend that had been built on the success of her 'screwball heroine' roles in films such as *Twentieth Century*, *My Man Godfrey* (Gregory La Cava, 1936) and *Nothing Sacred* (William Wellman, 1937). The main theme in the 'screwball' publicity that had become central to her star persona at this time was a 'crazy-like-a-fox' quality that rationalized her independence in business and her choice of career over marriage. Black offered a description of Lombard and Gable that resembles a screwball comedy:

> Clark and Carole themselves aren't bothering with even a semblance of a hide-up! You'll see them go careening down Ventura Boulevard in that dusty station wagon of theirs, both of them togged in dirty old overalls and farm clothes laughing like a couple of old sophomores.[13]

He noted that the couple is comfortable at rodeos or at Hollywood nightclubs, implying that the former is the more preferred place, writing: 'if you skip the Victorian conventions and get down to the real savvy of the situation, they ARE in love.' The core of the piece highlighted the healing effects of their modern mutual relationship: 'I believe Carole Lombard has done more, in a material and spiritual way, for Clark Gable than all the rest of his life added up. She has certainly done more to make his life worth the living than any of his other associations.'[14] These 'other associations' were Gable's two previous marriages, the first to Dillon, a theatrical director and his coach who was fourteen years his senior, and Langham, his then current wife, an oil heiress, who was seventeen years older than him. Black did not dwell on the age differences (which was well known at the time), but rather focused on the class connotations that each woman lent to Gable's persona:

> Neither of those women brought the fun the fun-loving Carole Lombard did. Carole is an ex Mack Sennett girl.[15] She has no social aspirations yet she is one of Hollywood's most sought after guests. She has no exalted ideas about histrionics

and yet she is one of Hollywood's top box office stars. Carole can and therefore does give Clark the social status Rhea gave and the theatrical standing and help Josephine gave – but in addition she also gives a whole-hearted companionship and good fellowship. … Carole is a man's girl. Clark is a man's man.[16]

Here Lombard offers a modern counterpart, read sexual one, to the potentially emasculating relationship with 'mothering types' that both Dillon and Lang represented.

Black's article traced the directions Lombard's and Gable's publicity strategies took in an attempt to negotiate their romance within the cross-currents of discourses associated with marriage and sexuality that had been swirling since the onset of the Great Depression. He focused primarily on Lombard as a career woman in control of her image, balancing the demands of her profession with the demands of the industry's perception of a potentially disapproving, and distinctly 'old fashioned', conservative, primarily rural, audience. Lombard's independence was pitched alongside Gable's 'über-masculinity' which, through his marriages to older women, held the potential to be undermined by implicit readings of the 'mothering nature' of their relationships.[17] Black depicted his marriage to Dillon as nurturing his theatrical talent while Langham, coming after his rise to stardom, introduced him to 'how things are done in the upper tiers of social life.' Dillon and Langham are portrayed in a gender reverse of the Pygmalion myth, where the modelling clay is metaphorically the 'salt of the earth', that is, the commonplace origins of Clark. Their roles become the necessary steps to be taken in arriving at the 'right' relationship with Carole the previously 'vulgar' Mack-Sennett girl who provides business acumen and an equal star stature to his. The Lombard–Gable couple in this formulation are an escape from the convention represented by his previous wives, into a relationship characterized by both utility and 'fun' thanks to Lombard's influence.

Marriage and divorce in the Great Depression

'Fun' is characterized by Tina Olsen Lent as a primary ingredient in the shifting discourse of romantic love in 1920s' and 1930s' America. She points to the efforts of social observers in the 1920s, both scholarly and popular, to redefine the concept of marriage: 'The aims of the ideal contemporary marriage were romantic satisfaction achieved through sexual gratification and friendship …'[18] The screwball comedies of the 1930s seem to be responding to these changes, often pitching the antics and antagonisms between the couple against conventional, usually wealthy, parental figures and family. Lent argues that the restrictions of the Production Code[19] reoriented the sexuality of the flapper of the 20s towards 'stories of courtship, where friendship developed along with love'.[20] To this it might be added that the 'gold-digger' of the 1920s and pre-Code early 1930s, whose 'targets' were primarily rich middle-aged men and exemplified by comedy dramas such as the Anita Loos-scripted *The Red Headed Woman* (Jack Conway, 1932) as well as melodramas like *Baby Face* (Alfred E. Green, 1933), were also displaced by the combination of the Code and the changing attitudes towards marriage. *It Happened One Night* (Frank Capra, 1934) and *Hands Across the Table* (Mitchell Leisen, 1935), exemplified a post-Code production trend of screwball comedies where a hyper-valuation of youth culture, with an emphasis on displaced sexual gratification through fun, afforded a solution to the problems the Code presented. They replaced gold-diggers and old guys with young couples and fun.

Throughout the 1930s, film fan magazines, like the producers and scriptwriters of the films themselves, were able to negotiate the tastes and sensibilities of their varied audiences via a sophisticated form of double coding. Explicit readings, which on the surface seemed to endorse generally accepted values, at the same time provided probable interpretations that either cut against or deepened them. In the case of Lombard and Gable, their personas individually, as with all stars, drew upon an amalgam of their film roles and their private lives. Their persona as a couple, as Black's article demonstrates, played off the screwball comedy sensibility and, in a more nuanced way, utilized the single and independent professional image of Lombard as a central ingredient in making their relationship particularly modern. Euphemisms for sexual relationships, such as that employed by Black in his reference to Lombard as having 'done more to make [Gable's] life worth the living than any of his other associations', exemplify the double coding style of fan journalism. Lombard, albeit within the bounds of patriarchy – 'a man's girl' – offers the complete version of coupledom that includes both spiritual and physical plenitude.

It is clear from both Lent's and Carman's work that these representational strategies belong to a broader discourse surrounding marriage and divorce, and the changes in the Hollywood industry being brought about by independent stars such as Lombard, as well as Barbara Stanwyck and Miriam Hopkins. However, it is illuminating to explore, through the examination of statistics, the impact that the Great Depression had been having on circumstances of women's employment and the conditions under which choices about marriage and divorce were being made more generally. Lombard's role as an independent star who made Gable's 'life worth the living' has a stark resonance when cast against the background of the emasculating effects of unemployment for many men during the Depression, and the notion that she had a positive effect on Gable, the cypher of ultra-masculinity, was timely. The impact of the Great Depression on marriage and divorce rates demonstrates the role that economic factors played during that period. Looking back to the 1930s at the end of the decade, Frederick Lewis Allen wrote:

> It pushed to the forefront of attention a relatively new problem: What was the future of the jobless young man and his girl, who loved each other deeply and really wanted to marry? Were they to postpone marriage and live resolutely apart? … As a result, many young couples accepted as an alternative to immediate marriage an occasional night in a cheap hotel room or an auto-tourist cabin. … Hating the furtiveness of such meetings, hating the conventions which made them furtive, these young couples nevertheless felt their behaviour was right – a response to necessity.[21]

Allen's illustration demonstrates the social background for screwball comedy scenes such as the 'Walls of Jericho' gag in the auto-tourist cabin between Gable and Claudette Colbert in *It Happened One Night* (1934). Matthew Hill, an economic historian who has compared Gross Domestic Product levels with marriage rates in the United States across the period 1928–40, lends Allen's scenario statistical support. Marriage rates dropped along with the GDP between the period of the stock market crash of 1929 and the election of Franklin D. Roosevelt in 1932. Following this period from 1932 to 1935 there was a slow recovery of employment and GDP, and retail sales returned to about 95 per cent of the levels of 1928, at which time there was a commensurate rise in marriage rates. This was followed by a recession in 1937–39. His findings indicate that during the 1928–33 period unemployed males of marriageable age were less likely to enter into marriage, and women of marriageable age were inclined to put off getting married. Throughout the period of recovery from 1932 to 1935 the age of marriage increased alongside the rates of marriage, which 'is consistent with the idea that marriage was delayed. If some of the women who had forgone marriage during the marriage downturn of 1930–33 married in the recovery period from 1933 to 1937, then these women would be a few years older and would thus push the average marriage age from 1934 to 1937 upwards.'[22] While in 1937 the marriage levels had returned to those of the late 20s, the recession of that year correlates to a decline in marriage rates in 1938, although they rise back to the 1937 level by 1940. Hill's study points out that the effects of the Depression were reflected in the convulsive economic climate but overall '… the effects were not long lasting. Marriage rates rebounded during the economic recovery: marriage was merely delayed, not foregone.'[23]

Two related phenomena had been ongoing prior to the Depression. The first was a rise in clerical positions and office work since 1900, of which 24 per cent were occupied by women by 1930. Another was a rise in high school graduation rates, which went from 26 per cent in 1928 to 52 per cent by 1938. Social historian Claudia Goldin argues that, '… the increased demand for clerical workers and the increased supply of high school graduates meant that, prior to marriage, young women entered nicer, cleaner, shorter-hour, and thus more "respectable" jobs. Some remained employed after marriage, although levels were insubstantial until the 1940s.'[24] Goldin points to the widespread practice of 'marriage bars' or regulations that required women who married to leave their jobs. These, however, had almost completely disappeared by the early 1940s.[25] Nevertheless throughout the 1930s the marriage bar, combined with the economic strife outlined by Allen and Hill acted as an effective disincentive for young employed women to marry. The Lombard–Gable relationship, their decision to remain unmarried, carried an underlying relevance to unmarried couples, albeit via the Hollywood fantasy scenario they inhabited. Even before her relationship with Gable, Lombard had been frank about the effect of marriage on the working woman: 'The woman who earns her own living has a definite set of problems … she isn't seeking a lax uncontrolled life. She is only searching for happiness, some exaltation of her spirit and body, which she has not been able to find by being a stay-at-home.'[26] Lombard couched her pragmatic solution within an appeal to self-determination and an implicit endorsement of choices being made by young women in the face of economic and ideological realities.

The economic climate of the Depression forced changes in relationship conventions but these were for the most part practical solutions rather than progressive choices. They offer a backdrop to the Lombard–Gable marriage and the star constructions of both that led up to it. For the most part the publicity depicted their out-of-wedlock coupling as 'legitimate' in that Lombard was divorced from William Powell and Gable was a man trapped in a loveless marriage. Both in differing ways had prepared 'narratives' which depicted them as in line with modern attitudes towards marriage, divorce and independent adult relationships. Lombard's persona reflected the social changes outlined by

Hill and Goldin. Following her divorce from Powell, fan magazines reported the story in a way that worked to simultaneously reinforce marriage as an institution with the challenges faced by independent working women. Sonia Lee, in her introduction to the article where Lombard spoke about the conflicts of her professional and personal life, outlined the issue: 'The modern wage-earning woman has arrived at a moral and emotional cross-roads. Marriage no longer holds for her the conventional values.' Lombard is a '... modern woman who has expanded mentally and spiritually ... she asks for a new set of moral values and a new marriage code.'[27] Presenting Lombard as a 'modern working woman' could speak to single women, working or not, who up to that time may have been delaying marriage whether by necessity or design. How this might have played in Black's 'hinterland' then may have been a moot point. In 1940 Frederick Lewis Allen, looking back at the attitudes towards marriage and the family in the Depression referred to those 'less fortunate' than the college-educated middle class:

> Even here there was something new about the mood. ... The dilemma was practical. One managed the best one could. ... If the conventions were in abeyance, it was simply because the times were out of joint and no longer made sense; but that did not mean that one might not long for wedded security.[28]

From this perspective, the out-of-wedlock relationship of Lombard and Gable acted out imagined solutions to the real scenarios that many couples faced during the recovery period where marriage was only just becoming economically viable. Further it imbued choices made to delay marriage with a moral rationale centred on necessity.

A cross-class screwball

Lombard's role in the public narrative of their coupledom was as an equal partner, if not actually being more in control. The ideological tap dance that the publicity campaign performed was as complicated as any of Fred and Ginger's routines, with Lombard doing everything in the eponymous phrase 'backwards and in high heels.' In 'A Loud Cheer for the Screwball Girl' for *Life* magazine, Noel Busch opened with the statement, 'A nation's state of mind is reflected in its entertainments', and in the process set Lombard within the apparent contradiction of 'champion attractive screwball ... proved by the fact that she gets $150,000 per picture. ...'[29] The article spent most of its copy outlining Lombard as 'neurotic' but attached her behaviour to being like that of 'most U.S. women' and that 'far from being a liability' these neuroses 'are worked off in productive channels and cause their possessors to be not only more amusing but more efficient'. Turning the 'neuroses' from a malady to an asset that every U.S. woman shares, the article confirmed her connection with everyday working people. According to Busch, Lombard spent considerable time on the set greeting '... propmen, mechanics, assistant directors and electricians on the rafters. ...' He praised her ability to connect with the labourers in her workplace while at the same time characterized the whole industry as in touch with the nation: '... it is impossible not to be democratic in a business which requires $5000-a-week actresses to make funny faces in close proximity with $10-a-day labourers, and actresses who try to be dignified merely succeed in being absurd'.[30] Lombard was a cut above the would-be star that 'put on airs'.

Presenting Lombard as approachable brought her persona in line with the 'hinterland' and countered potential disapproval with tacit support for Roosevelt's New Deal programmes. She announced to *The New Yorker* in 1938 that she '... gave the Federal Government 65% of my wages last year, and I was glad to do it too'.[31] This came at a time when Roosevelt's government was attempting to raise the marginal rate of tax from 63 per cent to 79 per cent arguing that concentrations of wealth led to 'undesirable concentrations of control' and were not good for the economic health of the country.[32] It also came at a time when other stars such as Charles Laughton were being investigated for tax evasion.[33] In 1938, the country was feeling the effects of a downturn in the economy that had disrupted the slow recovery from the Crash of 1929. These were felt most acutely in the Midwest.[34] While this strategy indicates an astute understanding of the discursive drift across both city and hinterland audiences, it was, in retrospect, a canny continuation of the kind of roles she had built her career on. The characters she played were often able to cross class boundaries. In *Twentieth Century* she played Mildred Plotka, a former lingerie model from the sticks, in *Nothing Sacred* she was Hazel Flagg, a small town girl from Warsaw Vermont who desperately wants to come to the city, and in *My Man Godfrey* she took the role of Irene Bullock, the heiress whose empathy for 'forgotten man' Godfrey, played by William Powell, is the centrepiece of the film's romance plot.

Lombard had begun the retooling of her persona as she was negotiating the contract with Selznick International for the film *Nothing Sacred* in 1937. The William Wellman film, scripted by Ben Hecht was an early Selznick package.

The film's publicity put Frederic March and Lombard on equal billing and the tagline was 'See the Big Fight! Lombard vs March'. This was partly a result of the publicity that had been generated by Lombard's negotiations with Selznick that had run in the trade and fan press throughout 1937. However, this feistiness and equal punching power was both a reality in the business, given her newly negotiated independent contracts, and a feature of the characters she had had the most success with. This was the case in her breakthrough film *Twentieth Century* with John Barrymore and again in *My Man Godfrey* with, her by then ex-husband, William Powell. In *Twentieth Century* she played an amateur whom Barrymore, as grand theatrical director Oscar Jaffe, turns into a star (Lily Garland). She then develops her own ideas, takes control of her own stardom, and leaves the eccentric and arrogant Jaffe, a comic Svengali who loses his ideal to the vulgarities of Hollywood. In *My Man Godfrey* she picks up Godfrey who is down on his luck, living at the city dump and takes him to a high society 'scavenger party' as her 'find'. Lombard/Irene is cast as compassionate against her sister Cornelia, played by Gail Patrick, who is cold-hearted. It is Cornelia who first finds Godfrey and he refuses to go with her, insulted by the cruel indifference of such a proposition. As she leaves, Lombard/Irene has a more honest discussion with him and he agrees to go, where he makes a point of chastising the idle rich who make fun of other people's misfortune. However, from the outset Irene and Godfrey understand each other. The film's moral centre is Godfrey who is revealed as having come from a well-to-do family and has found a deeper sense of value through his experiences living rough and down and out. He acts as a sage to Lombard and her family, and in the process exposes the shallow and precarious nature of the wealthy.

These earlier films were made not by her home studio Paramount but by Columbia and Universal respectively. She had been loaned out on both occasions. Irene and Lily have proactive control of their fate, which Lombard and publicist Birdwell built upon. She played women who possess self-determination and, particularly relevant in the depression years of the 1930s, a consistent rejection of 'airs'. Her persona was often that of a working woman who transcended class boundaries. In *Hands Across the Table* (Mitchell Leisen, 1935), her first of four films with Fred MacMurray, she played Regi Allen, a manicurist in a swanky hotel. Regi is convinced that romance is a foolish and dangerous notion and is determined to find a rich man. She sets her sights on Theodore Drew III (MacMurray) whom she thinks is wealthy but is actually a penniless playboy. When he convinces her to let him sleep on her couch for a week until his rich fiancée returns to town, she discovers that he is, in the words of the *New York Times* reviewer, 'a Depression baby', that is, the offspring of previously wealthy parents who have been ruined in the Crash. They fall in love, he leaves his fiancée, and the film ends with him promising to look for a job. The film was a financial and critical success, and further evidence of Lombard's acumen at both understanding her appeal and at choosing projects. The *New York Times* review of the film underscored her cross-class appeal: '"Hands Across the Table" is precisely the kind of maid-servant literature which permits the disinherited to dream of happiness in this worst of all possible worlds.'[35] It also represents, through the emotional journey of Regi, a transition from gold-digger to the role of equal partner central to screwball comedy romances.

Lombard's status as the screwball queen aided the cross-class appeal, not least because of the general reception of screwball comedies as 'sophisticated', which implied a knowingness in the treatment of sexual matters through humour, although screwball comedies were less explicitly sexualized than the flapper comedies of Clara Bow or Coleen Moore. They were also send-ups of 'Victorian conventions' and 'hinterland prudishness'. Screwball heroine roles had been developed against the background of the perceived excesses of the 1920s. Frederick Lewis Allen's account of the 1930s, *Since Yesterday*, spent a good deal of attention on the changes in the ideal modern woman from the 'reckless' 1920s. Compared to the 'bored-looking' affectation fashionable in that decade, the woman of the early 1930s was 'alert looking'. 'She had a pert, uptilted nose and an agreeably intelligent expression. ... She conveyed a sense of competence. ... This was the sort of girl who might be able to go out and get a job ... when her father or her husband's income stopped.'[36] He might have been describing Lombard's star persona throughout the 1930s.

Photoplay was more succinct: 'She's as delectably feminine as Eve but watch out! That's no apple in her hand, it's a blackjack!'[37] She was capable of taking care of herself and she was a resourceful, equal companion. In Lent's words '... the flapper depicted gender inequality (She had strength of character, while he [the older rich man] had social and economic power), the screwball comedy depicted greater gender equality.'[38] The transitional role of Regi in *Hands Across the Table* was followed a year later by Irene in *My Man Godfrey*. Both exemplify Allen's description of this post-flapper woman of the new decade. Although Irene comes from an upper-class family, she is down to earth. She is contrasted with her sister Cornelia whose arrogance serves as a foil for Lombard's Irene, a boundary-less but insightful and empathetic woman who alone sees not only that Godfrey has value and feelings, but so do all the other forgotten men on the dump. Similarly, in *Nothing Sacred*, Hazel Flagg gets involved with an elaborate publicity hoax along with Frederic March. She plays a character who is apparently dying of an incurable disease and wins the hearts of the public as a poor girl whose luck has run out. Troubled by the genuine grief of the public she ultimately sabotages the hoax and remains honest and unfazed by the money she stands to lose. Characters such as these combined glamour and resourcefulness with empathy and independence, as Lombard's role in the Lombard–Gable couple did. In this way, Lombard's persona offered a positive response to problems that many women faced in their real-life situations within couples, married and unmarried, and the hard choices forced by economic hardship.

Gable, 'Two Dimes, A Nickel and a Heart Without Fear'

Gable also had been able to negotiate the inherent contradiction of the fabulous wealth of Hollywood stardom and the masculine 'everyman' appeal. In the early years of the decade, he had mainly played villains and romantic leads such as that alongside Greta Garbo in *Susan Lennox* (Robert Z. Leonard, 1931). Adela Rogers St. Johns provided the template for his 'uber-masculine' image in her article entitled 'The Great God Gable' for the March 1932 edition of *Liberty Magazine*. Emphasizing his heterosexuality she pointed out: 'Gable has a hot temper and he hits like Dempsey. No one has yet dared call him a matinee idol to his face.'[39] The popular boxer Jack Dempsey had exemplified a brute physical masculinity throughout the 1920s and was known for his aggressiveness in the ring. Gable bore a slight physical likeness and was often compared to him. In 1935, 'hardboiled' writer (and real-life hobo) Jim Tully referred to Dempsey in an article on Gable: 'He resembles Jack Dempsey … he wears his clothes as easily as a tiger wears its skin. …' A more tender side, though, tempered the ultra-masculine image: 'He also has the great fighter's tolerance for people and his love of little children. I have been close to both men for many years, yet I have never known either to do a deceitful act or say an unkind word.'[40] His status as a man's man was developed from this contrast between playing heavies in films such as *Night Nurse* (dir. William A. Wellman, 1931) and an everyman with compassion, as in his breakthrough film *A Free Soul* (dir. Clarence Brown, 1931). In that film, he stole the show from Leslie Howard as a 'rough but lovable' man who pushed Norma Shearer around. The brutish nature image held until *It Happened One Night* demonstrated a comic side to his character, which brought him an Academy Award in 1934 and established him as a top star.

Gable's performance in *It Happened One Night* of a resourceful guy, down on his luck cemented his type of masculinity. He plays Peter Warne, a journalist, in a similar kind of newspaper sensation story to *Nothing Sacred*. In *It Happened One Night*, his conflict lies with his employer, the newspaper magnates, represented by Colbert's father. He is fired from his job and in the process provided poignant reminders to Depression audiences. Tully's article, which appeared after Gable's Academy award for the role, drew an equivalence between the unemployed but optimistic Warne with Gable's own life story as an out-of-work actor who 'pounded the streets of Hollywood in hope and hunger.' The road, travelling rough, and the romance of the hobo-life were Tully's stock in trade. He had written *Beggars of Life* in 1925, a set of stories that related his own experience as a hobo. Tully drew on this to exemplify Gable's resilience in telling his life story as a means of negotiating the inherent threat to masculinity that acting, and particularly male stardom presents. He emphasized the itinerant and precarious existence of actors: 'The company (was) stranded in Butte Montana. ... He had two dimes, a nickel and a heart without fear.'[41] Calling Gable a 'hobo-actor', Tully recounted the numerous odd jobs he had undertaken when he was out of work, from forest engineer to working for the telephone company. In 'The Great God Gable' Rogers St. Johns was explicit about the potential distaste for the matinee idol image:

> The smell of the soil clings to him, the desire for down-to-earth hearty living and eating and drinking and loving. There are no complexes, no inhibitions, no fixations no phobias about Clark. His greed for life, for pleasure, for battle, for conquest, for money, is normal and honest and it vibrates in a room and wipes out the pale lavender scent of pseudosophistication.[42]

This last veiled homophobic reference seems designed to drape Gable's masculinity with a protective cloak of heterosexuality; and yet both Rogers St. Johns and Tully introduce Gable as having been the construct and choice of women. In fact, Rogers St. Johns' article was subtitled 'A close-up of a Man's Man Whom Women Have Made a Star of Stars'. She wrote: 'A woman – his stepmother – first woke in him the joy of living. A woman – his first wife – warmed him to his first real confidence in himself ... and Minna Wallis, actors' agent – who first recognized his great picture possibilities.' Finally Rogers St. Johns invokes 'the women of America, fed up with antiquated or pleasant but slightly devitalized stars, forced their demand for him upon that arbiter of all movie destinies, the box office.'[43] Jim Tully continued the theme in his article: 'As women and children are blamed for all that is wrong with films, they must be credited with discovering and retaining Clark Gable. When they found a real man in the house of celluloid, they held him until the critics came.'[44] Tully's shading of Gable's masculinity as having a 'touch of the road' and chosen by women implicitly referred to a version of the romance of the hobo as free and unbounded by the confines of employment and in the process exposed social graces and sophistication as vapid facades.

Attaching the dirt of the road to Gable set him into that twilight between adolescence and manhood occupied by what, by that time, had become a distinctly American version of 'carefree and rootless masculinity', perhaps best exemplified by Mark Twain's Huck Finn, who does anything to avoid becoming 'civilized', a state often represented by a woman. In the comic frame of the screwball comedy, his type of boyish truculence offered a fruitful foil to the heroine, who can see through him yet all the while falling for him. Attaching a romantic version of drifting and homelessness to Gable's character had the effect of ennobling and re-masculinizing the image of the forgotten man of the Great Depression. Coupling him with a resourceful and independent woman, either in his films or in the fan magazine version of his real life had a resonance, intended or not, with the experience of couples in the 1930s.

A good fellowship

The Lombard–Gable couple was primarily a construct of the fan press guided by the template of the screwball comedy couple. They did not actually appear together in a film after *No Man of Her Own* in 1932. Fred Black's 1939 article was emblematic of this strategy and brought the various strands of their star personas together. He built on earlier foundations concerning Gable's masculinity within the context of Carole Lombard's 'screwball but clever' persona. She offered another more modern sexualized partner than his previous wives while in the pattern of the screwball couple she offered a more equal, modern partner. In the Lombard–Gable manifestation, Gable's uber-masculinity remained intact through her understanding, and tolerance, of his Huck Finn proclivities. 'He's no social butterfly, he'd rather wear dungaries and hunting khaki than tails and an opera hat. He'd rather engage in some utterly hilarious and unmentionable clowning … than take part in a la-de-da cocktail fight at Madame La Ritz's society soiree.'[45]

Figure 3.2 Lombard and Gable on their San Fernando Valley ranch 'Roughing it interests me most in the cosmopolitan world, says Clark Gable', *Cosmopolitan Magazine*, July 1941.

Lombard's value to him was both personal and professional: 'When she isn't working herself she spends much of her time on the sidelines, as Clark works. She gives him help, coaches him from her own innate sense of stagecraft. She rehearses his lines with him.' Black goes on to cite a number of things that she has done to aid his career such as helping him to be more discerning in choosing his roles and to insist on script changes that enhance his career: '... it's pretty generally accepted that Carole is Clark's professional mentor far and away beyond what appears on the surface'[46] Lombard, the glamorous star and astute business woman, is depicted as managing Gable, the ultra male star. Black's article, then, is an example of the kind of publicity work that these magazines did but it is also possibly more of an indication of how the star system was changing as the origins of the package unit system began to take shape. As such, Lombard's move to short contracts and single picture deals anticipates the shape of the industry in the future where 'packages' of scripts, directors and stars are put together by independent producers and then 'sold' to larger studios. David O. Selznick had left MGM and formed Selznick International Pictures in 1935. Lombard, on leaving Paramount was represented by the agent Myron Selznick and signed with his brother David to do *Nothing Sacred* with Selznick International Pictures. All of her pictures thereafter were made on this basis.

Lombard's role in the couple replaced maternal nurturing with glamour and sex. But Lombard also echoed the new woman of the 1930s who worked and aided her husband. While this is an extension of the role of mentor that characterized Gable's previous marriages, Lombard modernized it and demonstrated a version of the new couple as stretching convention, if not breaking it. Their relationship – through the fan press, their films, and their previous star personas – was geared to relate to the concerns of Depression audiences. They appeared to be a couple that mirrored the changes in courting and marriage wrought by the Crash. Lombard's clear shift from the flapper to the working girl complemented Gable's move from brute to virile but compassionate underdog. Gable is cited in Black's article as having to buy expensive clothes but these were a business expense: 'Outside of business he puts on no big act. With Carole he goes to neighbourhood movies rather than snooty operas or symphonies. That ranch of his that you read so much about – it's only a two acre spot in the San Fernando Valley, much smaller than many a lesser movie name boasts.' (see Figure 3.2)[47] Here they are a working, yet unmarried, couple living together on their small ranch. Their choice not to marry is presented as pragmatic and offered as an implicit riposte to Victorian convention and hinterland moral righteousness. In this mutually supportive relationship and pooling of resources, the business savvy of Lombard guides and protects Gable, whose type of masculinity greets the 'scent of pale lavender' of the matinee idol with the smell of the soil. Whether that soil signifies the 'pleasures of the outdoors' or the 'smell of hope and hunger' is left indeterminate. As such, Lombard–Gable were able to be both the star couple and the working couple that the hard times demanded.

Notes

1   Frederick Lewis Allen, *Since Yesterday: The Nineteen Thirties in America* (London: Hamish Hamilton, 1940), 111.

2   Sonia Lee, 'Carole Lombard Tells Why Hollywood Marriages Can't Succeed', *Motion Picture Magazine*, May (1934), 28.

3 Adele Whitely Fletcher, 'A Heart to Heart Letter to Carole Lombard and Clark Gable from Adele Whitely Fletcher', *Screen Guide*, November (1936): 5.

4 Fred Black, 'Will Clark Gable Ever Marry Carole Lombard', *Motion Picture Magazine*, February (1939): 31.

5 Ibid., 31.

6 Emily Susan Carman, 'Independent Stardom: Female Stars and the Studio System in the 1930s', *Women's Studies* 37 (2008): 597.

7 Carman, 607–08.

8 Ibid., 598.

9 Lee, 80.

10 Ibid., 28.

11 Dorothy Calhoun, 'How Many Marriages for Clark Gable', *Movie Classic*, September (1931): 41.

12 Carole Lombard, 'I'm a Gay Divorceé, as told to Dorothy Manners', *Hollywood*, September (1934): 61.

13 Black, 49.

14 Ibid., 73.

15 In 1928 Lombard had worked for slap stick comedy producer and director Mack Sennett in shorts released by Pathe Exchange.

16 Black, 73.

17 The private life of Gable as reported in the fan press tended to have an underlying inflection of dependence, positioning his older wives as career nurturers and enablers rather than sexual partners. An article from *Photoplay* in 1934 entitled 'Clark Gable Cuts the Apron Strings' is an example of this.

18 Tina Olsen Lent, 'Romantic Love and Friendship: "The Redefinitions of Gender Relations in Screwball Comedy"', in *Classical Hollywood Comedy*, ed. Henry Jenkins and Kristine Brunovska Karnick (London: Routledge, 1995), 314–31 (321).

19 The Production Code Administration (PCA), a part of the Motion Picture Producers and Distributors Association, was a self-regulating body which enforced the Production Code introduced in 1934. The Code was a set of guidelines for films setting out what was deemed morally and socially acceptable. Film scripts were vetted by the PCA before they were put into production.

20 Lent, 321.

21 Allen, 114–15.

22 Matthew J. Hill, 'Love in the Time of the Depression: the effect of economic conditions on marriage in the Great Depression', paper given at the All-UC Spring Economic History Conference at Cal Tech. 2011, 6.

23 Ibid., 23.

24 Claudia Goldin, 'The Quiet Revolution That Transformed Women's Employment, Education, and Family', *American Economic Review* 96, no. 2 (May 2006): 6.

25 Goldin, 'Marriage Bars: Discrimination against Married Women Workers from the 1920s to the 1950s', in *Favorites of Fortune: Technology, Growth, and Economic Development since the Industrial Revolution*, ed. Patrice Higonnet, David S. Landes and Henry Rosovsky (Cambridge, MA: Harvard University Press, 1991), 511–36.

26 Lee, 28.

27 Ibid., 28–29.

28 Allen, 114–15.

29 Noel F. Busch, 'A Loud Cheer for the Screwball Girl', *Life*, 17 October (1938): 48.

30 Ibid., 63.

31 Alva Johnston, 'Public Relations – IV', *New Yorker*, 9 September (1944): 31.

32 Eric Hoyt, 'Hollywood and the Income Tax: 1929–1955', *Film History* 22 (2010): 5–21.

33 Ibid., 10.

34 Joshua L. Rosenbloom and William A. Sundstrom, 'The Sources of Regional Variation in the Severity of the Great Depression: Evidence from U.S. Manufacturing, 1919-1937'. *The Journal of Economic History* 59 (September 1999): 714–47.

35 Andre Sennwald, 'Hands Across the Table': A Sprightly Romantic Comedy at the Paramount', *New York Times*, 2 November (1935): 8.

36 Allen, 118.

37 Hart Seymore, 'Carole Lombard Tells "How I live by a Man's Code"', *Photoplay* LI, no. 6 (June 1937): 12.

38 Lent, 320.

39 Adela, Rogers St. Johns, 'The Great God Gable', *Liberty Magazine*, 12 March (1932): 66–67.

40 Jim Tully, 'He went Places', *This Week*, 30 June (1935): 10.

41 Ibid., 10.

42 Rogers St. Johns, 66.

43 Ibid.

44 Tully, 10.

45 Black, 73.

46 Ibid., 75.

47 Ibid.

Part Two

Kinship

Shelley Cobb and Neil Ewen

The most common image of family – the nuclear family of married mom and dad, and two (maybe more, maybe fewer) kids – holds a central position in contemporary western media culture, and has done since at least the earliest days of television. From *Leave it to Beaver* (1950s) through *The Cosby Show* (1980s) to the current *Modern Family* (2009–), many successful TV shows, structured by the nuclear family, have marked the medium's history in America and beyond.[1] Television has been particularly associated with the image of the family because of its status as a hub of domestic community, and the anxiety that has sprouted as a result of recent technological changes – with the rise of personal media devices undermining television's historical hegemony – is often explicitly linked to the supposed disappearance of the family unit sitting together in front of the TV set. Of course, television is only one medium among many that reproduces the nuclear family as normative; but its assumed value as a familial and cultural glue remains strong in the multimedia era. Today, television's intersection with celebrity culture is perhaps most obviously illustrated by the rise of the reality TV family in shows like *The Osbournes, Living Lohan, Hogan Knows Best, Snoop Dog's Father Hood* and *Keeping up with the Kardashians* (see Alice Leppert's analysis of the celebrity momager, Kris Jenner, in this section).[2]

The attendant rhetoric of 'family values' attached to the idealized image of the family has had significant cultural power as a discourse since the onset of (the ongoing) culture wars of the 1980s, particularly in the US and the UK. Margaret Thatcher's (in)famous comment in 1987 that 'there is no such thing as society. There are only individual men and women, and there are families'[3] neatly expresses the ways that capitalism in the neoliberal era rhetorically uses the family as cover while enacting economic policies that have, over the last few decades, eviscerated public institutions, weakened historical community ties, and effected change on the traditional family unit itself. The rhetoric's hollowness is exposed by the fact that since neoliberalism took hold, increasingly fewer households in the US and UK comprise married couples with children; the blended family has become more prominent; and the number of single-person households has increased.[4] This is, in our view, at least partly because neoliberalism has wrought increasing income inequality, wage deflation and more precarious employment conditions for the vast majority of ordinary people: all of which make the idealized nuclear family more difficult to achieve. Celebrity families can often appear to portray fantasy versions of cohesive, normative and wealthy households. However, though many are members of what is known, in the parlance of our times, as 'the 1%', celebrities also experience divorce, remarriage, troubled children and financial ruin. Whether made up of traditional or non-traditional kinship formations, whether wealthy or ruined, whether functional or dysfunctional, celebrity families multiply the heights of celebrity fantasy and identification in the ways they do and do not reflect our experiences of being a parent, child or sibling.

Over the last 150 years the nuclear family has been repeatedly interrogated by some of intellectual history's most famous names. Marx and Engels, for example, argued that the foundations of the bourgeois family were 'On capital, on private gain',[5] while in their *Anti-Oedipus: Capitalism and Schizophenia* (1972) Deleuze and Guattari argued that the family under capitalism was a key agent of social repression transforming individuals into docile servants of a system that exploited them economically and chained them to servitude by repressing desires in childhood.[6] The family and its capitalist structures were also, of course, critiqued by Marxist-feminists who directly linked gender inequality to the capitalist foundations of family life.[7] Though the chapters in this section do not take explicitly radical approaches, all of them to a greater or lesser extent consider the celebrity family's relationship with capitalism as one of commodification, and recognize that, as the content of a popular reality TV show, as a valuable media brand for the individual stars involved, as a mini industry of celebrity production, or as a dynasty of successful stars, the celebrity family both sells itself and the individual members within it.

Feminists and critical race scholars have pointed out how the 'family values' mentioned above have been used repeatedly to stereotype, if not vilify, women and persons of colour. 'Family values proselytizers' (as Hannah Hamad calls them in her chapter under this section) perpetuate a discourse of the family in crisis that is at best simplistic in its analysis and at worst is a self-fulfilling prophecy. For example, the 'crisis discourse' blames the break-up of the bourgeois family on feminists and blames the break-up of the black family on feckless fathers and lazy welfare mothers. These, and other gendered and racialized cultural stereotypes of parenting, also play out in the media's representations of celebrities, often in contradictory ways. Whether in the sexualized dysfunction of Ryan and Tatum O'Neal, the blended families of Eddie Murphy and Will Smith, or the profit-oriented mother of Kris Jenner, several of the analyses in this section consider how celebrities perform and sometimes trouble the cultural politics of sex, gender and race in parent–child relationships.

Beginning with a queer reading of the celebrity portmanteau and a reminder that 'show business dynasties have emerged from the studio era and the post-studio period alike', Maria Pramaggiore, in her chapter 'Filial Coupling, the Incest Narrative, and the O'Neals', investigates the notion of the 'filial couple' and considers how we might analyse the celebrity couple that is not structured explicitly by romance or sex. Her particular focus on Ryan and Tatum O'Neal and on the 'docu-series' in which they appeared together in 2011 on the Oprah Winfrey Network – 'The O'Neals' – articulates how their filial coupledom is constructed by 'the discourses of family dysfunction and incest trauma', and offers a template for understanding how the 'practices of celebrity should also be considered in relation to collective, familial dynamics'.

Following on from Pramaggiore's claim that 'dynastic celebrity exposes historically and culturally specific beliefs regarding genetics, breeding, and reproduction, parenting and childhood, youth and old age', Racher Dwyer, in her chapter 'A Star is Born?: Rishi Kapoor and Dynastic Charisma in Hindi Cinema', takes the idea of dynastic stardom to Bollywood and considers the narrative of the Kapoor family in Hindi cinema that has produced four generations of film stars, 'asking if there is anything particular or unusual about stardom in Hindi cinema which accounts for the Kapoor family's durability and dominance'. Dwyer specifically focuses on Rishi Kapoor (1952–), who, she suggests, 'lived his life in the eye of the media, destined for stardom from birth', but throughout the chapter she explores how both the men and women of the family, across its various generations, negotiate their individual styles with the Kapoor 'family charisma'.

Bringing us back to Hollywood, Hannah Hamad, in her chapter, 'The (Post-) Racial Familial Politics of Hollywood Celebrity Couples', analyses how the 'celebrity identities of Will Smith and Eddie Murphy, as they pertain to the politics of racial discourse at the dawn of the Obama era, are charged with meaning' and how this 'comes into clearest view when seen through the frame of coupledom and familial politics'. She closely considers how both men's family lives are differently, and problematically, narrativized in the celebrity media through the 'family values rhetoric that paints and pathologizes the black family as perennially "in crisis"'. Her close analysis of the Smith family also looks at the 'industrial mobilization of their coupledom and their family dynamic, enabled by the couple's partnership in their [own] production company' in order to take into account how their children's careers contribute to the Smith family's image of dynastic celebrity.

The 'industrialial mobilization' of kinship relations in the commodification of the celebrity family is exemplified by the Kardashians and their 'momager' Kris Jenner in Alice Leppert's 'Momager of the Brides: Kris Jenner's Management of Kardashian Romance'. Jenner serves as manager for all six of her children (and a few husbands/partners) while also being a celebrity in her own right. Jenner has been strongly criticized in the press for holding the dual position of mother and manager, the latter of which she profits from financially. But, as Leppert shows, 'Jenner's acceptance of this villainous role simultaneously works to protect her clients, as she sacrifices her own image and reputation in order for them to appear more sincere'. Jenner's management and commodification of various family weddings allows all of the family 'to profit from images of "fairy-tale romance," a fairy-tale in which Jenner, in her own capacity as a celebrity, often plays the role of the villain'.

Notes

1   Muriel G. Cantor, 'The American Family on Television: From Molly Goldberg to Bill Cosby', *Journal of Comparative Family Studies* 22, no. 2 (Summer 1991): 205–16.

2   For an analysis of the construction of celebrity fatherhood in many of the reality TV shows mentioned here, see Hannah Hamad, '"Hollywood's Hot Dads": Tabloid, Reality and Scandal Discourses of Celebrity Post-Feminist Fatherhood', *Celebrity Studies* 1, no. 2 (2010): 151–69.

3   See Margaret Thatcher, 'Interview for *Woman's Own* ("no such thing as society")', Margaret Thatcher Foundation', http://www.margaretthatcher.org/document/106689.

4 See Debra Caruso and Sandra Timmerman, 'The Disappearing Nuclear Family and the Shift to Non-Traditional Households Has Serious Financial Implications for Growing Number of Americans', Huffington Post, 25 January 2013, http://www.huffingtonpost.com/debra-caruso/retirement-plan-the-disappearing-nuclear-family_b_2534622.html; and Hannah Richardson, 'Nuclear Family in "decline"', figures show, BBC online, 2 July 2010, accessed at http://www.bbc.co.uk/news/10487318.

5 Karl Marx and Friedrich Engels, *The Communist Manifesto* (London: Pelican, 1967), 100–01.

6 Gilles Deleuze and Felix Guattari, *Anti-Oedipus: Capitalism and Schizophrenia*, reprinted. (Minneapolis: University of Minnesota Press, 1983).

7 Two key examples of the latter are Shulamith Firestone's *The Dialectic of Sex* (1970) and Michèle Barrett and Mary McIntosh's *The Anti-Social Family* (1982).

4

Filial Coupling, the Incest Narrative and the O'Neals

Maria Pramaggiore

It's been a traumatic couple of decades.

Tatum O'Neal, 'The O'Neals'

I fight with everybody Tatum, not just you. It's not personal.

Ryan O'Neal, 'The O'Neals'

During the first two decades of the twenty-first century, fan magazines and web sites became incubators for the conjoined celebrity name, a linguistic trope that revealed the continuing significance of heteronormative coupling within the discourse of stardom. The trend, which, Michael Williams argues in this volume, may have begun as early as the late 1920s with *Gilbo*, took hold in earnest after 2002, with the corporate and coital mergers known as *Bennifer*, *TomKat*, *Brangelina* and *Kimye*.[1] Television scholars Martha Nochimson and Nancy San Martin have argued that these supercouple conflations began with the soap opera *General Hospital* in the 1980s.[2] Taking stock of the coupled naming convention for *Huffpost Celebrity* in 2012, Erin Clements lays out the synergistic and multiplicative logic of the 'uni-name': it embodies a process of accumulation of a form of 'equity' that exceeds the value associated with the two stars as individuals.[3]

Because the portmanteau so thoroughly endorses heterosexual hegemony, it might be thought of as a paradoxical development or a sign of retrenchment in an era in which traditional sexualities and family structures were openly challenged by popular TV programmes such as *Modern Family* and *Glee* and films such as *The Kids Are All Right* (Cholodenko, 2010), not to mention the growing number of 'out and proud' gay and lesbian celebrities such as Neil Patrick Harris and Ellen Page. Gay and lesbian celebrities entered the pantheon of Hollywood power couples in this period as well: *TV Guide* placed Ellen De Generes and Portia Di Rossi on its list of Hollywood power couples in 2007, and *Forbes* included them on its list of top-earning power couples the following year.[4] Despite attaining this elite status and marrying in 2008, however, the lesbian pair failed to earn a conjoined name.

The portmanteau affords some flexibility in the nature of the connection it implies, which may include sexual, romantic and quasi marital-familial relationships. Its joining of first names – as opposed to the conventional sharing of the last name within heterosexual marriage – allows it to circumvent traditionalism, aligning it with a glamorous, freer, sexier, Hollywood version of union. This no-strings-attached form of para-matrimony represents a complete mystification, of course, because the capital that most celebrities amass makes their pairings and break-ups, whether formalized through marriage or not, extremely complicated legal and financial affairs.

The conjoined name, as a speech act, falls short of achieving what legal marriage accomplishes, of course: its emphasis on romance rather than reproduction – the latter implied by the single surname in traditional marriage – does not explicitly establish the dyad as the basis for the generation of a new family. My interest in the portmanteau trend in the context of the filial celebrity couple rests precisely with the way the conjoining of *first names* elides the old-fashioned and un-sexy trappings of the romantic couple when it becomes a family unit (even if prospectively), even as it consolidates the affective and cultural power of the star couple. In other words, the naming device suggests a desire to create not new couples but a new kind of couple, one that might transcend the process that transforms the (young and exciting) romantic couple into a (sedate) family unit.

For the celebrity pairing that explicitly signifies the family unit – the filial coupling of parent and child – family bonds rather than sexual attraction define the relationship. The members of a filial couple often share a name, and they sometimes enjoy the same synergistic dynamics as romantic couples, whereby the pairing amounts to more than the sum of its parts. Although this couple is not defined through romance, the discourse of sexuality that attaches to stardom returns, in surprising ways, to construct aspects of even this 'sacred' bond.

Fan interest in the literal reproduction of stardom – evident in the ubiquity of baby bumps, post-baby bodies, yummy mummys and mini-mes in the tabloid press of the late twentieth and early twenty-first centuries – is nothing new. The Hollywood film industry, one of the most important engines of modern celebrity, began to capitalize on the parent–child relationship as early as the 1920s, through vehicles such as the two-reel comedies directed by Madeline Brandeis of Pathé.[5] In 1927, the *LA Times* reported on the short film *Young Hollywood*, which displayed a stable of talent birthed by Hollywood royalty, including Erich Von Stroheim, Jr, Tim Holt (son of Jack Holt), Billy Reid (son of Wallace Reid), Eileen O'Malley (daughter of Pat O'Malley) and Barbara Denny (daughter of Reginald Denny). Show business dynasties have emerged from the studio era and the post-studio period alike, and include the Chaplins, the Barrymores, the Hustons, the Carradines, the Fondas, the Redgraves and, more recently, the Derns, the Sheens and the Smiths.

These dynasties are the breeding ground for filial couples; however, famous families do not automatically produce filial celebrity couples. I propose a narrow definition of the filial couple: they are parent–child couples whose fame is invariably inflected by, and possibly even dependent upon, the filial relation. In the argot of our therapy-saturated culture, the filial couple's fame is generated through codependency. The parent generally earns celebrity prior to and independently of the child, but once the child enters the public arena, their star texts develop jointly, with frequent reference to the filial relation.

I am adopting this admittedly queer angle on celebrity coupling in order to explore the underlying structure of coupled stardom more fully and, particularly, the inevitability of its sexualization. There are other, equally productive ways to queer the celebrity couple: investigating gay and lesbian couples to test the constraints of heteronormativity or considering trans identities to probe the dynamics of fame and gender, to name only two. These would be worthy projects, indeed. My goal here, however, is to understand the dynamics of coupling when it is not explicitly contextualized by sex or romance, and to ask if that is even possible. Examining the filial couple also provides an occasion to examine notions of family love and affection that contribute in important ways to defining heteronormative sexuality. In arguments for marriage equality, for example, the promise of family bonds – stable couples and parents with children – has frequently been marshaled to normalize queerness, to the delight of some and the dismay of others.

Finally, the filial couple offers an occasion to probe the way that celebrity culture rests upon practices of capital accumulation and beliefs about genetic inheritance, while contradictorily touting stardom as a democratic process. In *Celebrity*, Chris Rojek argues that modern celebrity has everything to do with democracy, and he establishes an opposition between achieved and ascribed celebrity; the latter refers to those whose 'status typically follows from bloodline'.[6] Sociologist Karen Sternheimer argues that celebrity culture 'seems to provide a continual reaffirmation that upward mobility is possible in America and reinforces the belief that inequality is the result of personal failure rather than systemic social conditions'.[7] This, despite the fact that celebrity discourses routinely refer to media sensations as America's royalty, challenging that democratic ethos. Sternheimer addresses this contradiction, writing 'despite the belief that success is primarily the result of our own actions, being born into the right family can make it easier to become a celebrity, a part of the American caste system that we seldom recognize'.[8]

The broader context for this chapter is my interest in dynastic celebrity, the economic, cultural and affective practices associated with the accumulation of financial and cultural capital through celebrity. Dynastic celebrity mediates concepts of naturalness, inheritance and birthright, and, in the US context at least, must manage the tension created between celebrity exceptionalism and the democratic discourse of the American Dream.

Dynastic celebrity, along with dynasties of other kinds, is consistent with the political economy of oligarchy, plutocracy and nepotism, dynamics that blatantly contradict the American Dream narrative of merit and mobility. Filial relations are bound up with the capitalist practices and neoliberal ideologies that have reinvigorated the family as a locus of economic activity in recent decades. A mode of capital accumulation that pre-existed industrialization and mass media, the family unit has re-emerged in the wake of the global financial crisis, rising unemployment and rising (student) debt levels that have created the situation of 'boomerang' children who never quite leave home. In 2014, *The New York Times* reported that one in five people in their late 20s or early 30s is living with her or his parents.[9]

In addition, dynastic celebrity exposes historically and culturally specific beliefs regarding genetics, breeding, reproduction, parenting, childhood, youth, old age, and the role of the family in shaping individual and cultural experiences. These historiographical concerns distinguish the filial couple from the romantic celebrity couple. In *Valences of the Dialectic*, Fredric Jameson argues that history manifests itself at the level of the individual through the feeling of belonging to a generation. 'The experience of generationality,' he contends, 'is a specific collective experience of the present: it marks the enlargement of my existential present into a collective and historical one.'[10] Within the realm of celebrity, the filial couple contributes in unique ways to the experience of generationality because its parent–child dynamic enlarges the existential present both diachronically, through lineage, and synchronically through the structure of the nuclear family. It is not inconceivable that, at different points in time, depending upon their personal experiences, fans would identify with both children and parents in filial celebrity couples. Because they speak to family legacy, filial couples are bound up in our experiences of collectivity and continuity.

Thus, the filial couple helps to position those who consume celebrity culture within a specific cohort, such as 'the 60s generation' or 'baby boomers' or 'millennials' while also contributing to the definition of those constructs. For example, in *Parenting Culture Studies*, Charlotte Faircloth describes 'intensive parenting', as a trend linked to the new momism, which Susan Douglas and Meredith Michaels have identified as a dominant influence in the lives of women at the end of the twentieth and beginning of the twenty-first century.[11] This paradoxical investment in mothering in an era in which growing numbers of women joined the paid workforce has generated political discussions and triggered the mommy wars. Some sociologists have taken aim at idealized 'celebrity mom spreads in glossy magazines'[12] as perpetuating norms of attachment through which women, in particular, must establish their identities in the contemporary cultural landscape.

Along with baby bumps, second and third generation celebrity became a pronounced feature of the media landscape in the early twenty-first century. Dynastic celebrity uses the patina of glamour and luxury to reflect back the increasing concentration of wealth in the US economy, a concentration noted by economist Thomas Piketty, who points to the greater importance of inherited wealth relative to income earned from labour to the distribution of wealth in the US.[13] Reality TV in particular has been an important breeding ground for consolidating second (and third) generation celebrity with programmes such as *The Osbournes, Living Lohan, Hogan Knows Best, Gene Simmons' Family Jewels, Keeping Up with the Kardashians* and the programme that is the subject of this chapter, *The O'Neals*.

From the Generation Gap to gap kids

Acknowledging that there are a number of permutations possible within filial celebrity, I offer two brief sketches that suggest how filial celebrity couplings function, using one Hollywood studio era example, that of Henry and Jane Fonda, and one reality TV example, that of Kourtney Kardashian and Mason

Disick, before moving to an analysis of Ryan and Tatum O'Neal, celebrities whose conjoined star text spans post-studio Hollywood, television and reality TV. What initially emerges from all three pairings is the impossibility of disentangling sexuality from filial stardom. Some of the implications of this sexualization of filial stardom are borne out within the example of the O'Neals through the elaboration of a traumatic incest narrative.

The case of Henry and Jane Fonda may have established the father–daughter filial couple pattern in the post-war era.[14] Evidence for the codependent and multiplicative fame of the Henry–Jane pairing derives from both the tabloid press and the critical establishment, both of whom invariably represented Jane as an emblem of the political rebellion of the 1960s generation against the values of Henry's Greatest Generation. The narrative that informed this couple inevitably took the form of, and in turn naturalized, the idea of the Generation Gap. Tellingly, until Henry's death, neither figure's romantic relationships or marriages, not even Jane's partnership with activist Tom Hayden, eclipsed the filial connection in their star discourses.[15]

Writing on the family romance in 1908, Freud argued that the 'whole progress of society rests on the opposition between successive generations'.[16] This dynamic of opposition broadly informs one aspect of the Fonda narrative of father–daughter celebrity in the post-war era. In celebrity culture, where personas are products, brand continuity and commercial viability are maintained across celebrity generations through the careful orchestration of norm and deviation, and, within the family, through the dialectic of estrangement and reunion. Intergenerational conflict has been a touchstone of American culture since the post-war invention of the teenager; and the filial star text of Henry and Jane Fonda dramatized this dominant narrative of twentieth-century US social history. This narrative harks back to both Oedipus and Odysseus, with the parable of the Prodigal Son thrown in for good measure: a voyage and return pattern of youthful rebellion and subsequent reconciliation.

In the case of father–daughter couples, including the Henry and Jane Fonda pair, this pattern is often tinged with sexual tension. From her earliest days working in theatre and film, Jane was compared to or conflated with her father Henry, often in oddly physical terms, which I have discussed elsewhere:

> A review of Fonda's 1960 film debut in *Tall Story* established a strange yet definitive image for her early stardom that endured well into the seventies. Playing the role of a husband-hungry college cheerleader, she was 'a second generation Fonda with a smile like her father's and legs like a chorus girl'.[17]

By the 1970s, the press couched Jane's antiwar activism in the terms of the needy and rebellious daughter. Her activities were viewed as especially dangerous because of her insistence on encouraging soldiers to talk about the war, a strategy that resonated as an especially problematic parallel with Henry's own military career on a Navy destroyer during the Second World War. Jane's political work, and Henry's disapproving response to it, became a central theme in both star personas from the late 1960s until Henry's death in 1982.

For the Fondas, reconciliation came in the form of their shared, and Henry's final, film, *On Golden Pond* (Rydell, 1981), which encouraged the two to enact their filial relationship on screen. On 12 April 1982, *People Magazine* published a piece entitled 'Daddy's Girl: For Jane Fonda, Those Days on *Golden Pond* Brought Her and Her Dad Together at Last.' Driving the project, Jane had purchased the rights to an Ernest Thompson play, thus permitting the actors to not only explicitly perform their father–daughter dysfunction but also to relive the theatrical sensibility of their one prior performance together, at the Omaha Playhouse where Jane had made her theatrical debut at the age of eighteen. *On Golden Pond* was widely understood as a vehicle for the two actors to resolve their complicated relationship, as evidenced by the comments of the film's director Mark Rydell: 'Perhaps unconsciously [Jane] purchased [the rights to the play] to give herself an opportunity to resolve some of the distance that existed between her father and herself before the end.'[18] Both Fondas were nominated for Academy Awards for the film; Jane accepted the Best Actor award on behalf of an ailing Henry, cementing their legacy as a filial celebrity couple.

Another entrant in the filial coupling category, this time a mother and son pairing, are Kourtney Kardashian and Mason Disick. Kardashian's relationship with her firstborn child has been constructed as a threat to her long-term liaison with boyfriend Scott Disick. Although the source of Kourtney's fame is familial, and, more specifically, paternal and sororal, her work on the family's three television programmes has been mediated primarily through her relationship with Scott Disick, as an on-again, off-again couple.

The economic value of celebrity children as an asset has been foregrounded in tabloid press estimates of the earning potential of Kourtney's son Mason, already proclaimed a fashion icon like his mother, at $3 million. Mason's middle name, 'Dash', is the name of the first chain of Kardashian clothing stores for children, reflecting the confluence of commercial interests and familial intimacy. In a recent interview, Kardashian's mother and manager Kris Jenner reflected on the literal value of the family within the postfeminist neoliberal economy: 'Who knew it would be this profitable? I should have had more kids.'[19]

Focusing on the filial coupling of Kourtney and Mason also reveals the narrative of similarity combined with sexual tension that emerged in the Fonda star text: the two are treated as fashion mavens with Oedipal romance lurking in the background. A November 2012 cover story in *Us Weekly* entitled 'The Worst Week of My Life' hinted at Kourtney's struggle to balance two relationships – the romantic coupling with Scott and the filial coupling with Mason – by making reference to Kourtney's preference for sleeping with Mason and relegating Scott to the guest room. A few weeks earlier, Disick's purported abandonment of the family had provided fodder for another magazine cover. Here, the potential for celebrity as a parent–child dyad competes with that of the traditional romantic couple. In the era of thoroughgoing commercial exploitation of celebrity offspring, the possibilities may be that the filial relation, presumed to be a lifelong connection, might serve as a stable and potentially more lucrative platform for long-term celebrity than the relatively impermanent romantic dyad.

In both of these examples, a parent–child relationship assumes central importance to the stardom of both individuals. In both cases, genetic replication (similarity) and sexual tension (difference) inform these cross-gender relationships. The press subjects Jane and Henry Fonda to odd bodily conflations and to frequent comparisons of their smiles and their blue eyes. Kourtney Kardashian's investment in her son is depicted as a replication of her own interests in fashion (the first business she and Kris Jenner started was the children's clothing store Dash) and a threat to her sexual partnership with the child's father. The Fonda example is pervaded by the post-war rhetoric of rebellion and reconciliation, whereas the Kardashian–Disick dyad reveals the post-millennial practice of intensive parenting, as both a personal and professional matter, not only by Kardashian but also by her Momager, Kris Jenner. Clearly, there is more work to be done to investigate the complexities of family stardom and filial couples. Nevertheless, these two cases establish patterns of familial similarity and sexual tension that structure the filial coupling of Ryan and Tatum O'Neal and inform a narrative of incest and competition encompassing personal and professional relationships.

The incest narrative and the O'Neals

Ryan and Tatum O'Neal's individual star texts became inextricably intertwined when they co-starred in Peter Bogdanovich's *Paper Moon* (1973), a film in which Ryan O'Neal plays a man who refuses to acknowledge his paternal relationship to the girl Addie, played by daughter Tatum. Like the Fondas, but without the political agenda, the discourse surrounding the O'Neals has centred on their combative, dysfunctional relationship from the time of Tatum's teenage years throughout her adulthood. The pair engaged in their own version of a performative reconciliation by starring in and co-producing a short lived, 8-episode reality show called *The O'Neals*, which aired on the Oprah Winfrey Network (OWN) between June and August 2011. The programme focuses on reconstructing a normative father-daughter relationship that seems never to have existed, because the pair was dogged by implications of both competition (the dark side of filial replication) and incestuous closeness. A father–daughter pair that shares some of these elements is that of Jon Voight and Angelina Jolie; however, their fame is far less codependent than that of the O'Neals. Although Voight played Jolie's father in the first *Tomb Raider* film, echoing Ryan O'Neal's turn in *Paper Moon*, Jolie had already established her career independently, winning an Academy Award for *Girl, Interrupted* (Mangold, 1999) six years earlier.

The stardom of Ryan and Tatum O'Neal has always been situated within the discourse of family – Ryan O'Neal's parents, Blackie and Patricia, and his wives Joanna Moore (Tatum's mother), Leigh Taylor Young, and partner Farrah Fawcett, were all in show business. The O'Neal star discourse has also characterized celebrity as the family business and tragedy as the family avocation, hinting at what Misha Kavka describes as fame addiction as the family curse.[20]

Ryan O'Neal established his career in the late 1960s and early 1970s by transitioning from his role as a rich WASP (White Anglo-Saxon Protestant) bad boy Rodney Harrington on the soap opera *Peyton Place* to a rich WASP Harvard Law graduate Oliver Barrett III in *Love Story* (Hiller, 1970) and WASP musicologist Howard Bannister in *What's Up Doc?* (Bogdanovich, 1972). He reached the height of fame and box office clout in the 1970s with performances as a feminist man, playing opposite strong women such as Ali McGraw and Barbra Streisand in romance and comedy films.

The early 1970s penchant for nostalgia – evident in Lucas's *American Graffiti* (1973) and Polanski's *Chinatown* (1974) – generated momentum for Ryan O'Neal's career in 1973, when Peter Bogdanovich cast him and Tatum, then 9, in the depression era comedy *Paper Moon*. Playing not quite father and daughter – in the sense that Moses Pray, the charming huckster played by Ryan O'Neal, never admits paternity – Tatum stole the show and won an Academy Award for Best Supporting Actress, becoming the youngest recipient of that award in competition. In her 2004 memoir, *A Paper Life*, she reports that, when Ryan heard about her nomination, he jealously punched his daughter in the arm.[21] Her grandmother Patricia O'Neal accompanied Tatum to the Oscars' ceremony because neither her father nor director Bogdanovich chose to attend. Bogdanovich stated later that he 'knew it was going to be the beginning of a lot of problems'.[22]

Paper Moon had a significant impact on the careers of both O'Neals, father and daughter, and cemented them as a couple in fan culture. Tatum went on to become the highest paid child actor at that time in *The Bad News Bears* (Ritchie, 1976). As Tatum's career took off, her father's hit a plateau after the release of Stanley Kubrick's *Barry Lyndon* (1975), the director's least commercially viable film and one that O'Neal himself pointed to in a 2009 interview as causing a slump from which his career never recovered.[23] Ryan was relegated to playing slightly less hunky bachelors in unsuccessful films such as *Green Ice* (Day, 1981), *So Fine* (Bergman, 1981) and *Partners* (Burrows, 1982). By the 1980s and 1990s, he moved into parental roles with *Irreconcilable Differences* (Shyer, 1984), foreshadowing his stint as the titular character's unlikely father on the television programme *Bones* (2006–14).

The defining feature of the fame-inflected filial relationship of the O'Neals is not only a discourse of similarity and competition, but also a sexualized, incest narrative, with Tatum repeatedly cast (and sometimes casting herself) as the sexual and romantic partner to Ryan, the heedless womanizer. In a 2002 *People* magazine cover story, Michelle Tauber quotes Tatum as saying that Ryan, from whom she had been long estranged and who had recently been diagnosed with leukemia, was 'the love of my life'.[24] In articles published about the long, rocky romance between O'Neal and Farrah Fawcett, Ryan admitted to an affair with a young actress whom he thought of as a daughter. 'She was more a daughter to me than a lover,' O'Neal tells *Vanity Fair's* Leslie Bennetts, 'and my own daughter had flown the coop, so here was this replacement'.[25] In a shocking and highly publicized encounter, when Tatum appeared at Fawcett's 2009 funeral, her father, who later claimed he did not recognize her because they had been estranged for so long, propositioned her.[26]

In terms of the filial coupling of the O'Neals, the late 1970s and early 1980s were crucial to establishing the foundation for the incest narrative, as Ryan, whom Bennetts describes as 'a notorious Lothario who spent decades effortlessly seducing beautiful women into throwing themselves at his size-13 feet,' began his affair with Farrah Fawcett-Majors, which broke up her marriage

Figure 4.1 Ryan and Tatum O'Neal present competing family histories during a joint therapy session on their reality programme *Ryan and Tatum: The O'Neals*, Oprah Winfrey Network, 2011. Screen grab.

to television star Lee Majors and turned them into the 'Angelina and Brad of their day'.[27] O'Neal abandoned the teenaged Tatum, with whom he had shared his bed and his drugs, and moved in with Fawcett, creating a long-lasting rift the two O'Neals address in joint therapy sessions in their reality TV series (Figure 4.1). Tellingly, in one episode, Tatum refers to herself in the therapy session as 'the *Paper Moon* girl', while Ryan mentions that they always worked well together. Both actors reference the 1970s and the projects on which they worked together, which amount to only one film beyond *Paper Moon*, Bogdanovich's *Nickelodeon* (1976); their shared nostalgia reveals their fond memories of the decade in which their stardom peaked and suggests the way in which their work became inseparable from their filial relationship. Another example of this conflation of fame and family appears in Ryan's comments on making *Paper Moon*. He claims that he thought working with his nine-year-old daughter would enable them to 'be connected for life'.[28]

O'Neal's bad boy reputation grew amid his tempestuous romance with Fawcett and his arrests for drugs and violent behaviour sustained his celebrity more than his performances did. Although he worked steadily in film and television from the 1970s to the 2010s, including appearances in a star-studded series in the early 1990s, *Good Sports*, in which he and Fawcett played sports anchors engaged in a love–hate dynamic, he never regained the level of adulation he had achieved in the 1970s. In fact, he was nominated for a Golden Raspberry ('Razzie') award for the year's worst performance for his turn in *Tough Guys Don't Dance* (Mailer, 1987). Before his appearances on *Bones* and *The O'Neals*, O'Neal's legacy might have rested with his much mocked performance from Mailer's film. A YouTube clip from *Tough Guys Don't Dance* depicting a distraught O'Neal, who has just been asked to kill his wife and her lover, repeating 'Oh God, Oh Man,' has garnered more than four million hits under the title 'Worst Line Reading Ever.'[29]

Tatum's career also peaked during the 1970s, and her star text since then has been dominated by her troubled marriage to tennis player John McEnroe and her bouts with drug addiction. In *Spectacular Girls: Media Fascination and Celebrity Culture*, Sarah Projansky argues that Tatum O'Neal was a 'key girl star of the 1970s' but has been marginalized in relation to other stars of the same era such as Brooke Shields and Jodie Foster.[30] Projansky proposes that, in the 1970s, O'Neal's whiteness, her gender, and her sexuality elicited an 'anxious ambivalence'[31] that manifests in her 1970s star text as both the concern and pleasure associated with reporting on her difficult, 'tortured' childhood.[32] Whereas Projansky argues that the press sexualized and spectacularized Tatum O'Neal, I would return to the seminal text of the O'Neals' filial stardom to suggest that the way Ryan and Tatum, as Moses and Addie Pray, engage in the 'erotic, sexual banter commonly found in screwball comedies'[33] is the troubling source of that sexualization. Addie is explicitly constructed as a foil to Moses's romantic coupling with Trixie (Madeline Kahn), which is played for laughs rather than sexual tension. I would argue that the film that cemented the critical importance of the familial bond to their star texts was also one that introduced, in a public way, the incest narrative, a story that would build and develop in a variety of ways in the ensuing decades. Ryan's love interests would inevitably be cast against his responsibility to his daughter; her whirlwind romance and early marriage to a narcissistic, bad boy tennis player read as evidence of her daddy complex (Ryan was also a tennis player).

Extending Projansky's useful work, I would also argue that one critical element contributing to Tatum O'Neal's continuing iconicity and marginalization is precisely the fact that her stardom was established within the context of an incestuous filial relationship to Ryan O'Neal, a figure who similarly remains both iconic and marginalized. The incest narrative that played a role in establishing the star personas of the two actors may also have thwarted their attempts to reascend to A-list celebrity, together or alone. From the outset, they are marked by the patina of perversity, referenced by Projansky in her analysis of Sam Blum's 1973 *Redbook* article, 'The Real Love Story: Ryan and Tatum O'Neal,'[34] in which the journalist asks Ryan about living an Oedipal fantasy. While Projansky convincingly reads this process of eroticization in the context of the girl star,[35]

I would argue for the value of taking a closer look at these filial dynamics in their own right, to fully account for the gendered and sexual implications of casting a (tomboyish) girl as a partner to her own celebrity father.

In addition to the incest narrative, the dynamic of rejection and reconciliation that we have already seen at work in the Fonda family romance similarly attends the filial coupling of Tatum and Ryan O'Neal. Freud's writing on the family romance is concerned with the (male) child's assertion of independence from his parents. The term refers to the child's belief that his parents are exalted beings, a belief that ratifies the adolescent's own sense of significance in the world. According to Freud, the child imaginatively substitutes other people of higher status for his parents, and, especially his father, since maternity is presumed to be indisputable. Freud concludes that the fantasy of replacement is merely a reflection of a wish for an earlier time when the child perceived the father to be noble: 'The whole effort at replacing the real father by a superior one is only an expression of the child's longing for the happy, vanished days when his father seemed to him the noblest and strongest of men.'[36] In the case of Tatum and Ryan O'Neal, as delineated in the former's first autobiography, *A Paper Life*, Freud's 'happy vanished days' correspond to the period in which Ryan, a young, single Hollywood star, rescued Tatum from her alcoholic mother Joanna Moore, and, after a brief stint in a boarding school in Arizona, brought her to live with him in his Malibu bachelor pad. In the memoir, Tatum recounts sleeping in her father's bed and waiting outside a locked door when he entertained women friends.[37]

Ryan's failed fatherhood – manifested in his rocky relationship with Tatum and the constant tension and brawling between Ryan and Griffin, Patrick and Redmond (the three boys he fathered with Joanna Moore, Leigh Taylor Young and Farrah Fawcett, respectively) – has come to dominate the star text of every O'Neal family member, in what Leslie Bennetts calls 'the family pathology'.[38] For forty years, from the mid-1970s through 2012, tabloid headlines have proclaimed family troubles as the defining trope of O'Neal celebrity, and repeatedly situate Ryan and Tatum at the centre of the fray. In its 6 October 2008 issue, *People* published a multipage spread entitled 'The O'Neal Family: Hollywood Tragedy.'

The discourses of family dysfunction and incest trauma converged to produce Ryan and Tatum O'Neal's *The O'Neals*, which was billed as their last attempt to reconcile (as Ryan was seventy in 2011) and functioned as a way to capitalize on their recent TV work (Ryan on *Bones* and Tatum on *Rescue Me*) in roles which themselves drew upon ideas about familial dysfunction. The reality programme aired on OWN in 2011 and revisited the father–daughter incest theme through joint therapy sessions that disinter a troubled past, as the two return again and again, primarily at Tatum's prompting, to Ryan's abandonment of Tatum when he became involved with Farrah Fawcett.

Jen Shelton, in her work on James Joyce, defines incest in relation to narrativity as 'a structure of conflict over control of a child's body and narrative'.[39] This structure of conflict animates the public relationship between Ryan and Tatum O'Neal: Ryan's access to Tatum's childhood body enabled the O'Neals' most successful Hollywood endeavours. The incest narrative, created in conjunction with press and publicity over decades, was brought into relief by the publication of Tatum's two autobiographies, in 2004 and 2011, in which she airs the details of their competitive and codependent relationship.

This conflict over Tatum's body and her narrative emerged once again in the reality TV series. In an episode entitled 'The Final Revision', which focuses on Tatum completing her second memoir, business manager and family friend, Bernie Francis, raises the spectre of Ryan's probable objection to her statement that her father had 'abdicated his role'. Tatum breaks down in tears, wearily asserting 'This is really my story, and I don't think my dad should have control over what I write or how I write it.' (See Figure 4.2) But she finally acquiesces in light of Bernie's admonition to 'have a little more patience with your father' who is 'not strong enough to face up to some of the things with you and your family.' She narrates to the camera in a scene shot later that she had an 'aha moment' in which she realized that 'it's about today … [not] the backstory stuff.'

Figure 4.2 Tatum tears up in response to Ryan's challenge (by proxy) to her narrative. *Ryan and Tatum: The O'Neals*, Oprah Winfrey Network, 2011. Screen grab.

The dynamics of bodily and narrative control play out here – through the distinctive world of celebrity – when Ryan describes their relationship in terms that confound and conflate family, stardom, and intimacy:

> You and I, we're not just father and daughter, we're co-stars. And so we have a relationship that differs from a lot of people. It's far more intimate. She could finish my sentences; that's how close we were. It was a perfect union. It was better than any one I'd ever had with my wives or girls. I'd sure like to get that back.

Tatum diagnoses the pathology of the category confusion that her father embraces, complaining, 'he does this thing where he doesn't differentiate me as a daughter, I'm just kind of a woman, or a chick, or a female.' She recalls that, during her adolescence, 'I was far too close to him, I had gone to every party with him.' Ryan, however, again attributes the boundary issue to their professional status: 'we never had any boundaries; we couldn't.' He then asserts, 'We worked together; actors don't always have the same kind of boundaries.' A statement summarizing Ryan's version of their shared story appears on the OWN website: 'her grudge is that I left her for another woman'.[40]

What's at stake in the reality TV iteration of the conflict over Tatum's body and narrative is not family reconciliation, but, instead, the possibility of continued access to fame itself, the substance to which these two are mutually addicted. As Misha Kavka brilliantly notes in her work on star damage, when the substance to which one is addicted is fame itself, rehabilitation and redemption can no longer be sought through corrective action and public confession.[41] Instead, damage control paradoxically demands the hyper-performance of that damage in the context of media culture, which characterizes the OWN network's staging of the father–daughter family romance of *The O'Neals*.

As I hope this chapter begins to suggest, filial stardom provide us with an occasion for understanding the way celebrity coupling both reflects and informs our understanding of family, gender, sexuality and generational belonging. In his introduction to the *Celebrity Culture Reader*, P. David Marshall writes, 'Celebrities serve as the lingua franca of identity' because fans 'interpret the meaning of the celebrity … on the dimensions of individuality and identity in contemporary culture.'[42] In this chapter I have argued that practices of celebrity should also be considered in relation to collective, familial dynamics that influence the construction of individuality and also contribute to the psychic economy and the political economy of fan generations.

One key element of late-twentieth-century and early-twenty-first-century therapeutic discourse in the US has been the exploration of family trauma, due in part to feminist interventions and often enacted through the naming of domestic violence and child abuse. The O'Neals offer one striking example of the ways in which the incest narrative can be engendered and enabled by a form of codependent celebrity that depends upon the eradication of boundaries.

Notes

1   Vanessa Díaz examines the dynamics of the conjoined name in 'Brad, Angelina … and Now Brangelina!: the Linguistic, Economic and Social Significance of the Blending of Celebrity Names', in this volume.

2   Martha P. Nochimson, *Screen Couple Chemistry: The Power of 2* (Austin: The University of Texas Press, 2002); Nancy San Martin, *Queer TV: Framing Sexualities on US Television* (Ann Arbor: UMI, 2002).

3   Erin Clements, 'Kimye, Brangelina, Bennifer: The Evolution Of Celebrity Couple Nicknames', *Huffpost Celebrity*, 18 April 2012.

4   See Lacey Rose, 'Hollywood's Top Earning Couples', *Forbes*, 10 November 2008, http://www.forbes.com/2008/11/19/hollywood-jayz-beyonce-biz-media-cx_lr_ls_1119couples.html/. For a compelling analysis of the convergence of postfeminism, queer politics, and celebrity coupling, see Shelley Cobb's 'Ellen and Portia's Wedding: the Politics of Same-Sex Marriage and Celesbianism', in this volume.

5   See Tom Mole's work on celebrity in the Romantic era for an account of the pre-history of mass media celebrity: *Byron's Romantic Celebrity: Industrial Culture and the Hermeneutic of Intimacy* (Basingstoke: Palgrave Macmillan, 2007). For another historical view of the long history of celebrity, see Leo Braudy's *Frenzy of Renown: Fame and Its History* (Oxford: Oxford University Press, 1986).

6   Chris Rojek, *Celebrity* (London: Reaktion Books, 2004), 17.

7   Karen Sternheimer, *Celebrity Culture and the American Dream: Stardom and Social Mobility* (New York: Routledge, 2011), 3.

8   Ibid., 12.

9   See Susan Douglas and Meredith Michaels, *The Mommy Myth: the Idealization of Motherhood and How It Has Undermined All Women* (New York: Free Press, 2005).

10   Quoted in Benjamin Kunkel, 'Into the Big Tent', *London Review of Books* 32, no. 8 (22 April 2010): 16.

11 See Adam Davidson's 'It's Official: the Boomerang Kids Won't Leave', *The New York Times Magazine*, 20 June 2014. www.nytimes.com.

12 Charlotte Faircloth, 'Intensive Parenting and the Expansion of Parenting', in *Parenting Culture Reader*, ed. Ellie Lee, Jennie Bristow, Charlotte Faircloth and Jan MacVarish (New York: Palgrave Macmillan, 2014), 28.

13 Thomas Piketty, *Capital in the Twenty First Century* (Cambridge, MA: Harvard/Belknap Press, 2014), 237.

14 The pair comprising Peter and Henry Fonda does not conform to my definition of a filial star couple, but the coupling of Jane and Henry does. While Peter was clearly understood as a Fonda, his star persona was not built specifically upon the notion of his relationship with his father – for one thing, the triangulation of Henry, Jane and Peter was a pervasive element of his star text.

15 In 'Jane Fonda, Power Nuptials, and the Project of Ageing', in this volume, Linda Ruth Williams discusses the way Fonda presents her celebrity in her autobiographies, which focus on her three marriages.

16 Peter Gay, *The Freud Reader* (New York: W.W. Norton, 1995), 298.

17 Maria Pramaggiore, 'Jane Fonda: from the Graylist to the A List', in *Hollywood Reborn: Movie Stars of the 1970s*, ed. James Morrison (New Brunswick, NJ: Rutgers University Press, 2010), 17.

18 John A. Gallagher, *Directors on Directing* (Westport, CT: Greenwood Press, 1989), 216.

19 See Alice Leppert's 'Momager of the Brides: Kris Jenner's Management of Kardashian Romance', in this volume.

20 Misha Kavka, 'Celebrity Damage', research paper, SCMS annual conference, Boston, MA, March 2012.

21 Wendy Leigh, 'Is Ryan O'Neal the worst father in Hollywood?' *Mail Online*, 6 February 2007. www.dailymail.co.uk.

22 Michelle Tauber, 'To Hell and Back', *People* Magazine 58, no. 2 (8 July 2002), http://www.people.com/people/archive/article/0,,20137470,00.html.

23 Leslie Bennetts, 'Beautiful People; Ugly Choices', *Vanity Fair*, September 2009, http://www.vanityfair.com/culture/features/2009/09/farrah-fawcett200909.

24 Tauber, 'To Hell'.

25 Bennetts, 'Beautiful People'.

26 Ibid.

27 Ibid.

28 Quoted in Sarah Projansky, *Spectacular Girls: Media Fascination and Celebrity Culture* (New York: New York University Press, 2014), 47.

29 'Worst Line Reading Ever', *YouTube* video, 0.36. 31 October 2007, http://youtu.be/Y9KyBdPeKHg.

30 Projanski, *Spectacular Girls*, 25–27.
31 Ibid., 49.
32 Ibid., 48.
33 Ibid., 49.
34 Ibid., 50.
35 Ibid., 56.
36 Gay, *The Freud Reader*, 300.
37 Tatum O'Neal, *A Paper Life* (New York: Harper Entertainment, 2004), 57.
38 Bennetts, 'Beautiful People'.
39 Jen Shelton, *Joyce and the Narrative Structure of Incest* (Gainesville: University Press of Florida, 2006), 23.
40 'OWN Preview: Ryan and Tatum Reunited on *The O'Neals*', http://www.oprah.com/spirit/OWN-Sneak-Preview-Ryan-and-Tatum-The-ONeals.
41 Kavka, 'Star Damage'.
42 P. David Marshall, *Celebrity Culture Reader* (New York and Oxon: Routledge, 2006), 3.

5

A Star is Born?: Rishi Kapoor and Dynastic Charisma in Hindi Cinema

Rachel Dwyer

Rishi Kapoor (1952–) is one of the biggest stars in the Hindi film industry (now known as Bollywood). He has acted in around 100 films, beginning as a child actor, before becoming a leading romantic hero, now opting for a variety of often challenging roles. Rishi married his co-star, Neetu Singh, and they remain a popular couple in the public imagination, appearing in several films today. This chapter concentrates on Rishi Kapoor's stardom as part of the famous Kapoor family, which has now produced four generations of major film stars. I explore the idea of individual stardom within the wider context of the Indian star dynasty, asking if there is anything particular or unusual about stardom in Hindi cinema which accounts for the Kapoor family's durability and dominance.

Indian film stardom

Star theory was developed mostly in the context of Hollywood[1] and has proved productive in exploring ideas of stardom in Indian cinema.[2] The concept of the star is based on two main sets of theories, one which privileges the text[3] and one which is the study of the star as part of the industry.[4] While both of these approaches inform this chapter, the text of the star and the wider cultural meanings of stardom in Indian society form the main focus.

Bollywood is the name by which the mainstream Hindi film industry based in Bombay/Mumbai is now known, perhaps best considered as a brand of the culture industry,[5] in which the star plays a major role as a focus of spectacle and desire, who structures the text but whose intertextual role is constantly referenced, while also exceeding the film text itself, notably in other media.

In India, despite the advent of celebrity culture the movie star still has an excess of celebrity. Film in India dominates other media including popular music, fashion, television and advertising, where stars are brand ambassadors. They overlap with other celebrities in sports – many of them owning Indian Premier League (IPL) cricket teams – they host reality shows and competitions. The wealthy need a film star to make their parties special and like to be photographed in the presence of stars. Many film stars are enthusiastic users of social media; leading stars such as Amitabh Bachchan and Shahrukh Khan have millions of followers. This media saturation also creates stories in the news and even those who claim not to follow Hindi film or its stars seem remarkably well informed about their lives.

This ubiquity of film stardom in India is not managed by agencies and studios but mostly by the stars themselves. Perhaps this is because the films themselves heighten the stars' presence, showing them as archetypes, the epitome of every quality, with an emphasis on glamour rather than character, while the melodrama allows them to perform as stars rather than acting in roles of characters so they 'play themselves'. The famous song and dance sequences, with the added input of choreographers (dance directors), music directors (composers and conductors), playback singers, with special locations (often extra-diegetic, such as the 'dream sequence'), and multiple costume changes, heighten the star's presentation of sexuality and glamour.

Indian stardom shares features of the two types of status that Chris Rojek,[6] following Durkheim,[7] suggests for celebrities. The first is what he calls 'achieved' based on the person's accomplishments in open competition, while the second is 'ascribed', that is it follows the bloodline though an individual may add achieved celebrity to his/her status derived from lineage. This is seen clearly in the star family of Hindi cinema: the Bachchans (two generations of two star couples), the Roshan-Khans (three generations of Roshans and two of Khans), the Samarth-Mukherjee-Devgns (who have produced many top female stars over three generations) and, of course, the Kapoors.

These star families form dynasties, which are not unique to India, being found from royal families to political dynasties, showing that the idea of birth entitlement is widely accepted, albeit also strongly contested. Yet, it may be that Indian culture is more favourable to creating and supporting dynasties. South Asia has produced several multigenerational political dynasties, such as the Nehru-Gandhi family in India, the Bhuttos of Pakistan and others. Many of India's leading businesses are family owned over many generations by sets of cousins and brothers.[8] Writing this chapter in 2014, the year in which the dynasty of the Nehru-Gandhi Congress Party suffered a major defeat, perhaps the current feeling is that one has to earn one's celebrity.

The dynastic stardom of the Kapoor family, from the silent period to the present, makes them one of the most significant dynasties in cinema in the world. Film dynasties occur in other cinemas, such as Shivaji Ganesan's in Tamil cinema, or the Fairbanks and the Barrymores of Hollywood, yet few if any of them compare in longevity and superstardom to this extraordinary family.

In India, stardom follows other cultural trends in putting the family before the individual. Ideas of links of blood, kinship and caste are part of the nature of dynasties which seems premodern and even anti-democratic in many ways, as family values contest the rights of the individual, yet dynasties are much celebrated by the fans and viewers as well as by the family. In traditional Indian society the primary bond is not necessarily or even usually between the conjugal couple – though there are important alliances in the Kapoor family – but between males in the family, not just fathers and sons but also with brothers and cousins and nephews and uncles.

The modern joint family in India can be one that does not actually live together but meets for ritual and other purposes. India also has embedded nuclear families, with all the usual quarrels, closeness, shared traits and differences. These provide an endless source of interest to fans and film viewers and the fandom and fun of knowing the dynasties of Indian cinema is reminiscent of Britain's royal watchers. The Kapoors remain the outstanding dynasty of Indian cinema so in this chapter I focus on one of its pivotal members, Rishi Kapoor, a star in his own right but also a star son, brother, nephew, cousin, father and husband.

The Kapoor *khandan* (family)

Film stars are always one of the favourite topics of journalists and biographers, and there are several books about the Kapoors. Two of the youngest generation of female Kapoors have written their own lifestyle books.[9] Among these many offerings, Madhu Jain's excellent book[10] contains biographies of the first generations of the family, for which she conducted solid research and detailed interviews over many years. Much that is 'known' about the family comes from other interviews, gossip[11] and is largely in the public domain.

The film story of the dynasty begins with Prithviraj (1906–72), who acted in India's first talkie, *Alam ara*/Light of the world (dir. Ardeshir Irani, 1931). Prithvi possessed heroic good looks, an athletic physique, and the light skin, hair and eyes that distinguish the family. He was a dashing hero throughout the 1930s, the heyday of the film studio, when he worked first in New Theatres in Calcutta.[12] He moved to Bombay where he continued these roles in *Phool*/The flower (dir. K Asif, 1944), where he plays a young man who goes to fight for the Caliphate and the title role in *Sikandar*/Alexander the Great (dir. Sohrab Modi, 1941), two great films of the period.

Prithviraj's roles were mostly in the popular genres of his day, historicals, mythologicals and Arabian-nights fantasies, which fell from favour in post-independence India. He began to take roles as patriarchal figures, including in two classic films, *Awaara*/The vagabond (1951, directed by his son Raj Kapoor), where he plays his screen father and *Mughal-e Azam*/The great Mughal (K Asif, 1960), where he plays the Great Mughal Akbar, father to Dilip Kumar's Salim. In both films, his authoritarian manner and overbearing and somewhat Oedipal relationship with his son are reinforced by his old-fashioned histrionic style.

Although a celebrated film star, Prithvi's real interest lay in theatre, and these were the days of IPTA (Indian People's Theatre Association), part of the cultural wing of the Indian communist party. He ran a theatre group where he starred in every production and in which his children played roles too.[13]

Prithvi roped all his offspring into performing but the only one who had a lifelong interest was his youngest son, Shashi (Balbir Raj Kapoor, 1938–), who married into the Kendal dynasty of actors – his wife Jennifer was the daughter of Geoffrey and sister of Felicity – but who also worked in mainstream cinema, where he usually played a very Anglicized or upper-class Indian, as well as acting in international cinema, notably the Merchant Ivory productions, such as *The Householder* (1963), *Shakespeare-Wallah* (1965), and *Bombay Talkie* (1970), and *Sammy and Rosie Get Laid*, (dir. Stephen Frears, 1987). Shashi's sons, Kunal (1960–) and Karan (1962–) and his daughter Sanjana (1967–) tried acting in films but had little success. Kunal married into the Sippy film family while Sanjana ran Prithvi Theatres from 1993 to 2012.

Prithvi's middle son, Shammi (Shamsher Raj Kapoor, 1931–2011), worked very rarely with his brothers, instead leaping around sets, with his trademark 'Yahoo' (*Junglee*, dir. Subodh Mukherjee, 1961), and becoming India's Elvis Presley, famed for his exuberant dances and his wild antics. Tall and fair, fashionably dressed with styled hair, he was one of the top stars of the 1960s, creating a new type of masculinity with his strutting and pouting and unstoppable energy. Shammi's style was widely imitated and loved. He acted with many of the leading ladies of the 1950s – Sharmila Tagore, Asha Parekh, Saira Bano –and was the first Kapoor to marry a film star, eloping with Geeta Bali, a bigger star than him when they married. Shammi had an arranged marriage after she died but remained known for his hunting, hypermasculinity and association with music. Like the other male Kapoors, he gained weight as he aged, and took only character roles, with decreasing frequency, although his last role, even though small, with his great-nephew Ranbir (see below) was much appreciated. Although Shammi defined a certain youth culture and masculinity, little has been written about him, beyond Jain,[14] although Ramani[15] remembers her romance and subsequent friendship with him.

However, Prithviraj's son who is most important in the history of Indian cinema was his eldest, Raj (Ranbir Raj Kapoor, 1924–88). He rose to fame in the late 1940s when he was not only a star but also a director and producer at a very young age. This was when the studio system was collapsing and giving rise to the independent producer, but he set up his own studio, RK Studios – still run by the family – which allowed him important creative control not just as a star. He had considerable worldwide popularity, particularly in USSR, and in China, his film *Awaara* being one of the greatest international hit films of all time.[16]

Raj Kapoor has received the most attention from writers on Hindi cinema, mostly journalists and academics[17] but also by his publicist, Bunny Reuben[18]; and his daughter.[19] There was much gossip about his romances, in particular that with his leading lady of the 1950s, the star, Nargis,[20] though he was married to Krishna Kapoor, the sister of actors Rajendra Nath and Prem Nath (through whom there are further star connections, as the latter married Bina Rai while Prem Chopra married another of their sisters). Stories about him circulated widely before the existence of tabloid papers, the gossip magazine and the internet, although they are widely held to be true.[21]

Best remembered as the 'Showman of Indian cinema', Raj Kapoor's films embody the struggle of the young against the old, his deep ambivalence about dichotomies of tradition and modernity, western and Indian, the worthiness of the poor and the glamour of the rich, being part of the tension in his films. Raj Kapoor defined beauty, romance, eroticism and passion set to some of the most memorable song and dance sequences in Indian cinema.

Raj played 'himself' in his films, Mr Raj, an ordinary man, an *awaara* (tramp, *Awaara*, 1951), a '420' (trickster, *Shree 420*, 1955), an *anari* (simpleton, *Anari*, dir. Hrishikesh Mukherjee, 1959), who is on the side of good, although he may don the clothing of the rich and successful to move between different worlds. When Raj became too old to continue playing the hero, he essayed one last time in his magnum opus, *Mera naam joker*/I'm called a clown (1972) in which Rishi played his young self. Stung by its box office failure, and short of cash, he cast Rishi as his star, and to a great extent, his replacement, in the blockbuster classic, *Bobby* (1973); then his youngest brother, Shashi, played the hero in *Satyam Shivam Sundaram*/Truth, auspiciousness, beauty (1978) (Shashi had played the young Raj in Raj's films in the 1940s and 1950s such as *Aag* [1948] and *Awaara* [1951]); Rishi starred again in *Prem Rog*/Love fever (1982), while his youngest son, Rajeev, in *Ram teri Ganga maili*/Ram, your Ganges is polluted (1985). This interchangeability between family members is reinforced by their striking physical resemblance over and across generations which made their stardom seem transferable and given at birth.

Raj's oldest son, Randhir (1947–), directed *Kal aaj aur kal*/Yesterday, today and tomorrow (1971), a clash between the three generations, starring Prithviraj, Raj and himself. He also acted in a few major hits, being one of the top-paid stars after his *Jawani deewani*/Crazy youth (dir. Narender Bedi, 1972). Rajiv (1962–), the youngest son, enjoyed huge success with *Ram teri Ganga maili*/Ram, your Ganges is polluted, in 1985 but has not had much of a career subsequently.

Randhir married his co-star, Babita (Babita Shivdasani, 1948–), a non-Punjabi (she has a Sindhi father and European mother) and then withdrew into running his father's studios. The family was said to have agreed to the marriage on condition that she gave up her career. Babita has remained a figure of interest in the press, as she and Randhir separated, though never divorced, and recently moved back together after many years apart. Babita brought up their daughters, Karisma (1974–) and Kareena (1980–), the first female stars in the family, again the leading stars of their time. While Karisma, whose success was initially in mass entertainment movies with Govinda, she went on to become a major star of the 1990s, and after a supposed engagement to Abhishek Bachchan, married a Delhi businessman and gave up movies. Now divorced, she made an unsuccessful comeback effort, *Dangerous Ishhq*/Dangerous love (dir. Vikram Bhatt, 2011), and writes 'Yummy mummy' books. Kareena continues to work as a leading heroine after her marriage, retaining her role as *the* diva of Hindi cinema. Her husband, Saif Ali Khan, is part of another dynasty, being the son of the captain of the Indian cricket team, the Nawab of Pataudi and superstar Sharmila Tagore, who acted in Satyajit Ray's films as well as being a major Bollywood star and related to Nobel Laureate Rabindranath Tagore. (Raj Kapoor's grandson by his daughter, Ritu, married Shweta, the daughter of Hindi cinema's megastar Amitabh Bachchan.)

Rishi Kapoor, Raj's second son, married his co-star, Neetu Singh, a major star who worked with his father, their romance being a big item in the gossip circles of the 1970s. They married in 1980 and she stopped acting in 1983, a decision she says she took without family pressure. She returned to the screen in 2009, with a surprise appearance in *Love aaj kal*/Love today (dir. Imtiaz Ali, 2009), and has since appeared in a couple of other films.

Their son, Ranbir (1982–), began his career in 2007 with *Saawariya*/Beloved (dir. Sanjay Leela Bhansali), which has many references to the Kapoors and their films. It includes a famous towel/bathing scene to display his body, though subsequently he has gone against the trend for the gym-built hero, playing gentle, introverted and complex characters, often musicians or closely associated with music, continuing the Kapoor family star image, despite his close resemblance to his mother, Neetu, rather than to the Kapoor males. In films such as *Ajab Prem ki gazab kahani*/The wonderful story of amazing Prem, dir Rajkumar Santoshi (2009) and *Barfi!* (dir. Anurag Basu, 2012), he performs the Chaplin slapstick loved by Raj Kapoor, famously in the fire extinguisher sequence of *Shree 420*. Another of Ranbir's films, *Bachna ae haseeno*/Run for your lives, my beauties! (dir. Siddharth Anand, 2008), uses the title of a song his father performed in *Hum kisise kam nahin*/We're not inferior to anyone (dir. Nasir Hussain, 1977). In *Rockstar* (dir. Imtiaz Ali, 2011), he plays a rock musician who is a disciple of music *ustad* (master) played by his great-uncle, Shammi.

Women who marry into the family have largely prioritized their marriages over their careers. Krishna Kapoor, Raj's wife, has often appeared in public, where she is known for her white clothes, but keeps a low profile, as does Shammi's second wife. Shashi's wife, Jennifer Kendal, an actress of British parentage, continued with her career after marriage while Randhir's wife, Babita, and Rishi's wife, Neetu, stopped working, said to be at the insistence of Raj Kapoor.

Raj Kapoor's daughters, however, have continued the dynastic legend. Reema Jain, a well-known figure in Bombay, helped launch her son Armaan Jain in *Lekar hum deewana dil*/With our joyful hearts (dir. Imtiaz Ali, 2014). Ritu Nanda (1948–), whose son, Nikhil Nanda, married into the Bachchan family, is a businesswoman based in Delhi, who wrote about her father. Shashi and

Jennifer's daughter, Sanjana, is well known for her work with Prithvi Theatres. She is married to tiger conservationist and writer Valmik Thapar, himself from a dynasty of Delhi intellectuals which includes the editors of *Seminar* magazine and celebrated historian Romila Thapar.

Rishi Raj Kapoor (1952–)

This chapter looks at the public star, not at the private person. The analyses here are all from mediated accounts rather than direct interviews, although I have met Rishi and interviewed him for the LSE India week.[22] Rishi has lived his life in the eye of the media, destined for stardom from birth. Rishi and his siblings, Randhir and Ritu, make a brief appearance in one of the most famous songs of Hindi cinema: 'Pyar hua, ikrar hua'/We fell in love, in *Shree 420*/The trickster (dir. Raj Kapoor, 1955). Raj Kapoor gave Rishi his first major role in *Mera naam joker*/I'm called a clown (dir. Raj Kapoor, 1972), a semi-autobiographical film where Rishi plays the young Raj. This was the last film in which Raj cast himself as a hero, using Rishi for Bobby and *Prem Rog*/Love fever (1982).

Little is known about how Raj encouraged younger members of his family to act, or if they had any say in doing so, or why Raj focused on Rishi rather than Randhir, and why Rajiv did not continue. It would be interesting to know how the dynasty responds to the stardom of its other members and how it supports or hinders them, but this remains unclear. One would also like to know what life as Raj Kapoor's son was like. It is said that Raj was a domineering father, himself dominated by his father. Neetu, Rishi's wife, says he was scared of his father.[23] For Rishi this life was normal, and he never lived apart from Bombay and its cinema. He grew up as a celebrity, meeting all the major stars of the day and the media focused relentlessly on his life. It is never clear what he wanted for himself and if that was the same as what his father wanted for him. Media reports, such as those documented in Jain suggest the family was highly patriarchal and one had to submerge oneself in it or keep at a distance.

Rishi's first lead role was as the teenager, Raj Nath (note the use of his father's name and his relatives' surname) in *Bobby* (1973). It marks not just a change of star, with the son replacing the father who was now too old to play a romantic hero, but also a change of theme and concerns. *Bobby* was written by K. A. Abbas who had turned out screenplays for earlier films for Raj Kapoor, including *Awaara* and *Shree 420*, which portrayed romance and eroticism, mixed with leftist politics and support of the masses, focusing on Raj's tramp persona, a kind of Charlie Chaplin figure of innocence, all set to some extremely popular Hindi film music. Although this film paid lip service to love being worth more than money in its theme, it is best remembered for its fun, glamour and fashion.

The film is not named for Rishi's character but the heroine who is called Bobby and was the debut outing for Dimple Kapadia, who abandoned her career before the film released in order to marry the then superstar Rajesh Khanna. This is said to have infuriated Raj who counted on his young heroine looking innocent in some of the skimpiest clothes seen in Hindi cinema of this time. She and Rishi were actual teenagers playing their age, and Rishi established his own image in the film as the son of Raj Kapoor, albeit young and carefree, fun. Even though he brought glamour as a good-looking star son, he was also the boy next door – not an athlete or a superhero, but a nice guy, safe, romantic, known for his fashion and gaudy knitwear.

The naming of the film perhaps suggests Rishi began by playing second fiddle to the heroine as well as to his father. Although Rishi was involved with RK Studio and continues to be so, he was a freelance star throughout most of his career. From *Bobby* to 2000, that is, for nearly twenty years, he played the lead romantic hero in ninety-two films, forty-one in multi-hero films and fifty-one as sole lead.

As a solo hero, Rishi played a romantic lead, seeking romance and happiness against a background of music and dance. He was closely associated with two major musical genres, the *qawwali* (a type of Sufi devotional song), including the celebrated 'Hum kisise kam nahin' from the film of the same name (see above) and 'Purdah hai purdah'/There is a veil in *Amar Akbar Anthony*, based on an Islamic devotional song, as well as disco, including his still celebrated 'Om Shanti Om' in *Karz*/Debt (dir. Subhash Ghai, 1980).

In his solo films, Rishi worked with leading female stars including Dimple, Zeenat Aman, Sri Devi and Tina Munim. He acted with Neetu Singh, later his wife, in many films. Their off-screen romance was often seen as being an extension of their life in films and the glamorous star couple featured in gossip and discussion about romance, arranged marriage and the family in new fan magazines such as *Stardust* which began in the 1970s.

Rishi and Neetu's alleged marital difficulties surfaced in the 1990s, which was when domestic conflict and violence began to be talked about publicly. Their reconciliation has also been of interest as ways of working out problems and family conflicts rather than finding a happy-ever-after lifestyle.[24] Perhaps it is the stories of these problems that make their fans more sympathetic towards them, and the common comfort that beauty, fame and wealth do not remove life's problems.

Rishi as a co-hero

Rishi's roles as second heroes are perhaps more interesting than his solo films, at least for examining his off-screen stardom. He often played second hero to the biggest star of Hindi film in the 1970s, Amitabh Bachchan, allowing Rishi to embody an alternative masculinity – gentler, more romantic in some ways but full of a stereotypical Punjabi joie-de-vivre, boisterous and fun-loving.

Bachchan's peak years as a hero in the 1970s and 1980s was in the era of 'multi-starrers', in that they had multiple heroes and heroines. Amitabh also starred in many films of the great director, Yash Chopra, in the 1970s. He often appeared with Shashi Kapoor, who first acted in a Yash Chopra film in 1961. Amitabh and Shashi worked together in many films including some of the greatest all-time hits of Hindi cinema, namely *Deewaar*/The wall (1975), *Kabhi kabhie*/Sometimes (1976) (see Figure 5.1), *Trishul*/Trident (1978) and *Kala Patthar*/Black coal (1979).[25] They also appeared together in *Silsila*/The affair (1981), whose lack of initial success has been compensated by its long afterlife.

Figure 5.1 Rishi Kapoor and Neetu Singh in *Kabhi kabhie*/Sometimes (Chopra, 1976). Screen grab.

The 1970s superstardom of Amitabh Bachchan cast a shadow over all other male heroes.[26] He played the angry and brooding young man who often had to die after taking the law into his own hands in order to avenge a wrong done to him or to his family. Romance was usually secondary for this character consumed with anger so the romantic lead was often the other hero, Shashi (see above) or sometimes Vinod Khanna, in classics such as *Muqaddar ka Sikandar/ Man of destiny* (dir. Prakash Mehra, 1978). Rishi began to take the role of the other hero alongside Amitabh, first with Vinod Khanna as well in *Amar Akbar Anthony* (dir. Manmohan Desai, 1977), then in Desai's *Coolie* (1983).

Rishi played one of the heroes in Yash Chopra's flop multi-starrer *Vijay* (1988) alongside Rajesh Khanna and Anil Kapoor but he regained ground with *Chandni* (1989), where he was paired again with Vinod Khanna. Rishi was coming to the end of his career as a romantic hero, although he played a double hero role with the newcomer Shah Rukh Khan in *Deewana/*Crazy (dir. Raj Kanwar, 1992), where they both courted Divya Bharti, who was twenty-three years younger than Rishi.

Rishi was cast in these movies not as a second lead but to portray another kind of masculinity from that offered by Amitabh Bachchan and the more macho heroes. Rishi played the romantic role, the good guy, the younger guy, a happy character rather than the brooding figure of Bachchan. He was much loved for these roles, with female fans adoring him as a cuddly hero while for many male devotees he played a more realistic character whom they could emulate,[27] in particular wearing his famous knitwear.[28]

Other roles

Rishi admits that success went to his head. He has acknowledged his love of food and drink, which have led to the weight issues that plague the family.[29] This was when stories of his troubled marriage surfaced in the press. Rishi tried his hand at directing but *Aa ab laut chalen/*Come, let's return (1999) was unsuccessful and many thought this was the end of the road, but he bounced back as he moved from romantic hero to father figure – often one who could teach the younger generation the meaning of true love.

Amitabh Bachchan had also been struggling to find a new role in cinema that suited his continuing superstardom and it came in 2000 with Aditya Chopra's *Mohabbatein/*Loves, the same year he found success as host of *Kaun banega* *crorepati?*/Who wants to be a millionaire? While Amitabh's roles were as a stern patriarch that built upon his earlier roles as an angry young man, Rishi played a very different kind of father, a warm loving hero, which built on his romantic image as a star, his willingness to fight for love. These roles included *Hum tum/ Me and you* (dir. Kunal Kohli, 2004), where he plays father to Saif Ali Khan (later his nephew by marriage), convincing him to follow his dreams. In *Luck by chance* (dir. Zoya Akhtar, 2009) Rishi plays a film producer in a comedy role for which he was highly acclaimed. In *Love aaj kal*/Love nowadays (dir. Imtiaz Ali 2009), Rishi plays a restaurateur who teaches the hero, played by Saif Ali Khan (his future nephew-in-law mentioned a few lines above), to hold on to love rather than give in to pressures, urging the younger generation to pursue their love and their dreams as he had done for his beloved. The film delighted its audience with a surprise appearance of Neetu as his wife at the end, her first appearance for many years.

This unexpected return of Neetu with Rishi led to further roles for the couple. In *Do dooni char*/Two twos are four (dir. Habib Faisal, 2010) they play a lower middle-class couple struggling to upgrade their scooter to a small car in order to look good at a family wedding. This film emphasizes family relationships in the face of the rising consumerist culture of new India, and, while outside the mainstream Bollywood, was well received. Neetu and Rishi deployed their stardom in the film rather than playing parents to stars, which was very unusual, in particular because of their total lack of glamour in the film, with the film's iconic image being of Rishi, the maths teacher, on a motorbike in an unfashionable sweater and a crash helmet, very different from his image in *Bobby*.

If *Do dooni char* was surprising for its lack of glamour and for having no other star, Rishi acted in other roles which were even more at odds with his star character. These included a gay dean in *Student of the Year* (dir. Karan Johar, 2012) and, for the first time, a villain. He played Rauf Lala, a butcher and a pimp in the remake of *Agneepath* (dir. Karan Malhotra, 2012), which was out of character, although he performed a *qawwali,* 'Shah ka rutba'/The magnificence of a king in a performance as good as any in his heyday; and he played a role which suggests the terrorist/gangster Daud Ibrahim in D-day but the famous *qawwali* (Sufi song) 'Dum mast Qalandar'/Intoxicated Qalandar is not pictured on him.

In Yash Chopra's last film, *Jab tak hai jaan*/As long as I live (2012), Rishi and Neetu play a couple who fall in love, with the mother leaving her husband

and baby daughter for her new lover. The grown-up daughter is played by an actor said to be their son's partner – Katrina Kaif – which, along with rumours that Rishi and Neetu were not on speaking terms during the filming, added to audience enjoyment.

Rishi and Neetu have acted once with their son, Ranbir, in the box office flop, *Besharam*/Shameless (dir. Abhinav Kashyap, 2013), which they have said they regret accepting. Ranbir is now one of the biggest and most talented stars of his generation as an all-rounder able to act well in emotional or comical scenes, and to dance, as well as bringing his stardom and glamour.

Rishi plays his star persona

One film which did not receive a great deal of attention is the strangest role which Rishi has performed in his career – *Chintu Ji* (dir. Ranjit Kapoor) (no relation, I believe), released on Rishi's 57th birthday in 2009. Chintu is Rishi's nickname, and he plays himself as a very unattractive character. The film is set in a fictional Indian small town (Hadbahedi), where locals discover that Chintu was born. As he enters politics, he accepts their invitation to visit as a canvassing opportunity. The locals are in awe of the star so run around after him while he behaves dreadfully, demanding booze and non-vegetarian food, being rude and behaving like a spoilt celebrity. However, after he slips on the ice brought for his whisky, he is grounded. His film producer comes to finish the shoot there while Rishi gets involved in local politics and corruption. Then Ksenia Ryabinkina, the Russian star of Rishi's first film, *Mera naam joker,* arrives in the village to teach him a lesson, giving him an album of photos from the sets of that film.

Chintu ji is a very strange, though delightful, Hindi movie. Film critic Rajeev Masand says: '[It is a] clever satire that stars Rishi Kapoor as an exaggerated version of himself.'[30] Not many stars would agree to play themselves, 'warts and all', or rather play their star persona as the character has many features that are said to be those of Rishi Kapoor from his love of alcohol and non-vegetarian food.

The film has memorable moments such as the Bengali doctor who attends to Rishi and reads his script to the star. The film within the film involves shooting a song in the style of a 'tribal dance', with an 'item' star, whose lyrics are entirely composed of internationally acclaimed film directors, 'Akira Kurosawa, Vittorio de Sica; Tarantino, Wilder, Capra, Ozu ...', with the song coming to a stop when Rishi says his only words: 'Satyajit Ray'.

Rishi Kapoor has probably played the most varied roles of all Kapoor stars, and remains hugely adored today. His films from the 1970s are now seen as classics, such as *Bobby*, and have new lives – *Amar Akbar Anthony* is about to have its own book, written by three academics [forthcoming], while his famous song, 'Om Shanti Om', from *Karz* is the name of a film which parodies and pastiches the period in Hindi film (dir. Farah Khan, 2007). Rishi's stardom and his changing star text throughout his life, from child actor, to romantic hero, a screen couple, a father figure and a maverick, is part of the dense networks of stardom within the Kapoor dynasty.

What is it that allows the building of such a dynasty? The founding member, Prithviraj, can be looked at as other stars, that is, the combination of talent, hard work, charisma, glamour and luck. Prithviraj was particularly handsome and had a muscular body suited to the roles of the time. Raj did not begin working with his father or drawing on his contacts but set himself up as actor as well as director and producer at a very young age and was already successful in his early twenties. Shammi set up his own stardom outside the family, although it took him some time to find his star image and success; Shashi was known for his more serious, actorly views and was reluctant to commit to Hindi films, a star image bolstered by his marriage to one of the Kendals. All the boys were handsome and well connected, and all three fulfilled Geraghty's three categories of star: star-as-celebrity, where biography and lifestyle are important, but box office failure is not; star-as-professional, where the focus is on the body of work and there is a stable star image; star-as-performer, where particular acting skills or physical type (e.g. action) are important.[31]

The dynasty has long been acknowledged by the family, with Prithviraj as the patriarch. Raj Kapoor built his production house, RK Films, where he chose the logo of him and Nargis in his 1949 hit *Barsaat*/The rains, but his films began with his father performing a *pooja*, or ceremony of worship, of Shiva.

The third generation did not all become leading stars although they all had at least one hit, and stardom transferred seamlessly to the fourth generation as Karisma's star was rising while Rishi's had a temporary dip. She was popular for her dancing and comedy films with Govinda (*Coolie no. 1* [dir. David Dhawan, 1995]) and Salman Khan (*Andaz apna apna*/Each to his own [dir. Rajkumar Santoshi, 1994]). Initially mocked for her ungroomed looks, Karisma appeared transformed in *Raja Hindustani*/Indian king (dir. Dharmesh Darshan, 1996), and became a fashion icon with a huge following among younger women. Kareena soon achieved fame for her glamour, in particular after *Kabhi khushi kabhie gham*/Sometimes happiness, sometimes sorrow (dir. Karan Johar 2001), and is now regarded as the most glamorous diva in Bollywood. Their cousin Ranbir is now a top male star, while another cousin, Armaan Jain, recently launched his career with support from the Kapoor dynasty. Rishi retains a considerable presence in character roles that often become a major feature of any film in which he appears.

The transference of stardom, discussed above, is echoed by the family's striking resemblances to one another which helps to reinforce their star image. The Kapoors embody the Indian standard of good looks, being tall and fair-skinned with light hair and eyes, not looking very 'Indian' but resembling old India's elites.

The visual image of the star is always important but Hindi film also creates a musical association around major stars. The Kapoors have always been closely linked to the musicians in the industry, Raj Kapoor with the composers Shankar-Jaikishan and later Laxmikant-Pyarelal, as well as the singers Mukesh and Lata Mangeshkar. The family are famous as dancers, said to have a sense of rhythm and dance which is needed to carry the music. They often become associated with particular instruments and styles of music, so Raj Kapoor played the violin in *Barsaat*, but was usually linked with the accordion, the piano, the *dafla* (a hand-held drum), and among the musical styles associated with him, the waltz is the most common. Shammi was India's rock'n'roll or Elvis, while Rishi most often sang qawwalis and was a disco dancer, while Karisma and Kareena are known for their dancing prowess.

Although the Kapoors do not perform their own songs, which are sung by playback singers, they have well-known and recognizable speaking voices, using mostly a formal Hindi with shades of Urdu as well as speaking excellent English.

Yet, despite all this talent, looks and connections, there seems to be something else which is not manufactured but seems to be inherent in the Kapoors. This may be identified as stardom or as charisma[32] although the definition is often circular, with stardom giving charisma and charisma making stars. But it is unclear what this charisma is and if there is anything in Indian culture to explain it or whether Hindi film reinforces charisma in any way. This may be to do with a particular ability to convey emotion in the Hindi melodrama but other possibilities need exploring.

The Kapoors have mostly relied on family management of their star images through the media. Raj is the only one to have had any sort of political connections when he was seen as a cultural ambassador of India, especially to the Soviet Union, and met Nehru and other statesmen. The Kapoors have given interviews regularly and written books (and Rishi is writing his autobiography) but none of the Kapoors has a big presence on social media today unlike stars such as Amitabh Bachchan or Shahrukh Khan. Rishi is very frank with the media and spoke directly to the press to ask the photographers to leave Ranbir alone. Then Rishi said that of course his son has affairs at his age, and there are plenty of them.[33]

The Kapoors are proud Punjabis, loving music and dance, food and drink. They are associated with the old Punjab, which is felt to have largely vanished. The Kapoors are often called 'Hindu Pathans' as they lived in Peshawar but the family is originally from Punjab, but the part which is now in Pakistan. The family is further associated with the Punjab lost to India, at least until Rishi's generation, as they speak Hindi with many Urdu words. Perhaps Rishi's association with the *qawwali* is part of this background, although Ranbir and Shammi were both associated with Islamicate music in *Rockstar*.

Like other Punjabis they are seen to be modern and traditional at the same time. While they are modern urbane stars, always fashionably dressed, they are known to be very conservative in their deference to elders, and their view of women's roles. The family is known to unite for events such as weddings, festivals and launches of younger family members.

Perhaps in view of the family values the films espouse, the family nature of the industry – with its caste networks, long histories of family involvement and dynastic marriages – it is not surprising that the dynasty is central to the Hindi film industry, which remains largely a cottage enterprise. There have been some attempts to corporatize, but it remains family-dominated. Such family networks extend beyond the Kapoor family, to include distant relatives, such as the star Anil Kapoor (whose fame in the west soared after *Slumdog Millionaire* [dir. Danny Boyle, 2008]) and his star children; while many of the Punjabis in the film industry are of the Punjabi Khatri caste whose surnames include Kapoor, Chopra, Tandon, Khanna – that is a substantial number of key figures although the role caste plays remains obscure.

The truism remains that the easiest way to get to be a star is to be a star child. Of the major stars today only Shahrukh Khan had no industry connections. Yet connections and networks are not enough and the individual has to have the charisma and other requirements of stardom to succeed.

The Kapoors do not all live together but they can be seen to form a 'Hindu Undivided Family', or joint family, which still remains an ideal for many in

India. They attend events together and are known to meet on special occasions. The fans like this appearance of a normal, though somewhat idealized, family, perhaps something like a royal family. However, there is no king or queen. In the Punjabi family, the oldest male leads. This was the case with Prithvi then Raj but now authority in the family is dispersed – Krishna, Raj's widow is the matriarch, while Shashi is the oldest surviving Kapoor but Rishi, although junior to Randhir, remains the bigger star.

Yet even given connections, talent and hard work – and even 'luck by chance' – the family has been remarkable by any standards. It seems that charisma may be transferable by hereditary networks, with the children destined for stardom from birth, given their looks and style, their talents at acting and music, the family's passion for films and its work ethic and they gain entry and are sustained by the family's social networks. Yet while the individuals may remain celebrities by virtue of their birth, to become stars they need the right kind of charisma and the right career decisions. Many star children are launched but few reach the level of stardom of the new generation of the Kapoor family. The Kapoor dynasty of Indian cinema remains one of the greatest star phenomena to date and, with two leading stars and another just launched, shows no signs of weakening.

Acknowledgements

Thank you to Sanam Arora and LSE SU SPICE for inviting me to chair a talk with Rishi Kapoor in LSE India Week, 2012; Kulraj Phullar for inviting me to present the first draft of this chapter at the KCL Stardom Film Conference, 2013; and Rohit Dasgupta for inviting me to speak at the London College of Fashion. Thanks to Beth Watkins (Beth Loves Bollywood) for providing me with the screengrab.

Notes

1   Richard Dyer, *Stars* (London: British Film Institute, 1979/1998); Richard Dyer, *Heavenly Bodies: Film Stars and Society* (London: British Film Institute, 1986); Richard DeCordova, *Picture Personalities: the Emergence of the Star System in America* (Urbana and Chicago: University of Illinois Press, 1990/2001); Christine Gledhill, ed., *Stardom: Industry of Desire* (London: Routledge, 1991); Jackie Stacey,

Star Gazing: Hollywood Cinema and Female Spectatorship (London: Routledge, 1993); Christine Geraghty, 'Re-examining Stardom: Questions of Texts, Bodies and Performance', in *Reinventing Film Studies*, ed. Christine Gledhill and Linda Williams (London: Arnold, 2000), 183–202; Paul McDonald, *Hollywood Stardom* (Oxford: Wiley-Blackwell, 2013).

2   Beroze Gandhy and Rosie Thomas, 'Three Indian film stars', in Gledhill, *Stardom*, 107–31; Neepa Majumdar, *Wanted Cultured Ladies Only!: Female Stardom and Cinema in India, 1930s-1950s* (Urbana: University of Illinois Press, and Delhi: Oxford University Press, 2009); Ravi Vasudevan, *The Melodramatic Public: Film Form and Spectatorship in Indian Cinema* (Ranikhet: Permanent Black, 2010); Rachel Dwyer, 'I love you when you're angry: Amitabh Bachchan, the star and emotion in the Hindi film', in *Stars in World Cinema: Screen Icons and Star Systems Across Cultures*, ed. Andrea Bandhauer and Michelle Royer (London: IB Tauris, forthcoming 2015).

3   De Cordova, *Picture Personalities*; Dyer, *Stars*.

4   Danae Clark, *Negotiating Hollywood: the Cultural Politics of Actors' Labor* (Minneapolis: University of Minnesota Press, 1995); Barry King, 'Stardom as an occupation', in *The Hollywood Film Industry*, ed. Paul Kerr (London: Routledge and Kegan Paul, 1986), 154–84; Barry King, 'The star and the commodity: notes towards a performance theory of stardom', *Cultural Studies* 1, no. 2 (1987): 145–61.

5   M. Madhava Prasad, 'Surviving Bollywood', in *Global Bollywood*, ed. Anandam P. Kavoori and Aswin Punathambekar (New York: New York University Press, 2008), 49.

6   Chris Rojek, *Celebrity* (London: Reaktion, 2001).

7   Emile Durkheim, *The Elementary Forms of Religious Life*, ed. Mark S. Cladis, trans. Carole Cosman (Oxford: Oxford University Press, 1912/2008).

8   Ritu Birla, *Stages of Capital: Law, Culture, and Market Governance in Late Colonial India* (Durham, NC: Duke University Press, 2009).

9   Karisma Kapoor, *My Yummy Mummy Guide: From Getting Pregnant to Being a Successful Mom and Beyond* (New Delhi: Penguin, 2013); Kareena Kapoor, *The Style Diary of a Bollywood Diva* (New Delhi: Penguin, 2013).

10   Madhu Jain, *The Kapoors: the First Family of Indian Cinema* (New Delhi: Viking, 2005).

11   Rachel Dwyer, 'Shooting stars: the Indian film magazine *Stardust*', in *Pleasure and the Nation: the History, Politics and Consumption of Public Culture in India*, ed. Rachel Dwyer and Christopher Pinney (New Delhi: Oxford University Press, 2000), 247–85.

12   Kidar Sharma, *The One and Lonely Kidar Sharma*, ed. Vikram Sharma (New Delhi: Bluejay Books, 2002).

13   Shashi Kapoor with Deepa Gehlot, *The Prithviwallahs* (New Delhi: Roli Books, 2004).

14 Jain, *The Kapoors*.

15 Bina Ramani, *Bird in a Banyan Tree: My Story* (New Delhi: Rainlight, Rupa, 2013).

16 Gayatri Chatterjee, *Awåra* (New Delhi: Wiley Eastern, 1992); Michael H. Hoffheimer, 'Awåra and the post-colonial origins of the Hindi law drama', *The Historical Journal of Film, Radio and Television* 26, no. 3 (2006): 341–59; Ashish Rajadhyaksha, 'The Curious Case of Bombay's Hindi Cinema: The Career of Indigenous "Exhibition" Capital', *Journal of the Moving Image* 5 (December 2006): 3; Ahmet Gürata, '"The Road to Vagrancy": translation and reception of Indian cinema in Turkey', *BioScope* 1, no. 1 (2010): 67–90; Nasreen Munni Kabir et al., *The Dialogue of* Awaara: *Raj Kapoor's Immortal Classic* (New Delhi: Niyogi Books, 2010); Rachel Dwyer, 'Fire and Rain, The Tramp and The Trickster: Romance and the family in the early films of Raj Kapoor', special issue of *The South Asianist, Journal of South Asian Studies* 2, no. 3 (December 2013): 9–32.

17 Wimal Dissanayake and Malti Sahai, *Raj Kapoor's Films: Harmony of Discourses* (New Delhi: Vikas, 1988); Saadat Hasan Manto, *Stars From Another Sky: the Bombay Film World of the 1940s* (New Delhi: Penguin, 1991); Hutokshi Jall, *Raj Kapoor and Hindi Films: Catalysts of Political Socialization in India* (Calcutta: Statesman, 1995); Rachel Dwyer, 'Bombay ishtyle', in *Fashion Cultures: Theories, Explorations and Analysis*, ed. Stella Bruzzi and Pamela Church Gibson (London: Routledge, 2000), 178–90; Jain, *The Kapoors*; Rachel Dwyer, 'Depictions of and by religious practitioners in films: Hinduism', in *The Routledge Companion to Religion and Film*, ed. John Lyden (New York: Routledge, 2009), 141–61; Dwyer, 'Fire and Rain'.

18 Bunny Reuben, *Raj Kapoor: the Fabulous Showman* (New Delhi: Indus, 1995).

19 Ritu Nanda, *Raj Kapoor: His Life and Films Presented by his Daughter* (Bombay: RK Films and Studios, 1991).

20 T. J. S. George, *The Life and Times of Nargis* (New Delhi: Indus, 1994).

21 Gandhy and Thomas, 'Three Indian film stars'.

22 Available online at http://www.youtube.com/watch?v=Ebt6cKfcL24, viewed 29 September 2014.

23 Jain, *The Kapoors*, 291.

24 See Khushboo Motihar, 'The Love Story of Neetu and Rishi Kapoor', *BollywoodShaadis.com*, available online at http://www.bollywoodshaadis.com/articles/the-love-story-of-neetu-and-rishi-kapoor-1713, viewed 29 September 2014.

25 'Shashitabh' according to several blogs including 'Beth Loves Bollywood', available online at http://bethlovesbollywood.blogspot.co.uk/2009/07/shashitabhiness.html, viewed 29 September 2014.

26 Dwyer, 'I love you when you're angry'.

27 Stacey, *Star Gazing*.

28 Available to view online at http://rishisknits.tumblr.com/, viewed 29 September 2014.

29 Geeta Rao, 'The Reinvention of Rishi Kapoor', *Verve Magazine* 20, no. 6 (June 2012), available online at http://www.verveonline.com/109/people/rishi-kapoor. shtml, viewed 29 September 2014.

30 Rajeev Masand, 'Masand's movie review: Chintuji', *IBN Live*, 5 September 2009, available online at http://ibnlive.in.com/news/masands-movie-review-chintuji/100691-8.html, viewed 15 July 2014.

31 Geraghty, 'Re-examining Stardom'.

32 Max Weber, *Max Weber: Essay in Sociology*, ed. and trans. H. H. Gerth and C. Wright Mills (New York: Oxford University Press, 1946); Dyer, *Stars*, 30–32.

33 Afsana Ahmed, 'Like Ranbir, I also had many girlfriends and link-ups: Rishi Kapoor', *Hindustan Times*, 14 April 2013, available online at http://www. hindustantimes.com/Entertainment/Tabloid/Like-Ranbir-I-also-had-many-girlfriends-and-link-ups-Rishi-Kapoor/Article1-1044156.aspx, viewed 29 September 2014.

6

Eddie Murphy's Baby Mama Drama and Smith Family Values: The (Post-) Racial Familial Politics of Hollywood Celebrity Couples

Hannah Hamad

I really believe that a man and a woman together, raising a family,
is the purest form of happiness we can experience.

Will Smith, *The Voice*, 1997

We're not together any more.
And I don't know whose child that is until it comes out and has a blood test.

Eddie Murphy, *RTL Boulevard*, 2006

I had people calling me a gold digger, saying that I got pregnant on purpose.
It was a horrible time.

Melanie Brown, 'Mel B: Spice Mom', *Mel B: It's a Scary World*
(Style Network, 2010)

When Barack Obama delivered his keynote address to assembled delegates of the Democratic National Convention on 27 July 2004, asserting 'There's not a black America and white America and Latino America and Asian America; there's the United States of America,'[1] it not only signalled his imminent rise to prominence within the Democratic Party, it also heralded a shift towards the cultural and political normalization of post-racial discourse, culminating in Obama's election to the presidency on 4 November 2008 as the first person of colour to hold this office in the nation's racially charged history. Through espousal of rhetoric that purports not to see racial difference, Obama's election was, as racial justice advocate Tim Wise argues, achieved in part on the back of 'a rhetoric of racial transcendence' and an 'agenda of colorblind universalism.'[2]

Also symptomatic of the purported end of racial discourse in popular culture was Forbes' naming of cross-media celebrity Will Smith as the highest paid actor in Hollywood in 2008.[3] Smith was also voted most bankable star of that year in the annual film exhibitors' poll conducted by the International Motion Picture Almanac.[4] He was only the third African American to attain this level of stardom by the latter measure, and the first since Eddie Murphy, himself the third highest paid actor in Hollywood in the year of Obama's election,[5] who topped the poll in 1987.[6] Hence, as arguably the biggest African-American stars in Hollywood during the period leading up to the Obama presidency and beyond, the celebrity identities of Will Smith and Eddie Murphy, as they pertain to the politics of racial discourse at the dawn of the Obama era, are charged with meaning. This comes into clearest view when seen through the frame of coupledom and familial politics, as articulated through the public identities and personae of these stars. The cultural politics of coupledom and family have always been particularly racially charged spheres of debate where African Americans have been the subjects. And as encapsulated in the epigraphs that open this chapter, the opposing extents to which Smith and Murphy are seen through mediation of their romantic relationships and their attendant self-conceptualizations as fathers to espouse and live up to normative family values, are highly revealing of their embodiments of (post) racial discourse.

Smith, partnered by wife and fellow Hollywood actor Jada Pinkett Smith, was hailed during this time as the emblematically post-racial star for Obama's America, and the Smiths, including children Jaden and Willow, as a model family. Whereas Murphy, whose persona always carried more overt racial charge than Smith's but whose image had been recuperated as racially benign and family-oriented by the early 2000s, became embroiled in a highly publicized paternity dispute. This followed his brief relationship with British singer and reality star Melanie Brown, best known in the 1990s as a member of girl group, The Spice Girls. And its mediation positioned his celebrity alongside damaging stereotypes of African-American family life, divesting his persona of the veneer of colour-blindness and racial transcendence that had heretofore characterized this phase of his career. This chapter therefore explores the racial and postracial cultural politics of coupledom and family as they pertain to the celebrity discourse surrounding Will Smith and Eddie Murphy at the germination of the Obama era. It argues that, notwithstanding claims made for their racial transcendence or colour-blind appeal to crossover audiences, both stars remain firmly located within the discourse of race, which manifests differently through mediated dynamics of coupledom and family.

In his discussion of the relationship between post-racial discourse and celebrity culture, Ellis Cashmore makes clear what is at stake in this dialogue, writing that

> black celebrities have sold the idea that America is no longer manacled to ... a history pockmarked by racism, segregation and victimization. Undeniable progress since civil rights has promoted the ideal of what many call the postracial society, a place where racism and other forms of bigotry have no purchase. The election of Barack Obama, himself a political celebrity... , seemed to validate if not the arrival, then the imminence of the postracial society.[7]

It would therefore be injudicious to interrogate the U.S. cultural politics of celebrity coupledom and race since the mid-2000s without acknowledging the semiotic power of Barack and Michelle Obama, along with their children Malia and Sasha, and the extent to which mediation of this family set a new benchmark for the widespread negotiation of post-racial discourses of colour-blindness and racial transcendence in celebrity culture. As an upshot of their pre-election mediation, the Obamas joined the pantheon of couples fuelling the economy of the cross-media celebrity gossip industries, across the spectrum of relative levels of cultural distinction, ranging from tabloid to top-end journalism and the lowest to highest forms of cultural criticism. Noteworthy examples from the higher end that underscore the extent of the cultural valence of the Obamas' celebrity coupledom include *Time*'s decision to feature Michelle in its recurring 'Celebrity Spotlight' cover feature in May 2009,[8] and Jodi Kantor's profile of the first couple for *The New York Times Magazine* in October 2009.[9] At the other end, *People* profiled 'The Obamas at Home' in August 2008,[10] while *US Weekly* showcased the couple under the banner 'Why Barack Loves Her' in June 2008.[11] As Caroline Streeter states in her explanation of how such media imagery of the Obamas was harnessed on the campaign trail:

> Obama's charm was legendary, yet consistently chaste. His wife ... beautiful, intelligent, articulate, along with attractive and appealing daughters ... seemed a made-to-order first black family. Obama's embodiment of ideal husband and father put him above reproach without dimming his sex appeal.[12]

But pointing to what was at stake in doing so, Angela Nelson highlights that much of the post-racial charge of mediating the Obamas in terms of their coupledom and as a normatively configured family, lies in the function of such imagery to 'allow America to see a *functional* (rather than dysfunctional) black family',[13] at odds with entrenched and pernicious rhetoric that paints and pathologizes the black family as perennially 'in crisis'. Since the publication of sociologist E. Franklin Frazier's *The Negro Family in the United States* in 1939,[14] followed by the infamous Moynihan report *The Negro Family: The Case for National Action* in 1965,[15] and the 1995 'Million Man March' on Washington by massed African Americans organized by Nation of Islam leader Louis Farrakhan (the major flashpoint of the 1990s fatherhood responsibility movement), African Americans have come under fire as deficient from family values proselytizers. Over time, evidence of this purported absence of family values has been attributed to births out of wedlock, a correspondingly high proportion of single mothers with attendant dependency on welfare, matriarchal kinship networks, and chronic levels of fatherlessness, paternal irresponsibility and domestic violence, often linked to the high numbers of African-American men in the US prison system. Perniciously gendered and racialized cultural stereotypes of African-American families thus emerged from this 'crisis' rhetoric. It is in this context that the media framing of the (post-) racial familial politics of Murphy/Brown and the Smiths must be understood.

Eddie Murphy's baby mama drama

The Murphy/Brown paternity scandal unfolded in a post-Katrina America, newly reminded in catastrophic circumstances of the urgent need to see and acknowledge racial discourse, albeit one poised to embrace the fantasy of post-racial transcendence to which the ascendance of Obama was giving rise. The media spectacle of this scandal is productively understood in relation to the racially charged term 'baby mama drama' – widely understood slang that positions African-American coupledom and out-of-wedlock parenthood as pathologically dysfunctional. It articulates the aforementioned culturally entrenched historical discourses that situate black people as lacking in the family values valourized under white hegemony, which are compulsory for the successful articulation of a post-racial identity. As one irreverent definition of the term has it: 'Baby mama probably got pregnant on purpose thinking she could hold on to the man – finds out ain't nothin' happening and gets mad.'[16] Noteworthy pop culture reference points for this discourse are Daz Dillinger's

1998 record 'Baby Mama Drama' in which a man bemoans the requirement to make support payments to the mother of his child, who is presented as having filed for child support as a vindictive act following his refusal to marry her; and Dave Hollister's 1999 R&B record 'Babymamadrama', the lyrics for which similarly lament the plight of a man whose personal finances are being drained by his child's mother. Both are analysed by black popular culture scholar Mark Anthony Neal as symptomatic examples of 'baby mama drama', which he presents as the structuring discourse of black sexual politics in millennial culture, arguing that it demonizes black single mothers, making appeals to victim status for absent black fathers.[17]

The profile of discursive excoriations of black women through the structuring discourse of 'baby mama drama', was raised considerably the year before the Murphy/Brown paternity scandal, following the success of the song 'Gold Digger' by hip-hop star Kanye West featuring Hollywood actor Jamie Foxx, the lyrics for which reiterate the discourse thus: '18 years, 18 years/She got one of your kids, got you for 18 years,'[18] going on to lament the payment by fathers to mothers of child support, advocating for the necessity of prenuptial agreements as a safeguard against the eventuality of the loss of 'half' his fortune to his 'baby mama'.

Parallels to be drawn with Murphy's own 'baby mama drama' are striking and clear. 'Baby mama drama' is hence the charged frame through which to understand the gender and racial politics of Murphy/Brown and the furore surrounding the paternity of their daughter Angel Iris Murphy Brown. But to understand how Murphy's persona came to embody these persistent discourses of African-American masculinity that characterize black men as promiscuous, misogynist, materialistic irresponsible partners and fathers whose default position is to deny paternity of their children or flee its consequences, it is necessary to observe how he negotiates the politics of coupledom through his celebrity persona over time.

Murphy's twenty-first century 'baby mama drama' vividly recalls the misogynist vitriol, suffused with racial charge, which characterized the better-known portions of his 1980s stand-up comedy in the films *Delirious* (1983), and especially *Raw* (1987). Here Murphy infamously rails against what he performatively perceives to be the mercenary sexual machinations of women who deliberately tie themselves to moneyed men, through disingenuous marriage and/or the calculated conception of their children, to obtain wealth and the subsidization of their lifestyles in divorce settlements, and through payment of alimony and child support. Thus, in *Raw*'s most famous moment, Murphy delivers a blistering excoriation of African-American women: 'They'll get it. They'll get half your money, your house, your car, alimony, child support, and your children.' With its gendered, raced references to the manipulative and/or fraudulent acquisition by black women of unearned assets, this diatribe bears troubling comparison to pejorative 'welfare queen' rhetoric that then characterized Reaganite discourse about the economic dire straits of poor black single mothers.[19] Thus, through his performed narrative of the breakdown of a romantic relationship via the new archetype of the 'baby mama', Murphy is complicit in the cultural construction of what Patricia Hill Collins calls 'controlling images', of African-American femininity, which 'reflect the dominant group's interest in maintaining Black women's subordination'.[20]

In one of many instances that twin his performative persona with the mediation of his personal biography, the strength of Murphy's misogynist feeling was attributed to his recent break-up with then partner Lisa Figueroa. As one journalist reported, 'It was said that Murphy's friends convinced him that she liked his money more than him,' and 'he later said Figueroa inspired *Raw*'s diatribes against grasping, fortune hunting women.'[21] The routine takes a more disturbingly gendered, racialized turn as Murphy posits a solution to his coupling dilemma:

> If I ever get married, I'd have to go off to the woods of Africa and find me some crazy, naked, zebra bitch that knows nothing about money. She got to be butt naked on a zebra with a big bone in her nose and a big plate lip and a big fucked-up Afro. ... And I'm gonna bring her home and lock her up in the house.

As Herman Beavers notes in his intersectional analysis of Murphy's persona, in *Raw* Africa is thus construed as 'a primitive and pre-capitalist space' that is also 'synonymous with submissive women' commensurate with the misogyny of Murphy's performance of his conceptualization of the ideal dynamic between a black heterosexual couple.[22] Making clear what is at stake with respect to the politics of race and gender, Beavers continues:

> Murphy asserts that he wants to go to Africa and find Umfufu, the 'bush-bitch.' But in doing so he works out a contemporary version of the Triangle Trade: he goes to find a woman who lacks the wherewithal to resist or emasculate him [unlike the excoriated but legally enfranchised American women of his

divorce settlement tirade]. As a black man who performs the cultural labor of entertaining the masses, Murphy's African woman serves the same purpose as the African American woman in slavery: as a breeder and economic entity subject to his whim.[23]

Some aspects of this dynamic are vividly realized in the mediation of Murphy's break-up with Brown and the ensuing scandal concerning his alleged, later proven, paternity of their child.

Having divested his persona of this racially charged sexism through his reinvention as a family man, both in films with his successful late 1990s turn towards family comedy in lucrative and racially inert vehicles like *Dr Dolittle* (1998), *Daddy Day Care* (2003) and *The Haunted Mansion* (2003), and in his publicity image through media profiles of Murphy with his wife and children,[24] this modified image began to crack following the breakdown of his marriage. But it unravelled spectacularly after his whirlwind romance with Brown amid the acrimony of their split. Just weeks after publicly declaring himself 'madly in love' with her,[25] Murphy abruptly ended the relationship and openly questioned the paternity of the unborn child,[26] including, famously, in an interview on Dutch television during which he made the statement contained in the epigraph attributed to him at the outset of this chapter. The media framing of the paternity dispute had the recidivist effect of recalling the Eddie Murphy of old, who gleefully performed the above recounted racially charged misogyny, what Bambi L. Haggins describes as 'black on black social critique' devoid of 'larger sociopolitical context',[27] construing women's romantic interest in him and claims of his paternity of their children as predatory and covetous. As the couple entered into a bitter legal dispute, papers filed revealed Murphy's claims that Brown had demanded 'a $9 million ... house, plus living expenses for 18 years in exchange for her silence while she was pregnant'.[28] In February 2009, Murphy was ordered to pay Brown £7million (approximately $11.4 million) in child support in monthly instalments until Angel is eighteen.[29]

Thus, notwithstanding his mid-career interlude in deracinated family comedies and a family-oriented publicity image that chimed well with the shift towards the post-racial, the discourses of coupledom and family that circulate around Murphy's celebrity ultimately fix his public identity in relation to racially charged familial politics. They also invoke some of the worst cultural stereotypes of African-American masculinity, in stark contrast to the familial idyll of post-racial transcendence contemporaneously offered up by the Smiths.

Smith family values

Despite appearing to have followed life scripts that lend themselves to negative, racially charged media framing, by being open about his mistrustfulness of unfaithful women,[30] fathering a child in a marriage that quickly failed, and fathering another child out of wedlock in subsequent relationship to Pinkett, Smith rose to A-league stardom in the 1990s largely free of imbrication with pernicious discourses of black masculinity that attached themselves to Eddie Murphy (and to which he was complicit in attaching himself). Instead Smith and his second wife, thereafter Jada Pinkett Smith, proved adept in negotiating family values through mediation of their relationship. And, to the extent that by the time Smith was named the most bankable star in Hollywood in 2008, they along with children Jaden and Willow (usefully named after the couple, anchoring their public identities to one another enabling easy brand recognition) were celebrity culture's emblematic black family for America at the dawn of the purportedly post-racial Obama era.

Since his sitcom fantasy of class mobility *The Fresh Prince of Bel-Air* (NBC 1990–6), Smith's persona had flirted with discourses of racial transcendence. Critics, scholars and audiences have differently attributed the extent of his success to his supposed ability to transcend race and embody masculinity beyond it. Sean Brayton cites Richard Corliss pointing to Smith's 'panracial' popularity as stemming from being black, but considered beyond blackness.[31] Janani Subramanian states that Smith 'combines contrary qualities that simultaneously mark his blackness while foreclosing its narrative significance and … potential political significance'.[32] And Lorrie Palmer cites journalism that attributes Smith's crossover appeal to his ability to invoke racial discourse, only to dismiss it, historicize it or render it irrelevant.[33] Will Smith's celebrity embodiment of African-American masculinity has always been more racially marked than the innumerable platitudes that espouse his transcendence of racial discourse can take into account. Much of his success comes from his appearances in a particular kind of African-American star vehicle that Haggins terms the 'comedy of colour-coded colour blindness',[34] in which a black protagonist is placed in a 'white liberal'[35] narrative context that 'does not engage black culture and identity in any direct or significant manner',[36] but makes superficial gestures to signify race. In Smith's case, they are not always comedies, but employ the same devices of racial containment, as can be seen in the laboured musical interludes in *I, Robot* (2004) and *I Am Legend* (2007) that confirm Smith's characters' proclivity for black music by having him diegetically listen to records by Stevie Wonder and Bob Marley respectively. Another trope is that the black protagonist is Othered through possession of a 'gift' that 'becomes a mark of difference but also operates as a signifier for identity,'[37] for example, Smith's cybernetic arm in *I, Robot*, his immunity to the deadly virus in *I Am Legend*, and his superpowers in *Hancock* (2008). But the emblematic example of the 'comedy of colour-coded colourblindness' for Smith is *Hitch* (2005), in which he plays Alex Hitchens, a 'date doctor' whose gift is seduction, which is employed to enable the narrative trajectory and romantic relationship of an affluent white couple.

Furthermore, a noteworthy phenomenon of Smith's screen persona that gives truth to the lie of the fantasies of colour-blindness and racial transcendence attached to his celebrity is the nature of his screen coupledom with female co-stars. Specifically, with exceptions accounted for below, Smith is never (yet) romantically or sexually coupled with white women, commensurate with long-standing cultural fears of miscegenation that excoriate interracial coupling between black men and white women through pernicious cultural stereotypes of black male predatory sexuality, and white female virtue and victimhood. A significant exception is CG animation *Shark Tale* (2004) in which Smith's character is romantically paired with a character voiced and facially modelled on Renée Zellweger. But the cultural stakes of their interracial coupling are nuanced through the film's use (typical in animated family films) of anthropomorphism, which sublimates tensions arising from fears of miscegenation, and is a common device used in animation to negotiate or sidestep questionable politics of identity in characterization.[38] Another exception is *Hancock* in which, as trade paper *Variety* reported during its week of release, Smith plays 'a black man who, at some point in the past, was married to a white woman.'[39] Industry reporter Peter Bart viewed this as evidence of Hollywood's racial progressivism, noting that this 'story detail … in generations past, would have sent the movie censors into a panic.'[40] He thus situates miscegenation anxieties as a phenomenon of history, consigning them to the past in a gesture towards what he understands to be, where screen couples are concerned, the post-racial present.

However, something Bart declines to mention in his generous reading of *Hancock*'s racial politics of coupledom is the anxious manner in which this relationship is articulated, and the racially recidivist means by which it is revealed. Smith plays Hancock, an alcoholic ageless amnesiac with superpowers who befriends Ray (Jason Bateman) and his wife Mary (Charlize Theron). Spending the evening at their house Hancock and Mary are drawn together, and with Ray passed out drunk Hancock leans in to kiss her. But before their lips meet,[41] Mary reveals her own superpowers, grabbing Hancock and violently throwing him through the window (we later learn of their past romance). The implied perceived threat of sexual violence is clear. But thus construed as a plot point, the miscegenation anxieties attendant to the scene are neatly sidestepped as devoid of racial charge. Persistent anxieties over the depiction of this permutation of interracial coupling – between black men and white women – is thus a way in which Smith's persona is racially marked, recalling the worst of Hollywood's racist archetypes of black masculinity as sexually threatening to white femininity, in tension with the discourse of post-racial transcendence underpinning his cross-media celebrity.

Off-screen (and occasionally on) the coupledom of Smith and Pinkett Smith has informed their mediation in celebrity culture since reports of their romance surfaced in 1995,[42] especially for the latter about whom nary a profile is published that does not hierarchically situate her as the subservient member of this celebrity couple: as 'Mrs Will Smith',[43] 'the wife of Will Smith',[44] 'Will Smith's other half',[45] etc. This gendered phenomenon is underscored by the fact that Pinkett Smith has been open about her decision to scale down her career and downshift her public sphere expectations of herself following marriage and motherhood. In a 2004 interview, she stated that despite the fact that when she met Will she 'wanted to be the biggest female star in the world', she later realized that 'the sacrifice that you have to make, especially as a woman, to live that dream [of normative family life] is going to hit your professional life hard'.[46] And she was willing to make that downshift because 'My relationship with Will and my family is much too sacred'.[47] Pinkett Smith thus speaks of the Smith family unit and the relationships therein in reverential pseudo-religious terms, over-determining their normativity as a functional black family, commensurate with what later becomes the post-racial discursive function of the celebrification of the Obamas. Her noteworthy public sphere downshift can therefore be productively twinned with that of Michelle Obama, whose career as an executive with the University of Chicago Hospitals took a backseat to marriage, motherhood and the campaign trail, following her husband's nomination for the presidency.

Also symptomatic of the Smiths' determination to self-present in terms of normative family values is Pinkett Smith's adoption of her husband's last name. In contemporary celebrity culture we are well accustomed to seeing female celebrities eschew this patriarchal tradition.[48] For the female member of straight celebrity couples, this is often as much about retaining the established brand identity of her celebrity than about making a feminist political gesture.[49] The case of Jada Pinkett Smith therefore stands out. As such, issues of proprietary nomenclature, gendered celebrity hierarchies and the decision by women in celebrity couples of whether to take their husbands' names come to the discursive fore. In August 2014, Pinkett Smith attracted media attention when she addressed this issue for her fans in a Facebook status update:

> The dilemma you face whether to change your last name to your husband's is a timely one. I have always believed that an empowered woman is one that can stand on her own two feet and has the strength to trust her personal code of womanhood and not necessarily the code that a collective creates as the standard to which an independent woman must adhere to [sic], to actually be identified as … independent. Each woman carries a different code so that she may never be replicated and is assured her individuality and freedom. As long as your decision reflects your personal code towards building the woman you want to be in this world … congrats …[50]

This depoliticized pseudo-feminist rhetoric of personal empowerment, freedom of choice and individual self-determination is entirely in step with the neo-liberal ideological underpinnings of their post-racial discursive function as a celebrity African-American couple and family. And it works to negotiate the recidivist gender politics of patriarchal proprietary nomenclature, and the circular logic of neoliberal self-governance.

At the time of writing, Smith and Pinkett Smith have starred together as a couple on-screen only once in the Muhammad Ali biopic *Ali* (2001), in which Smith plays the iconic boxer. It was not a big box office hit, but it enhanced the cultural capital of his film stardom through industry recognition when it led to his first Academy Award nomination for Best Actor. Pinkett Smith plays Sonji Roi, Ali's first wife (of four), and the romantic screen time they shared here did much to solidify the currency of their celebrity coupledom becoming as it did a noteworthy part of the media buzz surrounding the film's release. It also prefigured Smith's later screen pairings with their children, giving rise to the evolution of their celebrity coupledom into a fledgling form of what Rachel Dwyer and Maria Pramaggiore call 'dynastic stardom'.[51]

The Smiths' celebrity coupledom was earlier incorporated into Smith's stardom in 1998, when a heavily pregnant Pinkett Smith appeared in her husband's music video for his record 'Just the Two of Us'. Pinkett Smith rests on the lap of her seated husband, who looks to the camera smiling and stroking her distended belly, while she looks down on him stroking his neck (see Figure 6.1).

Figure 6.1 Will Smith, Jada Pinkett Smith and an unborn Jaden Smith appear together in the music video for 'Just the Two of Us' in 1998. Screen grab.

This laid the foundations for what subsequently became the industrial mobilization of their coupledom and their family dynamic, enabled by the couple's partnership in their production company Overbrook Entertainment, which Smith founded with producer James Lassiter in 1997. This has provided them considerable agency at an industrial level, ensuring their ability to foster the 'dynastic stardom' of their family, through the production of films that they produce and/or in which they and/or their children star. So far they include (but are not limited to): the aforementioned *Ali*; *The Pursuit of Happyness* (2006) in which Will and Jaden play father and son in an upward mobility narrative of post-racial transcendence and colour-blindness; *I Am Legend*, a post-racial apocalyptic fantasy in which Will is the emblematic last man on earth and which features Willow playing his daughter in flashback; *The Karate Kid* (2010), a transnational narrative of cultural appropriation – a vehicle for Jaden but with Jada on board as producer and taking a lead role in the film's global promotion; and *After Earth* (2013) which co-stars Will and Jaden, who are billed alongside one another as father and son. Also significant from this standpoint is Will and Jada's creation of the television series *All of Us* (UPN 2003–6; The CW 2006–7), a sitcom of African-American family life which ran for four seasons and was inspired by the Smiths' own 'blended' family dynamic that included Smith's son Trey from his marriage to his first wife Sheree Zampino. The significance of this level of industrial agency to the Smiths' ability to fashion a self-determinedly post-racial image for their familial stardom therefore cannot be overstated.

Conclusion

The over-determination of the Smiths as a model black family for Obama's America has been somewhat destabilized by media reportage in 2013 of their 'open' marriage, which followed celebrity gossip media rumour mongering about Pinkett Smith's alleged sexual affair with pop singer (and then husband to Jennifer Lopez) Marc Anthony in 2011. Since then reportage of the imminent implosion of the Smith marriage has been intermittently recurrent. Alongside this, Smith's heretofore unshakeable box-office bankability has been similarly destabilized following the underperformance and critical excoriation of *After Earth*, which has been attributed, in part, to backlash against the Smiths' nepotistic championing of their children's stardom. Joseph Tompkins contends that the Smiths' cultivation of Jaden's stardom belies the discourse of meritocracy on which Will's purportedly racially transcendent celebrity was built.[52] And shifting the focal point of the Smith dynasty to Jaden brings his privilege into view, destabilizing the discourse of meritocracy that has so successfully circulated around Will. How the Smiths will negotiate post-racial familial politics through their celebrity from here on remains to be seen. But what is certain is that Smith's celebrity, like Murphy's, is far more tied to the politics of race than any notion of post-racial discourse makes possible, and that this comes into sharp focus through the lens of coupledom and family.

Thus viewing the racial politics of contemporary celebrity culture through the charged framing discourses of coupledom and family, this chapter therefore illustrates just one of the ways in which we remain far from achieving a culture or society capable of operating without recourse to racialized structures of thought and feeling. What is further revealed by examining the cultural politics of coupling as they manifest through the celebrity identities of African-American A-listers like Eddie Murphy and Will Smith is that there remains a very real need to see and acknowledge the continued negotiation of racially charged discourse. Such discourse persists in spite of the disingenuous rise to prominence of post-racial notions of racial transcendence and colour-blind universalism. Both these celebrities' identities have at different times adhered to the surface disavowal of racial rhetoric through their articulation of family values while also evoking racially charged discourse. Eddie Murphy's sharp fall from public grace following both the Murphy/Brown paternity scandal and his fleeting prior embodiment of the post-racial familial ideal was highly revealing of the extent to which celebrity culture is primed to fall back on familiar cultural scripts underpinned by racial rhetoric, as it leaned heavily on and reached readily for the discourse of 'baby mama drama' to re-anchor his celebrity within racial discourse. And while at the same time Will Smith appeared on the surface to transcend everything that Murphy then embodied with respect to a racially marked celebrity identity, closer interrogation of the way coupledom and family values have been negotiated through his public persona is equally revealing of how tied his celebrity is to race-based assumptions about familial cultural politics.

Notes

1 'Transcript: Illinois Senate Candidate Barack Obama', *The Washington Post*, 27 July 2004, accessed 28 September 2014, http://www.washingtonpost.com/wp-dyn/articles/A19751-2004Jul27.html.

2 Tim Wise, *Colorblind: The Rise of Post-Racial Politics and the Retreat from Racial Equity* (San Francisco: City Lights Books, 2010), 16.

3 Lacey Rose, 'Hollywood's Best-Paid Actors', *Forbes*, 22 July 2008, accessed 28 September 2014, http://www.forbes.com/2008/07/22/actors-hollywood-movies-biz-media-cx_lr_0722actors.html.

4 'Top Ten Moneymaking Stars of the Past 82 Years', *The 2014 International Motion Picture Almanac* (La Jolla, CA: Quigley Publishing, 2014), accessed 10 August 2014, http://www.quigleypublishing.com/MPalmanac/Top10/Top10_lists.html.

5 Rose, 'Hollywood's Best-Paid Actors'.

6 'Top Ten Moneymaking Stars of the Past 82 Years'.

7 Ellis Cashmore, *Beyond Black: Celebrity and Race in Obama's America* (London and New York: Bloomsbury, 2012), 2.

8 Nancy Gibbs and Michael Scherer, 'The Meaning of Michelle', *Time*, 21 May 2009, accessed 10 August 2014, http://content.time.com/time/magazine/article/0,9171,1900228,00.html.

9 Jodi Kantor, 'The Obamas' Marriage', *The New York Times Magazine*, 29 October 2009, accessed 10 August 2014, http://www.nytimes.com/2009/11/01/magazine/01Obama-t.html. This was later expanded into and released as a full-length book, *The Obamas: A Mission: A Marriage* (New York: Allen Lane, 2012).

10 Sandra Sobieraj Westfall, 'The Obamas Get Personal', *People*, 4 August 2008, accessed 10 August 2014, http://www.people.com/people/archive/article/0,,20221617,00.html.

11 Susan Scheiber, 'Camelot: The PR Campaign', *Zapwater Communications*, 23 June 2008, accessed 28 September 2014, http://blog.zapwater.com/2008/06/.

12 Caroline A. Streeter, 'Obama Jungle Fever: Interracial Desire on the Campaign Trail', in *The Iconic Obama, 2007-2009: Essays on Media Representations of the Candidate and New President*, ed. Nicholas A. Yanes and Derrais Carter (Jefferson, NC: McFarland, 2012), 177.

13 Angela Nelson, 'Popular Culture in the Age of Obama', in *The Iconic Obama, 2007-2009: Essays on Media Representations of the Candidate and New President*, ed. Nicholas A. Yanes and Derrais Carter (Jefferson, NC: McFarland, 2012), 13.

14 E. Franklin Frazier, *The Negro Family in the United States, Revised and Abridged Edition* (New York: The Citadel Press, 1948[1939]).

15 Lee Rainwater and William L. Yancey, *The Moynihan Report and the Politics of Controversy* (Cambridge, MA and London: Harvard University Press, 1967).

16 Tay-Tay, 'Baby Mama Drama', *Urban Dictionary*, 6 June 2005, accessed 28 September 2014, http://www.urbandictionary.com/define.php?term=Baby%20 Mama%20Drama.

17 Mark Anthony Neal, *Soul Babies: Black Popular Culture and the Post-Soul Aesthetic* (New York and London: Routledge, 2002), 77–85.

18 Kanye West featuring Jamie Foxx, *Gold Digger* © 2005 by Roc-a-Fella, Def Jam, digital download.

19 Neal, 75–76.

20 Patricia Hill-Collins, *Black Feminist Thought: Knowledge, Consciousness and the Politics of Empowerment* (New York and London: Routledge, 1991), 71.

21 Michael Gross, 'Big Ed', *Evening Standard Hot Tickets*, 3 October 1996, 3.

22 Herman Beavers, '"The Cool Pose": Intersectionality, Masculinity, and Quiescence in the Comedy and Films of Richard Pryor and Eddie Murphy', in *Race and the Subject of Masculinities* (Durham, NC and London: Duke University Press, 1997), 265.

23 Ibid., 265–66.

24 Karen S. Schneider, 'Bye-Bye, Bad Boy: Eddie's in Love', *People*, 22 March 1993, 71. See also Hannah Hamad, *Postfeminism and Paternity in Contemporary U.S. Film: Framing Fatherhood* (New York and London: Routledge, 2014), 124–28, and Hannah Hamad, '"Hollywood's Hot Dads": Tabloid, Reality and Scandal Discourses of Celebrity Post-feminist Fatherhood', *Celebrity Studies* 1, no. 2 (2010): 151–69.

25 'Eddie Murphy Declares He's "Madly In Love" With Mel', *Hello*, 26 September 2006, accessed 28 September 2014, http://www.hellomagazine.com/ film/2006/09/26/eddie-murphy-mel-b/.

26 Marla Lehner, 'Eddie Murphy Questions Paternity of Mel B's Baby', *People*, 12 May 2006, accessed 28 September 2014, http://www.people.com/people/ article/0,,1566035,00.html.

27 Bambi L. Haggins, 'Laughing Mad: The Black Comedian's Place in American Comedy of the Post-Civil Rights Era', in *Hollywood Comedians: The Film Reader*, ed. Frank Krutnik (London and New York: Routledge, 2003), 171–86.

28 '"I Won't See My Daughter Because Mel B Tricked Me Into Having a Baby" Says Eddie Murphy', *The Daily Mail*, 14 March 2008, accessed 28 September 2014, http://www.dailymail.co.uk/tvshowbiz/article-533139/I-wont-daughter-Mel-B-tricked-having-baby-says-Eddie-Murphy.html.

29 Nick Rutherford, 'Eddie Murphy Ordered to Pay £7 Million Child Support to Daughter He Had With Mel B', *The Daily Mail*, 8 February 2009, accessed 28 September 2014, http://www.dailymail.co.uk/tvshowbiz/article-1138923/Eddie-Murphy-ordered-pay-7million-child-support-daughter-Mel-B.html.

30 Nancy Collins, 'Big Willie Style', *Rolling Stone* 801, 10 December 1998, accessed 10 August 2014, http://www.rollingstone.com/movies/news/big-willie-style-19981210?page=5.

31 Sean Brayton, 'The Racial Politics of Disaster and Dystopia in *I Am Legend*', *The Velvet Light Trap* 67 (2011): 75.

32 Janani Subramanian, 'Alienating Identification: Black Identity in *The Brother from Another Planet* and *I Am Legend*', *Science Fiction Film and Television* 3, no. 1 (2010): 45.

33 Lorrie Palmer, 'Black Man/White Machine: Will Smith Crosses Over', *The Velvet Light Trap* 67 (2011): 34.

34 Haggins, 'Laughing Mad', 178.

35 Ibid., 181.

36 Ibid.

37 Ibid.

38 See for example Murphy's racially marked vocal performance as the jive-talking Donkey in the *Shrek* films (2001, 2004, 2007, 2010) and the sublimation of the 'Mammy' archetype into Gloria the hippo voiced by Pinkett Smith in the *Madagascar* films (2005, 2008, 2012).

39 Peter Bart, 'Superheroes Get Super Makeovers', *Variety*, 30 June to 13 July 2008, 3.

40 Ibid.

41 An alternative version of the scene was shot and cut in which the characters engage in a lengthy kiss, but it was edited out for the film's release.

42 'Star Tracks', *People*, 9 October 1995, accessed 10 August 2014, http://www.people.com/people/article/0,,20101745,00.html; 'Fresh Prince Finds Another Princess', *The Voice*, 7 November 1995, 27.

43 Julia Toppin, 'Home Girl's All Grown Up', *The Voice*, 21 September 1998, 41.

44 Stuart Husband, 'Ms Dynamite', *The Sunday Telegraph Magazine*, 2 September 2004, 25.

45 'Is This It?' *Guardian Guide*, 21 April 2007, 98.

46 Husband, 'Ms Dynamite', 25.

47 Ibid., 25.

48 British 'WAGs' are a noteworthy exception to this, as discussed by Shelley Cobb and Neil Ewen in their paper 'Behind Every Man? The Value of the Celebrity WAG in Western Media Culture', Celebrity Studies biennial conference, June 2014.

49 For discussion of this issue as politically charged see in this volume Shelley Cobb, 'Ellen and Portia's Postfeminist Wedding: Celebrity Couples and the Politics of Gay Marriage'.

50 Jada Pinkett Smith, *Facebook*, 8 August 2014, accessed 10 August 2014, https://www.facebook.com/jada.

51 See in this volume Rachel Dwyer, '"A Star is Born?" Rishi Kapoor and Dynastic Charisma in Hindi Cinema' and Maria Pramaggiore, 'Filial Coupling, the Incest Narrative, and the O'Neals'.

52 Joseph Tompkins, email message to author, 2 November 2013.

7

Momager of the Brides: Kris Jenner's Management of Kardashian Romance

Alice Leppert

'I'm trying not to be the controlling mother,' Kris Jenner proclaimed in *Vogue*, referring to her daughter, US reality television star Kim Kardashian, and rapper Kanye West's upcoming nuptials.[1] However, since 2007, when she successfully pitched *Keeping Up with the Kardashians*, a reality television series featuring her family, Jenner has maintained control of her daughters' commodified romantic entanglements, managing their careers through her company, Jenner Communications, Inc. She has leveraged her daughters' weddings and divorces for healthy profits, most notably releasing her memoir *Kris Jenner … and All Things Kardashians* the day after Kim filed for divorce from second husband Kris Humphries. As she notes in the tome's introduction, 'I'm a unique combination of mother and manager. I've actually trademarked the term "Momager," which is what I am.'[2] Jenner is indeed both a manager and a mother, but she is also a celebrity in her own right. Familial talent managers have become increasingly visible with the rise of reality television, marking the family as a potentially profitable site for the production of celebrity. *The Osbournes* (2002–5) featured Ozzy Osbourne's wife and manager, Sharon Osbourne, and launched her own celebrity image, which has proliferated on other reality and talk shows like *America's Got Talent* (2007–12) and *The Talk* (2010–present). Similarly, *Newlyweds: Nick and Jessica* (2003–5) featured Jessica Simpson's father and manager, Joe Simpson, as a meddling and often creepy father, overly invested in his daughter's sexual objectification, a role he reprised on *The Ashlee Simpson Show* (2004–5), which chronicled his younger daughter's budding music career. Both Sharon Osbourne and Joe Simpson serve as templates for Jenner's hybrid role as celebrity momager – both headed families that were already wealthy and had some degree of fame that they could capitalize on in order to build their own celebrity.

Though Jenner's high-profile role as momager has only recently made her famous, her skill at monetizing love and family is long-standing. A 1996 *People* magazine profile of her second husband, former Olympic champion Bruce Jenner, notes that Kris 'helped organize a family conglomerate comprising their infomercial (*SuperFit with Bruce and Kris Jenner*), exercise products (like stair-climbing machines) and an aircraft sales company'.[3] This momaging has received a significant amount of negative press, as both celebrity gossip and popular press journalists express disapproval of her calculated, entrepreneurial management of her daughters' personal lives. Yet, Jenner's management strategy has worked symbiotically with gossip media: she allows herself to be painted as the villain in order to promote her daughters' romantic relationships as authentic. Though the press often vilifies Jenner as an exploitative fame-monger, in fact, she fulfils the idealized role of the self-sacrificing mother, taking on the role of villainous mastermind and thus partially sacrificing her own celebrity image for the sake of her daughters' images. Through analysis of media coverage of the Kardashian family and their self-representation on reality TV, this chapter shows how Jenner has been uniquely successful in producing her own discrete celebrity image as momager while simultaneously managing her daughters' images and romances.

Jenner as celebrity manager

In pointing to the necessity for celebrity studies to examine the production and industry of celebrity, Graeme Turner claims, 'At the most pragmatic level, for the individual concerned, their celebrity is a commercial property which is fundamental to their career and must be maintained and strategised if they are to continue to benefit from it'.[4] In many ways, a talent manager's job is the maintenance and strategy of celebrity. However, managers also often maintain themselves as commodities. As Sasha David points out, 'talent managers must objectify themselves in order to objectify their clients'.[5] Following her research as a participant observer at a major talent agency, David argues that successful talent managers turn themselves into marketable products in order to effectively make connections and further the interests of their celebrity clients. And, following his own participant observation at a talent agency, Stephen Zafirau notes the importance of a talent manager's reputation, as he suggests that managers strategically shape their reputations in an attempt 'to fit industry-wide expectations regarding how talent agents and managers should present themselves'.[6] In marketing her daughters and herself, Jenner has accepted and commodified the stereotype of the momager, rather than attempting to paint herself in a more altruistic light. In doing so, she manages to escape some of the pitfalls of other stage mothers, in that her embrace and unabashed promotion of this role allow her to become a celebrity in her own right.

However, Jenner's acceptance of this villainous role simultaneously works to protect her clients, as she sacrifices her own image and reputation in order for them to appear more sincere. She fulfils the expectations of a momager – pushy, hungry for fame and using her children for her own gain – yet she also fulfils some of the industrial expectations for female talent managers. Zafirau observes distinctly gendered ideals of talent management, wherein female talent managers (a minority in the field) bring '"nurturing" skills, and less of the harder interpersonal tactics characteristic of their male counterparts' to their relationships with clients.[7] Simply by virtue of combining motherhood and management, Jenner's management style takes on a nurturing, maternal tone, and despite the fact that Jenner Communications, Inc. has office space, and Jenner has a home office, many of her meetings with her clients and non-familial business partners occur in her living or dining rooms.

Serving as the manager for all six of her children (in addition to Bruce and, at one time, son-in-law Lamar Odom), Jenner has successfully moulded eldest daughters (with ex-husband Robert Kardashian) Kim, Kourtney and Khloé into entrepreneurs and product-endorsers, with an expansive line of feminized goods including fashion lines, make-up, perfume and diet products, and younger daughters (with Bruce Jenner) Kendall and Kylie are embarking on a similar path. Jenner serves as executive producer on *Keeping Up with the Kardashians*, as well as its numerous spin-offs, including *Kourtney and Kim Take Miami* (2013), *Kourtney and Khloé Take Miami* (2009–10), *Kourtney and Kim Take New York* (2011–12), *Khloé & Lamar* (2011–12) and *Kourtney and Khloé Take the Hamptons* (2014), while she uses the reality programmes to promote the product and branding empire she has built with her family. As Leigh H. Edwards observes,

> Their branding practices have led industry magazines to insist that the Kardashians are a [*sic*] building a new, highly-influential business model based on the key elements of: the success of their reality shows, social media interaction

with fans, and profitable products and brand endorsements, all in the service of promoting the Kardashians as a brand.[8]

Jenner also carefully integrates her daughters' professional and romantic interests, capitalizing on both their relationships with men and the children these relationships produce. While talent managers routinely take ten per cent of their clients' earnings (and *Keeping Up with the Kardashians* references this fact repeatedly), Jenner's cut is much more substantial, as she seemingly manages herself as well as her clients. By turning herself into a celebrity momager, Jenner manages to profit not only from monetizing her family and their romantic relationships, but also by monetizing herself and producing herself as a commodity.

Criticism of Jenner's management of her daughters' careers and lives (which are collapsed due to their reality television-driven livelihoods) often position Jenner as greedy and desperate for youth and fame. In a 2011 skit on *Saturday Night Live*, Kristen Wiig played Jenner as a spotlight-stealing self-proclaimed 'fourth sister' to her three famous daughters. This representation of Jenner aligns with Shelley Cobb's analysis of the celebrity stage mother, whose 'grotesqueness is signified through both her own aging femininity and the selling of her daughter's youthful sexuality (both of which are played out in the public sphere) as an act of class aspiration.'[9] What sets Jenner apart from enterprising celebrity stage mothers like Dina Lohan and Lynne Spears is her class status – despite initially lacking fame, Jenner and her daughters were undeniably wealthy, and their pre-existing Southern California lifestyle clearly codes them differently than class usurpers from rural Louisiana (Spears) and Italian American Long Island (Lohan). Jenner's wealthy background and lifestyle make her transition to celebrity much smoother and her momaging appears somewhat less opportunistic as a result, although she still routinely faces scrutiny for exploiting her family.

Before *Keeping Up with the Kardashians*, Kim was the only marginally famous Kardashian, thanks to her spectacularly successful, supposedly leaked sex tape with ex-boyfriend, R&B singer Ray J. The pilot episode of *Keeping Up with the Kardashians* details Jenner and Kim discussing strategies for how Kim should respond to Tyra Banks' interview questions about the sex tape, where they carefully insist that the tape accidentally fell into the wrong hands unbeknownst to Kim. Despite this act of televisual damage control, as Alexandra Sastre points out, 'It was widely speculated that Kardashian and her mother Kris Jenner were themselves responsible for the leaking of Kardashian's sex tape and that they orchestrated a deal with Vivid Entertainment to distribute the video.'[10]

By using her daughter's pornographic performance to launch the careers of several family members as well as her own, Jenner marked her management style as one that was unabashedly exploitative of intimate moments. An episode in the first season bears out the implications of this strategy, as Jenner convinces a reluctant Kim to pose nude in *Playboy*. By positioning herself as the pushy, greedy momager, Jenner takes much of the heat for her daughter's over-sexed image, protecting Kim from some of the cultural backlash, while taking ten per cent of the profits. Through her paradoxical monetization of 'fairy-tale romance', Kris Jenner has produced not only a branded identity for her daughters and their romantic partners, but also cultural anxiety about and suspicion of women's prospects for successfully combining love and family with professional careers. At the same time, Jenner's reputation as puppet master helps bolster her daughters' images, allowing them to appear at least somewhat sincere in their romantic endeavours while Jenner appears unfailingly calculated, itself a key part of her production of her own celebrity. Despite the broad condemnation of Jenner's momaging, her success at turning herself and her family into eminently marketable commodities is symptomatic of neoliberal ideals of self-branding, a logic that is particularly endemic to celebrity gained from reality television.

Khloé & Lamar's 'Unbreakable Bond'

Journalist Jo Casamento encapsulates Jenner's strategy: 'Engagements, weddings, divorces and babies are flogged to the highest bidder and any opportunity for cross promotion is embraced.'[11] Jenner's most profitable ventures have been Khloé's and Kim's weddings. By the time Kim became engaged to Kris Humphries in 2011, Jenner had already honed her business strategy with Khloé's 2009 wedding to NBA player Lamar Odom. According to *The Hollywood Reporter*,

> *OK! Magazine* received the official photos and announcement for just shy of $300,000. Kris also had everything from the Lehr & Black custom invitations to Khloe's 9-carat engagement ring 'donated' for the lavish affair; sources say she promised vendors massive product promotion that would come from the media circus surrounding the wedding. In the event that an item wasn't gifted, E!, it is believed, picked up the tab.[12]

Despite all these opportunities for profit, Khloé and Odom's wedding special, which aired in November 2009, portrays a whirlwind romance devoid of ulterior motives, as Khloé largely leaves the wedding planning to her mother. Following the wedding special, Jenner became Odom's manager (of his 'off-court career pursuits'), and leveraged his and Khloé's marriage into a perfume deal that emphasized the supposed solidity of their relationship – a unisex fragrance called Unbreakable, followed by Unbreakable Joy, Unbreakable Bond and Unbreakable Love.[13] The process of creating the perfume was chronicled on the *Keeping Up with the Kardashians* spin-off *Khloé & Lamar*, executively produced by Jenner, and clearly a branding vehicle for the couple and their developing portfolio of product endorsements (which included shooting a television commercial for Wonderful Pistachios, which was itself chronicled on *Kim's Fairytale Wedding*).

Khloé & Lamar positions the perfume as Odom's brainchild, with a lead-in scene wherein the couple discusses his extensive cologne collection and his passion for fragrance. Odom suggests that they create a unisex fragrance while the camera cuts to a close-up of his and Khloé's hands seductively intertwined as he massages her. Khloé initially expresses concern about turning her marriage into a business relationship. In voiceover accompanying stock footage of Khloé arguing with her sisters over business matters, she worries that undertaking a business partnership will cause similar friction with Odom. The camera then cuts back to the couple as Odom lays Khloé on their bathroom floor and begins to do a series of push-ups over her body. Khloé makes a deal with him that if he does twenty push-ups, she will agree to join him in developing a fragrance. This sexualized scene effectively masks Jenner's work of brokering the deal, suggesting that the idea for the perfume sprung organically from Khloé and Odom's mutual passion. It also mirrors the marketing of the fragrance, which used images of the couple nude and embracing, thus emphasizing the authenticity of their love while simultaneously branding it.

Later in the episode, Khloé and Odom meet briefly with a representative for Lighthouse Beauty at Jenner's house, but once the deal is made, the couple go to a development meeting without Jenner, and test scents alone in their home. They then pick the bottle, which Khloé says she wanted to 'pick together', as though it were an intimate experience or important milestone. However, when Odom dislikes Khloé's choice of bottle cap, she storms out and calls Jenner in tears. She tells the viewer in a direct address interview that she just wants to go back to being 'husband and wife', that 'this business, bickering relationship, this isn't us'. Jenner, for her part, encourages Khloé to 'take [her] emotions out of it for a second'. This is a key scene that again marks Jenner as more concerned about the business aspect of her daughter's marriage than its emotional component, while allowing Khloé to appear sincere in her love. The episode concludes with Khloé and Odom engaging in some pseudo-bondage role-playing while picking their scent, with Odom blindfolded to ensure an honest opinion. Khloé sprays the perfume on her breasts and presses her chest into Odom's face. He breathes in deeply and approves, and the scene cuts to the press tour and promotional blitz. A montage of the photo shoot for the packaging and ad campaign mirrors earlier scenes as they embrace and massage each other while partially nude. A still image from the campaign briefly arrests the montage, symbolizing the effective blending of Khloé and Odom's sexual passion with their passion for business and profit. Khloé tells the viewer that she feels 'so much stronger in [her] relationship', while Odom tells a friend he feels 'unbreakable', again mixing their marriage with its commodified product.

When Kim's marriage to Humphries fell apart in late 2011, the Kardashian brand managed to save face thanks to the apparent stability of Odom and Khloé's carefully branded 'unbreakable bond'. The couple went so far as to walk away from the lucrative *Khloé & Lamar,* despite E!'s (and Jenner's) bid for a third season. *Us Weekly* suggested the couple chose 'real life over reality TV', a decision that was framed at the time as the two of them privileging their relationship over profit.[14] When revelations of Odom's serial cheating and drug abuse came to light, Jenner sprung into action, reportedly holding 'an emergency two-hour meeting with divorce lawyer Laura Wasser – who also took care of sister Kim Kardashian's legal separation from Kris Humphries – where they discussed the pair's prenuptial agreement'.[15] As Khloé's marriage unravelled, Jenner remained concerned about the effect on Khloé's career and assets, while Khloé struggled to cut ties with Odom, as she reportedly sought reconciliation on several occasions and delayed filing for divorce. *Us Weekly* quoted a source who spoke about Jenner's strategies for handling Khloé's divorce and mused, '[Jenner] is thinking about their brand and how they can recover: "When is Khloé ready to go back to work? When can she make appearances?"'[16] The magazine's coverage of Khloé's handling of the divorce, however, focused on Khloé's agonizing efforts to help Odom overcome his addiction and repair the damage his drug abuse and infidelity had caused to their relationship. Because of Jenner's meticulous management of the divorce (not to mention her foresight in arranging the prenuptial agreement), Khloé was free to continue representing herself as a hopeless romantic and a devoted, if betrayed, wife, while Jenner appeared more concerned about the bottom line. Still, the fact that what had long appeared to be the most stable Kardashian relationship imploded points to cultural anxieties about successful women combining career and family, which often leads to what Diane Negra calls the postfeminist 'time panic'.[17] This trope defined Khloé and Odom's relationship for years as they publicly struggled with infertility. Meanwhile, Jenner productively combines work and family in that she has made her family into her career, willing to embrace the roles of overbearing mother and castrating bitch for the sake of her children's success and profit, even at the cost of her own celebrity image, and seemingly, her own marriage.

Kim's Fairytale Wedding

Jenner replicated her profitable wedding formula in 2011, when Kim married NBA player Kris Humphries, and the details of Jenner's and the couple's earnings from the wedding quickly spread, especially when the speedy divorce sparked rumours of a publicity- and profit-driven stunt. Widely reported to have raked in at least $15 million worth of cash and goods, *Kim's Fairytale Wedding* is notoriously bursting with product placements ranging from the Palazzo and Venetian in Las Vegas (who paid Kim $50,000 for the privilege of hosting her bachelorette party) to Living Social, with Kim, Jenner and Humphries visiting one luxury wedding vendor after another, and bragging about their personal relationships with the likes of fashion designer Vera Wang and celebrity chef Wolfgang Puck. *The Hollywood Reporter* noted the unique value of a Kardashian wedding for the bridal industry:

> Vendors rarely receive the mass publicity a Kardashian wedding can provide, says celebrity event producer Tony Schubert, so many offer free goods. Because Kim is viewed among many brides-to-be and bridal hopefuls as a tastemaker, association with her is priceless. A single tweet from the star can get a brand's name in front of nearly 9 million followers (dress designer Vera Wang is already receiving frequent mentions), compared to the 200,000 circulation of a wedding magazine like *Brides*.[18]

Free publicity was abundant for Kim's wedding vendors, as gossip media followed her wedding planning process down to the tiniest detail, and speculated wildly about her selections for dresses, venues, jewellery and other paraphernalia.

Before the wedding, Kim promoted various vendors through her Twitter feed, and gossip magazines like *Us Weekly* reported on her cake tasting at Hansen's Cakes (where one article noted that Jenner had the final say), her dress fitting with Vera Wang and her personal training sessions with celebrity trainer Gunnar Peterson.[19] According to Amanda Scheiner McClain,

> Kim and Kris [Humphries] received at least the 'three Vera Wang dresses Kardashian wore during the ceremony and reception, worth $20,000 each, $400,000 in Perrier Jouet Champagne, and $10,000 worth of wedding invitations.' Moreover, *People* supposedly paid '$2.5 million for the exclusive rights to wedding photos and a further $300,000 for the engagement shots,' while '*OK!* Magazine is said to have paid $100,000 for exclusive pictures of the bridal shower.' Kim also released a bridal-themed limited edition perfume, named 'Love.'[20]

Despite the clear profit motivation behind the wedding special, Jenner and E! took pains to represent it as a romantic love story.

A key strategy in disguising this overtly commercial endeavour as fairy-tale romance was to align it with the wildly popular royal wedding that was televised in the US just three months before. Vague comparisons to Prince William and Kate Middleton's 2011 wedding abounded leading up to Kim's wedding, all playing on an American understanding of the British royal family as connoting a fairy-tale fantasy of wealth, luxury and fame, a discourse that effectively silences the complex political implications of the Queen's role as Head of State and the taxes that support their luxurious image and lifestyle. E!'s website was blatant in asking 'are the Kardashians the new royals?' with an accompanying photo essay comparing the Kardashians to major players in the royal wedding. Unsurprisingly, the site compared Jenner to Queen Elizabeth II, making note of their control over their respective families. *Us Weekly* ran two stories claiming Kardashian was seeking a cake resembling William and Kate's,[21] one announcing that her cake of choice 'costs a king's ransom: approximately $20,000 for the 10-tier white cake with chocolate-chip frosting!'[22] The same article established Kim's impressive (even royal) connections, '"This is going to be like the American royal wedding," says a source. With help from an actual princess! England's Beatrice – best known for her crazy hat at Will and Kate's I do's – introduced Kardashian to Google exec Eric Schmidt, owner of the wedding venue, a Spanish-style estate in Montecito, California.'[23] After the wedding, but before the wedding special broadcast, *Us Weekly* ran another story claiming that during the wedding itself, 'the reality queen [in this case Kim, not Jenner] kept boasting, "This is our version of the royal wedding!"'[24]

Kim's Fairytale Wedding goes to great lengths to paint Kim and the rest of the Kardashians as a royal family – Odom and Kourtney's boyfriend Scott Disick address the difficulties they had assimilating into the family and learning the Kardashian way of life, in much the same way that gossip swirled around Duchess Kate's royal training. Pointing to Humphries' position as a commoner in relation to Kim, his family is carefully pushed to the margins. Jenner arranges luxury cars to transport the Kardashian clan to the wedding venue, but when Humphries inquires as to his family's transportation, she admits she didn't even think about them. When Kim lists her bridesmaids for Khloé, Khloé dismissively asks, 'who's that?' when Kim lists Humphries' sister Kaela. And as much as the spectre of Princess Diana loomed large over the royal wedding, Kim's deceased father Robert Kardashian, Sr is invoked tearfully on numerous occasions, and appears in home video insert footage accompanied by wistful voiceover narration from Kim.[25] The wedding ceremony itself draws further parallels, with the bridesmaids all dressed in form-fitting white gowns reminiscent of Kate's maid of honour Pippa, and the bride changing out of her cumbersome ball gown into a more comfortable dress for the reception (though Kim upped the ante on Kate, having not only a reception dress, but also a first-dance dress). Lastly, *Kim's Fairytale Wedding* represents the wedding ceremony itself as a media circus, with helicopters circling overhead, celebrity guests greeted by photographers, and the bride carefully sheltered from prying eyes before her walk down the aisle. Throughout the wedding special, Jenner keeps her focus on the impact the wedding will have on Kim's brand and financial interests – insisting that Kim retain her maiden name for the sake of the family business, despite Kim's musings about following tradition and pleasing Humphries. This disagreement further allows Kim to appear invested in 'fairy-tale romance' while Jenner remains invested in profit, but it also speaks to postfeminist anxieties about combining career and family life. As Suzanne Leonard suggests, 'celebratory representations of marriage' in postfeminist media culture

> emphasize that if push comes to shove a woman's marital status is indeed *more* important than her career. Such portrayals frequently emphasize that female employment, far from being the sort of life necessity that feminists advocated, has the potential to be a hindrance to her 'feminine' aspirations.[26]

This tactic of privileging Kim's romanticized submissive idealism temporarily backfired on Jenner when Kim's marriage lasted only seventy-two days, with the divorce announcement made just three weeks after *Kim's Fairytale Wedding* aired. *Us Weekly* suggested that Humphries' lack of ambition for fame and reluctance to employ Jenner as his manager were to blame for his and Kim's marital problems. The gossip magazine quoted a family friend who remarked, '[Kim is] urging Kris to meet with her mom officially about what opportunities are out there.'[27] Jenner largely handled the publicity and fallout of the divorce while doing press for her book, making the rounds on talk shows denying that the family profited from the wedding, and instead claiming that they owed money.[28] Jenner's book tour strategically shielded Kim, as Jenner spoke to multiple media outlets on Kim's behalf. Jenner's appearances maintained the focus on *her*, not on Kim, so that Jenner could continue to play the role of the calculating momager and Kim could maintain a shred of romantic innocence in the fiasco. Moreover, *The Hollywood Reporter* suggested that the Monday morning timing of the divorce announcement was even more strategic, as 'most weekly magazines close out their issues Monday evening. ... The matriarch of the Kardashian clan, Kris Jenner, made sure that the news hit before the weeklies closed.'[29] Throughout the aftermath of Kim's divorce, Jenner used both her own celebrity as well as her role as mother/momager in order to manage Kim's scandal. In order to effectively manage her daughters' romantic relationships, Jenner combines her own status as a celebrity, her management of her family's celebrity, and her family more broadly, functioning as a protective mother attempting to shield her daughters from pain as much as she functions as a celebrity manager looking out for her clients' best interests.

Kimye

Jenner's careful shaping of Kim's relationships was challenged when Kim began dating Kanye West in April 2012. West seemed to revel in Kim's reality television stardom, appearing in several episodes of *Keeping Up with the Kardashians*, and referencing her fame in several of his songs. However, West also made it apparent that he intended to use Kim as his Barbie doll (calling her the 'number one trophy wife'[30] in a song), as in one episode he advises her to get rid of all of her clothes and replace them with a full wardrobe of his and his stylist's choosing, a move that Khloé immediately recognizes as controlling. He similarly 'steered [Kim] away from maternity clothing. He selected about 300 pieces – heavy on the

Figure 7.1 *Kimye* (Kanye West and Kim Kardashian), Los Angeles 11 July 2012. Photo: Galo Ramírez

black-and-white color scheme – from her closet and had them tailored for her body.' (see Figure 7.1)[31] West paraded Kim to a variety of fashion-driven functions including the Met Gala, thus using her to raise his profile in the fashion world, where, as Devon Powers points out, he has long yearned to be taken seriously.[32] As Christopher Bagley noted in a *W* profile of West, 'given West's current thirst for refined Euro cool, one might expect him to fall for some chicly cerebral French artist rather than a trash-TV queen who epitomizes the kind of branded mass culture he's rebelling against'.[33] Though Kim is most likely not the best choice for a man trying to break into European high fashion, their union did score West the cover of *Vogue* along with Kim (a controversial choice on editor Anna Wintour's part, as it inspired popular outcry against the magazine's seeming endorsement of the low-value celebrity Kim represents). Despite this controversy, West continued to insert himself into Europe's fashion scene, outfitting his bride and daughter in Givenchy Haute Couture, and enjoying a pre-wedding lunch hosted by fashion designer Valentino. West's careful reshaping of Kim into a bride worthy of an aspiring fashion icon began to encroach on Jenner's territory.

In contrast to Jenner's control of Kim's wedding to Humphries, multiple sources noted that West was running the show when it came to Kim's third wedding. West's influence reportedly infuriated Jenner, with the *New York Post* claiming that after West and Kim turned down multi-million dollar offers for publication rights to their wedding photos, 'Kim's money-hungry momager, Kris Jenner, was unhappy with their decision'.[34] Unsurprisingly, 'Kardashian klan [*sic*] mastermind Jenner, however, "very much wanted to sell the pictures," a source says, pointing out that Jenner gets commission on her kids' business interests'.[35] Although Kim and West also decided against selling rights to the first photos of baby North, Jenner managed to capitalize on North's birth in other ways. One journalist observed that Kim's due date was closely aligned with the launch of Kardashian Kids, a line of baby clothes for Babies 'R' Us. The journalist mused, 'It is the kind of serendipitous timing that not even Kim Kardashian's "momager," Kris Jenner, and the reality television producers could have concocted in their wildest script-drafting meetings'.[36] In perhaps a conciliatory move, West revealed the first photo of North on Jenner's short-lived talk show *Kris* (2013), where he also gave his first television interview in three years. This photo reveal seemed carefully crafted to suggest West and Kim were simply trying to help Jenner launch her talk show, rather than to profit, allowing them to maintain their moralistic pledge not to sell their baby photos. As usual, Jenner appears as though she is capitalizing on these intimate moments. Jenner's role as momager once again allows her daughters and their partners to sell themselves and their children without looking like they are selling themselves. Jenner takes the fall as the calculated, money-hungry manager while Kim and West appear almost magnanimous, willing to compromise their principles as a familial favour.

Kourtney and Scott

Of all the men who have come and gone in her daughters' lives, Kourtney's long-time boyfriend Scott Disick has proved to be both the longest lasting and the most challenging for Jenner. For the first four seasons of *Keeping Up with the Kardashians*, he was painted as a villain, as Kourtney and her sisters suspected infidelity, and despite Jenner's efforts to set Disick up with a job working for one of the Kardashians' business partners, she had to have him removed from a business dinner after he became belligerently drunk in a season four episode. Perhaps due to these tensions, as well as to the fact that Disick and Kourtney are not married, Jenner has expended more of her energy into branding grandchildren Mason and Penelope, conveniently launching an expansion of the Kardashian Kids baby clothes collection shortly after Kourtney announced her third pregnancy. According to *The Hollywood Reporter*, 'News of Kourtney's 2009 pregnancy was sold in a package deal for $300,000 to *Life & Style* magazine. That included multiple stories: the pregnancy announcement, sex of the baby, birth announcement, first baby photos and body-after-baby reveal.'[37] Of course, the value of this deal extends beyond $300,000, as the magazine coverage provides publicity for the television shows, product lines and brand. Jenner brokered a similar deal for Kourtney's second pregnancy, with *Us Weekly* running several features and cover stories on Kourtney's pregnancy, baby Penelope's birth and the coveted post-baby-body reveal. In a feature on Kourtney and Disick's 'babymoon' vacation to Mexico, the magazine quotes Jenner as gushing, 'They have this great relationship and they're just waiting for the new baby. ... He has been the most wonderful dad and a great partner for my daughter.'[38] The feature includes photos of Disck and Kourtney playing with son Mason, kissing and dancing on the beach, a far cry from Disick's infamously poor behaviour during Kourtney's first pregnancy, which aired on *Keeping Up with the Kardashians*, as in the episode noted above. The photos serve to promote the couple as a happy family and maintain an air of romantic spontaneity, despite their calculated arrangement for a magazine payday.

As Disick has proved his worth as a contributor to the family brand through his fathering of children, Jenner has worked more deliberately to monetize his relationship with Kourtney. One tabloid claimed that despite their lack of a formal engagement, Jenner was already planning their wedding and orchestrating it for maximum dramatic effect. The article cites an 'insider' who claims '[Jenner] has suggested that after they announce the wedding date, Kourtney should walk out on Scott. Then he'll have to win her back in time for the wedding.'[39] Indeed, Kourtney and Disick may be the most stable part of the Kardashian franchise, with the end of Khloé's marriage, Kim and West refusing to allow their daughter North to be filmed, and Bruce moving out of the family compound. With North carefully positioned just outside of the camera's purview throughout season nine of *Keeping Up with the Kardashians*, Kourtney and Disick seem poised to take centre stage in the Kardashian clan, with Kourtney announcing her third pregnancy in June 2014, and the ninth season of *Keeping Up with the Kardashians* heavily featuring the couple and their children moving into a massive, camera-ready house.

Kris and Bruce

Jenner's crumbling relationship with her husband Bruce brings her long-standing representation as castrating, calculating businesswoman full circle. Tabloid *Star* magazine celebrated the 2014 separation by proclaiming that Bruce was 'no longer under Kris' iron-fisted, almost psychotic control'.[40] As Maria Pramaggiore and Diane Negra point out, Bruce's role on *Keeping Up with the Kardashians* has long been 'awkward and insecure … a putatively henpecked househusband'.[41] In a 2013 interview with *Us Weekly* promoting her talk show, *Kris*, Jenner dismissively remarks, '[Bruce is] so excited for me! I stay away from his ideas, though, because his episodes would be golf and helicopters.'[42] The series regularly marginalizes his viewpoint and positions him as having very little control over his life and family. Before the announcement of the separation, Kris was already capitalizing on the palpable tension in their marriage, endorsing Zestra, 'a line of arousal oils [Jenner] says she uses to overcome those "Seriously? Not you again" moments with her husband'.[43] The image of Bruce as emasculated by his domineering wife became even more predominant as multiple gossip media outlets began speculating that Bruce is undergoing a gender transition, thanks to his decision to grow his hair and nails long, and to undergo a plastic surgery procedure called a laryngeal shave in order to reduce the appearance of his Adam's apple. *Us Weekly* noted his 'shocking new look', and quoted two sources who explained, 'he's "never felt comfortable in his own skin"', and 'He wants to have a more feminine appearance.'[44] While the announcement of the Jenners' separation played on the postfeminist trope of the failed 'work–life balance', the suggestion of Bruce's gender transition solidified Kris' image as a ball-busting, castrating bitch. Still, Jenner managed to capitalize on the separation, selling the story as an exclusive to *Us Weekly*[45] and publicly stepping out with former *Bachelor* star Ben Flajnik, winning herself another cover of *Us Weekly*.[46]

Conclusion

Though Jenner seems to be exploiting her daughters' intimate, private moments, the nature of the family's celebrity demands this branding strategy much more so than culturally legitimated celebrities like actors, musicians or athletes. The Kardashians are famous in the first place for making their private lives public in order to profit. Jenner's role is thus not only the productive combination of celebrity, momager and mother; she is also a *reality* celebrity and momager, an ideal role for the neoliberal moment wherein individuals are encouraged to market, brand and take responsibility for themselves. In this way, Jenner is less self-interested than she is often portrayed to be – she markets, brands and takes responsibility for her children (even if this is in part a strategy to market herself). Despite a bevy of negative press presenting her as excessively opportunistic and exploitative of her children, Jenner actually fulfils the ideal of the self-sacrificing mother. Though she has unquestionably profited handsomely from managing her children, by allowing herself to be represented as a controlling, relentlessly entrepreneurial momager (and in many ways helping to construct this representation as her own celebrity image), she allows her children's careers and brands to flourish. Jenner's own celebrity makes this management strategy possible, as she is in the public eye in her own right, and not only in her role as a manager. The manner in which Jenner has moulded her daughters' careers and personal lives allows them to profit from images of 'fairy-tale romance', a fairy-tale in which Jenner, in her own capacity as a celebrity, often plays the role of the villain.

Acknowledgements

I would like to thank Neil Ewen, Shelley Cobb, and Tony Nadler for their careful editing and helpful suggestions throughout the writing and revision process.

Notes

1 'Keeping Up with Kimye', *Vogue*, April 2014, 282.
2 Kris Jenner, *Kris Jenner ... and All Things Kardashian* (New York: Gallery Books, 2011), viii.
3 'Bruce Jenner', *People*, 15 July 1996, 93.
4 Graeme Turner, 'Approaching Celebrity Studies', *Celebrity Studies* 1, no. 1 (2010): 14.
5 Sasha David, 'Self for Sale: Notes on the Work of Hollywood Talent Managers', *Anthropology of Work Review* 28, no. 3 (2007): 10.
6 Stephen Zafirau, 'Reputation Work in Selling Film and Television: Life in the Hollywood Talent Industry', *Qualitative Sociology* 31 (2008): 100.
7 Ibid., 121.

8 Leigh H. Edwards, 'Transmedia Storytelling, Corporate Synergy, and Audience Expression', *Global Media Journal* 12 (2012): 5.

9 Shelley Cobb, 'Mother of the Year: Kathy Hilton, Lynne Spears, Dina Lohan and Bad Celebrity Motherhood', *Genders* 48 (2008), accessed 7 July 2014, http://genders.org/g48/g48_cobb.html.

10 Alexandra Sastre, 'Hottentot in the Age of Reality TV: Sexuality, Race, and Kim Kardashian's Visible Body', *Celebrity Studies* 5 (2014): 135.

11 Jo Casamento, 'The Business of Baby "Kimye"', *The Sun Herald*, 6 January 2013, 9.

12 Merle Ginsberg, 'Kim Kardashian Sells Engagement Photos to "People" for $300,000', *The Hollywood Reporter*, 1 June 2011, http://www.hollywoodreporter.com/news/kim-kardashian-sells-engagement-photos-193816.

13 'Odom Says He'll Avoid Tiring Himself with Show', *Orange County Register*, 6 January 2011, C.

14 Sarah Grossbart, 'Putting Family First', *Us Weekly*, 14 May 2012, 52.

15 'Here Comes Kris', *The Hamilton Spectator*, 29 August 2013, G3.

16 Kevin O'Leary, 'Khloé's Private Hell', *Us Weekly*, 23 September 2013, 68.

17 Diane Negra, *What a Girl Wants? Fantasizing the Reclamation of Self in Postfeminism* (London: Routledge, 2009), 47.

18 Leslie Bruce, 'The Business Behind Kim Kardashian's TV Wedding', *The Hollywood Reporter*, 18 August 2011, http://www.hollywoodreporter.com/news/kim-kardashian-kris-humphries-e-tv-wedding-224992.

19 Jennifer O'Neill, 'Prepping for The Big Day', *Us Weekly*, 29 August 2011, 54–55.

20 Amanda Scheiner McClain, *Keeping Up the Kardashian Brand: Celebrity, Materialism, and Sexuality* (Lanham, MD: Lexington Books, 2014), 65.

21 'Kim & Kris: Cake Test!', *Us Weekly*, 15 August 2011, 51; O'Neill, 'Prepping for The Big Day', 54–55.

22 O'Neill, 'Prepping for the Big Day', 54.

23 Ibid., 55.

24 Jennifer O'Neill, 'Inside Kim's Lavish Wedding', *Us Weekly*, 5 September 2011, 54–57.

25 For more on the posthumous adoration of Princess Diana, see Margaret Schwartz, 'Diana's Rings: Fetishizing the Royal Couple', in this volume.

26 Suzanne Leonard, '"I Hate My Job, I Hate Everybody Here": Adultery, Boredom, and the "Working Girl" in Twenty-First-Century American Cinema', in *Interrogating Postfeminism: Gender and the Politics of Popular Culture*, ed. Yvonne Tasker and Diane Negra (Durham, NC: Duke University Press, 2007), 103.

27 Eric Andersson, 'Kim's Final Warning to Kris', *Us Weekly*, 7 November 2011, 47.

28 Reuters, 'Kim's Wedding Real and Expensive: Mom', *The Calgary Herald*, 3 November 2011, E3.

29 Rebecca Ford and Lauren Schutte, 'Kim Kardashian Divorce: 10 Signs the Marriage Was One Big Hoax All Along', *The Hollywood Reporter*, 31 October 2011, http://www.hollywoodreporter.com/news/kim-kardashian-divorce-kris-humphries-media-publicity-255371.

30 Future, featuring Kanye West, 'I Won', in *Honest*, Epic Records, 2014.

31 Eric Andersson, 'Don't Call Me Fat!', *Us Weekly*, 1 April 2013, 42.

32 Devon Powers, 'From Civil Rights to Selling Rights: Kanye West and the Politics of Auteurism', unpublished paper.

33 Christopher Bagley, 'Kanye West: The Transformer', *W Magazine*, 19 June 2013, http://www.wmagazine.com/people/celebrities/2013/06/kanye-west-on-kim-kardashian-and-his-new-album-yeezus/.

34 Emily Smith, 'Kimye pix-nix Irks Kris', *New York Post*, 16 June 2014, 10.

35 Ibid.

36 Casamento, 'The Business of Baby "Kimye"', 9.

37 Judith Newman and Leslie Bruce, 'How the Kardashians Made $65 Million Last Year', *The Hollywood Reporter*, 16 February 2011, http://www.hollywoodreporter.com/news/how-kardashians-made-65-million-100349.

38 Kevin O'Leary, 'Kourtney's Mexican Babymoon', *Us Weekly*, 13 February 2012, 58.

39 Emma Powell, 'Roll Up, Roll Up! Circus Wedding Could Be On the Cards for Kourtney Kardashian and Scott Disick', *London Evening Standard*, 13 July 2014, http://www.standard.co.uk/showbiz/celebrity-news/roll-up-roll-up-circus-wedding-could-be-on-the-cards-for-kourtney-kardashian-and-scott-disick-9534117.html.

40 'Kardashians Empire Crumbles', *Star*, 31 March 2014, 41.

41 Maria Pramaggiore and Diane Negra, 'Keeping Up with the Aspirations: Commercial Family Values and the Kardashian Family Brand', in *Reality Gendervision: Sexuality and Gender on Transatlantic Reality Television*, ed. Brenda R. Weber (Durham, NC: Duke University Press, 2014), 83–84.

42 'Kris' New Day Job', *Us Weekly*, 22 July 2013, 70.

43 Jennifer O'Neill, 'Kim and Reggie: Back On?', *Us Weekly*, 27 February 2012, 61.

44 Sarah Grossbart and Jennifer O'Neill, 'Bruce Jenner: Shocking New Look', *Us Weekly*, 17 February 2014, 11.

45 Kevin O'Leary, 'It's Over', *Us Weekly*, 21 October 2013, 51.

46 Sarah Grossbart, 'Dating a Bachelor!', *Us Weekly*, 9 December 2013, 54–57.

Part Three

Marriage

Shelley Cobb and Neil Ewen

Chapter 16 of Stephanie Coontz's *Marriage: a History* is entitled 'The Perfect Storm: The Transformation of Marriage at the End of the Twentieth Century'. In it, Coontz outlines the trends that constitute a crisis in the institution of marriage across the western world since 1970: a steady decline in rates of marriage, a dramatic surge in the rates of divorce and 'a whole flood of new alternatives to marriage'.[1] As Anthea Taylor argues in her chapter in this section, however, 'Despite the western divorce rate widely conceded to be one in two, marriage retains its currency. Indeed, in many ways, it seems its stocks are on the rise, with marriage equality activists reinscribing its status as a desirable institution.' Though the fifty per cent divorce rate and the decline in marriage rates are sometimes contested, the cultural anxiety expressed through the media's repetition of this number seems to attest to a widespread fear in relation to the changing institution of marriage.[2] However, the media's intense focus on, scrutiny of and speculation about celebrity marriage (as well as divorce and remarriage) also suggests a deep cultural ambivalence about an institution that is regularly lauded as the foundation of society.

The currency of marriage in its ability to legitimize, and delegitimize, strikingly different types of coupled relationships is laid out and dissected by the chapters in this section through analyses of the ways celebrity couples dramatize these processes. As all of these chapters illustrate, marriage as an institution is a site of confluence between multiple different discourses, including the social, the cultural, the legal, the political and the economic. During a time when marriage is becoming in some ways more inclusive, *vis-à-vis* the expansion of same-sex marriage rights, it nevertheless remains a controversial and discriminatory institution. Logically, in its legitimization of some couples, it inevitably delegitimizes those couples and individuals who cannot or choose not to be married. And those who find themselves outside the institution (by choice or exclusion) are therefore positioned in cultural terms, to varying degrees, as abject.

The analyses of celebrity couples in this section expose some of the ways that marriage is complicit in producing and reproducing the restrictions of normative relations in the contemporary period across very different geographical and cultural contexts. They also illustrate the ways in which getting married, or not, can alter the economic and cultural value of both the individual celebrity and the celebrity couple. Taken together, these remarkably diverse case studies – from the British royal family, Australian parliamentary politics, North Korean political culture, 'celesbianism' and American hardcore pornography – reveal the ideological complicity between marriage and celebrity across a spectrum of environments.

Margaret Schwartz, in her chapter 'Diana's Rings: Fetishizing the Royal Couple', argues that 'the royal couple is a key site where tension between royal mystique and its perceived consequence of dysfunction and entitlement has played out in public discourse'. Schwartz suggests that Princess Diana's engagement ring, which Prince William later used to propose to Catherine Middleton, symbolizes the 'tension between royal coupling as producers of lineage, on the one hand, and on the other as producers of cultural "relevancy" in such forms as celebrity, gossip, and visibility'. In this reading, the ring represents the continuity of royal values from the married Princess Diana to the Duchess of Cambridge, while simultaneously disavowing the threat to the monarchy posed by the behaviour of the unhappily married and then divorced Diana.

In her analysis of Julia Gillard and her partner, Tim Mathieson, that focuses on during the period of Gillard's time as Prime Minister, Anthea Taylor moves the consideration of celebrity couples from the politics of the British monarchy to the parliamentary politics of Australia. The celebritization of politics is a growing area of scholarship within celebrity studies,[3] and Taylor's chapter adds an important perspective on the intersection of celebrity, politics and marriage by asking, 'If successful leadership is presumed to require a successful relationship (as in a state sanctioned, heteronormative one), what happens when the celebrity political couple is not so easily assimilated into these loaded gendered narratives?' By remaining unmarried (and child-free) while Prime Minister Gillard strongly disrupted the cultural expectations of how to be both female and a politician. Taylor shows how Gillard's relationship with Mathieson was constructed as illegitimate because it was not 'officially sanctioned by the

State', and how, as a result, 'their relationship effectively became a synecdoche for her "relationship" with the Australian people', which the media 'also discursively constructed as "illegitimate"'.

Keeping with the theme of politics, David Zeglen's chapter, 'It's the Thought That Counts: North Korea's Glocalization of the Celebrity Couple and the Mediated Politics of Reform', illustrates how the western media read the introduction to the world of the North Korean leader's wife Ri in terms of its apparent celebrity couple elements – fashion, pseudo-events and discussion of class background – as signs of reform within the closed and tightly-controlled regime. Exposing this process as flawed, as well as challenging celebrity studies as a discipline to be mindful of its own western-centricity, Zeglen argues that the flow of 'celebrity culture to North Korea should be understood as having undergone glocalization – a process that involves the selective borrowing of foreign styles which are then imbued with domestic meaning', and suggests that Ri and Kim's celebrity marriage 'should be understood as a cultural hybrid comprising celebrity signifiers ... that have been made to fit the local context of North Korean "gift culture"'.

Shelley Cobb's chapter, 'Ellen and Portia's Wedding: the Politics of Same-Sex Marriage and Celesbianism', moves the theme of politics to the United States where the debates about equal marriage rights have recently acquired a higher profile than ever before, partly, as her chapter suggests, through lesbian and gay celebrity couples who have married (in the states where it is legal) and who are now ubiquitous in celebrity media culture. Her particular focus on Ellen DeGeneres and Portia de Rossi's marriage interrogates the ambivalent politics of the celebrity lesbian couple who participate in, and are legitimized by, the normative narrative of the married couple – from dating, to engagement, to wedding, to married life – even as both DeGeneres and de Rossi have spoken up for national same-sex marriage rights since they wed. Cobb argues that while the visibility of the equal marriage campaign 'has relegated other fights for LGBTQ equality to the margins and elevated marriage as the key symbol of equal rights and citizenship ... the prominence of the fight for marriage equality also contributes to the cultural weight of marriage itself as the optimum form of sexual intimacy, social acceptance and legal protection of individuals'.

Finally in this section, marriage as a form of legal legitimacy is cannily explored by Beccy Collings through an analysis of the (formerly) married porn-star celebrity couple Audrey Hollander and Otto Bauer, in her chapter 'Audrey Hollander and Otto Bauer: The Perfect (Pornographic) Marriage?' Collings challenges celebrity studies' relative neglect of pornography as a site of celebrity production and argues that 'traditional notions of the public/private and frontstage/backstage divides (so crucial to academic discussions surrounding celebrity image and the marketing of celebrity personae) are problematized when applied to performers for whom the most private of backstage activities are necessarily the public element of their careers'. Her analysis considers how marriage seemed to affect perceptions of their work together, potentially influencing the outcome of an obscenity charge against their film *Filthy Things 6*. And she suggests that their transgression of the private/public divide exposes 'the prevailing paradigms of celebrity behavior and self-promotion' necessary for any 'successful "celebrity" status, coupled or otherwise'.

Notes

1   Stephanie Coontz, *Marriage, a History: How Love Conquered Marriage* (New York: Penguin, 2005), 263–80. Coontz notes that rates of divorce slowed in the 1990s, but that 'rates of marriage fell even faster' (277). Recent figures suggest that marriage rates have slowed further in the wake of the 2008 financial crisis.

2   Danielle Teller and Astro Teller, The 50% divorce rate is a myth, so why won't it die?", Quartz, 4 December 2014, accessed at: http://qz.com/306166/the-divorce-stat-that-just-keeps-cheating-50/

3   See, for example: Mark Wheeler, *Celebrity Politics: Image and Identity in Contemporary Political Communications* (Cambridge, MA: Polity, 2013).

8

Diana's Rings: Fetishizing The Royal Couple

Margaret Schwartz

The Duke and Duchess of Cambridge – Wills and Kate, if you're a royals watcher – toured Australia and New Zealand in May 2014 with their baby son George. A generation earlier, Prince Charles and Princess Diana had made the same trip shortly after William was born, though the baby prince stayed out of sight. This time around, Baby Prince George was centre stage. Both William and Catherine were photographed holding the baby, who also enjoyed such 'normal kid' activities as a trip to the zoo and a staged 'playdate' with several other children of his age. The royals were at obvious pains to show that Kate is a hands-on mother: every time their plane touched down in a new location, the Duchess walked to the tarmac with the baby in her arms. George's visibility during this official visit earned him the title of 'Republican Slayer' as his visit evidently coincided with a marked rise in monarchist sentiment among Australians and New Zealanders.[1]

If, as Engels observed in *The Origin of the Family, Private Property, and the State*, the family is the primary unit of capitalist social reproduction, then the royal coupling holds pride of place.[2] Its use value, within that mode, is to produce children as a means to secure succession and to guarantee purity of lineage. In what Foucault called a control society, the fecundity and health of the royal line metaphorically extends to the nation: it is the paradigm of biopolitical power.[3] Or it was, in a world where royal lineages wielded absolute political power. Today, royal power is exercised as influence within the government, which funds the monarchy differently (and more generously) than it does other public bodies. As the head of state, the Queen is still a political entity with veto power whose potential influence on democratic politics in the UK is the source of anxiety over the appropriateness of the monarchy in a modern democracy (as well as straightforward republicanism).[4] Nevertheless, the fact remains that the modern British monarchy occupies a much-reduced political role in comparison with the absolute sovereigns of yore.

Similarly, while royal lineage and legitimacy still have some meaning, they are no longer requirements for political power. Increasingly, royal relevancy is measured in increments of tabloid ink and images, royal power measured in terms of clickbait. In an effort to steer clear of the pitfalls of scandal, the palace has embraced social media and even hired a PR firm. In contrast to the mystique of the monarchy of old, today's royals, particularly the Duke and Duchess of Cambridge, offer a media accessibility carefully crafted to underline their function as public servants, not as role models.[5]

Royals are a unique form of celebrity, and their couplings are of heightened fascination because of the ancient tang of lineage and pomp. In Chris Rojek's seminal formulation, royalty is the quintessential form of ascribed celebrity.[6] If they happen to be talented or beautiful, so much the better, but their genre of celebrity is predicated on its arbitrariness, on the fact that it precisely isn't deserved in any way. The popularity of royals tends to be staked more to behaviour – whether they are adequately balanced between approachability and pomp, whether they humbly and seriously undertake their roles, whether they commit themselves to charitable work. Nevertheless this discourse only appears where a royal is visible in the world of tabloid celebrity, and this happens most often with regard to their couplings. The notion of a 'fairy tale made real' that drove the public narrative of Diana and Charles' marriage gets its grounding from the idea that after all, the Windsors must have an heir if the monarchy is to continue. The stakes are nationalist, traditionalist and, if I may be pardoned the expression, eugenicist.[7] The royal body, itself always a doubled and theological entity,[8] becomes all the more charged with that particular tension between the body politic and the messiness of human embodiment when it is coupled. The royal couple is thus a complex, overdetermined unit in which the investments in sexual difference, family, and gender roles mingle with the traditional and nationalistic imaginary.

At the same time, the royals are the royals because of this ancient tradition of lineage and succession. It is in some ways their anachronism that fascinates the public, and makes royal couplings such a unique focus of attention. The royal couple is a key site where tension between royal mystique and its perceived consequence of dysfunction and entitlement has played out in public discourse (largely in the tabloids). After a spate of spectacularly embarrassing de-couplings, the public relations challenge has been to craft a compelling royal love story that earns loyalty, not jeers.[9]

Part of this story is about contrition and normalcy. Windsor Castle now charges visitors admission and uses the funds as its own source of income (initially to pay for renovations after the 1992 fire). The Duchess of Cambridge reuses hats and dresses in a calculated gesture to assure the public that she is not squandering their money – some of which, anyway, is no longer tax exempt. Nevertheless her role is defined by the need to project glamour and exclusivity via the image.[10] If at any point this balance were to be improperly calibrated, republican rumblings – always present in a world where kings and queens are expensive figureheads – would gain traction. The UK royals do not, as is often assumed, necessarily drive the tourist industry in that country. Alongside the murkiness of the royal finances, this makes them expensive anachronisms.[11] If Charles and Diana made a spectacle of royal decadence in the 1980s and 1990s before their marriage dissolved, today's royal couple – William and Catherine – are called upon to win back the loyalty of their subjects by demonstrating their earthiness, their willingness to serve, and their marital stability.

This chapter takes as its starting point this tension between royal couplings as producers of lineage, on the one hand, and on the other as producers of cultural 'relevancy' in such forms as celebrity, gossip, and visibility. Though the royal couple as producer of future kings seems an archaic function, it is precisely the couple that generates the most value within tabloid media and the wider commodification of the royals that characterizes neoliberal society. Moreover, the royal couple is called upon to somehow force the messiness of procreation into the metaphorical realm of the body politic – a process that, in today's image-saturated celebrity culture, offers crucial insights about the representational strategies that allow these bodies, in their messiness, to matter in the service of a national and capitalistic ideal.

I argue for a fetishistic reading of the royal coupling, one in which an object – in this case Diana's diamond and sapphire engagement ring – both covers over and invokes the disavowed scandal of Diana's extramarital sexuality, most notably her public romance with the Egyptian billionaire Dodi al-Fayed, who was also killed in the car crash that ended Diana's life. This fetish of the royal couple denies the fact of her sexuality outside her marriage while, paradoxically, continually memorializing this sexuality as a problem that must be covered over. When Diana's son William proposed to Kate Middleton using the same ring, the gesture seemed in part designed to redeem Diana's legacy: to remember her as virgin bride and mother of kings, and not as a globetrotting divorcee whose love affairs are tabloid fodder. It is not a coincidence that William and Catherine's engagement portrait is nearly identical to that of Charles and Diana's, emphasizing the ring as the centrepiece of a coupling that will, this time, 'work'. At the same time, these obsessive repetitions invoke Diana's non-procreative sexuality by recalling the ring enshrined at Harrods, the one her lover Dodi al-Fayed allegedly gave Diana the night of her death. Reading the ring as a fetish allows an intervention into the capitalistic investments in the British monarchy. Rather than reading such couples as symbols of nationalism or the royalist tradition, my reading attends to the ways in which these couples produce cultural value as brands. Moreover, fetishized images such as the ring work to maintain a 'stable' or properly traditional monarchy and thereby maximize its value as commodity.

Rebranding the royal couple

Royal couples now circulate primarily as images in their own sphere of tabloid celebrity, similar to but not quite in the sphere of what Jeffrey Sconce has called the 'meta meta famous',[12] but also not called upon to justify their visibility through talent or beauty like Hollywood stars. Royals need not be particularly talented or deserving; after all, they inherited their status. At the same time, their visibility carries with it the mystique of tradition and the glamour of protocol, along with a stable of celebrity style events – charity fundraisers, polo matches, state dinners – that give the tabloid press regular reason to cover them. The narrativization of their celebrity therefore tends to look for scandal, for ways to tear them down as undeserving, since unlike 'regular' celebrities, who may lose revenue as well as relevance if their popularity declines, they are not subject in the same way to the vicissitudes of popular opinion.[13]

The worldwide popularity of the British monarchy is of course inseparable from the enormous appeal of the late Diana, Princess of Wales. As a royal celebrity, however, Diana's fame and persona was inseparable from the drama of her coupledom: first as virgin bride, then as doting mother, unhappy wife, and finally as a liberated divorcee finding new love in the arms of Dodi al-Fayed. Her estrangement and divorce from Prince Charles and the scandals that accompanied it made her a source of fascination and identification, as she spoke openly about her struggles with bulimia and postnatal depression. Diana and

Charles ultimately didn't work for the monarchy as a brand because they failed to uphold the sanctity of the marriage, even if they did produce children. In the famous 1995 'Panorama' interview with Martin Bashir, she blatantly played the part of the scorned wife, famously admitting, 'Well there were three of us in this marriage, so it was a bit crowded.' She spoke at length about the pressure to keep up appearances for the public, and the expectation that she cope with these pressures without complaint.[14] Diana's ultimate release from the confines of royal marriage suggested that the monarchy had conceded defeat in that they could not make the Princess be quiet or suffer in silence, and they could not make the Prince a faithful or even attentive husband.

Intrinsic to this argument is therefore the assumption that the female body plays a particular role in royal couplings, and that as a fetish object, the royal couple plays intrinsically to the drama of sexual difference on a stage where the stakes are not only personal but national and historical. In short, although Diana was a virgin princess and mother of the future king, her ultimate uncoupling from Charles made her body into a sexual object in a way that disrupted the royal couple to its core. The fetish object I describe here, Diana's engagement ring (or rings, for as we will see there is also a double), thus recuperates her body for the patriarchy and simultaneously enshrines that of her successor, Kate Middleton, as well.

Initially a low point in the public approval of the monarchy, Diana's death has been incorporated into its rebranding, her death rewritten as a martyr's redemption of its sins. In his eulogy, Diana's brother, Earl Spencer, pledged that he would 'continue the imaginative and loving way in which you were steering these two exceptional young men so that their souls are not simply immersed by duty and tradition, but can sing openly as you planned'.[15] These words drew applause, first from the crowds outside the Abbey listening on the radio, and finally from those attending the funeral. This populist moment, where public sentiment broke through protocol, has become the dominant narrative of Diana's death. Perhaps best exemplified by the Hollywood movie *The Queen* (Frears, 2006), Diana's death saves the monarchy by forcing it to break with some of its older, stiffer traditions: it emerges as a modern, hands-on, humanitarian and broadly relevant institution. To wit: the Queen parachuting into the 2012 Olympics Opening Ceremony on the arm of the actor Daniel Craig in his role as James Bond.[16]

There is a politics to these strategies of representation, and if they are distinctly monarchical, it is only insofar as the monarchy is a lucrative commodity. We might further assert that monarchical politics, in Great Britain particularly, articulate not only to a sense of tradition and national identity, but also to something we might call national branding.[17] As Britain shifted from being an industrial, colonizing polity to a post-industrial service economy, identification with and support for the monarchy throughout the United Kingdom took on complicated dimensions.[18] Today, royal relevancy isn't just about tradition or even class – it's also about neoliberal economics. Like the royal wedding of Catherine and William and the Queen's Jubilee that preceded it, the Queen's stunt at the 2012 Summer Olympics only cemented the value of the royals as commodity fetish. As such, both events are part of the currency paid to keep up the 'special relationships, the Commonwealth, and other old club subscriptions' that allow the UK to maintain a kind of post-imperial 'symbolic supranationality'.[19] That is, they are good for global capitalism because the reformed monarchy upholds the neoliberal standard of what Lilie Chouliaraki calls the 'theatricality of humanitarianism'.[20] Diana's legacy is that her performance of her own suffering, as in the 'Panorama' interview, became a model for building public service into the monarchy as nationalist lifestyle brand. As long as that brand continues to have global viability, the monarchy is, if not strictly lucrative, relevant.[21]

What better symbol for the new royals, poised between tabloid celebrity and ancient custom, than the engagement ring? At once an object of tradition and a commodity, the diamond and sapphire engagement ring worn first by Diana and which, after her death, her son William used to propose to Kate Middleton, exemplifies this tension between the royals as nationalistic institution and as tabloid celebrities. It is both a traditional symbol of love and fidelity *and* an object perfectly suited to the visual consumption of wealth typical of star culture. Indeed, tabloid consumption of non-royal couplings often centres around the engagement ring. This takes many forms – paparazzi shots of a starlet wearing a bauble on *that finger*, appearances in which the celebrity may show off her ring (or his, as Johnny Depp did, wearing his fiancées engagement ring on his pinky finger as a stunt for a late night talk show), even magazine spreads showing the ring in detail, its cost and composition and comparing it to other celebrity rings. It is, moreover, perhaps too obvious to state that the engagement ring functions as a kind of stand in for the exchange of women among members of a tribe – its weight and size and cost metaphorically indexing the value of the woman being exchanged.

Significantly, Diana was criticized as a young fiancée for buying this ring 'off the rack', instead of having one made.[22] A ready-made ring bought at the jeweller's counter was cheap, beneath her station, an example of her shoddy, provincial tastes. How different that critique sounds today, when Catherine, Duchess of Cambridge, Diana's successor in the public eye, is lauded for shopping off the rack as a symbol of her 'down to earth' normalcy. Middleton herself is rather an 'off the rack' choice of princess, a commoner whose parents made their money selling party supplies. This middle-class identity reads in the new monarchy not as cheap or inappropriate, but as a kind of grounding, a literal way for Prince William to keep in touch with the subjects he will someday rule. This new generation of 'people's princess' elevates the middle class rather than reaching out to them: Middleton's less-than-flashy though still very handsome looks, her long devotion to William over the course of ten years, and her apparent weight-loss regimen over the course of those years testify to a kind of Ruskin-esque uplift project. Thus the Duchess' example will ennoble the masses by setting the same example of self-care and unquestioning loyalty required of the neoliberal subject.

In all of these aspects, Catherine represents the opposite of Diana, the eighteen-year-old from one of England's oldest aristocratic families, her arresting good looks only marred, early on, by a certain clumsiness of style and, as would later haunt her, a remainder of adolescent chubbiness.[23] On the Duchess, Diana's ring does not project approachability or off-the-rack crassness but is rather the symbol of her royalness, of her exclusive status as chosen and separate and special. As a fetish object the ring stands in for an imagined body that has been lost: here, Diana the virginal mother of kings.[24] It incorporates one idea of Diana's body into the new narrative of a reformed monarchy, by invoking its opposite – Diana's body as unruly, sexual, castrating – only to disavow it. The ring marks the specialness of William and Catherine because it is the enshrined and effaced mark of Diana's suffering, because it conceals and memorializes the ways in which her body was other than maternal and virginal, and thereby consecrates their union.

What do I mean when I say the ring is a fetish? The notion of the fetish comes from nineteenth-century anthropology, meaning a physical object that is thought to have magical properties. The fetish was used as a metaphor by both Marx and Freud,[25] by the former to describe the magic of the commodity in capitalism, and by the latter to describe the sexual proclivity in which a special or 'magical' object is necessary to achieve orgasm (say, for example, a shoe).[26] What is important here is the idea that a physical object stands in for dynamics that are either capitalistic – the labour relations that make the commodity but which are concealed in its object character – or libidinal – the belief that the mother had at one time a penis which has been castrated, and for which the fetish object substitutes.

The ring operates on both these levels. The Freudian fetish is a kind of scar marking sexual difference. When the boy (and it is always a boy) sees the mother's naked body for the first time, he presumes that its difference from his own is the result of a horrible mutilation – a castration. The fetishist is someone trapped in this moment of trauma who substitutes a shoe or a piece of underwear for that phantom penis which he thinks has been lost. The object itself is crucial to his sexual release – but in the very act of 'bandaging' this wound, the fetish also memorializes and crystallizes the moment of trauma. This is what I mean when I say a scar: it covers over the wound, but it also marks it forever as a site of trauma. This trauma is not only the sight of the female 'wound' but the threat to the male body it implies. The ring on Kate Middleton's finger covers over the wound/trauma/threat of Diana's sexuality, but it also memorializes this castrating threat to the monarchy. We cannot see the ring without thinking of the *other* ring, the one at Harrods which signifies her non-maternal sexuality, her uncoupled sexuality, one that was for her own pleasure and not for the brand of the monarchy.

While it may be less obvious why Diana's engagement ring is a fetish in the Freudian sense, the Marxist sense is all too clear. The ring is a costly piece of jewellery that conceals, in our fascination with its objecthood (I can hardly think of a more iconic ring, or a more visible one), the social relations that make it meaningful. We imagine that it is a sentimental object – a token from a son of his late and beloved mother. The object itself only has meaning because of the libidinal and capitalistic dynamics described here that make Kate the redemption of Diana and the royal couple of Kate and William a redemption of the failed couple. At the same time, that failure is inscribed in the object, making the threat of Diana's uncoupled sexuality hang over William and Kate, indeed over their son, pressing him into the service of tabloid monarchism.

The ring's two bodies

'I literally would not let it go,' said William, speaking of the engagement ring that belonged to his mother and that he planned to give to Kate Middleton. 'Everywhere I went, I was keeping ahold of it because I knew, this thing, if it disappeared, I'd be in a lot of trouble.'[27] William's language here clearly makes the ring itself magical and powerful. The ostensive reason for his care with the ring is because he had it in his backpack while he and Catherine were on a safari vacation in Africa. There, on the decolonized soil that once would have been his birthright, William knelt and offered Catherine – a woman without aristocratic title – her role as mother of kings. The purpose of the story, therefore, is to show how different William and Kate's engagement is, how much earthier and more sincere, than that of William's ill-fated parents.[28] Yet the language here betrays a belief in the magic of the ring as if it were possible to re-inscribe Diana's reconstructed body on to poor 'Waity Katy', the girl with whom William had a relationship for nearly a decade and who came to the marriage as something other than a virgin bride.

In Prince William and Catherine Middleton's official engagement portrait, the two smile broadly, arms around each other. Kate's left hand rests on William's chest, prominently displaying the enormous sapphire and diamond engagement ring that first belonged to Diana. Both are wearing warm, neutral colours in soft, yellow-tinted light, making the ring stand out boldly against her skin and the beige of his sweater. 'This is my way of making sure my mother didn't miss out on today', said William to reporters when the engagement was announced.[29]

The photograph is strikingly similar to the official portrait of Charles and Diana's engagement, so much so that it must have been deliberate. William and Charles are to the left of the frame, Diana and Kate on the right, both with their hands strategically placed to display the ring. Kate and Diana are even wearing almost the same cream-coloured blouse. The difference is that Kate and William are clearly making an effort to look casual, 'down to earth', excited and warm. William is dressed casually, in a pullover and unbuttoned white shirt; in his father's engagement portrait, Charles wears a suit and tie. Their poses and expressions are far more sedate, though they are still smiling; Charles' left hand perches gingerly on Diana's shoulder, while William is embracing his fiancée with both arms.

Between the two portraits is the story of the rebranding of the royal couple. The narrative begins with tragedy in the most classical sense: with a prideful figure who is taken down by one of her own personality flaws. In this case, the flaw was the desire to be public, the need for recognition that both made her such a popular figure and led her to feel hounded, scrutinized and afraid. So the story begins with a woman who walked a tightrope line between the kind of 'codeless' intimacy that modern media promise and the kind of horrible, panoptic scrutiny that makes celebrity a paranoid fantasy.[30]

The picture of the soon-to-be Duchess of Cambridge wearing the ring is the end of this story in that it seems to indicate a discarding of Diana as a fetishized loss and the incorporation of her death into the psychic life of the nation. The ring symbolizes an end to grief because it indicates that William has grown into a healthy young man whose mother's death has not scarred him significantly enough to keep him from having his own life, finding a partner, having a family of his own and carrying on the tradition of the monarchy without ruining himself in the process.

The ring is particularly potent as a signifier/fetish because it references the uneasy swerving of Diana's body into the area of racial mixing, of non-maternal sexuality, of feminine desire. All of this is a castrating threat to the monarchy as patriarchal and colonial institution. The persistent rumour that Diana was pregnant with Dodi al-Fayed's child was taken up by the inquest into their deaths as late as 2007. The allegation, from al-Fayed's father, Mohammed, is that the couple were murdered to prevent the possibility of a royal half-sibling of Egyptian and Islamic descent.[31] As the means by which to make his mother present for his happiness, the ring invokes Diana as princess, wife and mother. The ring makes a literal closure for a metaphoric circle that begins with the (virginal) Diana being given to Charles and begetting William, the prince and heir to the throne.

In so doing, it effectively cuts out (and, of course, enshrines) the ways in which the body for which the ring stands deviated from these roles. Diana's infidelity during the course of her marriage is now a matter of public record – and indeed, she even talked about it herself in interviews. Her lover, James Hewitt, has written two books about his time with Diana, and fuelled rumours that the second son, Harry, may not be Charles' biological offspring.[32]

This 'anti-Establishment' narrative reaches its most extreme in Mohamed Al-Fayed's allegations that the Duke of Edinburgh told the British Secret Service to assassinate Diana because of her relationship with Dodi and her pregnancy. Rather than seeing Diana as the martyr who reformed the monarchy, she is seen as 'a heroine who embraced the modern, multi-cultural, multi-ethnic Britain without reservation',[33] in the words of Dr Trevor Phillips, Chair of the British Commission for Equality and Human Rights. Gay men identified with Diana and her image as a palace outsider, because they felt it echoed their own sense of exclusion.[34] Versions of this narrative animated the applause at Earl Spencer's assertion that Diana 'needed no royal title to continue her particular brand of magic'.[35] The anti-Establishment narrative, in short, sees Diana as an outlier in the royal tradition, as someone who had escaped from an institution that abetted her loveless marriage, sought to control the way she raised her children, and stifled or criticized her need for closer contact with everyday people.

This is the Diana that the ring both enshrines and disavows. The idea of Diana's body as not only available to multiple (male) partners but also possibly carrying a child of mixed race who would be half-sibling to the crown prince must be suppressed in order to bury her once and for all. The ring effects this suppression while of course insisting on it just enough to enshrine its opposite, that is, the unruly sexuality of a body that did not remain pure or maternal. Kate Middleton (whose virginity has not been discussed as far as I know) is reinscribed as a fetish object whose body is both racially and sexually pure, a willing and appropriate vessel for the ongoing lineage of British kings.

The engagement ring has its double: the putative engagement ring Dodi gave Diana and which she was wearing on the night she died. It is the fetish of that coupling, which symbolizes all that Diana meant to anti-royalist sentiment. The ring is the centre of the shrine to Diana and Dodi at Harrods, which also includes such relics as glasses they drank from on the night of the crash, and a life-size statue of the couple, arms intertwined and reaching towards a dove of peace. If the day I visited is any indication, this shrine is extremely popular. Tourists from around the world crowded around the case containing the ring, taking photographs and nudging one another out of the way to get a closer look. Unlike Diana's grave at Althorp or such palace-approved memorials as the playground at Kensington Palace, this site has a tawdry, tabloid feel. The people who come to see it don't behave in a decorous or respectful fashion – they gawk and shove and take selfies. Though the site is ostensibly in celebration of Diana and Dodi's love, they don't feel like a couple here. Rather, the shrine feels like the return of Diana's suppressed body – the body that had sexual desire, multiple partners, non-white partners, maybe even (at least in the public imagination if not in fact) a non-white sibling for the future king.

This other Diana, and the more radical, queer, anti-royalist feelings she symbolized, is precisely *not* coupled. It is her potential as a multiple partner, as a single woman enjoying her own body outside of the confines of royal couple. This body is the double and disavowed other of the imagined virgin mother enshrined in the ring worn by the Duchess of Cambridge, herself now the mother of an heir (and a spare on the way). Both of Diana's rings testify to the potential threat carried by her body to the capitalist imperialist patriarchy of the modern United Kingdom. It remains to be seen whether the repressed will return now that Duchess of Cambridge has fulfilled her use value by producing a male heir. What is certain is that whatever happens will unfold in the public eye, and with the brand identity of the British monarchy on the line.

Notes

1 '"Republican Slayer" Prince George Is Turning Australians Monarchist', *The Huffington Post UK*, accessed 26 June 2014, http://www.huffingtonpost. co.uk/2014/04/16/prince-george-republican-slayer_n_5158328.html.

2 Friedrich Engels and Tristram Hunt, *The Origin of the Family, Private Property and the State*, reissue ed. (London; New York: Penguin Classics, 2010).

3 Michel Foucault, 'The Right of Death and Power Over Life', in *The Foucault Reader*, ed. Paul Rabinow (New York: Pantheon, 1984), 258–72.

4 'Know the Facts', *Republic: Campaigning for a Democratic Alternative to the Monarchy*, accessed 16 October 2014, http://republic.org.uk/what-we-want/know-the-facts.

5 'How the Royal Family Embrace Social Media', *Royal Central*, accessed 21 October 2014, http://royalcentral.co.uk/blogs/how-the-royal-family-embrace-social-media-24812.

6 Chris Rojek, *Celebrity* (London: Reaktion, 2001), 17–20.

7 While I recognize that this term has ugly overtones, I do not raise them lightly, particularly when it comes to the discussion below of Diana's partnership with the Egyptian Dodi Al-Fayed and the possibility that she was pregnant with his child.

8 Ernst Kantorowicz, *The King's Two Bodies: A Study in Mediaeval Political Theology* (Princeton, NJ: Princeton University Press, 1957).

9 Caroline Davies, 'How the Royal Family Bounced Back from Its "Annus Horribilis"', *The Guardian*, 24 May 2012, sec. UK news, http://www.theguardian.com/uk/2012/may/24/royal-family-bounced-back-annus-horribilis.

10 'Your Bill to Refurbish Kate's Palace Now £4MILLION: New Kitchen, Nursery and Several Bathrooms Quadruples the Cost', *Mail Online*, accessed 26 June 2014, http://www.dailymail.co.uk/news/article-2664060/Your-bill-refurbish-Kates-palace-4MILLION-New-kitchen-nursery-bathrooms-quadruples-cost.html.

11 See http://republic.org.uk/what-we-want/monarchy-myth-buster/its-good-tourism and http://republic.org.uk/what-we-want/royal-finances.

12 Jeffrey Sconce, 'A Vacancy at the Paris Hilton', in *Fandom: Identities and Communities in a Mediated World*, ed. Cornel Sandvoss, C. Lee Harrington and Jonathan Gray (New York: New York University Press, 2007).

13 The same is of course true of figures like Paris Hilton or Kim Kardashian who will be wealthy and privileged no matter whether or not they are famous or visible. Paris Hilton may no longer be able to sell reality shows, but that won't diminish her inherited wealth, only her popularity. However the royals carry with them the residue of political power and as such are not quite subject to the whims of the court of public opinion. Whether or not they are a 'popular' royal, like Diana was, their ribbon cuttings and gala attendances will still be news, that is, still be visible in a particular way in the public sphere.

14 'BBC1 Panorama', *Interview with Diana, Princess of Wales* (BBC1, November 1995).

15 'Brother's Eulogy for Diana: "The Very Essence of Compassion"', *The New York Times*, 7 September 1997, sec. World, http://www.nytimes.com/1997/09/07/world/brother-s-eulogy-for-diana-the-very-essence-of-compassion.html.

16 There's so much to say here, not least of which the fact that the lines between real and imaginary are so spectacularly blurred in this bit. Pairing her with a fictional character makes Queen Elizabeth seem a bit fictional, while at the same time she lends James Bond – or the actor who currently portrays him, Daniel Craig – a bit of reality. The truth of both of these symbols of Britain is that they are lucrative global commodities that circulate by means of the image.

17 Melissa Aronczyk, *Branding the Nation: The Global Business of National Identity* (Oxford; New York: Oxford University Press, 2013).

18 Tom Nairn writes eloquently about the monarchy role in keeping up appearances in light of the 'half-honorable decline' of the former British Empire in the Foreword to the 2011 edition of his study *The Enchanted Glass: Britain and Its Monarchy*, 2nd ed. (London; New York: Verso, 2011).

19 Ibid., vii.

20 Lilie Chouliaraki, 'The Theatricality of Humanitarianism: A Critique of Celebrity Advocacy', *Communication & Critical/Cultural Studies* 9, no. 1 (March 2012): 1–21, doi:10.1080/14791420.2011.637055.

21 As mentioned above, one of the main arguments for the monarchy is that it is good for tourism, while one of the main arguments against is that it costs the British taxpayer. The former claim is contested, while the latter is hard to prove because of a lack of transparency in the way the Windsors income and holdings are taxed and attributed. See note 10.

22 Maggie Gee, 'Prince William, and Kate Middleton, and the Return of the Ring', *The Guardian*, 20 November 2010, http://www.guardian.co.uk/uk/2010/nov/20/prince-william-potency-of-engagement-ring.

23 For a discussion of the Spencer family lineage see Tina Brown, *The Diana Chronicles* (New York: Broadway Books, 2008), 114.

24 'I knew I had to keep myself tidy for what lay ahead,' said Lady Diana Spencer, as quoted in ibid., 92.

25 For an interesting analysis of the imperialist colonialist implications of both Marx and Freud's use of the term, see Ken Hillis, *Online a Lot of the Time: Ritual, Fetish, Sign* (Durham, NC: Duke University Press, 2009).

26 Karl Marx and Friedrich Engels, 'Das Kapital, Chapter 1, Commodities', in *The Marx-Engels Reader*, ed. Robert C. Tucker, 2nd revised and enlarged ed. (New York: W. W. Norton & Company, 1978); Sigmund Freud, 'Fetishism', in *The Standard Edition of the Complete Psychological Works of Sigmund Freud*, vol. 21 (London: The Hogarth Press and the Institute of Psycho-Analysis, 1953).

27 Today staff and wire, 'Untold Stories behind Kate's 18-Carat Sapphire', *TODAY. com*, accessed 10 August 2012, http://today.msnbc.msn.com/id/40217151/ns/today-today_news/t/untold-stories-behind-kates--carat-sapphire/.

28 The interaction with reporters on the day of their engagement has come to crystalize the public's perception of the marriage as doomed. When asked whether the two are in love, Diana answers immediately, 'Of course.' 'Whatever "in love" means,' adds Charles.

29 Melissa Castellanos CBS News, 20 August 2012, and 2:59 Pm, 'Kate Middleton's Engagement Ring Is Princess Diana's', accessed 28 October 2014, http://www.cbsnews.com/news/kate-middletons-engagement-ring-is-princess-dianas/.

30 J. D. Peters, 'Broadcasting and Schizophrenia', *Media, Culture & Society* 32, no. 1 (2010): 123–40.

31 'Was Princess Diana MURDERED by British Soldier? Metropolitan Police "Assessing Credibility" of New Claim Made in Court Martial of SAS Sniper Danny Nightingale', *Mail Online*, accessed 28 October 2014, http://www.dailymail.co.uk/news/article-2396208/Princess-Diana-MURDERED-British-soldier-Police-assessing-credibility-new-claim.html.

32 Anna Pasternak, *Princess in Love*, 1st ed. (New York, NY: Dutton Adult, 1994); James Hewitt, *Love and War*, 1st ed. (London: Blake Pub, 1999).

33 Brown, *The Diana Chronicles*, 467.

34 For an excellent discussion of Diana's resonance with the gay community, see William J. Spurlin, 'I'd Rather Be the Princess Than the Queen! Mourning Diana as A Gay Icon', in *Mourning Diana: Nation, Culture and the Performance of Grief*, ed. Adrian Kear and Deborah Lynn Steinberg (London and New York: Routledge, 1999), 155–68.

35 Brown, *The Diana Chronicles*, 478.

9

Behind Every Great Woman …?: Celebrity, Political Leadership and the Privileging of Marriage

Anthea Taylor

In the twenty-first century, the female politician – often still positioned as an anomaly – garners much mainstream media attention, largely focusing on her corporeality and her sartorial style. However, in line with the intense focus on private lives that marks the so-called celebritization of politics, media coverage is also preoccupied with her affective bonds. Much of this coverage reveals that women politicians continue to be anxiety-provoking figures, especially when they refuse to adhere to traditional gendered scripts around matrimony and maternity. Moreover, often the political partner/spouse comes to be celebritized in her or his own right, underscoring just how extensive this emphasis on the intimate lives of politicians can be. Drawing upon the example of Australia's first female Prime Minister, Julia Gillard, and her de facto partner, Tim Mathieson, this chapter considers the ways in which concerns around the 'legitimacy' of this relationship worked in tandem with other deeply embedded discourses about the 'illegitimacy' of her leadership within the Australian political and media spheres to call into question her credibility as prime minister. If successful leadership is presumed to require a successful relationship (as in a state sanctioned, heteronormative one), what happens when the celebrity political couple is not so easily assimilated into these loaded gendered narratives? Although much has been written about how, as PM, Gillard was subject to intense misogyny from other politicians, journalists and even 'ordinary' citizens via social media, this chapter seeks to interrogate what her representation reveals about the operations of contemporary celebrity culture as well as the ongoing privileging of marriage.

* * *

In June 2010, Julia Gillard – then Australia's Deputy Prime Minister – challenged Prime Minister Kevin Rudd for the leadership of the parliamentary Labor Party and won. Rudd had come to power three years prior with his enormously successful 'Kevin 07' campaign; he was immensely popular, until his style of leadership prompted speculation and, subsequently, the challenge from his deputy. In media coverage, Rudd's deposal was widely characterized as a profound act of treachery, with Gillard being positioned as at once a mere pawn of the Australian Labor Party's (ALP) powerbrokers (or 'faceless men') who had long been plotting the downfall of the allegedly autocratic, narcissistic Rudd and a ruthlessly ambitious, disloyal woman. Indicative of the latter, *The Herald Sun* suggested: 'When the opportunity came, the ambitious Gillard did not hesitate to take up the knife and plant it in Rudd's back.'[1] Two months after her ascension, a federal election was held; rather than serving to shore up Gillard's leadership by having her elected in her own right, the result proved disastrous for Australia's first female PM. Placing a massive dent in the considerable margin obtained by Rudd, the poll was so close that for days she was forced to negotiate with minor parties and independents in the hope of being able to form government, which she eventually did in September 2010. Although media hostility towards Gillard undoubtedly intensified after the coup, there is a longer history of rendering her choices (especially in her private life) problematic, as I will show.

The election result, then, served to buttress rather than undercut the dominant narrative that had come to circulate in the Australian mainstream media around Gillard's 'illegitimacy' as PM. Central to the maintenance and force of this narrative, I will argue, is the perceived *illegitimacy* of her relationship with the man who would come to be known as the 'First Bloke', Tim Mathieson. (Gillard and Mathieson have been in a de facto relationship for a number of years but are not married.[2]) In particular, I suggest that it is through the increased celebritization of politics that such a narrative was able to gain traction. However, it also needs to be seen in the context of an apparent wider discomfort with a female national leader and the way she came to power. That is, this narrative of illegitimacy was overdetermined. Of the media's often vitriolic attacks on Australia's first female Prime Minister, Anne Summers argued, 'they are an assault on her legitimacy and, because they rely on sexual and other gender specific attacks for their potency, I have branded this campaign "misogynist"'.[3] In terms of news coverage, the precarity of her leadership was consistently pronounced. The following newspaper article titles from 2011 to 2013, compiled by Kerry Ann Walsh, are emblematic in this regard: 'Gillard is finished as

Prime Minister'; 'Support for Gillard collapsing'; 'Gillard should resign now'; 'Gillard won't last another month'; and 'Nothing will save the PM'.[4] Such articles can be seen to function performatively, in that in many senses they helped bring into being the crisis and instability they claimed to be merely cataloguing. All of these pieces, just a sample of a much bigger intertextual conversation fixated on Gillard and her inadequacy, are indicative of the discursive assaults that regrettably characterized her leadership.

Celebrity and political women

As Graeme Turner argues, the point at which someone comes to be constituted a celebrity is when media engagement shifts from details of their public role to their private lives.[5] In the case of female politicians, there is indeed a clear focus on aspects of their lives beyond the political sphere. Given the enduring presence of romance mythologies in contemporary media culture and that the woman without a man is still seen as a deeply threatening figure requiring intense regulation and recalibration, the other key area of public concern appears to be the woman politician's intimate relationships. In this way, coverage of political leaders is also consistent with the broader pathologization of women who are not, or who have never been, married.[6] It also speaks to what is variously referred to as the increased 'personalization', 'mediatization' and 'celebritization' of contemporary politics. As Peter Dahlgren notes, 'Politicians can take on an aura of celebrity, equivalent to the stars of popular culture.' In such a context, popular representations of individual 'celebrity' politicians work to inform 'how audiences experience them and evaluate their performance, authenticity, and political capabilities'.[7] That is, the politician-as-celebrity comes to mediate our understanding and engagement with (and indeed judgement of) our elected representatives.

As a modern politician, Gillard existed – and was required to perform – in the media spotlight. Celebrity is central to the way contemporary politics is practised, but not without warnings from pessimistic critics about its potential to undermine representative democracy.[8] In addition to using the tools of marketing to effectively sell themselves or their policies, politicians are required to participate in, and indeed use to their advantage, public interest in personalized narrative and desire for access to their inner life.[9] For some, however, this focus on the individual works to 'personalize' politics in a way that can never be productive[10]; news coverage of the private lives of politicians is seen to come at the expense of substance.[11] While these assumptions about the inherent negativity of celebrity culture are problematic, it does appear that women in leadership positions are subject to often harsh public judgement in an explicitly gendered way. In this vein, Georgia Duerst-Lahti argues that women politicians are required to negotiate the 'hair, husband, and hemline problem'.[12] As she makes clear, it is through media attention to her appearance and relationships – rather than her politics or policy positions – that the woman politician becomes most visible. The celebritization of contemporary politics discussed above, has – as Lisbet Van Zoonen emphasizes – particular implications for women: 'the prominent attention given to the private persona and family life of female politicians runs the risk of attracting attention to their non-standard gender choices'.[13] This is precisely the case with Gillard, as well as other international women leaders.

Van Zoonen contends that women currently engaged in formal politics, unlike their early-twentieth-century counterparts, do so in 'profoundly mediated contexts'. As she continues, 'the key trends that presently distinguish mediated political cultures are popularization and personalization'.[14] Key, of course, to the latter is the foregrounding of their affective bonds. In her study, Van Zoonen finds that Finnish President, Tarja Halonen, and Angela Merkel, Germany's Chancellor, at times both effectively 'bypassed the personalization of politics', working to 'rigidly conceal their private lives'.[15] While Gillard certainly did not appear to actively mobilize her intimate relationships in a personalizing gesture, when she announced during the 2010 election campaign that she was going to provide voters access to the 'real Julia' – implicitly opposed to the mediated persona of the celebrity politician – it perhaps sanctioned questions from the Australian press regarding her personal life. As she remarked, 'It's time for me to make sure the real Julia is well and truly on display … I'm the Prime Minister, I'm the leader of the party and I obviously take responsibility. It's about me.'[16] It is important, therefore, to acknowledge the agency of individuals in performing particular celebrity selves. That is, politicians' active participation in the circuits of fame results from a strategic acknowledgement of media's capacity to engage voters in new ways, making them what Mark Wheeler has called 'reflexive celebrity politicians'.[17]

Women politicians have at best had an ambivalent relation to the Australian media, as a number of feminist scholars have demonstrated.[18] Along these lines, focus on Gillard's appearance was intense, with her flaming red hair being the butt of many journalistic jibes; her suit jackets even prompted public criticism from Australia's most famous feminist, Germaine Greer.[19] And when she shifted from wearing contact lenses to 'hipster' glasses it was deemed newsworthy.[20] Moreover, photographs of her sterile, seemingly foodless kitchen were used to call her domestic capital, and by implication her femininity, into question. The empty fruit bowl in her kitchen, the significance of which media debated for days after the photograph appeared in January 2005,[21] was appropriated as a completely unsubtle metaphor for Gillard's childlessness: 'Speculation moved to Gillard's career – could she possibly represent the Australian people if she's without husband, children or brushed aluminium fittings?'[22] Such speculation, of course, ramped up when she actually did become a leader. As remarked in *The Sydney Morning Herald*, 'the majority [of the Australian public] have largely closed their minds to Gillard – "a single woman, childless, whose life is dedicated to her career", she does not fit voter expectations.'[23] Symbolically, Gillard was effectively charged with a series of 'gender crimes', including that she appeared not to prioritize her relationship with Mathieson over all else (a 'crime', of course, with which male politicians are never charged).[24]

In addition to Gillard, over the past decade or so women leaders have been more visible than ever before, including incumbents such as Germany's Chancellor Angela Merkel (2005–); Cristina Fernandez de Kirchner, President of Argentina (2007–), as well as former First Lady (2003–7); the Brazilian President, Dilma Rousseff (2011–); Park Geun-hye, South Korea's President (2013–), as well as the US's former foreign secretary (2009–13) Hilary Clinton (and First Lady, 1993–2001); New Zealand's former Prime Minister Helen Clarke (1999–2008), and, of course, Gillard. In addition, although fictional women in positions of political power are on the increase – evidenced by recent television series such as *Borgen* (2010–), *State of Affairs* (2014–), *Veep* (2013–) and *Madam Secretary* (2014–) –[25] the dominant discourses and tropes through which the female politician comes to mean remain, in the very least, fraught. As Hall and Donaghue observed of Gillard, in many ways she did not 'conform to a straightforward political stereotype, a situation that provoke[d] public curiosity and provides a striking opportunity for news media to interpret the new leader for the Australian public.'[26] Women politicians, who clearly destabilize myriad assumptions around normative femininity, are positioned as problematic. As Donatella Campos argues, 'the fact that women leaders are wives and mothers is intensively scrutinized'[27] – likewise, I would add, is the fact that they are *not*. Indeed, it appears to be absence of husbands (for these discourses are remarkably heteronormative) and children that see such scrutiny amplified. This intense focus on women's intimate bonds, Campos argues, is perhaps part of assuaging fears about women as political actors – emphasizing 'matrimonial and maternal subjectivities',[28] aligning them with 'ordinary' women, arguably makes them seem less transgressive. But it is also about the continued, and intense, investment in marriage as a social and political institution with circumscribed gender roles, something that the case of Gillard–Mathieson brings into sharp relief.

Fear of the unmarried female politician

Despite the Western divorce rate being widely conceded to be one in two, marriage retains its currency. Indeed, in many ways, it seems its stocks are on the rise, with marriage equality activists reinscribing its status as a desirable institution. Moreover, the celebration of coupledom and romance is a constitutive element of postfeminist discourses that continue to reign in Western media culture.[29] As Angela McRobbie suggests, in a climate where women are not economically reliant upon marriage, much symbolic labour is being expended on 're-securing the terms of heterosexual desire' and the marital trajectory.[30] Emphasizing the recalcitrance of what she dubs the 'marital economy', Jaclyn Geller underscores the sheer unrepresentability of a woman who defies the married/single binary: 'So entrenched is the notion of marital femininity that we can only envisage women in terms of wedlock or its opposite.'[31] In such an economy, even de facto relationships are situated below marriage on what is a clear hierarchy of heteronormativity. Indeed, in the case of Gillard, publicly she was – despite being in a committed, monogamous relationship – routinely described as 'single'. For example, 'Ms Gillard is our fifth childless prime minister, but the first to be single.'[32] In many ways, Gillard occupied a liminal state – neither uncoupled nor married – and thus it was difficult to map existing interpretive frameworks onto her. The dominant life script for women yet requires that they become a wife (and mother), with those who fail to adhere coded as 'unhinged'. As Lauren Berlant puts it, 'People who are unhinged or unhitched, who live outside the normative loops of property and reproduction, are frequently seen both as symptoms of personal failure and threats to the general happiness, which seems to require, among other things, the positioning of any person's core life story in a plot of love's unfolding, especially if that person is a woman.'[33] As I have previously argued, marriage is seen as a choice that all citizens should make and that makes all citizens.[34]

As the example of Gillard reveals, it is not just coupledom that is valorized and seen as the only legitimate form of cathexis for women (along with motherhood) but marriage. As Nancy F. Cott contends, 'Marriage uniquely and powerfully influences the way differences between the sexes are conveyed and symbolized. So far as it is a public institution, it is the vehicle through which the apparatus of the state can shape gender order.' In such a context, 'the unmarried as well as the married bear the ideological, ethical and practical impress of the marital institution'.[35] These assumptions about what constitutes an authentic or appropriate form of intimate bond are mobilized to ensure that certain ways of being are privileged over others. In particular, 'Marital regulations have drawn lines between the citizenry and defined what kinds of sexual relations and which families will be legitimate.'[36] Even though the de facto relationship in Australia is sanctioned by the State, it clearly carries none of the symbolic weight of marriage. Rhetorically, the link between Gillard's suitability as a leader and her marital status was even invoked by Opposition Leader, Tony Abbott (now PM), who in parliament said: 'I think, Mr Speaker, if the Prime Minister wants to make, politically speaking, an honest woman of herself. ...' In her famous 'misogyny speech', Gillard took him to task for this comment, remarking that it 'would never have been said to any man sitting in this chair'.[37] The phrase, of course, has a long history in terms of how unmarried women with partners have been discursively constructed. And as Abbott's comments indicate, Gillard was represented as dishonest, both personally (being unmarried) and politically (especially after she had broken her election promise not to introduce a carbon tax): 'The expression "honest woman" thus serves a double purpose, as it reinforces Abbott's branding of Gillard as a liar.'[38] Moreover, in a Western sociopolitical context where marriage is overwhelmingly figured as a postfeminist 'choice' – now ostensibly a partnership of equals rather than a bond formed of necessity by economically subordinated women – Gillard's 'choice' to *not* choose marriage was seen to make little sense. As an 'unwife'[39] (and indeed 'unmother'), it was implied, how could she effectively represent the Australian people? In addition, in public discourse the male partner she did have was – like the relationship itself – repeatedly rendered inadequate.

A 'de facto' Prime Minister

The media coverage of Australia's first female Prime Minister thus revealed a series of anxieties – both Gillard's rise to power and her life choices were seen to mount a challenge to normative femininity, and thus her ability to be an effective political representative.[40] She faced unprecedented destabilization, both from within her party and the media itself, suggesting that political ambition still appears to be gendered masculine.[41] In her third (and final) year as PM, she self-reflexively commented on the way she was being discursively positioned, quipping that she had told Barack Obama, 'You think it's tough being African-American? Try being me. Try being an atheist, childless, single woman as prime minister.'[42] Gillard's comments may have been in jest; however, she sagaciously identified the three interlocking subject positions that rendered her problematic in public discourse. Further, the way she attained leadership (as outlined above) – as well her gender – ensured that she would be scrutinized in a way that a democratically elected leader would not: 'From the outset of Gillard's term in office, it was clear that some sections of the Australian community were deeply uncomfortable with both the manner of her ascendency and her lack of appropriately feminine traits.'[43] Central to this 'un-femininity', I suggest, was her lack of an appropriate husband.

Not being officially sanctioned by the State, their relationship effectively became a synecdoche for her 'relationship' with the Australian people, also discursively constructed as 'illegitimate'. That is, Julia Gillard was not simply Tim Mathieson's de facto, she was effectively a *de facto* Prime Minister. In relation to political leadership, 'de facto' underscores illegitimacy. According to the legal definition, a de facto government or leader is one 'who is in actual possession of the office or supreme power, but by usurpation'. The term is used to characterize 'an officer, a government or state of affairs which exists actually and must be accepted for all practical purposes, but which is illegal or illegitimate'.[44] In media coverage – due to the way she came to power (by 'usurpation') and failed to secure a majority at the subsequent federal election – Gillard's leadership was primarily figured in these terms. Therefore, both her government and her relationship were at very least seen to be morally troublesome.

Rendering her even more suspect, Gillard's refusal to support gay marriage was seen to augment her threat to marriage as an institution; not only did she personally not invest in it, she argued against its accessibility. Her own personal 'failure' to marry was just one of the ways in which Gillard's behaviour was figured unfeminine, especially given marriage and family life have routinely been used to position politicians as 'just like us'. In this vein, Charlotte Adcock has shown how the media representation of Tony Blair – '"Blair the normal person"' as she puts it – 'was very much grounded on constructions of "normal" *masculinity*'.[45] In contrast, in both the public and private spheres, the unmarried Gillard was overwhelmingly seen to embody an 'abnormal' femininity. That is, she was effectively seen as a 'failure' because she did not exhibit feminine traits like 'political passivity, truthfulness, motherhood, and legitimated sexuality'.[46] It is this 'failure' regarding an appropriate relationship, and how processes of celebritization helped discursively produce it, with which I am preoccupied here.

As Garcia-Blanco and Wahl-Jorgensen remark, 'the celebritization of politics has brought the families of politicians and their qualities as parents and partners centre stage'.[47] Increased instances of women as leaders in the West have concomitantly produced a relatively new form of celebrity: the male political spouse or partner. While there has been much critical engagement with the figure of the 'political wife' (especially the US's first lady), less has been said on the political husband (unsurprisingly perhaps, since that most political leaders historically have been and continue to be heterosexual men). Given the way powerful women continue to be anxiety-provoking figures, what of the men who are defined primarily (at least in terms of their celebritization) in relation to them? Does this figure, like his powerful partner, evoke discomfort in public discourse? Is he too seen as an aberration? Does he come to function as a celebrity in his own right, and how? What is presumed to be the role of the male political partner, in relation to both his significant other and the nation itself? In comparison, the role of the political spouse has been fleshed out in relation to women, most notably the First Lady in the US. As 'First Lady, it is necessary to play into the role of the nation's mother'.[48] However, the 'first man' is more complicated than a simple inversion – he is not seen as the nation's father. Furthermore, compared to the First Lady, prime ministers' wives in Australia historically have not had such a clearly delineated role vis-à-vis the national imaginary or its maintenance. With no precedent available, and given that Mathieson both reaffirmed and challenged certain assumptions about Australian masculinity, the news media appeared unsure how to construct him as a male political consort (or indeed Gillard as a female leader). Moreover, Gillard's relationship with Mathieson was not only characterized as illegitimate because of its de facto nature but because of its inability to be read in terms of a stable, hierarchal masculine/feminine binary; media representations of Mathieson were central to this discursive process.

An 'Illegitimate' partner?: Representing the 'First Bloke'

During her time in public office, Gillard's partner, Tim Mathieson, was regularly referred to as Australia's 'first bloke', a characterization that coexisted, contradictorily, with assumptions that he otherwise failed to adhere to what R. W. Connell refers to as 'hegemonic masculinity'.[49] Before engaging with media portrayals of Mathieson, it is worth briefly attending to the contrasting sources of Gillard and Mathieson's celebritization. In the case of the former PM, her celebrity was a product of her exceptionality in the political field, making her what Chris Rojek would call an 'achieved celebrity'. Mathieson, however, was celebritized only because of his association with her, and could therefore be classified as a 'celetoid'. For Rojek, a celetoid denotes 'any form of compressed, concentrated, attributed celebrity'.[50] 'Celetoids', unlike achieved celebrities, may fade from public view quite quickly (as Mathieson has): 'Evanescence is the irrevocable condition of celetoid status, though in exceptional cases a celetoid might acquire a degree of longevity'.[51] Moreover, we could appropriate Daniel Boorstin's phrase to help describe the kind of celebrity-by-association embodied by figures like Mathieson: he came to public attention only because of Julia's 'well-knownness'.[52] As one newspaper put it, 'what is he famous for? Going out with someone famous'.[53] And in both the case of achieved and attributed celebrity, as this couple found, they 'surrender a portion of their veridical self, and leave the world of privacy and anonymity behind'.[54] As celebrities, the media visibility (and judgement) of their relationship was assured.

While women in the public spotlight are recruited into 'first woman to' narratives,[55] this was also the case with Mathieson – he was remarkable as the first *man* to occupy The Lodge (the name of the prime ministerial home in Canberra). As an article in *The Australian* remarked, 'Never before has there been a First Bloke, let alone a live-in hairdresser boyfriend of four years standing'.[56] In these representations, Mathieson – as mere 'boyfriend' and hairdresser – was as much of an anomaly as his politico partner and judged to be an inappropriate occupant of The Lodge. (The persistent reference to him as Gillard's 'boyfriend', as above, worked to further trivialize their 'unofficial' relationship.) No public language via which to discuss the partner of a female leader of the nation existed, so a series of familiar tropes came to be mobilized around him – the most obvious of which was 'bloke', of which Gillard herself remarked: 'It's a good Australian term.'[57]

It has been suggested that the figure of the First Lady is often represented as an 'everywoman'[58]; the same can be said of Tim Mathieson, as an 'everyman'. In Australia, this figure is often seen as the 'knock about aussie bloke' or what is often referred to as a 'larrikin'. As Melissa Bellanta shows, the term 'larrikin' in its earliest usages signalled a ruffian subculture and served as a moniker one would definitely wish to avoid.[59] Its meanings, she comprehensively demonstrates, have significantly shifted throughout the many decades of its public deployment. In the present, in terms of Australian masculinity, it is celebrated, signalling a good bloke, with a sense of humour (a 'scallywag', as Bellanta says), who knows how to enjoy himself – not least through the consumption of an activity that continues to be valorized in Australian culture: sport. In the years of Gillard's leadership, there were constant news references to Mathieson's commitment to 'manly' sports. He was reportedly 'mad for cricket' and 'far happier discussing the V8 Supercars than the G20 roundtable of economic superpowers, his passion is an electoral bonus for tertiary-educated Gillard, who needs to massage male voters in middle Australia'.[60] (At other times he was seen as a liability, making Prince Philip style public gaffes.) He was variously described as a 'blokey bloke'[61]; a 'man's man'; and a 'really good bloke'.[62] Although he was at times referred to as Gillard's 'man bag' in the press, journalists also underscored his masculine cultural preferences: 'He would prefer to hang out with mates at a cricket match than sit through the cultural programs offered up to spouses of dignitaries at world forums.'[63] This over-emphasis on his 'blokey-ness' illuminated an anxiety about the ways in which their relationship worked to destabilize gender binaries.

The domesticated bloke

Given that the celebrity political spouse is primarily made visible as a source of personal (and sometimes public) support; that women, problematically, continue to be seen as caregivers and emotional labourers; and that Mathieson's profession (hairdressing) has traditionally been gendered feminine, the 'first bloke' was often feminized and his heterosexuality called into question. Media conjecture about his sexuality, including from Perth 'shock jock' Howard Sattler who asked Gillard live on air if Mathieson was gay, revealed the extent to which celebrity politicians are subject to the same kinds of surveillance and judgement as other forms of celebrity[64] – and perhaps more so as their private selves and lives are believed to speak to their capabilities in the public sphere, especially in the case of women. But it was also consistent with the characterization of their relationship, or 'unmarriage', as inauthentic.

However, despite these anxieties around Mathieson's masculinity, journalists often depicted Gillard as 'non-traditional' (and by implication 'unfeminine'). For example, the *Herald Sun* published an article focusing on Mathieson's desire to one day wed the PM. His comments also sought to shore up the masculinity that was elsewhere being called into question, suggesting he would want to be positioned in the traditional role of proposer: "'I don't think that she actually ever would ask me (to marry),' Mathieson said. "There's no pressure on either of us to do that, but I would want to do the asking."'[65] In journalists' fixation on whether the 'first bloke' would 'pop the question',[66] the agency of the country's leader was completely elided and traditional gendered dynamics were, if momentarily, reinscribed. Marriage, therefore, continues to be seen as 'a female dream and a male initiative'.[67] As Geller emphasizes, 'real men provide, grateful women receive ... real men redeem, "single" girls are rescued'. Gillard, however, was positioned as aberrant because there could be no guarantee she would accept his proposal: 'If Mathieson proposes, will she accept? On paper he seems an unlikely consort for the former schoolgirl swat and prefect who studied law at university and single-mindedly pursued a career.'[68] These comments resonate with other popular postfeminist narratives around women's misguided focus on their careers being responsible for their lamentable singleness. They also reveal something about class dynamics, as the journalist wondered whether the highly educated, professional Gillard would marry someone whose own career trajectory and level of educational attainment failed to match her own.

In June 2011, Gillard and Mathieson were interviewed together for the first time by Australia's *60 Minutes*. Television, as Van Zoonen argues, represents the key site through which audiences come to engage with politics, so performances such as this are especially important.[69] During the course of the interview, like any celebrity couple, they construct a narrative about their romantic life, each professing to be deeply in love with the other. The revelation of such intimacy in the media can be productive for the female leader, as it involves 'the public through the expression of feelings and emotions that is culturally accepted and appreciated for women'.[70] Inevitably, they are asked about their marriage plans: 'And Prime Minister, of course every girl enjoys a good wedding?' Gillard successfully dodges the question, while Mathieson, reiterating that he would expect to do the asking, responds 'not anytime soon'.[71] So while she does publicly express tenderness towards her partner, the relationship is still found wanting as it is not a marital one.

As part of this wider discursive strategy of rendering their relationship problematic, press coverage consistently emphasized the non-traditional gendered dynamics at play at The Lodge: 'A week after he revealed he draws Ms Gillard baths and blow-dries her hair before taking his place on the lounge to watch parliament, Mr Mathieson has deflected criticism, including that he is an "old-fashioned wife".'[72] This emphasis on Mathieson's role as 'homemaker' conflicts with that other prevalent way of constructing him: as a hyper-masculine Aussie 'bloke', underscoring the contradictory discourses in which he became enmeshed. In a biography of Gillard, he was also firmly located in the private sphere: 'He often does the cooking in the townhouse she stays in, not far from Parliament. "She eats out all week so it's nice for her to come home to something healthy," he has said.'[73] By situating these domestic activities as 'unconventional male pursuits' such comments served to further police the boundaries of appropriate masculine and feminine behaviour.[74] Alongside this emphasis on Mathieson's role as care-giver, Gillard's domestic ineptitude was a common trope, be it through the loaded image of an empty fruit bowl in a stark, implicitly little-used kitchen or through explicit statements like this: '[Julia is] a domestically challenged gal who once used oven cleaner instead of polish on her dining room table.'[75] In particular, the fact that she was unable to cook was a gendered transgression seized upon by the media,[76] and the limits of her domestic capital (her very 'unwifeliness') came to be emphasized: '"He's in it as the first bloke and he'll make sure Julia is cared for at home." And that means doing all the cooking for Gillard, who has said her culinary specialty is toast ....'[77] No matter the political heights she had reached, such comments implied, in terms of meeting gendered expectations she was much less successful. Gillard's occupation (not to mention Mathieson's) was seen to lamentably produce these apparent gendered anomalies.

Another key textual site for this ongoing feminization of Mathieson, and his positioning as a kind of 'wifely' figure,[78] was the satirical series, *At Home with Julia* (ABC) (see Figure 9.1). Throughout the series, originally aired in 2011, these assumptions about Gillard and Mathieson's interactions being structured along 'reversed gender lines'[79] were thoroughly reinscribed. The angst-ridden character

Figure 9.1 Opening titles of *At Home With Julia* (ABC, 2011) with Amanda Bishop as Julia Gillard and Phil Lloyd as Tim Mathieson. Screen grab.

of Tim, depicted initially at home doing chores, seems to be experiencing a kind of masculinity crisis; with, 'Mr Julia' and 'Mrs Prime Minister', as schoolchildren dub him, being defined in opposition to his high-profile partner. He appears to feel neglected, uncertain about both his public and private roles. The series' 'humour' (for it is decidedly unfunny) relates to Tim's discontentment about being unmarried; he is ridiculed for this 'feminine' preoccupation with matrimony, while Julia's reluctance to marry is also scrutinized. As he listens to the radio while driving, the commentator, indicative of the media interest in politicians' affective bonds, asks: 'Come on Julia, what else has he got in his life?' The narrative implies, as Stevenson argues, that 'if the pair were to become a committed, married couple, their gender role "confusion" would subside and the gender hierarchy could be restored'.[80]

During his birthday celebrations in the penultimate episode, Tim mistakenly thinks they are going to announce their engagement rather than a government job she has organized for him: 'Manager of the Headlice Taskforce'. Following the confusion, and Tim's very public humiliation, the couple subsequently separate. In the final episode, the PM appears in her office dishevelled, the strain and affect of the break-up clearly written on her body. Once learning the news about their break up has become public, she loses her voice. This fictional incident presumes that women – including the country's most powerful – have no authority to speak unless partnered; only when they reunite does she regain her voice.[81] Indeed, this idea was explicitly articulated earlier in Gillard's parliamentary career when Senator Bill Heffernan publicly argued that she could not understand or effectively respond to the concerns of the electorate because she was unmarried and, more importantly from his perspective, had no children; as he put it, 'deliberately barren'.[82] With no man, and especially no husband or children, a woman – as *At Home with Julia* so blatantly literalized – is voiceless.

Conclusion

On 26 June 2013, following months of destabilization from Kevin Rudd and his supporters, Australia's first female Prime Minister was ousted from the position in the same way she had ousted her predecessor (and successor). Throughout her brief tenure as PM, public discourses around her relationship with Tim Mathieson circulated in a wider intertextual network in which her suitability to lead the nation was persistently called into question. Neither Gillard nor her partner adhered to clearly delineated gender roles, for which they were both – celebrity politician and celebrity political consort – heavily scrutinized. The 'personalization' of politics, via celebrity culture, permitted the focus on their relationship, which revealed how certain affective bonds continue to be subordinated to marriage. Gillard was repeatedly rendered inadequate and illegitimate, in terms of both her public and private subjectivities – something that the voracious appetite for celebrity couple narratives helped fuel. Even after she was deposed, media preoccupation with her romantic relationship and its viability did not wane. In September 2013, Britain's *Daily Mail* asked: 'Has Julia Gillard split up with her hairdresser boyfriend?' It continued: 'First she lost her job as Australia's Prime Minister, then her party lost this month's general election – and now reports are suggesting Julia Gillard has lost her man.'[83] That the loss of a partner is equated with the loss of Prime Ministership suggests just how deep the public investment in the private, and especially romantic, life of female political celebrities continues to be – as well as revealing how a leader without a man (and especially without a husband) is seen as inadequate not just as a political representative but as a woman.

Acknowledgements

Thanks to Graeme Turner, as well as the editors, Shelley Cobb and Neil Ewen, for their valuable feedback on drafts of this chapter.

Notes

1 Laurie Oakes, 'A Liberal Dose of Bad News', *Herald Sun*, 26 June 2010. See also Lauren J. Hall and Ngaire Donaghue, '"Nice girls don't carry knives": Constructions of ambition in media coverage of Australia's first female prime minister', *The British Psychological Society* 52 (2013): 631–47.

2 In Australian law, the term 'de facto relationship', according to the *Family Law Act 1975* applies to those who 'have a relationship as a couple living together on a genuine domestic basis' (Section 4AA).

3 Anne Summers, *The Misogyny Factor* (Sydney: University of New South Wales Press, 2013), 107.

4 Kerry Ann Walsh, *The Stalking of Julia Gillard* (St Leonards: Allen & Unwin, 2013), 297–304.

5 Graeme Turner, *Understanding Celebrity* (London: Sage, 2014).

6 Anthea Taylor, *Single Women in Popular Culture: The Limits of Postfeminism* (Basingstoke: Palgrave Macmillan, 2012).

7 Peter Dahlgren, *Media and Political Engagement: Citizens, Communication and Democracy* (Cambridge: Cambridge University Press, 2009), 137.

8 See Mark Wheeler's *Celebrity Politics* (London: Wiley Blackwell, 2013) for a critique of this position.

9 John Street, 'Celebrity Politicians: Popular Culture and Political Representation', *British Journal of Politics and International Relations* 6 (2010): 435–52.

10 Street, 'Celebrity Politicians', 441.

11 Darrel West and John Ormond, *Celebrity Politics* (New Jersey: Prentice Hall, 2003).

12 Duerst-Lahti 2006, 37.

13 Lisbet Van Zoonen, 'The personal, the political and the popular: A woman's guide to celebrity politics', *European Journal of Cultural Studies* 9 (2006): 287–301 (299).

14 Van Zoonen, 288.

15 Ibid., 295.

16 Cited in Simon Benson and Philip Hudson, '"I'll do it my way", Julia Gillard says, breaks tradition to show the real Julia', *Daily Telegraph*, 2 August 2010.

17 Wheeler, *Celebrity Politics*, 15.

18 Julia Baird, *Media Tarts: How the Australian Press Frames Female Politicians* (Melbourne: Scribe, 2004); Kathy Muir, 'Political cares: Gendered reporting of work and family issues in relation to Australian politicians', *Australian Feminist Studies* 20, no. 46 (2005): 77–90; Summers 2013.

19 On Australia's *Q&A* television program, Greer said that Gillard's jackets accentuated her 'fat arse'.

20 'Julia Gillard sports "hipster" glasses at National Press Club', 30 January 2013, *Herald Sun*. As the article notes, a Twitter account featuring the glasses even appeared.

21 Andrew Honery and Bonnie Malkin, 'Gillard Bares It All', *Sydney Morning Herald*, 24 January 2005.

22 Kate Crawford, *Adult Themes* (London: Palgrave, 2006), 131–32.

23 Gillian Guthrie, 'Put a stop now to mother of all insults', *Sydney Morning Herald*, 6 March 2012.

24 Linda Grant, *Fundamental Feminism* (New York: Routledge, 1993).

25 *Borgen* (2010–, Adam Price, DR1) and *Veep* (2012–, Armando Iannucci, HBO), *Madam Secretary* (2014–, Barbara Hall, CBS).

26 Hall and Donaghue, 'Nice girls', 631.

27 Donatella Campos, *Women Politicians and the Media* (Basingstoke: Palgrave Macmillan, 2013), 94.

28 Diane Negra, *What a girl wants: Fantasizing the Reclamation of Self in Postfeminism* (New York: Routledge, 2009).

29 Taylor, *Single Women*, 2012; Angela McRobbie, *The Aftermath of Feminism* (London: Sage, 2009); Negra 2009.

30 McRobbie, *The Aftermath of Feminism*, 62.

31 Jaclyn Geller, *Here Comes the Bride: Women, Weddings and the Marriage Mystique* (New York: Four Walls, Eight Windows, 2001), 10; Chrys Ingraham, *White Weddings* (New York: Routledge, 1999).

32 Alan Howe, 'Tim Mathieson reveals he wants partner and Prime Minister Julia Gillard to be his wife', *Adelaide Now*, 14 May 2011.

33 Lauren Berlant, *The Female Complaint: The Unfinished Business of Sentimentality in American Culture* (Durham: Duke University Press, 2008), 172.

34 Taylor, *Single Women*, 20.

35 Nancy Cott, *Public Vows: A History of Marriage and the Nation* (Cambridge, MA: Harvard University Press, 2000), 3.

36 Cott, 4.

37 Cited in Anna Goldsworthy, 'Unfinished Business: Sex, Freedom and Misogyny', *Quarterly Essay*, June 2013, 12.

38 Goldsworthy, 12.

39 Anna Kingston, *The Meaning of Wife* (New York: Farrer, Strauss & Giroux, 2005).

40 For detailed analysis of media treatment of Gillard, see Goldsworthy 2013; Hall and Donaghue 2013; Stevenson 2013; Summers 2013; and Walshe 2012.

41 See Hall and Donaghue 2013.

42 Cited in Philip Coorey, 'PM v Obama: who has it harder?', *Sydney Morning Herald*, 2 April 2012.

43 Jennifer Rayner, 'Was Julia Gillard a "real" female prime minister, or a leader who was female?' *The Conversation*, 26 June 2013. See also Anna Stevenson, 'Making Gender Divisive: "Post-Feminism", Sexism and Media Representations of Julia Gillard', *Burgmann Journal* Issue 1 (2013): 55.

44 'de facto', *Black's Law Dictionary*, Second Edition, thelawdictionary.org, accessed 12 October 2014.

45 Charlotte Adcock, 'The Politician, The Wife, The Citizen and Her Newspaper', *Feminist Media Studies* 10, no. 2 (2010): 147, original emphasis.

46 Stevenson, 60.

47 Garcia-Blanco and Karin Wahl-Jorgensen, 'The discursive construction of women politicians in the European press', *Feminist Media Studies* 12, no. 3 (2012): 425.

48 Lisa Guerrero, '(M)Other in Chief: Michelle Obama and the Ideal of Republican Womanhood', in *New Femininities*, ed. R. Gill and C. Schraff (Basingstoke: Palgrave Macmillan, 2011), 74.

49 R. W. Connell, *Masculinities* (Sydney: Allen & Unwin, 1985).

50 Chris Rojek, *Celebrity* (London: Reaktion, 2001), 20.

51 Rojek, 22.

52 Daniel Boorstin, *The Image: A Guide to Pseudo Events in America* (New York: Atheneum, 1971).

53 'Tim Mathieson: why is Australia's "first bloke" in the headlines?', *The Guardian*, 30 January 2012.

54 Rojek, *Celebrity*, 20.

55 Sandra Lilburn, 'Representations of Feminism in the Australian Print Media: The Case of Pat O'Shane' Digital Collections Library, Australian National University Open Access Research (1999), 1–14, accessed at: https://digitalcollections.anu.edu.au/handle/1885/41414.

56 Kate Legge, 'Nation Adjusts to PM's First Bloke', *The Australian*, 24 July 2010.

57 *Sixty Minutes* interview, Nine network, June 2011.

58 Guerrero, '(M)Other', 79.

59 Melissa Bellanta, *Larrikins: A History* (Brisbane: University of Queensland, 2012).

60 Kate Legge, 'Man about the House', *The Australian*, 9 March 2013.

61 Ibid.

62 Kerry-Ann Walsh and Mathew Benns, 'First bloke's a man's man', *The Australian*, 27 June 2010.

63 Legge 2013.

64 Marshall makes this point about celebrities generally, 2010.

65 Howe, 'Tim Mathieson', 2011.

66 Ibid.

67 Geller, *Here Comes*, 99.

68 Legge, 'Nation Adjusts', 2010.

69 Lisbet Van Zoonen, *Entertaining the Citizen: When Politics and Popular Culture Converge* (London: Rowman & Littlefield, 2005), 78.

70 Campos, *Women Politicians*, 104. As she argues, though, too much emphasis on one's male partner can be read negatively.

71 Transcript of the interview, http://sixtyminutes.ninemsn.com.au/stories/8259727/the-first-bloke.

72 Gemma Jones, 'Tim Mathieson carries the bags as Julia Gillard flies the flags', *Daily Telegraph*, 20 November 2012.

73 Jacqueline Kent, *The Making of Julia Gillard* (Sydney: Viking, 2000), 274.

74 Stevenson, 54.

75 Legge, 'Nation adjusts', 2010.

76 Julia Baird, 'Comment: Julia Gillard', *The Monthly*, August 2010, 11.

77 Walsh and Benns, 'First bloke's a man's man', 2010.

78 Stevenson, 57.

79 Ibid.

80 Ibid., 56.

81 Ibid., 57.

82 Cited in Greg Bearup, 'Hard man of the Hill', *Good Weekend Magazine*, 27 May 2006.

83 Richard Shears, 'Has Julia Gillard split up with her hairdresser boyfriend? Magazine: former Australian PM's lover is living alone in a caravan in the bush', *The Guardian*, 23 September 2013.

10

It's the Thought That Counts: North Korea's Glocalization of the Celebrity Couple and the Mediated Politics of Reform

David Zeglen

The danger here is North Korea has now developed celebrity couple technology, and America has always been the undisputed superpower of celebrity couples.

Stephen Colbert[1]

In July 2012, North Korean state media broke from the long-standing tradition of keeping the leader's wife from public view by announcing that the identity of the fashionable young woman who had been publically accompanying Supreme Leader Kim Jong-un for the past several weeks was none other than his wife, 'Comrade' Ri Sol-ju.[2] Over the next five months, state media amplified this historically unprecedented public display of coupledom by running non-stop coverage of Kim and Ri. Because of the recognizable elements of celebrity culture apparent in the representation of Kim and Ri in the North Korean media – appearances at pseudo-events, fashion politics and discourses of social background – the Global North media seized upon the North Korean media coverage and argued that North Korea was beginning to open up, reform and converge with the Global North.[3] In fact, even before the North Korean media officially announced Ri's status as the leader's wife, *The New York Times* had already coded Kim and Ri as a power couple intent on reforming their country, arguing that Kim's likely decision to marry a young, beautiful and fashionable woman indicated that North Korea would be moving 'in a new direction with some sort of opening to the West.'[4]

Given North Korea's long-standing hostility to the Global North, it is difficult to imagine why the regime would suddenly incorporate facets of celebrity culture into its own culture. Yet, Kim Jong-un inherited a country that exists in a world that is very different from the world his father, Kim Jong-il, and grandfather, Kim Il-sung, knew when they ruled the country, as a twenty-first-century framework for global democratization has started to emerge: the establishment of the Rome Statute in 2003; the passage of the United Nations doctrine of 'the responsibility to protect' (R2P) in 2005; the theoretical articulation of a global parliamentary assembly[5]; UN-sanctioned international coalition interventions in Afghanistan and Libya; and civil war in Syria have all brought the increasingly difficult maintenance of a dictatorship into sharp relief.[6] Indeed, several authoritarian regimes have begun to utilize an array of propaganda strategies, including branding dictators and their wives as celebrity couples, to give the appearance of political and cultural convergence with the Global North. For example, in March 2011, *Vogue* published an article profiling Syria's 'first lady', entitled 'Asma al-Assad: A Rose in the Desert'. Although the article focuses on Asma's individual beauty, smart fashion sense and 'wildly democratic principles', *The Atlantic Weekly* succinctly summarizes the article's underlying intent:

> It lists one detail after another portraying Bashar and Asma al-Assad as fun, glamorous, *American-style celebrities*: trips to the Louvre, a story about the couple joking with Brad Pitt and Angelina Jolie, Asma's effort to give Syria a 'brand essence', the fact that all three Assad children 'go to a Montessori school', and countless references to Christianity.[7]

A month after the *Vogue* article was published, an investigative report discovered that in November 2010, Brown Lloyd James, an international public relations firm, had signed a $5,000-per-month contract with the Syrian government to help arrange the article and photo shoot for *Vogue* magazine.[8] The Syrian example provides a powerful illustration of how a contemporary dictatorship framed its authoritarian leader and wife as a celebrity couple in order to convince the world it had reformed. Likewise, from July to December 2012, North Korea also decided to experiment with celebrity couple branding while eschewing the strong man model in order to present an image of reform in response to a nascent democratic global political arena. Commenting on the evolving PR strategies of modern dictatorships, Pedro Pizano rightly observes that 'in today's increasingly connected and informed world, dictators can no longer hide behind a cloak of secrecy. They are forced to find new, creative ways to convince the world that they are benevolent rulers.'[9]

Unfortunately, theories of the historical emergence of celebrity culture also reinforce the determinist assumption that the appearance of celebrity tropes coincides with the internalization of Global North values. Chris Rojek attributes the rise of modern celebrity culture to the democratization movement initiated by the French Revolution in conjunction with the expansion of consumer culture,[10] while David P. Marshall asserts that celebrity 'resonates with conceptions of individuality that are the ideological ground of Western culture'.[11] Even studies of formerly autarkic states like China and Russia implicitly suggest that the Global North-inspired political and economic reforms of Deng Xiaoping, Mikhail Gorbachev and Boris Yeltsin helped produce burgeoning national celebrity cultures.[12] Undoubtedly, Global North cultural forms, ideas and practices are increasingly infiltrating the local livelihoods of millions of people in the Global South. However, Global South nation states are more than simply passive receptors that readily internalize the value systems of foreign cultures. As the anthropology of globalization has revealed, domestic cultural norms, social structures and historical trajectories respond to cultural globalization through interpretation, translation and appropriation according to local ideological conditions.[13] In other words, celebrity culture in North Korea is not a priori in thrall to Global North values. It should therefore not be assumed that similar cultural practices that are being enacted in North Korea have the same underpinning values as the Global North. Instead, the flow of Global North celebrity culture to North Korea should be understood as having undergone glocalization – a process that involves the selective borrowing of foreign styles which are then imbued with domestic meaning.[14,15]

Therefore, to understand North Korea's first celebrity couple and offer a corrective to the Global North media's misreading of reform, Ri and Kim should be understood as a cultural hybrid comprising celebrity signifiers such as event appearances, fashion politics and social background, that have been made to fit the local context of North Korean 'gift culture'. A pillar of North Korea's official ideology, North Korea has developed a mode of domination based on rationing social goods and then bequeathing them as gifts to the public from the leader.[16] Furthermore, North Korean gift culture presupposes a specific kind of labour from the leader that includes large expenditures of time, care, concern and attention to the North Korean people, which personalizes the material gifts bequeathed to the people.[17] As a result, the giver (the leader) acquires great power due to the moral obligations on the part of the receiver (the people) to reciprocate with deep gratitude and loyalty in response to the leader's personal care and attention. Indeed, so persuasive is North Korean gift culture that, as Heonik Kwon and Byung-Ho Chung point out, 'the very material fact of being a North Korean, and having a political home and enjoying a meaningful political life in that home, [becomes] fundamentally a gift from the leader's exemplary historical life'.[18]

Therefore, this chapter seeks to elucidate a neglected area of North Korean cultural studies by drawing upon the field of celebrity studies, itself a field that has not yet thoroughly considered celebrity culture within totalitarian regimes. By analysing how the North Korean media framed Kim Jong-un and his wife as a celebrity couple that in turn created a discourse of reform in the Global North media, this chapter will show that when viewed in the context of North Korea's propaganda iconography, the semiotics of North Korea's first celebrity couple is actually bound up in the cultural politics of reproducing the leader's gift culture to maintain hegemony.

Staging the social space: The pseudo-event

After officially confirming that Kim Jong-un and his new female companion, Ri Sol-ju, were in fact married, the North Korean media circulated several photographs of Kim and Ri together at various public spaces in Pyongyang, with the Global North media quickly responding in kind.[19] On 25 July 2012, the state media published several photos online of Ri and Kim together at the newly opened Rungna People's Pleasure Park, an amusement park vaguely modelled on Disneyland (see Figure 10.1).[20] *The Associated Press* stated that Kim and Ri's appearance at the park was a move towards 'more Western-style' leadership[21] while *The New York Times* commented that Ri Sol-ju's appearance at the park 'had all the trappings of a Kate Middleton moment' which presaged policy changes in North Korea.[22] On 31 August, the state media released photos of Kim and Ri at a new upscale grocery store and dining facility in Pyongyang. Accompanying the photos, the state media reported that Kim was pleased to see the restaurant 'serving varieties of dishes of different countries' as well as 'rooms arranged to suit the characteristic features of the relevant countries'.[23] Impressed by Kim's aphorisms endorsing a more cosmopolitan menu, South Korea's *Chosun Ilbo* bylined an article on Kim and Ri's restaurant visit with the tag, 'North Korean first family's Westernized habits'.[24]

Figure 10.1 In this Wednesday, 25 July 2012 photo released by the Korean Central News Agency (KCNA) and distributed in Tokyo by the Korea News Service Thursday, 26 July 2012, North Korean leader Kim Jong Un, centre, accompanied by his wife Ri Sol-ju, right, waves to the crowd as they inspect the Rungna People's Pleasure Ground in Pyongyang. (AP Photo/Korean Central News Agency via Korea News Service.)

Although the Global North media interpreted Kim and Ri's visits as possible instances of genuine reform, a prediction no doubt encouraged by Kim's declaration that North Korea aligns itself with the 'global standards'[25] of Western society, these new facilities are still deeply embedded in the country's gift culture.[26] Traditionally, the leader's visits to newly developed industrial, agricultural and military sites across the country were rendered with oil paint on large mural canvasses, with the mural occupying a wall in the space where the visit had occurred.[27] These mythologized visits also contain an idiosyncratic feature: a placard is typically installed in the place visited, which quotes a pithy statement made by the leader when he visited. For example, a published account of one of Kim Il-sung's on-site inspections had him remark only one sentence: 'rainbow trout is a good fish, tasty and nutritious'.[28] In one of Pyongyang's downtown middle schools, a placard above a piano in the music room Kim Il-sung once visited quotes him as having said during his visit, 'It is important to play the piano well'.[29] The direct inheritor of this style, Kim Jong-un similarly uses such platitudes during his visits. At his inspection of Rungna People's Pleasure Ground with Ri Sol-ju, Kim Jong-un remarked 'that tall trees are especially good for shade',[30] while his visit to a fitness centre in Pyongyang was honoured by a placard installed on one of the treadmills which read that Kim had personally inspected it.[31]

Yet, the substance of the leader's guidance is not nearly as important as the time he takes to personalize his visit and administer attention to his people, which is what is cherished in North Korean gift culture. This propaganda technique has a distinct advantage over Soviet propaganda: while materialist goods such as new roads, schools, houses or transportation lines were conceptualized as gifts from Stalin to the people, who in turn were required to reciprocate through labour, North Koreans do not expect material gifts because 'the most meaningful gift from the state became the individual leader's visit to the workplace, which constituted the ultimate public acknowledgement of their dedicated labor'.[32] In turn, Koreans reciprocate with their loyalty to, and love of, the leader, and unsurprisingly, the North Korean media has done an excellent job promoting this love while alluding to the visual iconography of Kim Jong-un's grandfather's on-site visits. In a well-known mural painting of Kim Il-sung visiting an officer's strategic planning quarters, the leader benevolently embraces a young soldier and presses him towards his bosom while wrapping his arms around him.[33] And in a visit to a pilot's barracks in January of 2012, a photograph taken by Korean Central News Agency (KCNA) showed Kim Jong-un similarly embracing two soldiers and pressed them towards his bosom like his grandfather did decades before him.[34] The official encyclopedia of North Korea even describes the leader of North Korea as 'the loving parent who holds and nurtures all Korean children at his breast'.[35]

However, for these kinds of photo opportunities, Ri is absent because the public's love can only be given to the leader. Since the Global North media is obsessed with Ri's presence in public social spaces, her purpose is to draw attention away from these public displays of individual fealty to Kim Jong-un. Indeed, during the five-month media blitz focusing on the North Korean couple, Kim Jong-un, like his father and grandfather before him, also individually visited heavy industry facilities, collective farms and military bases, while Ri's appearances with Kim were almost entirely limited to cultural locations centred on leisure, pleasure and consumption. By keeping her away from locations traditionally associated with North Korea's dictatorial past, the North Korean media used the sensationalism surrounding Ri to draw the Global North's attention away from social spaces inflected with Communist associations while shifting focus to images of cultural prosperity imbued with the gestalt of the Global North. Both kinds of on-site visits therefore function as both a display of reform to the Global North that appears legitimate due to Ri's presence, while continuing the legacy of maintaining the requisite love for the leader because of his tireless efforts to visit his people.

Michael K. Goodman and Christine Barnes[36] note that the media technique of associating celebrities with specific development spaces confers the celebrity with an authenticity and expertise that belies common perceptions of the meretricious celebrity. However, the North Korean media's approach deviates slightly from this model: whereas Global North celebrities draw media attention to the plight of underdeveloped projects in the Global South, Ri's presence legitimizes the appearance of North Korea's convergence with the Global North. Nonetheless, Ri relies on the same mechanisms that 'development celebrities' like Chris Martin and George Clooney use to draw media attention to various development issues around the world.[37] For instance, showing physical proximity to political power (e.g.: Bono standing with Kofi Annan) is crucial: Ri legitimizes Kim's claims of convergence with global standards simply by being beside him in these social spaces as a non-traditional North Korean wife with access to the leader's political power – a familiar outsourcing of conventional authority to celebrity. Although the Global North media might have viewed Kim Jong-un's individual endorsement of projects like the amusement park and the restaurant as suspect, Ri's inclusion with Kim conferred them with the status of the recognizable celebrity couple, simultaneously drawing attention to, and legitimizing, the development of North Korea's reform projects into materialities of authenticity favourable to the Global North media. Thus, her authenticity as a 'first lady' committed to reforming and converging with the Global North legitimates Kim Jong-un's leadership by linking Ri's demotic celebrity aura with the spaces she and her husband inhabit. However, Ri's presence at Kim's on-site inspections is not without controversy among the North Korean public. According to sources based in the northern provinces bordering China,

> the appearance of Ri Sol Joo, who has no relation to the tasks of the Party whatsoever, is creating further negativity. … In the past when Kim Il Sung's wife Kim Sung Ae accompanied him on his guidance visits, the people considered it natural because she was the Vice-chair of the Union of Democratic Women, but Ri Sol Joo is just 'his woman.'[38]

This comment represents some of the tensions that have emerged as a result of the indigenization of celebrity culture in North Korea. In order for Ri to be successful at legitimizing Kim's pseudo-events for the Global North, she must eschew any pretensions of behaving as her predecessors did, which means tacitly rejecting the ideological social duties expected of her as the wife of the leader. By rejecting these duties, Ri takes on the role of the supportive, rather than revolutionary, political wife that is more in line with the traditional political wives of the Global North. Since the success of this image is heavily reliant upon Ri's self-conscious sartorial decisions, the North Korean media must provide enough coverage of her in order to entice the Global North media to pore over the meaning of her fashion choices.

Let them wear Christian Dior trousers

A few weeks after Ri Sol-ju's first public appearance with Kim Jong-un, the style section of *The Huffington Post* had already begun speculating on Ri's future fashion appearances, while warning other Western fashion-sensible first ladies like Samantha Cameron, Carla Bruni, Valerie Trierweiler and Angelica Rivera to 'watch out!' for the new first lady in town.[39] An article in *Der Spiegel* titled 'Is Dior the New Socialism?' also suggested that Ri's fashionable appearances indicated that 'the pull of globalization has reached even the world's last Stalinist holdout … and it is clearly beginning to corrupt socialist ideals'.[40] Even more provocatively, Ri's Western sartorial spectacles consisting of Chanel, Christian Dior and Prada were interpreted as vehicles for the liberation of North Korean women: in two separate articles in the South Korean *Chosun Ilbo*, Ri's style of polka dots, ruffles, ribbons and flower-shaped broaches, is considered outright defiant, as 'she gives the impression that she … does not like to be controlled'[41] and that there is 'a clash between her desire to be a responsible and well-behaved first lady and her desire to be a bolder fashion icon'.[42] One notable example of Ri's allegedly paradigm-shifting fashion statements occurred in September 2012, when Ri was 'spotted' wearing a black trouser suit on a routine visit to a tile factory with her husband. This fashion display symbolically contributed to the discourse of reform because North Korean female fashion, dictated by the state, maintained a conservative and traditional repertoire of skirts and dresses (even with regard to military apparel) to regulate traditional Korean femininity.[43] Therefore, the cultural politics of Ri's trouser-wearing expedition is encoded with several meanings. On one level, her pants suggest that North Korean women's bodies were being liberated from the shackles of state regulation, and that the country was beginning to reform its politics. A report from the *Korean*

Broadcasting System (KBS) in Seoul reflects this narrative of political reform based on Ri's new trouser expedition:

> The open-minded first lady has no particular objection to Western culture. She was even seen wearing pants, implying that she is against gender discrimination. By showing an active and practical part of women, she can also gain popularity with North Korean women and demonstrate to the outside world that North Korea is open now and there is no gender discrimination in the country.[44]

A *Telegraph* article on Ri's trousers also cited her 'flamboyant appearances' as evidence that Kim was planning to implement major reforms,[45] while the *Daily Mail* noted that Ri's appearance in a 'smart' trouser suit complimented her 'range of chic yet conservative outfits which recall the lady-like style of Kate Middleton or Carla Bruni',[46] revisiting the 'first lady' discourse legitimizing Ri as a wife in tune with Western democratic values. Thus the globalization of Western fashion appeared to offer North Korean women, represented by Ri, opportunities for new kinds of femininities outside of North Korean tradition.

In contrast, since taking power in December 2011, Kim Jong-un has not innovated his own sartorial style, instead opting for a more nostalgic look by appropriating his grandfather's black Mao suit. According to recent defector reports, within the country 'Kim Jong-il is associated both with the trauma of famine and crisis in the late 1990s'[47]; therefore, Kim Jong-un's adoption of the Mao suit is a likely attempt to visually model himself on his grandfather, who presided over great economic prosperity from the 1950s to the 1970s. However, Kim Il-sung's black Mao suit also intersects with the body politics of the Korean race. Unlike the muscular Christian body type of contemporary American celebrity politics that is used to construct leadership as a specific form of masculinity, the North Korean media has historically made no effort to hide the corpulence of their leaders. Commenting on Kim Il-sung, B. R. Myers summarizes the propaganda rationale behind this specific depiction of the leader:

> Kim appears in DPRK-themed pictures always as plump, if never quite as fat as he was in real life. Unlike Stalin and Mao, who personified the triumph of consciousness over the instincts, Kim had little need to pose as an ascetic. On the contrary, his plumpness symbolizes the race's newfound freedom to indulge its innocent instincts.[48]

Given this propensity for size and its intersection with the black Mao suit, Kim Il-sung's fashion style symbolizes the apex of North Korean political leadership and power in stark opposition to the athletic grace, virility and masculinity of Western constructions of political leadership.[49,50] Kim Jong-un has also reportedly undergone several plastic surgeries to reconstruct his face to match the corporeal perfection of chubbiness that his grandfather possessed, thus highlighting how politically significant it is to maintain this idealized body type of the North Korean leader.[51] The Mao suit's politics of nostalgia combined with the girth of the leader as the emblematic source of benevolence thus demonstrates the ideological significance of Kim Jong-un's own sartorial symbolism.

Kim Jong-un's inheritance of his grandfather's sartorial and physical sensibility coupled with Ri's fashion breakout takes on a particularly political meaning in light of the association Kim Il-sung and his Mao suit have historically taken in relation to the diversification of North Korean women's fashion. Starting in the 1980s, Kim Il-sung began encouraging light industry to develop in order to 'produce smart clothing that is up to the latest fashion',[52] meaning a shift away from traditional North Korean women's clothing. However, the North Korean media had to carefully construct their propaganda so that it still retained the leader's magnanimity, even in relation to diversifying women's fashion. Two propaganda paintings from the 1980s deftly convey a subtle balance between traditional political authority vis-à-vis gift culture and an emerging diversification of female fashion. In a mural entitled 'the Pyongyang Polyvinyl Chloride Shoe Factory',[53] the corpulent Kim Il-sung, dressed in his Mao suit, stands on the factory floor holding a newly manufactured white high heel, and smiles approvingly at the work while four female labourers hover around him and beam in admiration of his sartorial sensibility. Another painting titled 'Fatherly Love Is Felt in Silk Fabric' situates Kim Il-sung in the middle of a textile factory floor, this time holding a roll of patterned silk fabric, while the female labourers again look upon the leader with a subservient gaze.[54] The composition of both paintings downplays the women's labour necessary to produce the manufactured products for female consumption and heightens the role of the leader in the production of said products. Since the corpulent leader is robed in the Mao suit, the diversification of women's fashion appears as a natural extension of the leader's instincts, while the look on the female labourers' faces indicates that these products almost magically manifested due to the leader's generous thoughts. Since Kim Il-sung's smiling approval of the textile pattern positions him as the sole authority on female fashion and beauty, the production of female fashion is converted by the presence of the corpulent leader in his Mao suit into a gift, which the women receive gratefully. When North Korean fashion styles began diversifying in the 1980s, it became crucial to position the leader in the middle of the production process so as not to displace the 'true' producer of the material. In this way, femininity in the form of fashion as arbitrated by the leader is continually a gift bestowed to them so that they may perform labour in service to the nation. In Ri's case, her performance in the media is a form of labour in service to the country, as she is required to continue the tradition of acting as the mediator between two contrasting realms. Now, Ri must function as a female figure that carefully negotiates between the state and the outside world, while shielding her husband, Kim Jong-un, from the world so that he can continue to nurture his Korean instincts. As a celebrity couple, the tradition of the Mao suit worn by the heavy-set Kim Jong-un intersecting with the designer labels worn by Ri Sol-ju literalizes the discursive relationship the leader has over feminine fashion and beauty. New paradigms of femininity can thus be seen as thoughtful gifts the leader continues to bestow on the people, rather than indications of a convergence with Western consumer culture's assumption of underlying democratic values. While Ri's trousers give the impression that she is setting new paradigms of femininity in North Korea as a bold fashion icon, it is instructive to remember that it was her husband, Kim Jong-un, who overturned the ban on women's trousers, thus allowing Ri to wear them in the first place.[55] As Kim Suk-young points out, 'In North Korea, the notion that femininity is a gift bestowed by the state ... has provided grounds for regulating gendered body practices.'[56]

However, this strategy has also come under internal pressure due to the gross juxtaposition between the opulence of Ri's fashion and her influence on Pyongyang's upper classes, and chronic food shortages that plague the country, casting doubt on the viability of Kim and Ri's current fashion configuration. Although it is difficult to know what most North Koreans think of Ri's choice of designer labels, there are some reports from North Korea's border provinces that are critical of the leadership's new sartorial direction. Although there are women wearing 'fashions popularized by the chic wife of North Korea's not-yet 30-year-old leader ... North Koreans interviewed recently across the border in China say the changes so far are superficial and have done little to ease the daily task of just staying alive'.[57] One North Korean who works in the border provinces remarked, 'Why would I care about the new clothing of government officials and their children when I can't feed my family?'[58] While many of the most critical accounts on North Korea's leadership come from the border provinces, many defectors have pointed out that the ostentation of Ri's fashion is limited to an exclusive elite living within the capital of Pyongyang.[59] Indeed, what is rarely discussed in the Global North media is the social classification system that divides North Koreans between the haves and the have-nots.

Songbun and the celebrity background check

Unlike its Communist neighbours, North Korea has successfully transferred power from father to son twice, a custom inherited from Korea's neo-Confucian period. North Koreans also see the leader as a gift from the Korean race back to its people, as official propaganda frames North Korean history as a prelude to the arrival of the Kim family, starting with Kim Il-sung. Narratives in North Korean literature, film and theatre set prior to 1948 (the foundation of North Korea) always contain laments about how there is no national figure to protect the Korean people. However, allusions to the sun, a symbolic reference to Kim Il-sung, cue to the reader/audience that in the future, Korea will be blessed with a leader who can protect them. The Kim family is also frequently associated with Mount Paektu, the mythical source of the Korean race. According to North Korean mythology, King Tan'gun, the ancestral father of the Korean race, founded the Korean people 5,000 years ago with his semen at the top of Mount Paektu.[60] The association of the mountain with the Kim family patriarchs legitimates their status as the paternal figures of all the North Korean people.[61] Myers notes that 'since the advent of Kim Il sung', propaganda encourages Koreans to 'indulge their pure childlike instincts now that a national father figure can protect them'.[62] The importance of the fatherly leader as a gift to the Korean people is so pervasive that the traditional father figure in North Korean propaganda is usually replaced with the presence of the leader. The painting 'Kim Il-sung Visits A Soldiers' Family'[63] illustrates how the leader has usurped the position of the traditional patriarch, who is off fighting the Japanese. The daughter clutches the leader while holding a photograph of her father, but her gaze is clearly fixated on Kim Il-sung; the wife listens and waits obediently by the surrogate's side. The leader is also firmly embedded in the centre of the frame surrounded by children and within the courtyard inside the walls of the household, leaving no mistake as to what role Kim Il-sung is fulfilling. Currently, the North Korean media is eager to frame Kim Jong-un as a paternal figure by attempting to mimic Kim Il-sung's displacement of the traditional patriarch and close association with children. In a well-known photograph taken in the late 1970s, Kim Il-sung walks arm in arm with several boys and girls of the Kim Il-sung Youth League, who laugh and cry with joy over being attended to by the father of the North Korean nation. In a nearly identical photograph taken over thirty years later, a patriarch of the Kim family, this time Kim Jong-un, is again at the centre of a flurry of children from the Kim Il-sung Youth League.[64]

But what role does the wife of the fatherly leader play in this context? Historically, the wife has played the role of a devoted mother from a revolutionary and/or military background who has made sacrifices for the good of the nation, and produced a male child worthy of succession. However, Ri's social background, which has drawn considerable attention in the Global North media, is anathema to the traditional role played by the wife of the leader. Although the North Korean media has not officially confirmed Ri's background, several sources in the Global North media have managed to cobble together bits and pieces of information about her past as a singer. According to several South Korean newspapers, Ri performed with the Unhasu Orchestra at a New Year's Eve concert for Jong-un and his father in 2010, and subsequently won the heart of Kim Jong-un with her singing during the performance.[65] An article in the *JoongAng Daily* also commented that it was Kim Jong-il himself that singled Ri out to become Jong-un's 'first lady'.[66] At a press briefing in July 2012, Jung Chung-rae, a South Korean member of parliament with connections to the Korean National Intelligence Service, stated that '[Ri Sol-ju] is just a daughter of an ordinary family, not of a high-ranking military official.'[67] Ri's 'ordinariness' was seized by the Global North media and Jung's quote was quickly referenced in many articles about Kim's new wife. As a figure coupled with Kim, *The Independent* wrote that Ri's ordinariness helps 'North Koreans to feel that their new ruler is an average guy' and shows Kim is inching towards 'Western-style leadership'.[68] Ri's seemingly pedestrian heritage from the creative class appears to converge with the Global North's celebrity culture in two ways. First, Ri occupies a specificity of her own outside of the 'royal' family of the Kims because she is not a Kim herself, and can be understood through a narrative of discovery similar to the way Kate Middleton, as an outsider, is continually defined by her non-royal and apparent middle-class background. Secondly, Ri's artistic background mirrors the Global North's increasing reliance on the artistic class to provide political guidance in areas where the public feels their leaders have failed them.[69] In effect, the Global North media interprets Ri as offering a stark symbolic counter to the entrenched elitism of the Kim family. Kim Keun-sik, a North Korea expert at Kyungnam University in South Korea, expressed that

Ri's appearance 'helped ease hostilities in South Korea toward the hereditary succession in North Korea'.[70]

Yet, celebrity can also be used to reproduce hierarchy and exclusivity under a veil of ordinariness.[71] That Ri could marry into the Kim family and come from an 'ordinary' family utterly defies songbun, North Korea's deeply ingrained caste system. Songbun 'means that each and every North Korean citizen is assigned a heredity-based class and socio-political rank over which the individual exercises no control but which determines all aspects of his or her life',[72] including marriage. North Korea's elites in the highest songbun category are forbidden from marrying people from lower songbun, as illustrated by Chang Kum-song, Kim Jong-il's niece, who was prevented from marrying a man from a lower songbun class, and as a result, committed suicide in 2006. In Ri Sol-ju's case, her entry into the artistic class was already governed by her songbun status, as people can only become artists if they are from the elite in the first place.[73] The Global North media also unearthed Ri's travel excursions to South Korea as a singing cheerleader for the 2002 Busan Asian Games and 2005 Asian Athletics Championship, visits deeply intertwined with the politics of reunification between North and South Korea. At the time, a *Daily Mirror* article gushed that South Korea 'bid an emotional farewell Tuesday to a North Korean cheering squad whose presence at the Asian Games ... has sparked a mood of reconciliation'.[74] In 2012, after the North Korean media had officially announced Ri's marriage to Kim Jong-un, the BBC dredged up Ri's past as a cultural ambassador to South Korea, and linked her visits to speculation that Kim Jong-un had 'a more international outlook than his father',[75] implying that he may be more open to reunification (i.e. convergence) due to the influence of his cosmopolitan wife. The South Korean *JoongAng Daily* also ran an article in July 2012 containing a large photograph of Ri Sol-ju leaving South Korea with her cheerleading delegation in 2005 while headlining the article with the title 'Jong-un May Make Ri Western-style consort'.[76] However, only those with the highest songbun are ever allowed to leave North Korea, while those from lower songbun are restricted from travelling abroad.[77] Furthermore, those who do temporarily leave North Korea are required to sign a pledge never to talk about what they've seen and heard in South Korea, and agree to accept punishment if they break their pledge. According to a 2006 article in *The Chosun Ilbo*, several cheerleaders that had accompanied Ri in 2002 and 2005 had been sent to political prison camps because they had broken the pledge and spoken about South Korea upon returning home.[78] Therefore Ri's visits to South Korea can be read as examples of her elite status as well as her loyalty to the Kim regime, as she clearly was not sent to a camp because she did not articulate any reformist tendencies by praising the south.

The limits of the celebrity couple in North Korea

While Ri Sol-ju's perceived status as a commoner with an artistic background in conjunction with Kim's political status is what makes their power as a celebrity couple so appealing to the Global North media, Ri's social background also clearly challenges the firmly established narrative in North Korea that legitimizes the Kim patriarch's absolute rule to a much greater extent than pseudo-events and sartorial choices. In order for Kim to be seen by the public as a unique gift to the Korean people, the wife of the North Korean leader must occupy a sacred maternal space with specific duties that ensure the continuation of the Kim family. Kim Tae Hong points out that,

> [Ri Sol-ju's] career as a musician is insufficient for a revolutionary leader's spouse. Kim Jong Eun's mother Koh Young Hee was a former dancer with the Mansudae Art Troupe, but this information was deliberately struck from the public record and she was portrayed as a strong woman supporting the people's leader, Kim Jong Il.[79]

A 2011 documentary on Kim Jong-un's mother, Ko Young-hee, entitled 'The Beloved Mother of the Great Songun Korea' also omits her background as a dancer and instead highlights how she instructed Kim Jong-un in weapons training, including handgun operation, while she also dutifully knitted clothing to protect the young Kim from the elements.[80] If the recent propaganda on Ko Young-hee is an attempt to continue the lineage of revolutionary mothers/wives of the leader, then it looks as if Ri's celebrity status may be soon be terminated. In September, nearly three months after Ri's first public appearance, the Propaganda and Agitation Department of the Korean Worker's Party forcibly seized and destroyed every CD and album containing any of Ri Sol-ju's recordings with the Unhasu Orchestra in a likely attempt to suppress her background as a singer.[81] Additionally, Ri's frequent public appearances with Kim Jong-un stopped abruptly, and she was not seen again until the end of October at a musical concert where she had toned down her sartorial choices and was visibly pregnant. It is possible that having reached the limits of the celebrity couple, the North Korean media has now shifted Ri into the familiar revolutionary/domestic mother figure that previous wives of the leader have occupied. Indeed, her appearances have continued to remain more and more infrequent and she continues to wear more subdued fashion styles. However, despite North Korea's attempt to scale back Ri's celebrity brand in favour of a more maternal domestic role, the North Korean media spent most of 2013 and the spring of 2014 attempting to quell rumours of a sex scandal from Ri's past that also involved the alleged execution of several members of the Unhasu Orchestra.[82] In response, the North Korean public has grown increasingly irritated with Ri's inability to conform to her motherly role in order to support the Kim dynasty. One source in Hysean, Yangkang Province states, 'the number of younger people who view comrade Ri Sol Ju negatively is rising. … How can a mere entertainer who just sang and danced become the "Mother of Chosun?"'[83] Ironically, given the public's propensity for tradition, North Korea's experiments with the celebrity couple reveal that contrary to the Global North media's narrative of the Kim couple, ideological control has not eroded, but instead still persists and is deeply entrenched in North Korean culture. Yet the question remains whether, in the long term, the North Korean media will be able to completely sublimate Ri's celebrity aura into the gestalt of North Korean gift culture. As evidenced by new media rumours of a second pregnancy,[84] it is clear that for the time being, Ri continues to be the gift that keeps on giving to a Global North media myopically looking for fissures that suggest reform or even revolution.

Acknowledgements

I am grateful to Shelley Cobb, Neil Ewen, György Péteri, Greg Scarlatoiu and Margaret Zeddies for comments on earlier versions of this chapter.

Notes

1 S. Colbert, 'Cold War Update', *The Colbert Report*, airdate: 24 July 2012.
2 'Kim Jong Un Married to Ri Sol Ju, North Korea State TV Confirms', *Associated Press*, 25 July 2012, http://www.politico.com/news/stories/0712/78950.html.

3 Rather than employing the terms 'Western media' and 'Western culture' this chapter will use 'Global North media' and 'Global North culture.' The 'Global North/Global South' divide is an international development term adapted from the Brandt report of 1980 on international development issues. See http://www. stwr.org/special-features/the-brandt-report.html While 'The West' and 'Western media' problematically emphasizes the dominance of Western (i.e. American and West European) viewpoints and culture in contrast to 'the Rest' of the world, 'Global North' is more diverse, as it includes countries in Eastern Europe as well as Japan, South Korea, Israel, Singapore and Russia. While no division of the world into broad categories is ever entirely satisfactory, 'Global North' ties together countries that have adopted the capitalist mode of production and as a result have greater cultural and political affinities with one another. Indeed, as this chapter demonstrates, common media discourses emerge about celebrity culture throughout the Global North, indicating that celebrity is not just a 'Western' cultural phenomenon. Furthermore, the addition of 'Global' to the Brandt report's 'North/South' divide indicates that both halves are drawn together into global processes such as cultural globalization, rather than strictly separated from each other, a problem the term 'the West' also perpetuates.

4 M. Fackler, 'On North Korean TV, a Dash of (unapproved) Disney Magic', *New York Times*, 10 July 2012, A4.

5 Andreas Bummel, 'Towards A Global Democratic Revolution: A Global Parliament and the Transformation of the World Order', *Cadmus Journal* 1 (2011): 103–08.

6 The Rome Statute established the International Criminal Court, an international tribunal with judicial power to prosecute individual political leaders for genocide, war crimes and crimes against humanity. R2P dramatically altered nation-state sovereignty, as it is no longer considered a right, but a duty for nation states to protect their citizens from mass atrocities. If the nation-state is not willing, or unable, to protect their citizens, the international community is regarded as having the authority to intervene. Additionally, William J. Dobson's excellent book *The Dictator's Learning Curve: Inside the Global Battle for Democracy* (New York: Anchor, 2012) chronicles the growing difficulty that authoritarian regimes around the world are having maintaining their power in a gradually democratizing world due to perceptual shifts in the nation-state's responsibilities to its own people. Dobson rightly suggests that in order to maintain power, these regimes are shifting towards more subtle forms of coercion.

7 M. Fisher, 'Vogue Defends Profile of Syrian First Lady', *Atlantic Weekly*, 27 February 2011, http://www.theatlantic.com/international/archive/2011/02/vogue-defends-profile-of-syrian-firstlady/71764/, emphasis added.

8   K. Bogardus, 'PR Firm Worked With Syria on Controversial Photo Shoot', *The Hill*, 3 August 2011, http://thehill.com/business-a-lobbying/175149-pr-firm-worked-with-syria-on-controversial-photo-shoot.

9   P. Pizano, 'Crooners and Their Dictators', *Huffington Post*, 19 October 2012, http://www.huffingtonpost.com/pedro-pizano/crooners-and-their-dictators_b_1982520.html.

10 Chris Rojek, *Celebrity* (London: Reaktion, 2001), 14, 29.

11 David P. Marshall, *Celebrity and Power: Fame and Contemporary Culture* (Minneapolis: University of Minnesota Press, 1997), x.

12 Louise Edwards and Elaine Jeffreys, eds, *Celebrity in China* (Hong Kong: Hong Kong University Press, 2010); Helena Goscilo and Vlad Strukov, eds, *Celebrity and Glamour in Contemporary Russia: Shocking Chic* (Oxon: Routledge, 2011).

13 Jonathan Xavier Inda and Renato Rosaldo, eds, *The Anthropology of Globalization* (Oxford: Blackwell Publishing, 2008).

14 Roland Robertson, *Globalization: Social Theory and Global Culture* (London: Sage Publications, 1992), 172.

15 This is not to argue that cultural hybridity implies a mixing of two or more previously 'pure' cultural forms or practices. On the contrary, hybridity theory seeks to reveal the trans-local nature of culture by demonstrating how territorialized notions of culture, be it local, national or global, are facades. Contrary to its own propaganda, since North Korea's inception, it has repeatedly adopted Chinese, Soviet, Russian, Japanese and Eastern European cultural forms and attempted to pass these forms off as its own indigenous culture with varying degrees of success.

16 A. Lankov, 'The Rationing System in North Korea', *Korea Times*, 26 August 2012, http://www.koreatimes.co.kr/www/news/nation/2012/08/304_118268.html.

17 North Korean ideology also has a strong ethnic nationalist component, contains principles of self-reliance, and incorporates Confucian elements from the feudal period. However, the ideological aspect of North Korea's gift culture is particularly relevant for the purposes of this chapter.

18 Heonik Kwon and Byung-Ho Chung, 'North Korea's Partisan Family State', *The Asia-Pacific Journal* 10, no. 28 (2012), http://www.japanfocus.org/-Byung_Ho-Chung/3789.

19 Curiously, the North Korean media did not cover the marriage itself, perhaps revealing the upper limits of the influence of American celebrity culture on North Korean culture.

20 S. Kim, 'North Korea's Kim Jong Un Shows Off New Wife Ri Sol Ju', *Huffington Post*, 26 July 2012, http://www.huffingtonpost.com/2012/07/26/kim-jong-un-wife_n_1705130.html.

21 S. Kim, 'Un Becomes 2: North Korea Confirms Kim Is Married', *Associated Press*, 26 July 2012, http://bigstory.ap.org/article/nkorean-state-tv-says-leader-kim-jong-un-married.

22 'That Mystery Woman in North Korea? Turns Out She's the First Lady', *New York Times*, 26 July 2012, A1.

23 'Kim Jong Un Visits Haemaji Restaurant', *Korean Central News Agency*, 31 August 2012, http://www.kcna.co.jp/item/2012/201208/news31/20120831-28ee.html.

24 'North Korean First Family's Westernized Habits', *Chosun Ilbo*, 3 September 2012, http://english.chosun.com/site/data/html_dir/2012/09/03/2012090301206.html.

25 Kim Jong-un Calls On Nation To Catch-up With Global Trends', *Yonhap News Agency*, 8 August 2012, http://english.yonhapnews.co.kr/national/2012/07/08/12/0301000000AEN20120708002400315F.HTML.

26 Domestic state television reported that the restaurant was in fact an 'eternal gift to the people by our great leader.' J. Cho, 'Kim Jong Un Attempts to Rebrand North Korea', *ABC News*, 2 July 2012, http://abcnews.go.com/International/kim-jong-attempts-rebrand-northkorea/story?id=16662917#.UMS9LIW6Ay4.

27 On-the-spot inspections may have originated with Kim Il-sung's wish to see things for himself rather than trust reports by others, a precaution learned during his guerilla years when his bands were frequently infiltrated by Japanese spies who would feed him false information.

28 B. R. Myers, *The Cleanest Race: How North Koreans See Themselves – And Why It Matters* (Brooklyn: Melville House, 2010), 81.

29 Bruce Cumings, *North Korea: Another Country* (New York: The New Press, 2004), 147.

30 'Kim Jong-un Visits Rungna People's Pleasure Ground', *Korean Central News Agency*, 24 July 2012, http://www.kcna.co.jp/item/2012/201207/news24/20120724-12ee.html.

31 C. Harlan, 'At The Tongil Fitness Center, in Pyongyang, the treadmill has a placard showing Kim Jong Un Personally Inspected It', *Twitter*, 16 June 2013, https://twitter.com/chicoharlan/status/346510859050299392/photo/1.

32 Kwon and Chung, *North Korea's Partisan Family State*.

33 Unknown, 'Worrying About Even One Soldier's Health', *digitalpostercollection.com*, http://digitalpostercollection.com/propaganda/1945-1991-cold-war/north-korea/worrying-about-even-one-soldiers-health/#main.

34 'Kim Jong-un Inspects KPA Air Force Pilot Training', *Huanqui Shibao*, 23 January 2012, http://world.huanqiu.com/photo/2012-01/2378385_4.html.

35 Myers, *The Cleanest Race*, 82.

36 Michael K. Goodman and Christine Barnes, 'Star/Poverty Space: The Making of the "Development Celebrity"', *Celebrity Studies* 2 (March 2011): 69–85.

37 Ibid.

38 S. M. Choi, 'Kim Caught Fiddling As Rome Burns', *DailyNK*, 6 August 2012, http://www.dailynk.com/english/read.php?cataId=nk01500&num=9636.

39 E. Cheung, 'Ri Sol Ju, North Korea's First Lady, Remains a Style Mystery', *Huffington Post*, 25 July 2012, http://www.huffingtonpost.com/2012/07/25/ri-sol-ju-kim-jong-un-wife-marriage_n_1703210.html.

40 S. Koelbl, 'Is Dior the New Socialism?', *Der Spiegel*, 8 October 2012, 41.

41 'Kim Jong-un's Wife a Style Icon for Pyongyang Women', *Chosun Ilbo*, 6 September 2012, http://english.chosun.com/site/data/html_dir/2012/09/06/2012090600984.html.

42 'Fashion Mavens Dissect North Korean First Lady's Style', *Chosun Ilbo*, 9 September 2012, http://english.chosun.com/site/data/html_dir/2012/09/07/2012090701148.html.

43 Suk-Young Kim, *Illusive Utopia: Theater, Film, and Everyday Performance in North Korea* (Ann Arbor: University of Michigan Press, 2010), 228.

44 'North Korean Leader's Highly Publicized Moves', *Korean Broadcasting System*, 13 September 2012, http://world.kbs.co.kr/english/event/nkorea_nuclear/now_02_detail.htm?No=1425.

45 J. Ryle, 'North Korean First Lady Steps Out in a Trouser Suit', *The Telegraph*, 3 September 2012, http://www.telegraph.co.uk/news/worldnews/asia/northkorea/9516637/North-Korean-First-Lady-steps-out-in-trouser-suit.html.

46 R. Seales and D. Gayle, 'Nothing Jong With That: North Korea Leader's Wife Causes A Stir By Ditching Skirts for Trousers', *Daily Mail*, 4 September 2012, http://www.dailymail.co.uk/news/article-2198026/Nothing-Jong-North-Korea-leaders-wife-causes-stir-ditching-skirts-trousers.html.

47 C. K. Armstrong, 'Kim Jong-il: Leadership and Legacy', *opendemocracy.net*, 19 December 2011, http://www.opendemocracy.net/charles-k-armstrong/kim-jong-il-leadership-and-legacy.

48 Myers, *The Cleanest Race*, 78.

49 Marshall, *Celebrity and Power*, 218.

50 Predictably, the infamous Kim waistline has also provided the Global North media with fodder to level criticism at the regime. 'South Koreans Ridicule Fat Kim Jung-un', *The Telegraph*, 1 October 2010, http://www.telegraph.co.uk/news/worldnews/asia/northkorea/8036407/South-Koreans-ridicule-fat-Kim-Jong-un.html.

51 T. K. Ha, 'Kim Jong-un's 6 Plastic Surgery Procedures: The Making of a Mini-Kim Il-sung', *Open Radio For North Korea*, 3 July 2011, http://english.nkradio.org/news/403.

52 Kim Gui-ok, Kim Seon-im, I Gyeong-ha and Hwang Eun-ju, *How Do North Korean Women Live?* (Bukhan yeoseongdeul-eun eotteoke salgo isseulka) (Seoul: Dangdae, 2000), 152.

53 Rüdiger Frank, ed., *Exploring North Korean Arts* (Austria: University of Vienna, MAK Vienna, Verlag für moderne Kunst Nürnberg, 2011), 268.

54 Kim, *Illusive Utopia*, 257.

55 J. Cho, 'Kim Jong Un Attempts to Rebrand North Korea', *ABC News*, 2 July 2012, http://abcnews.go.com/International/kim-jong-attempts-rebrand-north korea/story?id=16662917#.UMS9LIW6Ay4.

56 Kim, *Illusive Utopia*, 161.

57 B. Demick, 'North Korea's Progress Seems to Be More Style Than Substance', *The Los Angeles Times*, 14 October 2012, http://articles.latimes.com/2012/oct/14/world/la-fg-north-korea-life-20121014.

58 A. Jacobs, 'North Koreans Say Life Has Not Improved', *New York Times*, 14 October 2012, http://www.nytimes.com/2012/10/15/world/asia/north-koreans-say-life-has-not-improved.html?pagewanted=all.

59 '"Daring" North Korean Fashion', *Radio Free Asia*, 6 October 2010, http://www.rfa.org/english/news/korea/fashion-06012010141022.html.

60 Myers, *The Cleanest Race*, 27.

61 Although Mao and Stalin also employed paternal rhetoric for political purposes in their propaganda, neither regime so successfully associated the paternal leader with the nation-state like North Korea. Kim Suk-young traces the historical development of why this occurred in her book (2010: 134–40).

62 Myers, *The Cleanest Race*, 56.

63 Kim, *Illusive Utopia*, 144.

64 Kim Il-sung had an advantage by relying on paintings while Kim Jong-un must rely on photographic media coverage that can be quickly reproduced and circulated. A photograph of Kim Jong-un with a rural family made the Global North media rounds due to the apprehension, anxiety and fear clearly visible in the faces of the family. 'Kim Jong Un Family Photo: North Korean Leader Poses With Terrified-Looking Family', *Huffington Post*, 20 August 2012, http://www.huffingtonpost.com/2012/08/20/kim-jong-un-family-photo_n_1812069.html.

65 'North Korea: Kim Jong Un "fell in love with new wife at music performance"', *The Telegraph*, 26 July 2012, http://www.telegraph.co.uk/news/worldnews/asia/

northkorea/9428048/North-Korea-Kim-Jong-un-fell-in-love-with-new-wife-at-music-performance.html.

66 'Kim Jong-un's First Lady Visited South in 2005', *JoongAng Daily*, 27 July 2012, http://koreajoongangdaily.joinsmsn.com/news/article/article.aspx?aid=2956960.

67 'North Korea Newsletter No. 221', *Yonhap News Agency*, 2 August 2012, http://english.yonhapnews.co.kr/northkorea/2012/08/01/70/0401000000AEN20120 801009000325F.HTML.

68 S. Kim, 'North Korea Confirms Kim Jong-un's Marriage to Ri Sol-ju', *The Independent*, 25 July 2012, http://www.independent.co.uk/news/world/asia/north-korea-confirms-kim-jonguns-marriage-to-ri-solju-7976506.html.

69 Goodman and Barnes, 'Star/Poverty Space'; Rojek, *Celebrity*.

70 'Kim Jong-un's Wife Is His Greatest Asset', *Chosun Ilbo* (http://english.chosun.com/site/data/html_dir/2012/09/07/2012090701110.html, 7 September 2012).

71 Graeme Turner, *Understanding Celebrity* (London: Sage, 2004), 83.

72 Robert Collins, *Marked for Life: Songbun, North Korea's Social Classification System* (Washington, DC: The Committee for Human Rights in North Korea, 2012), 14.

73 'Jong-un May Make Ri Western-style Consort', *The JoongAng Daily*, 27 July 2012, http://koreajoongangdaily.joinsmsn.com/news/article/article.aspx?aid=2956951.

74 'Busan Says Goodbye to North Korean Cheerleaders', *The Daily Mail*, 17 October 2012, http://archives.dailymirror.lk/2002/10/17/sports/2.html.

75 'North Korea's Ri Sol-ju "may have visited South Korea"', *British Broadcasting Corporation*, 26 July 2012, http://www.bbc.co.uk/news/world-asia-18993917.

76 'Jong-un May Make Ri Western-style Consort', *JoongAng Daily*, 27 July 2012, http://koreajoongangdaily.joinsmsn.com/news/article/article.aspx?aid=2956951.

77 Collins, *Marked for Life*, 115.

78 'North Korean cheerleaders Banished to Camps', *Chosun Ilbo*, 16 February 2006, http://english.chosun.com/site/data/html_dir/2006/02/16/2006021661019.html.

79 T. H. Kim, 'The Why of Ri at Rungra Resort', *DailyNK*, 26 July 2012, http://www.dailynk.com/english/read.php?catald=nk00400&num=9587.

80 This dichotomy is reminiscent of Kim Il-sung's first wife, Kim Jong-suk, who also deftly displayed a balance between domestic and revolutionary labor (Kim 2010: 148).

81 S. G. Park, 'North Korea Collecting Songs By Ri Sol Joo', *DailyNK*, 18 September 2012, http://www.dailynk.com/english/read.php?catald=nk01500&num=9817; S. Y. Kim, 'The Burden of an Art Troupe Past', *DailyNK*, 20 September 2012, http://www.dailynk.com/english/read.php?catald=nk02900&num=9827.

82 M. J. Kang, 'Ri Sol Ju and Unhasu Back in the News', *DailyNK*, 10 October 2013, http://www.dailynk.com/english/read.php?catald=nk01700&num=11063.

83 M. J. Kang, 'Ri Sol Ju Failing to Impress', *DailyNK*, 26 February 2014, http://renewal. dailynk.com/english/read.php?cataId=nk01500&num=11573.

84 S. Tomlinson, 'Kim Jong-un "expecting a second child" as his wife is spotted in public wearing a maternity dress (so will he finally have to give up the cigarettes?)', *Daily Mail*, 24 February 2014, http://www.dailymail.co.uk/news/article-2566574/ Kim-Jong-expecting-second-child-wife-spotted-public-wearing-maternity-dress-finally-cigarettes.html.

11

Ellen and Portia's Wedding: The Politics of Same-Sex Marriage and Celesbianism

Shelley Cobb

For most of history it was inconceivable that people would choose their mates on the basis of something as fragile and irrational as love. ... When someone did advocate such a strange belief, it was no laughing matter. Instead, it was considered a serious threat to social order.

Stephanie Coontz[1]

I always call Ellen DeGeneres the gay Rosa Parks. If Rosa Parks had one of the most popular daytime TV shows, I'm sure the civil-rights movement would've moved a little bit faster too.

Chris Rock[2]

In August 2008, within the short span of time that California issued marriage licenses to same-sex couples – between 17 July 2008 and the passing of Proposition 8 on 4 November 2008 – 'everyone's favourite lesbian', Ellen DeGeneres, married television actor Portia de Rossi.[3] When DeGeneres first announced the wedding on her talk show, the audience greeted the news with a standing ovation. Jennifer Reed argues that the wedding 'create[d] a new public space for the enactment of, and discussion about, gay marriage with a figure of goodwill and friendship'.[4] I consider Reed's positive evaluation a valid view. I am more interested here, however, in how the goodwill gesture is constructed through an appeal to conservative neoliberal views of identity and marriage that are highly commodified and circumscribed by postfeminist and homonormative tropes. Of course, Ellen and Portia DeGeneres (de Rossi changed her name in September 2010) are not the only celebrity same-sex couple who have married and shared their wedding publicly in the years since the legal challenges to Proposition 8 seemed to set off a wave of court decisions, proposed laws and political party statements both for and against same-sex marriage. Since 2008, gay and lesbian celebrity couples have become more ubiquitous in the media. Married couples include Neil Patrick Harris and David Burtka, Jesse Tyler Furgeson and Justine Mikitia, Cynthia Nixon and Christine Marinoni, Rosie O'Donnell and Michelle Rounds, and George Takei and Brad Altman, among several others. Arguably, the DeGeneres's are the only couple in which both partners were previously individually recognized celebrities. Their marriage has increased the value of DeGeneres's identity as 'everyone's favourite lesbian' as well as added value to de Rossi's celebrity identity, creating a valued coupled celebrity brand in the midst of the resurgent debates about and legal wrangling over gay marriage.

The fight for same-sex marriage has acquired an increasingly high visibility in the mainstream media and across key social media platforms such as Facebook and Twitter since the campaign against California's Proposition 8 in 2008, a visibility that has relegated other fights for LGBTQ equality to the margins and elevated marriage as the key symbol of equal rights and citizenship. Consequently, the prominence of the fight for marriage equality also contributes to the cultural weight of marriage itself as the optimum form of sexual intimacy, social acceptance and legal protection of individuals. After briefly summarizing key changes in the history of marriage that are the background for the important role it currently plays in neoliberal constructions of citizenship and identity, I set out some of the debates over same-sex marriage as a good thing for gay and lesbian persons. (Like Jocelyn Leimbach I leave out the BTQ of LGBTQ because the mainstream marriage debates largely figure those queer persons as irrelevant.)[5] Within this context, the images of the couples' lesbian wedding play a role in sentimentalizing the discourse for same-sex marriage, while other elements in the production of their coupledom draw on neoliberal discourses of individualism and self-care. Consequently, this chapter argues that the images of Ellen and Portia's same-sex wedding refigure lesbian identity within the 'postfeminist culture [that] both assumes and creates a female subject who desires marriage'.[6] At the same time, their high-profile celebrity wedding helped to mainstream the same-sex marriage equality campaign through their mutual celebrity brand. Paradoxically, then, their celebrity lesbian marriage is both a political act against heteronormativity and a neoconservative image of homonormativity and postfeminist female identity. If, as Dana Heller has shown, the 'celesbian' (defined as a celebrity who is 'known or alleged' to be a lesbian) is a 'disruptive laborer within the affective economies that organize the intimate celebrity logic of capitalism', then the 'celesbian couple' can function as the ultimate labour force within neoliberal capitalism for their ability to 'make queer feeling (or feeling queer) appropriate through performances that allow them to draw together that which has been kept apart – the homo and the hetero, the celebrity system and queer politics – within the norms of global capitalism'.[7]

Individual rights and marriage history

In her book, *Marriage, a History: How Love Conquered Marriage*, Stephanie Coontz outlines the history of marriage as a social contract, in which it 'united not just two mates but two sets of families', and love, as the epigraph of this chapter makes clear, was not a concern for those involved until the eighteenth century.[8] This is not an unknown history of course, but in the context of the political movement towards, and in debates about, same-sex marriage rights, which is often sentimentalized by the rhetoric that the fight for equal marriage laws is a fight for the right to love whomever one chooses, it is relevant to remember that the social acceptability of a man and a woman becoming husband and wife based on love and individual choice was already itself a drastic change to the institution of marriage. Coontz also importantly reminds us that the male bread-winner family that was and is still 'seen [as the] traditional and permanent form of marriage' was unique to 'the long decade of the 1950s' when 'never before had so many people agreed that only one kind of family was "normal"'.[9] The notions of traditional marriage and normal family were, of course, strongly critiqued by feminists and other counter culture critics in the 1960s. But the Civil Rights era was also time of pressure for more individual rights for and within marriage. Priscilla Yamin, in her book *American Marriage: A Political Institution*, demonstrates that 'as a right, marriage is meant to secure liberal freedoms and the privileges of full citizenship'.[10] Those liberal freedoms included the end of 'head and master' laws that redefined marriage as being between two equal individuals, of opposite gender, rather than a union of the 'distinct and specialised' roles of a man and a woman.[11] And the privileges of citizenship were extended to mixed-race couples with the 1967 US Supreme Court decision in *Loving v. Virginia*, which declared that marriage is 'one of the "basic civil rights of man" fundamental to our very existence and survival'.[12]

The fight for those freedoms and privileges in marriage for gay and lesbian individuals has been a longer time coming, even though a lawyer pointed out to

President Nixon that the court's declaration opened the possibility of same-sex marriage.[13] Throughout the first decade of the new millennium, there has been a continual back and forth, across the country, between moves towards legalizing same-sex marriage and moves to ban same-sex marriage. As soon as some states made laws in favour of equal marriage or their courts ruled that there was no constitutional reason to ban same-sex marriage, other states would introduce and then pass laws to write bans into their constitutions.[14] Not only has there been a back and forth between states in the progress towards same-sex marriage, there are also many instances of a back and forth within states. California's saga of the fight over Proposition 8 was one of the most high profile, in part because celebrities like Ellen DeGeneres and George Takei wed during the brief 2008 window when same-sex marriage was legal. In 2009, the California Supreme Court ruled the proposition constitutional, then in 2010 a Northern California District Court ruled that the proposition was unconstitutional. Proponents of the law challenged the 2010 ruling by petitioning the US Supreme Court to take the case, and on 26 June 2013, the Supreme Court ruled that the proponents had no standing in the case because the law had not caused them any injury, which meant that the 2010 ruling stood. On the same day, the United States Supreme Court declared section 3 of the Defense of Marriage Act unconstitutional. Since that ruling several state statutes legalizing same-sex marriage have come into force and the courts have declared unconstitutional a series of state bans on same-sex marriage.

The neoliberal logic of marriage

And yet, as Yamin also shows, marriage is not only an individual right; it is also 'an obligation' and as such, 'marriage is seen to structure social, sexual, political, and economic relationships'[15] in part because it is 'defined by its upholders as the "foundation of society" or the "foundation of civilization"'.[16] Consequently, marriage as the legally, socially and, for many, religiously sanctioned form of romantic love and coupledom, as well as the social foundations of parenthood, family and community might seem to be the nation's last bastion against the exclusively individualist ethic of neoliberalism. In its dualistic identity as both 'a romantic contract that individuals make for themselves and the contract which religion and the state impose upon them, a contract of mutual support and responsibility', marriage, especially with children, brings individuals together in groups.[17] The idealized version of the family group based on marriage suggests several things about those individuals: married couples with children live together; the married couple share their resources with each other and their children (and, if able, with parents and siblings in need); adult members of the family who are able, take care of those who are too young, too ill or too old to take care of themselves; all members provide emotional and psychological support; and they are loyal to each other in spite of any differences between them – all because they *love* each other. Admittedly ad hoc and superficial, this sketch of idealized family relationships fits Mary Evans's counter to accounts of neoliberalism that repress the reality of relational needs:

> Conventional accounts of neo-liberalism, and indeed the market economy, all portray the ideal citizen of these worlds as autonomous, self-defining and independent: the kind of person who stands on their own feet, looks after themselves and does not expect others to take care of him or her. Given the human condition, this person is a nonsense: we all need care from birth, through youth and the years of work and parenthood and into old age.[18]

As a group of people whom we expect to care for each other and remain in relationship out of love, married couples and families are often romanticized as being outside of and transcending economic values and market forces.

This view of marriage and the concomitant family is in line with the individual rights development of marriage laws that seem to suggest that marriage is a private sphere that has been removed increasingly from control of the state and separated from the neoliberal economy. However, marriage's relationship to individual rights and privacy is dualistically structured. As a personal commitment between individuals and as a religious institution, marriage exists within the private sphere, but as a legal arrangement formalized and legitimated by the state that offers legal rights and protections as well as tax breaks (over 1,000 in the USA) and financial incentives (e.g. health insurance) marriage is a public institution. Yamin argues that, 'marriage concerns the public realm of citizenship, national identity, civic membership, and economic independence as much as it does the private realm of sex, parenting, relations of dependency, familial roles, inheritance laws, or weddings.'[19] I want to note that money is an element of both these sides of marriage as she describes it: in the terms of 'economic independence', which she situates in the public realm, and 'inheritance laws', which she situates in the private realm. A key example of the state's use and promotion of marriage to implement economic policies is

The Personal Responsibility and Work Opportunity Reconciliation Act of 1996, which replaced the New Deal era federal assistance programme, Aid to Families with Dependent Children, enacted in 1935. The Act prioritizes marriage as the foundation of a stable family and declares that marriage is the best way to end dependence on government benefits.[20] It is not difficult to see how the logic of this programme also constructs other cultural and political expectations in the United States on marriage and the family to be the source of various forms of care and protection. Institutional care, whether residential or home care, for complex and/or long-term psychological and health issues, is not readily available or affordable.[21] Children with severe disabilities or health problems, ageing parents who are frail and/or suffering from dementia, and young adult children who cannot find work, among other myriad examples, are all expected to have families to depend on in their need. My claim then is that government promotion of marriage and family must be understood, at least in part, as neoliberal policy. Marriage, as Yamin argues, 'shapes notions of privacy and conceptions of economic independence from the state'.[22]

Same-sex marriage and homonormativity

Privacy and individual rights are key tenets of the fight for marriage equality, and in the context of marriage history, they can seem naturalized. Lisa Duggan shows how, during the 1990s, politically conservative groups such as the Independent Gay Forum and the Log Cabin (Republicans) National Leadership Conference 'invok[ed] a phantom mainstream public of "conventional" gays who represent the responsible center'. As such, they 'worked to position "liberationsists" and leftists as irresponsible "extremists" or as simply anachronistic'.[23] Through this delegitimization of queer activists, mainstream gay and lesbian rights have become 'a politics that does not contest dominant heteronormative assumptions and institutions but upholds and sustains them while promising the possibility of a demobilized gay constituency and a privatized, depoliticized gay culture anchored in domesticity and consumption'.[24] The neoliberal rhetoric of 'the new homonormativity' co-opts the language of equality, choice, and freedom in order to promote same-sex marriage and puts marriage forward as the most important, if not the only, signifier of equality and gay rights; marriage then, she argues, 'is a strategy for privatizing gay politics and culture for the new neoliberal world order'.[25] More recently, in her ethnographic research, Jaye Cee Whitehead has shown how grassroots activists in the marriage equality movement also use this rhetoric of neoliberal sexual politics established by the IGF and its associated writers. She focuses on 'the synthesis activists forge between "protections" and "responsibilities"'[26] and the 'strategies of self-governance that contemporary marriage embodies'[27]; these include: being the recognized next-of-kin; support during unemployment; independence from government benefits (one couple notes that they can both claim welfare since they can both claim head of household and that being married would save the government money); companionship and shared resources during major life events (e.g. parenthood, retirement). Additionally, they suggested that equal marriage rights were 'the solution to the fear of living as a socially stigmatized population' because they had accepted marriage as 'an institution with the productive, regulatory power to create normative acceptance of gays and lesbians as full citizens'.[28] Critics of mainstream same-sex marriage activism have pointed out that the exclusive focus on marriage as a route to these benefits has the potential consequences of reducing the benefits of gay and lesbian couples in civil unions who do not wish to get married.[29]

It is important to remember that as Michael Warner argues in his book *The Trouble with Normal*, 'Marriage … is selective legitimacy. … To a couple that gets married, marriage just looks ennobling. … Stand outside it for a second and you see the implication: if you don't have it, you and your relations are less worthy.'[30] However, marriage's power to include and exclude is so normalized and naturalized that we cannot easily resist its invitation. In his polemical book, *Single: Arguments for the Uncoupled*, Michael Cobb rightly argues against any simplistic patronizing of gay and lesbian couples who choose marriage where it is legal or to fight for it where it is not:

> the audacious and too-easy characterization of queers-gone-bad into the fight for wedlock does not take into account just how necessary the marriage form and its not-so-distant child, the couple form, are for intimate stability. And not only intimate stability: judicial, political, and cultural legibility that belongs to and exceeds official state regulation.[31]

No doubt many activists on both sides of the same-sex marriage debate feel ambivalence towards the institution of marriage in all that it offers and withholds. As a straight, married woman who wore a white dress on her wedding day, I can only confess my own ambivalence and internal fight over the feminist critiques of marriage that I hold true and the legal benefits and protections marriage allows me and my husband who are not citizens of the same country. But in the midst of that ambivalence we must recognize the hegemonic power of marriage to co-opt more of us into neoliberal forms of citizenship and community that are individualistic and exclusive. I would suggest that all married celebrity couples contribute to the image of marriage as the best route to intimate stability, but my focus here on Ellen DeGeneres and Portia de Rossi's situates that discourse in the extra-ambivalent image of the lesbian wedding and marriage.

Ellen and the spectacle of lesbian celebrity coupledom

Oprah Winfrey has said of Ellen DeGeneres, 'I don't believe she would have been as successful as she has become had she not come out.' Today, the audience figures for *The Ellen DeGeneres Show* (through which she has arguably taken over from Oprah as Queen of daytime television) alongside DeGeneres's various celebrity endorsement gigs, as well as her regular appearance in celebrity magazines and internet sites suggest that she is 'the most famous'[32] and 'the most popular' lesbian in America.[33] However, there was a time it seemed, after the 1998 cancellation of her sitcom and the public failure of her relationship with Anne Heche that, as Ellen herself remarked, coming out 'had destroyed her career'. Jamie Skerski articulates clearly how DeGeneres's career has followed a 'complicated rise, fall and resurrection' narrative that is marked by the politicization and depoliticization of her identity.[34] Published in 2007, before DeGeneres's marriage to De Rossi, Skerski's narrative of DeGeneres's career ends at a time when the talk show host declared to the *New York Times*, 'I'm just not a political person.'[35] Arguably, her marriage has brought politics back into her identity, though I hope to show that it is a politics produced through the affective work of her and De Rossi's combined identity as a married celesbian couple and circumscribed by commodity activism and celebrity branding.

DeGeneres and De Rossi's successful and sustained celesbian coupling contrasts sharply with DeGeneres's first celebrity coupling, which Skerski suggests, I think rightly, was one of the reasons the ABC network cancelled her sitcom *Ellen* in 1998. The year before, DeGeneres began dating Anne Heche, who was starring in the film *Wag the Dog* (Levinson, 1997) with Robert DeNiro and Dustin Hoffman. They acted like any other star couple, holding hands on the red carpet and getting photographed while shopping and putting their arms around each other at a White House dinner, which the *New York Times* called an 'ostentatious display of affection with her lover in front of President Clinton'.[36] But by virtue of their difference they became a Hollywood super-spectacle with several stories in *People* magazine closely surveilling their public displays of affection. It wasn't long until ABC cancelled *Ellen*, stating that the reason was not gayness, but sameness, because it 'became a program about a lead character who was gay every single week'. And yet, as Skerski argues, 'ABC could arguably control the content of *Ellen* … ABC had no way to constrain what DeGeneres and Heche did or said in public, nor what various media publicized about the couple … ABC had no way of responding rhetorically to DeGeneres' life *outside* the sitcom'.[37] In light of Christine Geraghty's suggestion that 'the term celebrity indicates someone whose fame rests overwhelmingly on what happens outside the sphere of their work and who is famous for having a lifestyle',[38] this, then, is effectively the moment when DeGeneres became a celebrity rather than a 'television personality',[39] when the media interest in her personal life superseded the interest in her television show. And though she and Heche may have been doing only all the 'normal' things other couples do in public, their spectacle as the first openly lesbian celebrity couple was inevitably abject within the terms of compulsory heterosexuality, a view confirmed for many when Heche had an infamous, psychotic break – she knocked on a stranger's door in her underwear and declared herself God – the day after they broke up. Irving Rein et al have suggested that 'industrialized celebrity [creates a space] in which individuals … can be elevated to a level of visibility unimaginable at any other time – and be compensated with imaginable rewards'.[40] Though the economic value of visibility for celebrities seems fairly obvious such a view cannot take into account the risks of visibility for persons of marginalized identities. The political value of 'coming out' as gay or lesbian has been a significant part of the gay civil rights movement, and though DeGeneres was lauded by many at the time, the swift and strong backlash from conservatives that peaked with the cancellation of her show and her very public break up with Heche meant that the value of her visibility plummeted and she did little work for two years. In an interview with Larry King, she said 'The phone stopped ringing and nobody was interested in anything to do with me'.[41]

The consequences of the high visibility of DeGeneres's coming out appears to have directly affected her decision not to be vocal about her sexuality in the early days of her new daytime talk show, *The Ellen DeGeneres Show*. In a 2004 interview, DeGeneres declared that she had 'no baby lust and no desire for legally sanctioned gay marriage' and that 'I never had that fantasy of a wedding'.[42] After the fallout from DeGeneres's coming out on both her show and on the cover of

Time magazine, her high-profile relationship and its break up, and the failure of her second sitcom, she told Larry King that 'a lot of station managers ... were afraid to buy the show, because they thought she's going to talk about being gay ... it's going to be political'. King replied, 'In fact, your show doesn't have an agenda, so to speak, you're not there to prove a point,' to which DeGeneres agreed.[43] Jennifer Reed suggests that 'the show seems to address stay-at-home moms and other people who are at home during the day, and thus is not exactly queer. ... On the other hand, the cultural work she is doing here, in part through the cumulative effect of her presence as a lesbian on television is allowing her to carve out space for lesbian subjectivity.'[44] Linda Mizejewski argues that this space – or this new, positive, visibility of her celebrity – is made possible by 'the niceness of DeGeneres's public image', which she suggests is 'not ... a diminishment or disavowal of her butch appearance but rather ... a powerful force that has impact through her butch-style body.'[45] Mizejewski persuasively analyses the potential political force of DeGeneres's body through the affective work that she performs through her dancing, easy-going interviews with kids and stars, and her self-deprecation in the humorous displays of her inability to perform femininity or fulfil the demands of heteronormativity (the latter of which appear both on her show and in her product endorsements). The political force of her 'butch' body – signalled through her dress style of trousers, t-shirts, blazers and sneaker – necessarily depends on the mainstream context of her show as articulated by Reed above.[46] The political force of her body is furthered in the juxtaposition with her 'femme' wife de Rossi, but it is also, as I suggest below, made consumable in that juxtaposition.

Ellen and Portia's postfeminist 'celesbian' wedding

Mizejewski says that, 'no matter how bourgeois and consumable some of her images may be, such as clowning with Justin Bieber on her talk show, it is impossible to unremember more transgressive images, such as posing with her bride on the cover of *People* magazine'.[47] Those images of DeGeneres and de Rossi's wedding in *People* magazine cannot help but disrupt the heteronormativity of the wedding photo genre in their undeniable lesbianism. In one photo from the time of their engagement, which appears to be at a red-carpet event, they stand cheek to cheek, while de Rossi holds up her left hand with the large diamond engagement ring on her fourth finger, which DeGeneres points at with her right hand. The pose recognizably signals that they have become engaged and they are smiling with the slightly sheepish grins of two people who cannot help but share how happy they are. It is easy to imagine a heterosexual couple in the same image. The wedding photos are glamorous, with the women in designer Zac Posen outfits, and in the *People* magazine spread they include an array of 'typical' wedding poses: standing with their arms around each other, smiles on their faces in the apparent moment after they have been declared; holding hands while walking across a lawn with their heads turned towards the camera behind them (a pose often used to show off the bride's wedding dress); forks with a bite of wedding cake raised as they are about to feed each other; and one with their foreheads touching, arms around each other's waists, an apparent first-dance photo. Like most wedding photos, they are romanticized through the emphasis on clasped hands and the use of soft focus, thereby both assimilating lesbian identity into heteronormative wedding culture and yet, importantly, still queering it in the image of two women, now married. The visibility of each women's individual celebrity, like with all celebrity wedding photos, is amplified in the process of coming together as a celebrity couple, while at the same time, their visibility as a butch/femme celebrity couple also makes visible their queerness: 'In a culture where heterosexuality has a naturalized status, butch/ femme visibility can be seen as destabilizing, constituting queer space through transgressive practices and gender performances.'[48]

Both the engagement and wedding photos are signifiers of 'the labors of celesbianism', which are defined by 'the perpetual production of good feelings that accrue value through their exchange'.[49] The affective labour of celebrity culture, and DeGeneres's celesbianism, materialized on her show when she announced the engagement to the studio audience, who spontaneously burst into applause. The inclusion of her audience and fans in the couples' personal life happens again through the wedding video they made and aired on DeGeneres's talk show. What, at the time of the event, was an intimate wedding for the couple and fewer than thirty guests, became an open invitation for their millions of fans to take part in this intimacy.

The widespread acceptance of that invitation may well be predicated on DeGeneres's 'white blondness' which 'is the iconic identity of the girl next door' and the ways her 'butch image plays perfectly well as tomboy next door' that make her show so hugely popular with so widespread a mainstream audience who see Ellen as just 'being herself'.[50] And yet, the video as a conduit of 'para-social' or 'second-hand' intimacy that is both a commodity of celebrity but also a relationship between 'star/celebrity and fan/consumer' that creates a 'productive, surplus emotionality that cannot be easily channeled or "sucked up" by capitalism, and which offers people transgressive models of identity' also invites the fans to be witnesses to, and by implication, supporters of a queer and, arguably, politicized event.[51] It may seem obvious to say, but because of the context of the same-sex marriage debates and the intimacy they offer to the public, the wedding photos and video cannot function exclusively as an expression of individualism. They are the public declaration of two persons becoming a couple, a new entity in the eyes of the law and the public. If, as Dyer says, stars and celebrities 'articulate what it is to be a human being in contemporary society',[52] then DeGeneres's and de Rossi's celebrity wedding invites viewers to see being lesbian as what it is 'to be a human being' because it situates transgressive sexuality within mainstream, heteronormative ideas of what it is 'to be a human being': love, romance and marriage.

At the same time, the photos and video also 'invoke ... credos of homonormativity, postfeminism, and neoliberalism' because they 'downplay homosexuality as a form of significant difference'. Joselyn Leimbach suggests in her analysis of television personalities Rachel Maddow and Suze Orman that 'homonormative conventions mark individuals within LGB communities as indistinguishable from heterosexuals ... and that they walk a fine line between remaining accessible to the masses while being open ... about their lesbianism'.[53] The engagement and wedding photos of DeGeneres and de Rossi can be read as downplaying the difference between homosexuality and heterosexuality through their butch and femme styles which seem to evoke heteronormativity: DeGeneres's trousers, collared shirt and vest along with her short hair marks her as the more masculine of the two, while de Rossi's low-cut dress, sparkly jewellery, long hair and make-up mark her as the feminine bride-to-be. The homonormative performance in the photos is reinforced by the heteronormative engagement script they followed: DeGeneres asked de Rossi to marry her and only de Rossi wore an engagement ring. In the wedding video, DeGeneres, in her white tuxedo, waits by herself in a courtyard; a moment later de Rossi appears at a door and walks into the courtyard revealing her as the bride – her hair is in an updo and the halter-neck satin dress she wears has a pale pink meringue skirt. The homonormativity of the imagery is buttressed by the performance of 'ordinariness': we see both women helping to set the long table for the few guests who will attend the wedding in their own home. The most important guests who are highlighted in the video include both women's mothers – each of whom speaks to the camera – and Ellen's father and brother whom we see in still photos spliced into the video. And yet, as much as the video works to remind viewers that the two women are 'normal' and just like us – they want to find 'the one' and get married in front of their family and friends[54] – it has to also remind us that they are not like us when it includes a few seconds of the pair 'running away' from the paparazzi. Trying to avoid the paparazzi is a key trope of the celebrity wedding – from Madonna and Sean Penn to Brad Pitt and Angelina Jolie – it functions simultaneously as an indicator of the celebrities' attempt to keep their private life private, while also making the official images that are taken worth much more as commodities of their celebrity identity.

Weddings, then, are a key episode in the narrativization of celebrity identity and its commodification. And weddings, as Diane Negra has argued, are a key stage in the postfeminist temporalization of women's lives around events that mark the achievement of sexual maturity and motherhood.[55] More importantly for this chapter, she points out that these lifecycle moments are governed by conformity and neo-traditionalism. Rosalind Gill and Angela McRobbie have also noted the resurgence of the white wedding and marriage culture – which, as Negra shows, includes multiple bridal showers, bachelorette parties and extended honeymoons – as indicative of postfeminism's double bind of independence and traditionalism as well as its emphasis on consumerism to signify both. However, all these critics understand postfeminism as being resolutely heteronormative. Yvonne Tasker and Negra have argued that postfeminism 'rejects lesbianism [except when] divested of potentially feminist associations and invested with sexualized glamour.'[56] It seems to me that from a feminist and queer critique the spectre that haunts DeGeneres's and de Rossi's wedding is the single person, particularly the single woman who is regularly set up as the straw woman of postfeminism.[57] Whether straight or queer, the single woman cannot fulfil the postfeminist ideal of the traditional family structure that tempers the threat of her success, if she is wealthy, or her failure, if she is poor. To some extent then, DeGeneres's and de Rossi's celebrity wedding photos alter the postfeminist media representation of the lesbian who used to be the bad object of postfeminism. The lesbian who was regularly represented as a caricature of radical feminism has now been co-opted into postfeminism through same-sex marriage. The postfeminist traditionalism and homonormativity that structures the narrative of their relationship – from the engagement ring to the frothy pink wedding – reached another plot point in 2010 when de Rossi legally changed her name to Portia DeGeneres.

Figure 11.1 Portia de Rossi visits *The Ellen DeGeneres Show* as a guest to promote her new sitcom and to celebrate the couple's seven-month anniversary. Screen grab.

As critics of postfeminism have shown, consumerism and the display of wealth (as long as it's within good taste) are at the heart of its project, especially before the financial crash of late 2008. The *People* magazine spread describes the wedding as intimate with only nineteen guests at the couples' own home. However, the images also show off the wealth and tasteful lifestyle of that home which has extensive and immaculate grounds and a large pool. The couple and their home were profiled in *Architectural Digest*, just like Brad Pitt and Angelina Jolie were, and the article and the photos show off the couple's good taste, their investment in the property, and highlights their healthy (they are both vegan) and eco-conscious living. The conspicuous consumption that structures a celebrity spread in *Architectural Digest* and the personal information about the couple's diet is emblematic of how 'contemporary culture is organized around the semiotics of elitism with a heavy stress on luxury commodities and experiences as transformative, renewing, and life-affirming'.[58] In the years before the Great Recession, as Diane Negra suggests, the most common luxury commodities on display for the middle classes and up the income scale were 'consumerist tokens of marriage and family life', such as showcase homes, SUVs and large diamond rings. In the context of Proposition 8, which ended same-sex marriage in California, the feature story, printed two years before equal marriage rights were restored in the State, cannot help but also carry some political meaning in its representation of the lesbian couple and the ways that 'femme style and presence more clearly marks butch and androgynous women as lesbian' and by extension, the femme as lesbian.[59] However, the conspicuous consumption, the hyperdomesticity, their coupledom and the DeGeneres's whiteness all work to soften the semiotic disruptiveness of their lesbianism.

Neoliberal ethics of self-care within marriage

The hyperdomesticity of postfeminist culture, as Negra says, is imbricated 'in a neoliberal political environment in which the family is increasingly charged with taking over the responsibilities of the state' and that 'at a basic level, postfeminist culture manages the decline of social health by emphasizing the importance of personal (physical and emotional) health in an individualized, isolated context'.[60] The latter point about emotional health in an individualized context shows how the twenty-first century postfeminist, neoliberal context structures de Rossi's coming out narrative in contrast to DeGeneres's in important ways. Before DeGeneres's coming out, both as her fictional character on television and as a celebrity in the public eye, there was widespread speculation about her sexuality and some critics argue that queer viewers regularly read between the lines of her show before the infamous episode when she admits she is gay to her therapist, played by Oprah Winfrey. Though her public coming out seemed to fail the political expectations on her when she disappeared from the public eye, it did, as Skerski has shown, make a 'mark on gay visibility', evidenced by the website After-Ellen.com which 'tracks lesbian and bisexual women's visibility in contemporary television and film'.[61] Meanwhile, as a cast member of the television show *Ally McBeal*, de Rossi kept her sexuality a secret from her family and all her co-workers; in her autobiography she says that the cancellation of DeGeneres's show convinced her that she could never come out and be successful in Hollywood.[62] Ultimately, tabloids outed her by publishing pictures of her and her girlfriend at the time. And yet, de Rossi specifically articulates her coming out within her relationship with DeGeneres by describing her first public appearance with DeGeneres at the 2005 Golden Globes award as 'the first time I'd stepped out as a gay woman, really'.[63] Since she had previously told Oprah Winfrey that hiding her sexuality 'ruined me ... really killed me', their coupledom is presented as central to her own individual identity and empowerment.[64]

In fact, de Rossi credits DeGeneres with saving her life. While playing the hard-nosed Nelle Porter on *Ally McBeal* de Rossi, like the show's star Calista Flockhart, was conspicuously thin. She reportedly got down to 82 pounds on her five-foot, eight-inch body. In her autobiography, *Unbearable Lightness: A Story of Loss and Gain*, de Rossi links her anorexia and her hidden sexuality. She tells the story of how, for a period, she saw a nutritionist regularly to try to stop her extreme fluctuations in weight from binging and purging and short-term diets of 300 calories a day before photo shoots. During one session, her nutritionist queries whether Portia is actually consuming the 1,400 calories she recommended and asks to see de Rossi's food journal. It turns out that de Rossi keeps two journals: one for her nutritionist that shows 1,400 calories of food for each day, and one for herself where she counts the 800 or fewer calories that she actually consumes each day. The latter has 'motivational' notes in it to herself. Many are variations on the harshest one she shares: 'YOU ARE A FAT UGLY DYKE.'[65] Not wanting to be a 'fat ugly dyke' were her motivations for staying so thin. Paradoxically, being so thin made her feel that she looked good in bikini photo shoots while also making her unattractive to men; she could keep working in Hollywood and avoid any sexual tension with the opposite sex in whom she was not interested.[66] Though she had recovered from her anorexia by the time she met DeGeneres (and she gives a lot of credit to her girlfriend Francesca Gregorini for helping her come to terms with her sexuality and her eating), she says that she still struggled with 'disordered' eating because she weighed 168 pounds and could not end her tendency to binge. She describes DeGeneres's love as emotional healing and self-acceptance: 'Ellen saw a glimpse of my inner being from underneath the flesh and bone, reached in, and pulled me out.'[67] She also writes that after reading a draft of de Rossi's autobiography, DeGeneres said that she wished she could have saved her. De Rossi responds to her in this way: 'You did save me. You save me everyday.'[68]

The publication of her autobiography was an occasion for her to be a guest on *The Ellen DeGeneres* show (see Figure 11.1). In their conversation about the book and de Rossi's anorexia, de Rossi talks about how ugly she felt, and immediately DeGeneres says that she thinks de Rossi is beautiful; de Rossi gets a bit teary and shy and they hold hands while the audience claps fairly wildly. I don't want to discount the authenticity of this moment for the couple, but it also contributes to the construction of their relationship as the restorative means by which de Rossi became well. The narrative fits squarely within the neoliberal insistence on individual self-care; but, importantly, in this instance it is self-care that is found in a relationship. The importance of DeGeneres's acceptance and love for de Rossi's health is magnified by the talk show audience's acceptance and approval of them as a couple; within the terms of the 'celesbian' couple's constant 'production of good feeling', the care of the self in the context of the couple is not complete until is also made public. This narrative of both personal and public acceptance and the commodification of their celebrity coupledom through the glamorous wedding photos and the promotion of de Rossi's book on the show means that they exemplify 'the fusion of celebrity emulation, luxury consumerism and self-care' of neoliberal postfeminist culture.[69] Doing so as lesbians means that they disrupt the compulsory heterosexuality of postfeminism while, at the same time, fulfilling its demands for hyperdomesticity and performing the neoliberal logic of marriage as a privatized source of health care, all of which, in the contemporary neoliberal culture, to justify the value of same-sex marriage and to be justified by it.

The politics of the celesbian couple

Since their wedding, being a celesbian couple has given both DeGeneres and de Rossi the opportunity to intervene in the same-sex marriage debate in the US. De Rossi in particular has spoken out in interviews for cover stories in *The Advocate, Out Magazine, LA Confidential* magazine and others. She has said, 'Gay marriage is the idea whose time has come … it really is the last civil rights issue we are going to have to deal with in this country.'[70] The latter point is naïve and problematic in its omission of everything from the rights of transgender persons to the regular infringement of the civil rights of persons of colour. However, it does fall in line with the history of marriage as a key signifier of individual rights in the United States and its power as a sign of cultural acceptance. DeGeneres draws on this language of civil rights and citizenship in her open letter 'brief' to the US Supreme Court in 2013 when it was deciding on the validity of the proponents in the case to uphold Proposition 8. In the jokey brief, she says that her marriage has not hurt anyone else's marriage; she mentions the 1,138 federal rights for married couples unavailable to her and de Rossi; she says that it will make 'kids feel better about who they are', and then she jokes that Benjamin Franklin said, 'We're here, we're queer, get over it.'[71] Before that her most high-profile intervention into the same-sex marriage debates was in early 2012 when the conservative group One Million Moms called for JC Penney to remove DeGeneres as their spokesperson. On her talk show, Ellen responded to the group's call by making fun of them. She says 'if they have problem with spokespeople, what about the Pillsbury Dougboy? He runs around without any pants on' and that 'they only have 40,000 members on their Facebook page; they're rounding up to the nearest million. I get that.' She shares comments on the group's Facebook statement (which declares the company will lose people with Christian values) from responders who now plan to shop at the store to support DeGeneres. More than once she states that she doesn't usually talk about these things on her show. She begins the bit by congratulating the

California Supreme Court for declaring Proposition 8 unconstitutional, which gets a strong applaud from the crowd. Halfway through she mentions that JC Penney rejected the call to drop her and stood by her as a spokesperson, which receives an even louder and longer audience applause that includes shouts and whoops.[72] The episode manifests the 'paradoxes of celebrity patronage and corporate philanthropy – both as showy spectacles that build brand loyalty, star iconicity, and profits and as openings for critical thought and action'.[73]

It is not insignificant that DeGeneres's coming out and the attention to her personal life with Anne Heche in the late 1990s temporarily ruined her career and threw her out of the public eye, functioning in Neil Ewen's terms as a 'bad celebrity couple',[74] and that, twenty years later, her lesbian marriage and personal life with Portia de Rossi has only increased her visibility as a celebrity. This new relationship has given Ellen a personal life that the public are interested in, which she is happy to include on her show, and which has prompted her to return to speaking about the politics of her sexuality as they are related to that personal life. This makes Ellen and Portia, in Ewen's terms, a 'good celebrity couple' (or, more to the point, a good 'celesbian' couple). It is also important to remember that though marriage performs citizenship in its inclusion of new members, it always excludes others as well. The homonormative imagery, postfeminist lifestyle and whiteness of the DeGeneres's as a high-profile celesbian couple inevitably contributes to the exclusion of those queer persons who are poor, persons of colour, transgender persons, and others who remain the scapegoats for the contradictory alliance of neoliberalism and social conservatism.

Since their marriage the DeGeneres continue to do the work of the 'perpetual production of good feeling' required of the celesbian (couple) in contemporary neoliberal culture. de Rossi regularly appears on DeGeneres's show: to debut her new haircut, to announce that she has become a US citizen, to give Ellen a birthday gift, to be interviewed about her new role on the show *Scandal* and more. Their celebrity coupledom continues to invest in that 'good feeling' that 'accrues value in exchange'. In the current context in which same-sex marriage is not yet national that value is inextricably both politicized and commodified. Most recently, rumours that the couple are expecting a baby circulated in the celebrity tabloid press, and in the midst of DeGeneres's interview with de Rossi about her new role on *Scandal*, the two responded to the rumours by pointing to a celebrity magazine that declared they were 'finally starting a family' and joking 'are people really that mad at us?' There is an implicit attempt in this moment to use the commodity value of their celesbian coupledom to resist this pressure to normative production of a family from a marriage. In the midst of the good feeling produced by the celesbian couple it remains true that,

> while legal debates surrounding marriage equality have effectively called attention to the fact that reproduction need not proceed from heterosexual unions in order for them to be recognizably legitimate, it should be noted that queer lives and pleasures remain to a significant extent measured negatively in terms of what they fail to reproduce, a valuation that has a long history of constructing queer pleasures as hedonistic, irresponsible, immoral, futureless, and failed.[75]

Several celebrity gay couples have brought children into their lives – from Elton John and David Furnis and Neil Patrick Harris and David Burtka to Jodie Foster and Cydney Barnard and Rosie O'Donnell and Kelli Carpenter. It remains to be seen if the DeGeneres's celesbian coupledom has enough commodity and political exchange value to continue to resist the demand for parenthood to be the logical next step in their marriage. By forgoing the next 'postfeminist lifecycle' of motherhood, the DeGenereses are realigned with the spectre of the single woman, mentioned above, and other married women who choose not to have children (both, in celebrity culture, exemplified by Jennifer Aniston). That opting out of motherhood draws single, married, straight and queer women together under the critical gaze of postfeminist culture suggests that 'the new momism' may well be the 'central, justifying ideology of postfeminism'.[76]

Conclusion

I began this chapter with Suzanne Leonard's claim that 'postfeminist culture both assumes and creates a female subject who desires marriage' and ended with Susan Douglas and Meredith Michael's claim that 'the new momism' is the ideological force behind postfeminism. As Diane Negra argues, 'such rituals … all celebrate the achievement of sexual maturity, marriage, or motherhood, and thus one of the consequences of the heightened ritualization milestones in the normative female lifecycle is that the lives of women without these experiences are temporarily unmapped'.[77] My analysis of Ellen and Portia's wedding suggests that, at least in today's media sphere of celebrity culture, lesbian women's exclusion from some of these milestones in the postfeminist lifecycle can no longer be presumed, bearing in mind the (geographically limited) availability of same-sex marriage. Of course, marriage is always, at best, ambivalent in its dualistic nature. As Yamin states: 'It is not merely oppressive and utilized to regulate behavior; nor is it simply progressively emancipatory and egalitarian. Marriage is a source of recognition, reward, and inclusion as much as it is a source of coercion, hierarchy, and exclusion.'[78] The affective labour of DeGeneres and de Rossi's celesbian coupledom functions queerly in the ways that it both performs homonormativity and transgressive lesbianism within what, we might argue, is the foundation of hegemonic heteronormativity: marriage. And though marriage can be seen to contrast the neoliberal aggrandization of the individual, it also can be used as a tool of neoliberalism and postfeminism to contribute to both legal and social exclusion. Lesbian and gay celebrity couples are clearly contributing to the campaign for equal marriage rights, but a close look at DeGeneres and de Rossi's celebrity coupledom shows that same-sex marriage is not exempt from the conservative ideologies of neoliberalism and postfeminism.

Acknowledgements

A profound thank you to Professor Dana Heller who graciously and generously shared a revised version of a paper on the 'celesbian' that she gave at the Celebrity Studies Conference in 2014. And many thanks to Neil Ewen for the advice and help in revising this chapter.

Notes

1   Stephanie Coontz, *Marriage, a History: How Love Conquered Marriage* (New York: Penguin Group, 2005), 15.

2   Frank Rich, 'In Conversation with Chris Rock: What's Killing Comedy. What's Saving America', *New York Magazine*, 30 November 2014, http://www.vulture.com/2014/11/chris-rock-frank-rich-in-conversation.html.

3   Jennifer Reed, 'Ellen DeGeneres', *Feminist Media Studies* 5, no. 2 (2005): 35.

4   Jennifer Reed, 'Lesbian Television Personalities – A New Queer Subject', *The Journal of American Culture* 32, no. 4 (December 2009): 312.

5   Joselyn Leimbach, 'Strengthening as They Undermine: Rachel Maddow and Suze Orman's Homonormative Lesbian Identities', in *In the Limelight and Under the Microscope*, ed. Su Holmes and Diane Negra (London: Continuum, 2011), 261, note 608, Kindle version.

6 Suzanne Leonard, 'Marriage Envy', *Women's Studies Quarterly* 34, no. 3/4 (Fall–Winter 2006): 55.

7 Dana Heller, 'Mixed Feelings: Queer Pleasure and the Labors of "Celesbianism"', unpublished paper from Celebrity Studies Conference 2014. Though 'celesbianism' is a term that appeared first in the media and has acquired some currency in academic scholarship, my use of the term is indebted to Dana Heller and her definition of it quoted here. Heller very generously sent me an updated copy of that paper, from which all the references to her work in this chapter are taken.

8 Coontz, *Marriage, a History*, 25.

9 Ibid., 229.

10 Priscilla Yamin, *American Marriage*, 1–2.

11 Coontz, *Marriage, a History*, 255.

12 Legal Information Institute, Cornell University Law School, sec: Supreme Court, http://www.law.cornell.edu/supremecourt/text/388/1.

13 When this was pointed out to President Nixon, he reportedly said: 'I can't go for that far – that's the year 2000!' See John Ehrlichman, *Witness to Power: The Nixon Years* (New York: Simon and Schuster, 1982), 239.

14 Priscilla Yamin argues that state marriage laws changing in waves is common throughout American history: 'states are influenced by each other, so that when one state passes a law, other states often follow suit. Witness how changes in state marriage laws occur in waves, such as the married women's property acts passed between 1848 and 1895, followed by the eugenic marriage laws that began in 1896 and were in existence until the mid-twentieth century, and the more recent proliferation of state constitutional and statutory bans on same-sex marriage'; see Priscilla Yasmin, *American Marriage: A Political Institution* (Philadelphia: University of Pennsylvania Press, 2012), 15.

15 Ibid., 2.

16 Ibid., 3.

17 Mary Evans, 'Love in a Time of Neoliberalism', OpenDemocracy.net, 6 November 2014, https://www.opendemocracy.net/transformation/mary-evans/love-in-time-of-neo-liberalism.

18 Mary Evans, 'Love in a Time of Neoliberalism'.

19 Priscilla Yamin, *American Marriage*, 6.

20 Quoted in ibid., 112.

21 Though Obamacare requires parity between mental and physical health care coverage, the resources for assistance for any long-term mental or physical health issue are scarce.

22 Ibid., 3–4.

23 Lisa Duggan, 'The New Homonormativity: The Sexual Politics of Neoliberalism', in *Materializing Democracy: Toward a Revitalized Cultural Politics*, ed. Russ Castronovo and Dana D. Nelson (London: Duke University Press, 2002), 179.

24 Duggan, 'The New Homonormativity', 179.

25 Ibid., 188.

26 Jaye Cee Whitehead, 'Risk, Marriage, and Neoliberal Governance: Learning from the Unwillingly Excluded', *The Sociological Quarterly* 52 (2011): 294.

27 Jaye Cee Whitehead, 'Risk, Marriage, and Neoliberal Governance', 297.

28 Ibid., 304.

29 See Katherine M. Franke, 'Marriage is a Mixed Blessing', *New York Times*, 23 June 2011.

30 Michael Warner, *The Trouble with Normal: Sex, Politics, and the Ethics of Queer Life* (Cambridge, MA: Harvard University Press, 1999), 82.

31 Michael Cobb, *Single: Arguments for the* Uncoupled (New York: New York University Press, 2012), 19.

32 Jennifer Reed, 'Ellen DeGeneres: Public Lesbian Number One', *Feminist Media Studies* 5, no. 1 (2005): 23.

33 Jamie Skerski, 'From Prime-Time to Daytime: The Domestication of Ellen DeGeneres', *Communication and Critical/Cultural Studies* 4, no. 4 (December 2007): 364.

34 Jamie Skerski, 'From Prime-Time to Daytime', 364.

35 Quoted in ibid., 363.

36 Quoted in Linda Mizejewski, *Pretty/Funny: Women Comedians and Body Politics* (Austin: University of Texas Press, 2014), 198.

37 Jamie Skerski, 'From Prime-Time to Daytime', 374.

38 Christine Geraghty, 'Re-examining Stardom: Questions of Texts, Bodies and Performance', in *Stardom and Celebrity: A Reader*, ed. Sean Redmond and Su Holmes (London: SAGE Publications, 2007), 99.

39 See James Bennett, *Television Personalities: Stardom and the Small Screen* (London: Routledge, 2011).

40 Irving Rein, Philip Kotler and Martin Stoller, eds, *High Visibility: The Making and Marketing of Professionals into Celebrities* (Lincolnwood: NTC Business Books, 1997), 1–2.

41 Interview with Ellen DeGeneres, CNN Larry King Live, aired 7 September 2004, cnn.com, http://transcripts.cnn.com/TRANSCRIPTS/0409/07/lkl.01.html.

42 Quoted in Jamie Skerski, 'From Prime-Time to Daytime', 376.

43 Interview with Ellen DeGeneres, CNN Larry King Live, aired 7 September 2004, cnn.com, http://transcripts.cnn.com/TRANSCRIPTS/0409/07/lkl.01.html.

44 Jennifer Reed, 'Ellen DeGeneres', *Feminist Media Studies* 5, no. 1 (2005): 33.

45 Linda Mizejewski, *Pretty/Funny*, 216.

46 It is important to remember that DeGeneres passed as heterosexual on her sitcom before the coming out episode, though her appearance has remained relatively consistent; see Helene A. Shugart, 'Performing Ambiguity: The Passing of Ellen DeGeneres', *Text and Performance Quarterly* 23, no. 1 (January 2013): 30–54. Her butch body, then, must be understood as such in the context of her coming out and in the context of postfeminism's emphasis on hyper-femininity as the norm for all women.

47 Linda Mizejewski, *Pretty/Funny*, 217.

48 Alison Eves, 'Queer Theory, Butch/Femme Identities and Lesbian Space', *Sexualities* 74, no. 4 (2004): 492.

49 Dana Heller, 'Mixed Feelings: Queer Pleasure and the Labors of "Celesbianism"', unpublished conference paper.

50 Linda Mizejewski, *Pretty/Funny*, 204, 208.

51 Sean Redmond, 'Intimate Fame Everywhere', in *Framing Celebrity: New Directions in Celebrity Culture*, ed. Su Holmes and Sean Redmond (London: Routledge, 2006), 38.

52 Richard Dyer, 'Heavenly Bodies', in *Stardom and Celebrity: A Reader*, ed. Sean Redmond and Su Holmes (London: SAGE Publications, 2010), 87.

53 Joselyn Leimbach, 'Strengthening as They Undermine: Rachel Maddow and Suze Orman's Homonormative Lesbian Identities', in *In the Limelight and Under the Microscope*, ed. Su Holmes and Diane Negra (London: Continuum, 2011), 243, Kindle version.

54 Suzanne Leonard argues that 'marital aspirations circumscribe understandings of female subjectivity, to the point that women who are not desirous of weddings and marriages, or who do not envy those women who can obtain them, are looked upon as "abnormal"'. See Leonard, 'Marriage Envy', 50.

55 Diane Negra, *What a Girl Wants: Fantasizing the Reclamation of Self in Postfeminism* (New York: Routledge, 2009). For the ways weddings construct heterosexuality, see Chris Ingraham, *White Weddings: Romancing Heterosexuality in Popular Culture* (London: Routledge, 2008).

56 Yvonne Tasker and Diane Negra, *Interrogating Postfeminism: Gender and the Politics of Popular Culture* (London: Routledge, 2007), 21.

57 See Anthea Taylor, *Single Women in Popular Culture: The Limits of Postfeminism* (Basingstoke: Palgrave-Macmillan, 2012).

58 Diane Negra, 125.

59 Eves, 'Queer Theory', 494–95.

60 Diane Negra, *What a Girl Wants*, 118, 134.

61 Skerski, 'From Prime-Time to Daytime', 365.

62 Portia de Rossi, *Unbearable Lightness: A Story of Loss and Gain* (New York: Simon & Schuster, 2010), 28.

63 Breeanna Hare, 'Portia de Rossi: The First Time I Truly Came out', cnn.com, 8 November 2013, http://edition.cnn.com/2013/11/08/showbiz/celebrity-news-gossip/portia-de-rossi-gay/.

64 James Nichols, 'Porita de Rossi Reveals Why She Just Didn't Want To Be a Lesbian', huffingtonpost.com, 1 November, 2013, http://www.huffingtonpost.com/2013/11/01/portia-de-rossi-lesbian-struggle_n_4192373.html.

65 Portia de Rossi, *Unbearable Lightness*, 168.

66 Ibid., 148.

67 Ibid., 304.

68 Ibid., 177.

69 Diane Negra, *What a Girl Wants*, 42.

70 Scott Huver, 'Sitting Pretty Portia de Rossi', *Los Angeles Confidential*, May/June 2013, http://la-confidential-magazine.com/personalities/articles/portia-de-rossi-arrested-development-netflix.

71 'Ellens Brief to the Supreme Court', ellentv.com, 1 March 2013, http://www.ellentv.com/2013/02/28/ellens-brief-to-the-supreme-court/.

72 'Ellen Addresses Her JC Penney Critics', ellentv.com, 25 June 2012, http://www.ellentv.com/videos/1-key75szi/.

73 Sarah Banet-Weiser and Roopali Mukherjee, *Commodity Activism: Cultural Resistance in Neoliberal Times* (New York: New York University Press, 2012), 3.

74 Neil Ewen, 'The Good, The Bad, The Broken: Forms and Functions of Neoliberal Celebrity Relationships', this volume.

75 Heller, 'Mixed Feelings'.

76 Susan J. Douglas and Meredith W. Michaels, *The Mommy Myth: The Idealization of Motherhood and How It Has Undermined All Women* (London: Free Press, 2004), 24.

77 Diane Negra, *What a Girl Wants*, 55.

78 Priscilla Yamin, *American Marriage*, 5.

12

Audrey Hollander and Otto Bauer: The Perfect (Pornographic) Marriage?

Beccy Collings

Otto Bauer and Audrey Hollander are Adult film actors active in the Los Angeles industry since 2003. Married to each other for over ten years (although now divorced), their high-profile relationship was bound up inextricably with their performing careers during that period. Their status as a real-life married couple saturated their own PR, and in this chapter I examine how they used their union to enhance their careers, analysing the potential importance of assumptions surrounding real-life coupledom in increasing their on-screen appeal, and exploring the extent to which their success rested upon their appearance as a perfect couple, *actually having* the fantasy sex of the 'pornotopia'[1] that is invoked in Adult texts. Importantly, Audrey and Otto's situation also raises wider questions surrounding celebrity studies and the Adult film industry, and I additionally consider how the traditional notions of the public/private and frontstage/backstage divides[2] (so crucial to academic discussions surrounding celebrity image and the marketing of celebrity personae) are problematized when applied to performers for whom the most private of backstage activities are necessarily the public element of their careers. How can examining the strategies used by these celebrities who reveal intimate private elements of their appearances, sexual behaviour and – in the case of real-life couples – sexual relationships in their public performance, enable us to see the functioning of frontstage/backstage activities and celebrity in new ways? The chapter contains three sections, first discussing the role of celebrity sexual appeal and behaviour within an Adult and mainstream context, before going on to examine the specific ways in which Otto and Audrey attempted to 'perform' both the perfect pornographic marriage and the role of a celebrity couple, and concluding with a consideration of the possible effects of these (sometimes contradictory) efforts on how they were perceived, with some suggestions as to what this reveals about the construction and policing of the successful criteria for mainstream celebrity.

The Adult industry has its own attendant celebrity industry, with red-carpet awards shows (such as the annual AVN Awards and XRCO Awards), print and online news media outlets and publications (Adult Video News and XBiz News being two of the biggest examples), countless official and unofficial performer, fan, and gossip sites, as well as the Internet Adult Film Database (an Adult version of the Internet Movie Database), all of which support the circulation of Adult celebrity information and recognition. Despite this, the industry has not yet attracted a great degree of interest in academic Celebrity Studies, and Adult industry celebrities are also often ignored or derided in mainstream media discourses of celebrity, reflecting the fact that the whole sector has been 'consigned to a space of supposed privacy and is not acknowledged as part of the cultural mainstream.'[3] This treatment is perhaps symptomatic of a wider urge to brush the scale and popularity of the industry under the carpet, it being a powerful reminder of sexuality and transgression (something that might also be regarded as a strong contributory factor to contemporary campaigns for legislation that would reduce access to and visibility of pornography on the internet), and the fact that few analyses of Adult celebrities exist can likely be attributed to the lowly status of the industry in general. Gertrude Koch has commented that 'attempts to have porn "taken seriously" by enhancing the genre with stars, festivals and directors should probably be seen not so much as a gimmick to attract a wider audience as an effort by an association of craftsmen to gain credibility.'[4] From a marketing point of view, the movement of the top level of the Adult film industry towards recreating the model of its geographical neighbour the Hollywood film industry, and the legitimation of its personnel go hand in hand; if mainstream films are sold to viewers on the promise of containing particular kinds of performances by known stars (e.g. Will Ferrell in a comedy) and this supports the image of those stars as skilled professionals in that area, then the marketing of Adult industry films today appears no different, and the celebrity personas of actors such as Audrey and Otto can be studied in exactly the same way that any mainstream celebrity can. Yet, each group's relationship to sexuality as an aspect of their celebrity is a complex differentiating factor between them.

There is an expectation that sex itself is part of private life; a backstage activity. Concomitantly however, the sex lives (including sexual indiscretions) of celebrities are of great interest to some fans. Tabloid newspapers, celebrity magazines and internet gossip sites frequently document them, and incidents such as the leaking of an explicit video featuring singer and former 'X-Factor' UK judge Tulisa Contostavlos, Paris Hilton's *1 Night in Paris* (Salomon, 2004), and Tommy Lee and Pamela Anderson's sex tapes attracted significant cross-platform media attention. Similarly, when Tom Cruise and Nicole Kidman starred together in *Eyes Wide Shut* (Kubrick, 1999), and Jennifer Lopez and Ben Affleck in *Gigli* (Brest, 2003), gossipy media speculation took place around how their simulated sexual interaction might evidence their real sexual attraction to each other. This interest in glimpses of the private, backstage world of the performers fits in with the notion of the celebrity as someone whose personal life is of equal or greater importance than their professional output, and with expectations that a fan might gain some kind of insight into the celebrity 'as a person' from their private life that it would not be possible to get otherwise. Graeme Turner, discussing the magazine publication *Celebrity Flesh* (which contains nude pictures of mainstream celebrities), and websites that collate images of naked celebrities sourced from paparazzi shots, copied from other publications, or faked, remarks that the 'interest satisfied by the nude celebrity sites and magazines constitutes one of the standard practices of the cultural consumption of celebrity. The desire to see what the celebrity is "really like" obviously has a substantial sexual dimension,'[5] and also notes that these sites commonly employ (or provide a venue for) discourses of shaming and deriding the celebrities which run alongside the assumption that such pictures will be titillating.[6] This highlights one of the issues surrounding celebrities as sex objects: if a star poses for an underwear shoot, or is snapped topless by a telephoto lens, then their (sexual) body, which would normally be considered part of the private sphere, is brought into the public eye. When it comes to nudity and sex, being too visible, too available or too open appears to be considered an undesirable situation that counters more positive constructions of 'celebrity'. Stars who become known for their sexual exploits, or the frequency with which private sphere actions relating to sex or nudity can be publically observed, are infamous as opposed to famous (popular media attitudes displayed towards the fame of reality star Kim Kardashian, or British glamour model Katie Price, exemplify this idea). It is possible that it is this placing of the private (sexual) life into the public sphere that activates distaste and disapproval more so than the specific bodies/images themselves, and this idea might help explain why Adult stars are often absent from the study of celebrities: the fact that the things they become known for are behaviours that are found distasteful as acts of celebrity means that they are routinely discounted as belonging to this group. In other words, in a hierarchy of taste where many pop culture figures are already considered to be of tenuous celebrity, it appears that Adult star celebrity is just a step too far down the ladder to be admitted. Unlike 'legitimate' celebrities, who (despite fan and media interest) are typically expected to speak about and treat the topic of sex modestly, with the impression of the private being preserved, Adult performers have to trade on sex and their performance of it, interest in it and lack of modesty concerning it. Chuck Kleinhans notes that 'even when presented as dramatic fictional narrative or as freewheeling fantasy, pornography has a fundamental core of documentation: this is it, this is sex, this is what it looks like.'[7] Therefore, when an actor in an Adult film is seen having sex, this *is* what it looks like when they have sex (in this particular way), and the sense of seeing something 'real' from what is usually considered the private sphere is particularly strong. While on one hand, their status as Adult performers gives them an obvious professional reason for their sexual behaviour to be on display in this manner, this also means that they cannot adhere to the 'rules' of the public/private divide by which celebrities are ordinarily constructed and consumed – simultaneously presenting a public persona alongside keeping details of their 'true' intimate private life hidden to be glimpsed at by fans or investigated by journalists – and their inability to conform to expectations of mainstream celebrity behaviour and the business of being a celebrity 'correctly' creates a struggle to be categorized as part of that group.

Presenting the perfect (pornographic) marriage

So, what do celebrities like Audrey and Otto stand to gain by making their real-life marriage (and its sex) into public property, and how does this fit in with ideas about celebrity? In order to answer, it is instructive to examine exactly how they presented themselves as a couple during the time they were married. First, they both talked frequently about the origins and development of their relationship in interviews, explaining how they met, how in love they were and how they depended upon each other's support to prosper. These discussions often emphasized the ordinariness of their married life and their roles within it (which appeared to be split along very traditional gender lines). Second, presenting their relationship as a fairy-tale romance, and having a romantic narrative of their love at first sight and Otto's marriage proposal that they both recounted in the same way in interviews, seemed to be a key element of their PR. For example, speaking to Gene Ross, Audrey said: 'Our eyes caught. Hmmm. He looks good and I was hoping he was thinking the same thing. … They came over and it was probably a matter of minutes and we were kissing. It was sparks.'[8] She tells Cindy Loftus the same story in further detail, adding: 'And later that evening, in the early morning hours, he proposed to me on the beach.'[9] By presenting their own whirlwind courtship in a manner that both echoes the fantasies of passion and immediacy integral to pornographic coupling-up, and accords to an idealized romantic progression in which encountering 'the one' leads neatly to marriage and official legitimization of sexual behaviour, Otto and Audrey set the tone for the great paradox (and potentially, the great appeal) of their relationship: their abundant sexual attraction and willingness to indulge it in impulsive ways is, however wildly it deviates from conservative conventions concerning fidelity and 'respectability', always firmly highlighted as belonging within that framework.

This carefully balanced dichotomy was also apparent in relation to the negotiation of Audrey's role as both 'traditional wife' and 'pornstar'. In the extra features of the film *Filthy Things 6*, Audrey describes herself as 'always a lady on the street and a whore in bed',[10] and gives a concise history of her sexual life. It appears highly constructed to cater to possible fantasies surrounding the ideal woman and ideal wife, yet also, the ideal 'porn chick' (as Jim Powers describes her in the same extras package). She describes how she grew up fooling around with girls on the cheerleading and gymnastics team, not guys, and reveals that she lost her (heterosexual) virginity to Otto after experiencing love at first sight, characterizing herself as a late bloomer and sexually naïve until marriage. She continues by explaining that her favourite sexual activities are anal sex and cum swallowing, and that she cannot believe how wonderful her life is in that she can have sex with her husband all the time and they are paid for it.[11] The paradoxical nature of Otto and Audrey's marriage (traditional vs. hard core) thus seems mirrored in her persona, which is highly marketable in terms of catering to pornotopian fantasies about ideal women who are sexually adventurous and keen to please, while also maintaining a modest public face that avoids the connotations of 'easy' behaviour that are frequently associated in the media (and society) with being undesirable in a woman. In an article referring to the duo as 'porn power couple Otto Bauer and wife Audrey Hollander', Dani Duran, owner of Mach 2 Productions, comments that on first seeing them, 'I thought, that's a special couple', and that, 'I always go, "Otto, you've got the perfect woman. She's the best of both worlds. She loves to cook, and then you've got a whore in bed".'[12] Certainly, 'the housewife has been a popular pornographic type – and trope – in stories, glossy magazines, and adult films and in amateur, reality, and gonzo porn,'[13] and Audrey's perfect pornographic wife persona seems clearly presented to evoke it; see, for example, the following exchanges between the couple and Dave Cummings in *Screw My Wife Please!! 38*:

> **Otto:** We've been married four years. What makes her special? Shit, man! Look at her... I mean, ... She cooks and cleans, and y'know...
> **Audrey:** I do windows!
> **Otto:** Yes. She does everything but drive.
> [Cummings asks her what they want to do on camera.]
> **Audrey:** I feel the need to be a nasty, nasty, naughty housewife. I want to be really bad.
> [Cummings asks if that's okay with Otto.]
> **Otto:** Yeah![14]

Another element of the presentational paradox between Audrey and Otto's 'traditional' marriage and their sexuality centred around their identity as swingers, and as a couple who enjoyed bringing other people into their relationship for threesomes or group sex, as part of their personal life. They even hinted that fans could 'get lucky' with them if the right situation were to come about:

> **Cindy Loftus:** Are you guys swingers?
> **Audrey:** We were before we got into the industry. I was going to school and I would bring him home little treats (girls). But now that we are in the industry we ... like to be responsible to our co-workers and make sure we are only with people that are tested. You are already having sex with so many partners, that it wouldn't happen often. If the right situation presents itself, we would use protection ...
> **Cindy:** So a fan could get lucky.
> **Audrey:** Yes.
> **Cindy:** Male, or female?
> **Audrey:** Oh yeah!
> **Cindy:** Like at a convention if someone catches your eye.
> **Audrey:** Yes.[15]

The fact that Audrey makes herself appear accessible to men (other than Otto) is a good marketing strategy in terms of attracting fans and sales at meet-and-greets and conventions, but would certainly present a challenge to the traditional and romantic narratives of the perfect marriage and the perfect wife that the couple have taken care to construct, were it not for the concept of pornotopia and the fact that part of being a perfect pornographic wife might in fact *involve* doing things like having sex with your husband's friends, for instance. A large number of films featuring the couple have basic storylines in which behaviour that would be considered infidelity in 'real life' is shown or implied to be acceptable for them. Frequently, this is achieved through Otto and Audrey playing themselves in the context of the Adult industry and implying that having sex with other performers, even outside a shoot, is an agreed acceptability in their relationship (see for example, *Audrey Hollander: Cock Star* [Powers, 2010] in which the narrative has Audrey relaxing at home with a friend/fellow Adult actor, and when the conversation turns to work she ends up demonstrating the Anal Nelson position to him).[16] On other occasions, the couple's desire to engage in acts that physically require multiple men, such as double penetration, is the explanation. However the avoidance of infidelity is achieved, viewers are encouraged to enjoy a transgressive act, overlooking any potential real-life social censure attached to it, and being assisted in that by the fact that the real-life marriage of the performers remains secure. Otto and Audrey's performances are therefore, in many ways, simultaneously a reinforcement *and* a challenge to traditional ideals surrounding marital sex. This dichotomy can also be linked back to the mismatch between the kinds of qualities useful to have on display in order to achieve mainstream celebrity in comparison to Adult success, and is perhaps symptomatic of Otto and Audrey's attempts to negotiate their own (and others') understanding of celebrity. In a mainstream celebrity context, where the perceived state of a famous couple's marriage can occasion a great deal of interest – particularly if infidelity is suspected – the idea that a couple would routinely have sex, unproblematically, with other people is hard to square up. Once more, the fact that the job done by Adult stars necessarily involves re-categorizing particular 'real', usually private, acts as public (and exempting them from real-life consequences) means that the 'glimpsing' and gossiping around private lives and sexuality that plays a large part in the consumption of celebrity for many is disrupted. To sell the authenticity of their work and take advantage of viewer curiosity, Otto and Audrey must promote the idea that their on-screen acts are merely an extension of their offscreen sex lives, but the sacrifice in doing so is to render their marriage as appearing highly *non*-conformant to the norms of mainstream celebrity (and, for that matter, to conventional expectations of marital sex). Therefore, their apparent concern to portray the rest of their marriage as conforming to highly traditional ideals may be read not only as an attempt to mitigate against the kind of infamy and mainstream derision that pornographic behaviour brings, but also perhaps as an attempt to protect the image of their marriage as respectable and conformant to consumption as a 'real' celebrity coupling.

Their marriage certainly seemed to have the power to affect perceptions of their work: a particularly strong illustration can be seen in the playing out of an obscenity trial that took place against the Adult distributors Five Star and JM Productions in 2007. Prosecutors were attempting to argue that a scene from director Jim Powers' *Filthy Things 6*, which featured Audrey being dominated by Otto and Rick Masters, was obscene and degrading to her. Legally, under the Miller Test,[17] determinations of obscenity must be made with the jury having viewed the alleged obscene material in its entire context. Accordingly, the court was shown the DVD in its entirety, including the extra features in which Powers and the actors discuss the direction of the contested scene, and in which Audrey refers several times to the fact that she and Otto are married to each other (see Figure 12.1). Adult industry journalist Mark Kernes described these moments in a report for Adult Video News: 'Among other things, the extras showed Audrey and Otto preparing for their scene, setting up the giant plastic dildo that would be shoved up her ass, discussing how the d.p. with Rick would be choreographed, and perhaps most importantly, letting the audience know that she and Otto were married.'[18] He noted that after this material was played, 'the entire mood in the courtroom seemed to change'.[19]

Figure 12.1 The behind-the-scenes footage of *Filthy Things 6* (Powers, 2005), part of the DVD release and used in evidence at the obscenity trial, shows Otto and Audrey's real-life relationship in distinction to the dominant/submissive characters they play in the contested scene. Screen grab.

Ultimately the scene was judged not to be obscene or degrading, and although Audrey and Otto's marital status was not the only reason for the jury's rejection of the obscenity charge,[20] its presence within the debate at all is intriguing: Kernes obviously found it sufficiently relevant to draw attention to it with his choice of wording ('perhaps most importantly') and the revelation certainly seems from his report to have affected the viewers in the courtroom. Tanya Krzywinska, speaking of filmed, real sex, suggests that:

> The manner in which an act … is lit and staged, the influence of genre, narrative structure, techniques such as innuendo, offscreen action, or strategies of disavowal built into the text, each play a role in the way that sexual transgressions are presented and rendered in accordance with cinematic values. The formal devices used to represent transgression are absolutely central to the meanings it is likely to convey to audiences. Such devices may make what would ordinarily be the object of our disgust palatable.[21]

It is very tempting to suggest that this could have been part of the case with *Filthy Things 6*: while the scene in question – featuring the actors in character – involved acts of domination, submission and extreme penetration, the DVD extras made visible the staged ('art') nature of the scene, its quality of being acted (even though the sex itself was real), and highlighted factors that spoke to the consensual, planned nature of the events; the interviews and candid backstage footage emphasized the real-life marital and friendship status of Audrey and Otto, Rick Masters and Jim Powers, and through these devices the BDSM – the transgressive sex act – could have been made more palatable and less easy to consider obscene or degrading.

Performing the celebrity couple

Otto and Audrey took care not only to present their marriage in a way that was appealing within the context of pornography, but also to market themselves *as* an Adult celebrity couple. They cemented their coupledom-as-a-brand through ensuring the consistent use of their names together as part of the titles of their own films, such as *Otto and Audrey Destroy the World* (Rinaldi, 2005), *Otto and Audrey On the Prowl* (Bauer, 2007) and *Otto and Audrey Out of Control* (Bauer, 2007), and on products they endorsed, as well as launching the 'Supercore' film line together, with their names always jointly credited for the venture. The efficacy of their marketing strategy is evident in the way the industry itself automatically recognized their couple status, with news articles, reviews and opinion columns often referencing their marriage when speaking of either individual: XBiz writer Steve Javors describes them as 'Hardcore adult power couple Otto Bauer and Audrey Hollander',[22] for instance, while fan discussion on internet review and video sites also frequently linked them,[23] and their status as a well-known Adult couple *and* as Adult celebrities was clear in the marketing of the 'Otto and Audrey Cyberskin Swing Town Swinger's Kit' as part of the Wildfire Celebrity Series of sex toys.[24] They were cast in a number of films where their marriage had some kind of relevance, such as *Screw My Wife Please!! 38*, and – most notably – in the XXX parody, *Everybody Loves Lucy* (Tanner, 2009). Indeed, many scenes filmed during their marriage featured a self-reflexive element, whereby they either played a fictional couple or played themselves, sometimes in their own home. They were also chosen to feature as 'the couple' in Jens Hoffmann's documentary film about the industry, *9 to 5: Days in Porn* (Hoffmann, 2008).

In *Everybody Loves Lucy*, Otto and Audrey were cast as the parody's Lucy and Ricky evidently not just because of their physical resemblance to Lucille Ball and Desi Arnaz (see Figure 12.2), but also because of other parallels between the two couples: both were known for playing (essentially) themselves

Figure 12.2 Otto and Audrey parody Lucille Ball and Desi Arnaz in *Everybody Loves Lucy* (Tanner, 2009). Screen grab.

in entertainment products; both couples consisted of a businessman/musician husband and an actress wife; they both presented a relationship divided along traditional gender roles; they both had their own production company and studio, and syndicated their products worldwide; her (Audrey and Lucille's) performance was considered physically innovative and highly successful; and in both couples, the personalities were considered larger than life. In this light, it seems like astute casting, and appears to show something about how Audrey and Otto were viewed, and what *Hustler* thought consumers would understand and buy into as well. Further, Audrey's descriptions of how she got together with Otto are similar in tone and content to the kind of interview material Lucille Ball gave concerning Desi Arnaz, marking a significant aspect in which the couples' marketing of their marriages overlaps. Lucy described her marriage by saying, 'I threw away all of my conservativeness and took the plunge because I loved him. It was the most daring thing I ever did.'[25] Desi and Lucy married spontaneously after a short courtship and even lived in Chatsworth in the San Fernando Valley (the centre of the US Adult film industry). While some of these elements are coincidence, it is perhaps easy to see why the industry itself observed parallels between the couples, and how the ways in which Ball and Arnaz used their union to further their careers (particularly by talking publically about their relationship, performing together, and in the way they attached the identities of both parties to their business ventures) might exemplify a pattern for creating the 'recognizable celebrity couple' that is knowingly reproduced by Otto and Audrey, among many others, in order to try and evoke this identity for themselves.

Speaking of Lucille Ball and Desi Arnaz, Lori Landay has identified a 'real life/reel life' or reality/fantasy blur from which they were able to benefit, and I suggest that Otto and Audrey parallel them here, as well: 'One of the attractions of *I Love Lucy* was its blend of reality and fiction, or "real life" and "reel life," as a 1953 *Look* article called it.'[26] 'By watching the show, the viewer participates in the act of loving Lucy, and voyeuristically enjoys the love between Ricky and Lucy, Arnaz and Ball.'[27] Many of Audrey and Otto's Supercore films trade on exactly this kind of 'real life'/'reel life' crossover. In reference to *Destroy the World*, for example, director Bobby Rinaldi stresses this angle in promotion for the series, suggesting that the films are favourably realistic: 'It's the kind of stuff they do in their personal life.'[28] This is echoed in promotion for their other projects: 'Real-life married couple and real-life porn stars Audrey Hollander and Otto Bauer ...;'[29] 'Starring real-life husband-and-wife team Otto Bauer and Audrey Hollander'.[30] This kind of presentation not only reinforces the idea that Otto and Audrey are one unit working together and that they are accessible (and pornotopian), but also blurs the reality/fantasy divide; in this way it might – to borrow Landay's quote – encourage the viewers to participate in the act of loving the performers, and to voyeuristically enjoy the love between Otto and Audrey. Additionally, this kind of blurring perhaps makes it easier to 'see' the presence of their real marriage in their performed acts, and to apply assumptions made about the former to the latter (as in the case of the obscenity trial). Otto and Audrey's attempts to perform celebrity married coupledom in conjunction with the content of their on-screen performances may even work to challenge conventional assumptions about marital sexual behaviour itself.

Bart Andrews, in his examination of the original *I Love Lucy*, recounts TV writer Jack Sher as saying, 'The captivating thing about Lucy and Ricky is the fact that they hold a mirror up to every married couple in America. Not a regular mirror that reflects the truth, nor a magic mirror that portrays fantasy. But a Coney Island mirror that distorts, exaggerates, and makes vastly amusing every little incident, foible, and idiosyncrasy of married life.'[31] Audrey and Otto may be seen to do a similar thing, only their distorting lens is that of the pornotopia, reflecting exaggerated forms of sex that, in their extreme supercore content, go beyond the magic mirror fantasy of 'ideal' sex noted by Krzywinska as 'the heterosexual committed partnership of a man and a woman, who orgasm neatly together through gentle and passionate sex',[32] and into the realm of 'Explicit Sex', which she uses to refer to films which go beyond a basic depiction of heterosexual coitus to foreground anal or kinky heterosexual sex, or non-heterosexual sex.[33] Considering the context of their performance is, like Lucy and Desi, as a real-life married couple revealing an extension of their off-screen lives, the 'foibles and idiosyncrasies' implied in Otto and Audrey's exaggerated public sex constitute an acknowledgement of the wide variety of sexual practices beyond the 'ideal' that exists in the private sphere of couples.

Consuming Audrey and Otto

In pornography, while the physical acts that appear on the screen can be described as staged, mechanical or repetitive, and seem designed to do very specific things (e.g. to allow the camera visual access to particular body parts in motion, to arouse viewers interested in specific fetish objects, etc.), the observation of things specific to individual performers – either in their appearance, personality or performance habits – can add another layer into the viewing that makes the 'celebrity' element of Adult performing become salient. Recognizing Audrey and Otto, and knowing that they are married, has the potential to add meaning to their performance that goes beyond the mere physicality or mechanics of their bodies. By making their coupledom highly visible in their marketing and their films, Otto and Audrey introduce the possibility of their scenes being read in more complex ways than just as 'any two actors having sex', and the viewer who is aware of their off-screen relationship can bring that knowledge to bear while watching, possibly reading significance into certain acts that would not be available otherwise. With this in mind, another key element of Audrey and Otto's presentation of themselves as a couple is the way they appear and interact with each other on-screen. It is the case (as with Audrey's construction as a 'perfect pornographic wife' who professes to adhere to a number of traditional gender stereotypes) that gender affects the ways they are made available for spectating, and within their scenes the conventions of filming pornography typically offer the viewer something different in respect of each of them. The films privilege shots of Audrey's face, breasts, genitalia and feminine costumes over shots of Otto's body. Audrey is available in closer detail and in a more sustained way as an individual, while Otto is available only in so far as he is physically in relation to her (for instance, his penis is in the frame as an object for her to engage with, or his face is in close-up only when he is performing cunnilingus on her). Similarly, the soundtrack is dominated by the sounds of her pleasure. This is not to say that Otto is not available for gazing at, however, just that the films themselves assume a male (heterosexual) gaze is at work, and provide images of Audrey accordingly. In some scenes Audrey acts submissively; in others she drives the action forward herself, but in either circumstance, both she and Otto enthusiastically signal their enjoyment and satisfaction at what is taking place. In these terms, while their relative 'importance' to the presentation of heterosexual pornography – as informed by their gender – is visible *in* that presentation, they are still both shown as gaining sexually from the acts in which they participate, and therefore a certain degree of equality of experience is also demonstrated.

José B. Capino has spoken of how the staging of porn can allow couples to show control and power in different ways, and offer readings that both support and challenge traditional ideas about power dynamics and objectification. For example:

> The reverse cowgirl, one of the most widely used sexual positions in heterosexual pornography, gives a full view of the woman's body (exploiting her "to-be-looked-at-ness") while also allowing her to maintain a dominant, woman-on-top position in which she controls her and her partner's sexual stimulation. ... Does the preponderance of these positions help create a pornotopia with more equitable gender relations?[34]

I would argue that in the case of Audrey and Otto, these kinds of visuals in combination with their signalled identity as a genuine couple (their 'real life'/'reel life' blur) contributes not only to a pornotopia which starts to seem accessible and attainable, but also to one in which the image of a couple who work with each other and affect each other's pleasure and success on multiple levels becomes visible. It is frequently the case that Audrey and Otto make verbal demands of each other during their filmed sex together, work together to achieve complicated positions and acts, and also work together to direct the behaviour of other participants in scenes with them; in this respect, they offer a picture of a couple drawing upon each other's skills to achieve shared sexual goals and to enhance their scenes. This aspect means that their on-screen performance is a literal display of their real-life coupledom at work, as much as it also seeks to fit within the conventions of pornographic presentation and fantasies concerning female behaviour and gender relations. Allied to this, while many of the DVD extra features and press interviews done by Audrey position her as traditionally feminine and cater to male fantasies about ideal sexual partners, these are frequently supplemented by materials such as the topical interviews on the *Everybody Loves Lucy* release, in which she demonstrates her knowledge of politics and current affairs, essentially proving herself as not conforming to other stereotypes surrounding female Adult performers. This facet of her persona could contribute to the impression of her capability in being an equal actor in respect of the couple's career choices, and mitigates against possible accusations that Otto is using her merely to further his own success; if she is seen to be intelligent, practical, informed, etc., it is harder to believe that she has entered the Adult industry naïvely.

It is additionally possible that Audrey and Otto's marriage gave them an advantage in relation to the lucrative couples' market pursued by the Adult industry in its production of certain kinds of videos (and even a means to attempt an expansion of the type of content normally regarded as suitable for pornography seeking to attract and reflect the interests of women and couples; often, 'a formula of softer, gentler, more romantic porn with storylines and higher production values'[35]). If it has been traditionally understood that the viewing of films featuring extreme sex acts is the preserve of a male porn audience,[36] then a couple trying to make a name in this area, as Audrey and Otto did with the Supercore brand, may have been able to hail and appeal to a wider viewership. By positioning Audrey as well as Otto as a key figure behind their films, and emphasizing their teamwork in the scenes themselves, the titles of the films and in their other publicity, the couple could once more have tapped into assumptions about marriage – and gender – that worked to temper the boy's club association of the extreme material, using their own 'real life'/'reel life' blur to suggest that this content is capable of reflecting and catering to the interests of all genders. It is certainly the case that the supercore nature of Audrey and Otto's performances together (and with the other actors they co-opt or induct into supercore), particularly with regards to extreme anal penetration, can be considered innovative or out of the ordinary, while at the same time their prolific appearance in films – especially in the mid-2000s – had the effect of making the acts themselves appear more common. However, as Kaarina Nikunen and Susanna Paasonen have pointed out, 'Commercial heteroporn production tends to be controlled by rigid conventions and norms that ultimately leave little space for repetitions with a difference.'[37] Perhaps it is therefore the case that stressing their status as a heterosexual married couple as such an important part of their identity was primarily effective in helping to insulate Audrey and Otto's more extreme sex acts within a comfortably commercial framework, with any widening of the audience encouraged by their presentation of a pornotopia underpinned by coupled teamwork being an added bonus for their career.

Conclusion

It has been noted that '[b]y trying to broaden their identity to include multiple and diverse roles, actors … risk being devalued and even rejected. As such, it might be preferable to assume a simple, focused identity.'[38] This is an idea that Otto and Audrey seem to have taken to heart, and their simple, focused identities are – first and foremost – bound up in each other. For the time their marriage lasted, their couple status was continually reinforced by a wide variety of presentational strategies both on- and off-screen, and the efficacy of these was clearly evident in the ways the industry itself recognized them. Particularly striking is how well Otto and Audrey were able to evoke (both specifically, and in a wider sense) the image of a 'celebrity married couple' as modelled by Lucille Ball and Desi Arnaz. The type and success of the strategies Otto and Audrey used demonstrates not only how *they* appeared to understand the notion of celebrity coupledom, but also points towards the presence of a more general understanding and awareness of celebrity coupledom as something with a history, and paradigms, and as capable of being attained and maintained through particular behaviours.

There is an unavoidable complicating factor in Otto and Audrey's participation and recognition within the sphere of celebrity, however, and this is the fact that their fame comes through pornography. Goffman states: 'In their capacity as performers, individuals will be concerned with maintaining the impression that they are living up to the many standards by which they and their products are judged,'[39] and Audrey and Otto – as performers in both a social and a professional context – had to publicize a private life that seemed to accord with the pornotopian ideals of their on-screen lives. By blurring the lines between the two, they could sell a particular kind of authenticity to viewers of their (sexual) products, and also attempt to temper possible negative reactions to their acts. They were, in other words, using various assumptions and associations surrounding coupledom as part of their strategy to increase their appeal and hence, to try and cement their celebrity. *But*, it is also the case that Adult performers frequently are *not* perceived and discussed as celebrities in the same ways as their mainstream counterparts. I suggest that having an overt display of backstage activities as a necessary part of their public persona means that Otto, Audrey and their fellow Adult stars struggle to fit neatly into prevailing paradigms of celebrity behaviour and self-promotion that are centred upon providing glimpses of private sphere information and activities that can be sought out and speculated upon in the course of consuming celebrity. Despite their attempts to present themselves in ways that replicate various aspects of mainstream celebrity behaviour, and to mitigate against possible negative reactions towards the open display of extreme sexuality, Adult performers cannot simultaneously adhere to the expected maintenance of frontstage/backstage and public/ private divides demanded by mainstream celebrity *and* be successful in porn. Therefore, by way of the example of Adult stars – in their exclusion from mainstream categories and discourses of celebrity, and invariable distinction as 'Adult celebrities', and not just 'celebrities' – the crucial importance of careful adherence to prevailing paradigms of celebrity behaviour and self-promotion is highlighted, and the conclusion can be drawn that it is *this* that currently constitutes the key component of successful 'celebrity' status, coupled or otherwise.

Notes

1 The term pornotopia was created by Steven Marcus to describe the 'non-place' where pornographic fantasy plays out, in which it seems that men 'are always and infinitely potent; all women fecundate with lust and flow with sap or juice or both. Everyone is always ready for anything … – no one is ever jealous, possessive, or really angry. All our aggressions are perfectly fused with our sexuality, and the only rage is the rage of lust.' In short, the convenient parallel world of sexual perfection that pornography attempts to portray. Steven Marcus, *The Other Victorians: A Study of Sexuality and Pornography in Mid-Nineteenth-Century England* (New York: Basic Books Inc., 1964), 273.

2 See, for example: Erving Goffman, 'The Presentation of Self in Everyday Life', in *The Goffman Reader*, ed. Charles Lemert and Ann Branaman (Oxford: Blackwell Publishers Ltd, 1997); or Graeme Turner, *Understanding Celebrity*, 2nd ed. (London: Sage Publications Ltd, 2014), 8.

3 Linda Williams, *Screening Sex* (Durham, NC and London: Duke University Press, 2008), 300.

4 Gertrude Koch, 'The Body's Shadow Realm', in *Dirty Looks: Women, Pornography, Power*, ed. P. Church Gibson and R. Gibson (London: BFI, 1993), 29.

5 Graeme Turner, *Understanding Celebrity*, 2nd ed. (London: Sage Publications Ltd, 2014), 140.

6 Ibid., 140–41.

7 Chuck Kleinhans, 'Pornography and Documentary: Narrating the Alibi', in *Sleaze Artists: Cinema at the Margins of Taste, Style, and Politics*, ed. J. Sconce (Durham, NC and London: Duke University Press), 97.

8 Gene Ross, 'A Blast from the Past; Now Back in the Business', *Adult FYI*, http://www.adultfyi.com/read.php?ID=56361.

9 Cindi Loftus, 'My Interview With Audrey Hollander', *Cindi's Naked Truth*, http://www.xcitement.com/blog/?p=1625.

10 *Filthy Things 6* (dir. Jim Powers, USA: Powersville Inc., 2005).

11 Ibid.

12 Mike Ramone, 'Mach 2 Productions: Otto and Audrey Exclusively at Twice the Speed of Sound', *Adult Video News*, http://business.avn.com/articles/video/AVN-COM-BUSINESS-PROFILE-200604-Mach-2-Productions-Otto-and-Audrey-Exclusively-at-Twice-the-Speed-of-Sound-44322.html.

13 Susanna Paasonen, *Carnal Resonance: Affect and Online Pornography* (Cambridge, MA: The MIT Press, 2011), 107.

14 *Screw My Wife Please!! 38* (dir. Bobby Rinaldi, USA: Wildlife Productions, 2006).

15 Loftus, 'My Interview With Audrey Hollander'.

16 *Audrey Hollander: Cock Star* (dir. Jim Powers, USA: JM Productions, 2010).

17 The Miller Test is well-explained in this entry from the Wex Legal Dictionary concerning obscenity: 'Currently, obscenity is evaluated by federal and state courts alike using a tripartite standard established by Miller v. California 413 U.S. 15 (1973). The Miller test for obscenity includes the following criteria: (1) whether 'the average person, applying contemporary community standards' would find that the work, 'taken as a whole,' appeals to 'prurient interest', (2) whether the work depicts or describes, in a patently offensive way, sexual conduct specifically defined by the applicable state law, and (3) whether the work, 'taken as a whole,' lacks serious literary, artistic, political, or scientific value.' Unknown Author, 'Obscenity', *Wex Legal Dictionary*, http://www.law.cornell.edu/wex/obscenity.

18 Mark Kernes, 'Inside the Five Star Video Obscenity Trial', *Adult Video News*, http://business.avn.com/articles/video/Inside-the-Five-Star-Video-Obscenity-Trial-27625.html.

19 Ibid.

20 As well as defending the scenes as artistic in nature, attorney Richard Hertzberg demonstrated that very similar material was openly on sale elsewhere in the local area without complaint, suggesting that 'contemporary community standards' would not find that the contested scenes appealed to 'prurient interests'. Mark Kernes, 'Five Star Case Goes To The Jury', *Adult Video News*, http://business.avn.com/articles/legal/Five-Star-Case-Goes-To-The-Jury-28405.html.

21 Tanya Krzywinska, *Sex and the Cinema* (London and New York: Wallflower Press, 2006), 109.

22 Steve Javors, 'Otto Bauer, Audrey Hollander Put 'Supercore' Online', *XBiz*, http://www.xbiz.com/news/22575.

23 See, for example, a review of the film *Catherine* (Ninn, 2005) posted by freddyandeddy.com that recounts a meeting between the eponymous website couple and Hollander and Bauer: 'Incidentally, we happened to meet the two leads in person

at the 2006 AVN Show in Las Vegas (see picture at right as proof), who are an actual couple who've been together for years, and they vouch for their mutual enjoyment of every minute on screen.' A. Denchasy and I. Denchasy, 'Catherine', *Freddy and Eddy*, http://www.freddyandeddy.com/videoreviews/ninnworx/catherinedvdreview.htm. Or, the fan review of *9 to 5: Days in Porn* that describes how 'Otto Bauer and Audrey Hollander, the porno couple, challenge middle-America's perception of marriage every time they fuck other people on porn sets.' A. Keys, 'I Watched "9 to 5: Days in Porn"', *High On Sex*, http://highonsex.net/post/3635931703/.

24 Unknown Author 'Topco's Wildfire Celebrity Series Raises the Bar on Replicas', *Adult Video News*, http://business.avn.com/company-news/Topco-s-Wildfire-Celebrity-Series-Raises-the-Bar-on-Replicas-354051.html.

25 Bart Andrews, *Lucy & Ricky & Fred & Ethel: The Story of I Love Lucy* (New York: E.P. Dutton & Co. Inc., 1976), 15.

26 Lori Landay, 'Millions "Love Lucy": Commodification and the Lucy Phenomenon', *NWSA Journal* 11, no. 2 (1999): 28.

27 Ibid., 36.

28 Mark Kernes, 'On the set: Otto and Audrey Destroy the World', *Adult Video News*, http://business.avn.com/articles/video/On-the-Set-i-Otto-Audrey-Destroy-the-World-i-44667.html.

29 Unknown Author, 'Audrey Hollander and Otto Bauer Debut With Flirt 4 Free Fetish Show', *Adult Video News*, http://business.avn.com/articles/video/Audrey-Hollander-and-Otto-Bauer-Debut-With-Flirt-4-Free-Fetish-Show-43021.html.

30 Unknown Author, 'Hustler Video Releases Their Latest Parody: "Everybody Loves Lucy"', *Adult Video News*, http://business.avn.com/company-news/Hustler-Video-Releases-Their-Latest-Parody-Everybody-Loves-Lucy-354541.html.

31 Andrews, *Lucy & Ricky & Fred & Ethel*, 15.

32 Tanya Krzywinska, '*Cicciolina* and the Dynamics of Transgression and Abjection in Explicit Sex Films', in *The Body's Perilous Pleasures: Dangerous Desires and Contemporary Culture*, ed. M. Aaron (Edinburgh: Edinburgh University Press, 1999), 193.

33 Ibid., 192.

34 José B. Capino, 'Seizing Moving Image Pornography', *Cinema Journal* 46, no. 4 (2007): 122–23.

35 Tristan Taormino, Celine Parrēnas Shimzu, Constance Penley and Mireille Miller-Young, 'Introduction: The Politics of Producing Pleasure', in *The Feminist Porn Book: The Politics of Producing Pleasure*, ed. Taormino et al. (New York: The Feminist Press, 2013), 11.

36 As noted by Linda Williams as the stance taken by anti-pornography feminists. Linda Williams, *Hard Core: Power, Pleasure, and the 'Frenzy of the Visible'* (Berkeley: University of California Press, 1999), 204.

37 Kaarina Nikunen and Susanna Paasonen, 'Porn Star as Brand: Pornification and the Intermedia Career of Rakel Liekki', *The Velvet Light Trap* 59 (2007): 36.

38 Ezra Zuckerman, Tai-Young Kim, Kalinda Ukanwa and James von Rittmann, 'Robust Identities or Nonentities? Typecasting in the Feature-Film Labor Market', *American Journal of Sociology* 108, no. 5 (2003): 1019–20.

39 Lemert and Branaman, *The Goffman Reader*, 22.

Part Four

Love

Shelley Cobb and Neil Ewen

The idea that love is a simple antidote to life's ills, both individual and collective, is one of the most familiar truisms in western culture. John Lennon's invocation that 'All you need is love / Love is all you need' is one of the most famous and explicit pop culture examples of this assumption, with The Beatles' manager, Brian Epstein, saying of the lyric: 'The nice thing about it is that it cannot be misinterpreted. It is a clear message saying that love is everything.'[1] But with respect to the late Mr Epstein, things become a little more complicated than he suggests when we begin to scratch the surface. Most obviously, there are many different kinds of love: romantic love, parental love, sibling love, sexual love and divine love, among many. Even (what we think was) Epstein's intention – to suggest that love is simply a force of 'good' over 'evil', and that Lennon was taking a pacifistic stance and urging the citizens of the world to unite in harmony – runs into trouble if we consider what Lennon himself had to say about the lyric:

> According to journalist Jade Wright ... when asked in 1971 whether songs like 'Give Peace a Chance' and 'Power to the People' were propaganda songs, he answered: 'Sure. So was "All You Need Is Love". I'm a revolutionary artist. My art is dedicated to change'.[2]

We can only speculate – and Lennon may very well have meant exactly what Epstein assumed – but what he is gesturing towards here, consciously or not, is that there is a politics of love that always lies beneath simplistic interpretations, that constantly informs the ways individuals relate to one another (and even think about their selves), and often does its best to remain uncovered.

The politics of love has in recent years become a hot topic in intellectual circles, as a particular strand of a wider blossoming of Affect Theory.[3] In 'The Politics of Love and its Enemies',[4] David Nirenberg illustrates that notions of love and affect have never existed on a plane free of politics. Nirenberg's fascinating analysis goes back as far as 'the dry farming societies of the ancient Mediterranean world that produced some of our earliest written records'. These societies, he suggests, 'were built on a vast array of reciprocal relations of varying degrees of formalization and asymmetry, ranging from master–slave at one extreme, through patron–client, lord–vassal, and creditor–debtor relations, to relations of hospitality, friendship, kinship, and marriage on the other'. Since there was no 'dedicated vocabulary for such relations', 'terms of kinship (such as *father* and *son*) and affect (such as *love* and *friendship*)', were (and here he quotes Raymond Westbrook) 'promiscuously employed ... for all manner of social, commercial, and legal reasons'. As such, these terms were 'incestuously related to one another' and are 'encompassed by the terms we now translate into English as *friendship* and *love*'. 'If today love can seem a liberation from possession and exchange', Nirenberg argues, 'it is because this ancient incest has been repressed'.[5] In light of this reading, we might suggest that contemporary celebrity couple culture dramatizes this repression: at once obscuring the reciprocal relations of exchange in discourses of romance and private intimacy, while making explicit for public consumption those very exchanges.

The chapters in this section each focus to a greater or lesser extent on romantic celebrity relations, and show how celebrity couplings, in their production, often seek to harness the power of discourses of romantic love and intimacy. As critical readings, however, these chapters also expose the complicated politics of love that structure these celebrity relations, as well as taking into account the affective power of their mediations. Laura Kipnis, in *Against Love: A Polemic*, provocatively suggests that romantic coupledom in western culture constitutes 'omnipresent propaganda beaming into our psyches on an hourly basis: the millions of images of love-struck couples looming over us from movie screens, televisions, billboards, magazines, incessantly strong-arming us onboard the love train', positioning all those who do not conform to this hegemony as abject.[6] Michael Cobb, meanwhile, articulates succinctly the importance of thinking critically about these issues by suggesting that they 'are not wedge issues but central biopolitical concerns that ferociously animate our present and future politics. Marriage, gay or not, and for that matter most forms of coupledom, are at the heart of this political life.'[7] Taken together, then, these chapters serve as injunctions to consider the affective power of romantic celebrity relationships and their roles in structuring the ways we imaginatively relate to others.

This section begins with Suzanne Leonard's chapter, 'The Return of Liz and Dick', in which she shows how the on-again/off-again romance (and marriage) of Elizabeth Taylor and Richard Burton has created 'a celebrity couple whose mythologized pairing, if anything, has accrued more mystique since Taylor's death in 2011'. She argues that this renewed contemporary interest in the couple must be understood within recent developments in celebrity studies and situates 'their coupledom in a wider milieu wherein the boundaries between performance, intimacy and sexuality are forever blurred'. As such, she suggests Taylor and Burton are an 'origin text of celebrity coupling' and that their 'perpetual claim to be escaping an invasive press' contributed to the aggrandizing of their infamous passion, which is the basis for their current cultural visibility across various mass-market media texts.

Vanessa Díaz, in her chapter '"Brad & Angelina: And Now … Brangelina!" A Sociocultural Analysis of Blended Celebrity Couple Names', offers an inside perspective of the celebrity press through her ethnographic study of celebrity magazine reporters and the phenomenon of the celebrity portmanteau. The reporters she interviewed suggest that the blended celebrity name is metonymic of what celebrity journalism does – 'We pair people up together and report on them as one unit' – and what it seeks to create – 'a new level of celebrity'. Through an analysis of cultural naming practices, Díaz argues that the portmanteau 'promotes (imaginary) intimacy between consumers and celebrity couples, thus encouraging the personal interest and investment of individuals in those couples'. She also gestures towards an explanation as to why it is almost exclusively the preserve of white, heterosexual celebrity couples.

Many of the most recognizable celebrity couples are in early middle age, not too young to suggest impermanency, old enough to be married (if they choose) and have children, but not too old to appear unsexed. Linda Ruth Williams, in her chapter, 'Jane Fonda, Power Nuptials and the Project of Ageing', considers the ways that Jane Fonda's 'three marriages inform her public profile and the phases of her career'. She particularly focuses on Fonda's marriage to Ted Turner as 'a story of competing celebrity between 50-something megastars', and argues that after their break up, Fonda developed a 'lifestyle philosophy of gendered aging' that she articulates in her late-life autobiographies. This performance of a lifestyle of ageing, which is not only found in her books but also in her celebrity endorsements and in social media profiles, is central to 'Fonda's negotiation of coupling as key to two rebrandings she has fashioned: from younger revered performer/sex-goddess/fitness guru to still-sexualized, still-fit *grande dame*, and – crucially – from star to celebrity'. Williams therefore shows how Fonda's romantic relationships with her successive partners can be read in terms of different stages of branding her celebrity, moving from a distant early stardom to shaping a more intimate relationship with her fans in recent years.

Shifting the focus to a much younger couple, Diane Negra offers a close analysis of *Robsten* – the now defunct coupling of Kristen Stewart and Robert Pattinson. In her chapter, 'The Making, Unmaking and Re-making of *Robsten*', Negra suggests that 'their celebrity couplehood largely borrowed its terms of intimacy from the *Twilight* film franchise in which the pair's fame was sourced, and shows how it was heightened by their frequent presentation as "hunted" paparazzi targets'. Furthermore, Negra claims that the apparent authenticity of the private space of the couple that the media seeks to expose, and the spectacle of that exposure, covers over the 'industrial and ideological power' of the celebrity couple. As such, Negra argues that 'the tremendous public investment in the couple was a function of the desire to retain an image of innocent romance while simultaneously acknowledging how fraught that conception is'.

The ideological implications of the public's and the media's obsession with contemporary celebrity couples and families is considered in broader terms by Neil Ewen in his chapter, 'The Good, the Bad and The Broken: Forms and Functions of Neoliberal Celebrity Relationships'. Ewen problematizes the notion that celebrity relationships provide relief from the anxieties of everyday life under neoliberalism, and suggests that this process is not an even one across all forms of celebrity alliances. As such, the media often configure certain couples as '"good" celebrity couples [that] articulate cultural desires for idealized relationships', and others as '"bad" celebrity couples [that] are examples of how not to live'. Inevitably, of course, upon close examination those distinctions unravel and the normative ideologies that underpin the fantasies of both types are revealed. Ewen concludes his chapter with a brief consideration of the 'broken' couple, or 'anti-couple': a concept that is useful in part in that it highlights both the artifice and structuring conservative discourses that elaborations of 'good' celebrity couples usually manage to hide.

Notes

1 'The Beatles. All You Need Is Love (3:46)', *Lastfm.com*, http://www.last.fm/music/The+Beatles/Yellow+Submarine/All+You+Need+Is+Love.

2 Ibid.

3 See, for example: Melissa Gregg and Gregory J. Seigworth (eds), *The Affect Theory Reader* (Durham, NC: Duke University Press, 2010); Lauren Berlant, *Cruel Optimism* (Durham, NC: Duke University Press, 2011); Kathleen Stewart, *Ordinary Affects* (Duke: Duke University Press, 2007).

4 David Nirenberg, 'The Politics of Love and its Enemies', *Critical Inquiry* 33, no. 3 (Spring 2007): 253–605.

5 Ibid., 575.

6 Laura Kipnis, *Against Love: A Polemic* (New York: Vintage, 2004), 33–34.

7 Michael Cobb, *Single: Arguments for the Uncoupled* (New York: New York University, 2012), 17–18.

13

The Return of Liz and Dick

Suzanne Leonard

Lizandick (liz n 'dik) n. pl. [contemporary usage fr. Liz and Dick, often followed by exclamation point, i.e., Lizandick!] 1. Archaic. Mythic American actress and Welsh actor whose names were eternally coupled despite their celebrated uncoupling(s). 2. Aging and forever expanding histrionic duo whose sum is greater than their individual parts, and whose mutual moves are perpetually played out in public (did you hear that ~ started a limited-run revival of Noël Coward's Private Lives in Boston last week?). 3. Any pair of people who come together, split, come together, split, until they seem to make a profession of it or until their acquaintances move past empathy to ennui

Richard Stengel, *People*, 18 April 1983

As cameo appearances go, Richard Burton's unexpected sauntering onto the pages of Jess Walter's 2012 novel *Beautiful Ruins* makes for a salacious addition to the long deceased actor's oeuvre. In this fictionalized account, a drunken Burton beds unsuspecting B actress Dee Moray during the filming of *Cleopatra* in Italy in 1962, though he is merely killing time while paramour Elizabeth Taylor entertains her husband (unnamed in the novel, but presumably Eddie Fisher) who comes to Rome for a visit. After finding out that he has impregnated Dee, Burton is not repentant but rather petulant, self-absorbed and careless: a characterization meant distinctly as a foil to the novel's sympathetic and humble Italian protagonist, Pasquale, who cares genuinely for the actress. Despite Burton's attempts to coerce Dee into aborting the pregnancy, she chooses to continue it, carrying in secret the reality that her son – also selfish, impulsive, infantilized – is Burton's love child.

This counternarrative is hardly the love story we have come to expect of the famed Burton and Taylor, a celebrity couple whose mythologized pairing, if anything, has accrued more mystique since Taylor's death in 2011. Particularly, to quite literally bastardize the story of the fated and torrid affair that erupted on the set of *Cleopatra* would seem to undermine one of the most basic premises of the Taylor–Burton legacy, notably the fact that upon meeting, the couple were at once mad about one another and irrevocably changed. This intentionally oppositional portrayal nevertheless has done little to stem the tide of the pair's hagiographic representation in twenty-first century media culture. In fact, the sort of irreverent fatigue suggested by the *People* magazine spoof, which serves as the epigraph to this chapter, has been almost wholly replaced by reverence for their coupledom. Specifically, the twosome has enjoyed a renewed cultural visibility in the 2010s, as evidenced by the release of two made-for-TV movies, Lifetime's *Liz and Dick* (2012) and the BBC's *Burton and Taylor* (2013), as well as the publication of a book devoted exclusively to their relationship: *Furious Love: Elizabeth Taylor, Richard Burton, and the Marriage of the Century* (2010).[1] This period also saw the release of two mass-market texts, *How To Be a Movie Star: Elizabeth Taylor in Hollywood* (2009) and *The Richard Burton Diaries* (2013), again testaments to the assumed public appeal of their individual lives and their incendiary pairing.[2] As this chapter will argue, such a plethora of movies, biographies and memoirs, as well as the reinvigorated fascination with Taylor after her death, demands to be viewed in the context of recent developments in celebrity studies. Situating their coupledom in a wider milieu wherein the boundaries between performance, intimacy and sexuality are forever blurred, I will first consider how Taylor and Burton's famed relationship marks a shift from studio-generated ideals of stardom to more modern-day notions of celebrity, wherein talent is less centrally prized than is hypervisibility and a willingness to commodify everyday life. Secondly, I look at their coupledom against the backdrop of the paparazzi and celebrity journalism, and suggest that the pair's perpetual claim to be 'escaping' an invasive press assisted in augmenting attributions of their renowned passion. The essay concludes by situating Burton and Taylor as an origin text of celebrity coupling, thanks to their exaggerated performances of eroticism, emotionality and consumption.

From studio darling to celebrity 'nightmare'

In a review of *Furious Love* that appeared in the trade publication *Variety*, critic Peter Bart makes the provocative claim that 'Elizabeth Taylor and Richard Burton in their heyday represented vestigial symbols of the star system and their headline-grabbing self-indulgence helped bring about its demise'.[3] Bart's insistence on the couple's toxic effects on the movie business ('all Taylor and Burton had to do was walk on a set and budgets would start hemorrhaging'[4]) is a view that has been widely perpetuated, thanks to their costly affair on the set of *Cleopatra*. In 1964, Fox sued the now-married couple for a total of $50 million, alleging that their 'conduct and deportment during and after the filming of *Cleopatra* lessened the commercial value of the motion picture'.[5] Of particular note is the fact that in the first claim against Taylor ($10 million of the suit was directed towards Taylor, $5 million towards Burton and $25 million against them both) she is accused of not reporting for work, not reporting for work on time, reporting for work in a 'condition that did not allow her to perform her services,' becoming 'disabled, incapacitated, or unphotographable' and 'suffering herself to be held up to scorn, ridicule, and unfavorable publicity'.[6] The lawsuit's language betrays not only the multiplicity of labours and duties expected of a Hollywood star, but also the extent to which reputation management figures as integral to such agreements. Not acting in a manner supposedly consistent with 'good publicity' is therefore a breach akin to more easily quantifiable transgressions such as missing or being unable to work. This lawsuit, moreover, effectively documents and concretizes in legal terms the turn Taylor and Burton made from compliant stars to 'celebrity nightmares'.

In Taylor's case, part of what made this transition so alarming was her status as a seasoned professional whose career stemmed back to her early childhood. Taylor made her first movie at the age of nine, and her close management by MGM, as well as a seventeen-and-a-half year career there, is often cited as an example of the tight control of the studio system. Ada Hozić calls Taylor MGM's 'most dutiful daughter', as evidenced by the fact that 'she went to school in the Culver City Studio, held her birthday parties on MGM's sound stages, and even met her first dates and husbands through studio publicists'.[7] Such behaviours were consistent with the historical period in which Taylor's early stardom proliferated: studios in the 1940s were well-oiled machines where star images were manufactured by authorized biographies and staged publicity events, and symbolically verified and legitimated by screen roles.[8]

By the late 1950s, a star system dependent on public appearances that buttressed a carefully calibrated public image had nevertheless begun sliding into obsolescence, and Taylor can be understood to have both hastened this change and yet also thrived under the system's redesign. Put differently, the Taylor–Burton affair chauffeured in a new paradigm, whereby the couple flamboyantly outlived (and even thumbed their noses at) older models of commercialized propriety and decorum. To understand this transition, we must first locate in Taylor's image the vestiges of an older model of stardom premised on the idea that stars possess that 'special something'. Studio-era stars were celebrated for their 'authentic, gifted self,' explains Joshua Gamson, and 'fame, based on an indefinable internal quality of the self, was natural, almost predestined'.[9] That Taylor once adhered to such paradigms was particularly evident in the rhetoric surrounding her death at the age of seventy-nine; *Time* magazine film critic Richard Corliss described her as 'indomitable and irreplaceable, embodying the movies' glamour, excess, and transcendence', and asserts, 'she was the Hollywood star'.[10] Similarly, *People* magazine's obituary quotes talk show host Larry King, who said, 'We lost the last of what can truly be called a "star."'[11] This investment in designating Taylor a 'star' can be attributed to a number of factors, including her longevity as an actress, her fruitful association with the studio system during its heyday, her natural beauty and seemingly innate glamour, and her willingness to live her life in accordance with her film roles. What, then, does it mean to say that thanks to her affair with Burton, Taylor inaugurated a new phase to her stardom, wherein the couple also became modern 'celebrities', too?

To begin, it is crucial not to paint too saccharine or innocent a picture of Taylor prior to her affair with Burton. Known even at the time of her childhood for her feisty energy, her transition to adulthood was marked by the suggestion of steamy sexuality. As Richard Dyer notes, even in roles where she seems concerned with assuring a man of her love, 'Elizabeth Taylor's voice, though, wants something else, her own pleasure, only what that is cannot be spoken or even known. Perhaps it is the voice of the clitoris in an age that spoke only of the penis.'[12] One might expand on Dyer's boldly anatomical suggestion, extrapolating it to the realm of the sociocultural since, for some, Taylor's brash assertions of her own agency resonated with the sexual revolution and the coming quest for women's liberation. A 'poster girl' for the new morality of the 1960s, Taylor challenged the Puritanism of 1950s America, argues Susan McLeland, and broke through repressive and sexist double standards which held that only men should be sexually desirous.[13]

This attribution of Taylor as a sexually adventurous and experienced woman was also instrumental to her casting in *Cleopatra*. Already four times married, Taylor demanded a salary of a million dollars – a first for a female star – and producer Walter Wanger insisted that he could not make the film without her.

The extent to which the studio quickly got more than it bargained for thanks to her affair with Burton, is, however, revealed in first hand correspondence from the set. While Wanger writes on 2 January 1962 that 'Liz and Richard Burton played their first scene together', and observes with pleasure that 'There comes a time during a movie when the actors become the characters they play. This merger of real personality into the personality of the role has to take if a performance is to be truly effective. That happened today'.[14] The overlap between life and art nevertheless quickly became a source of concern. Told by director Joseph Mankiewicz on 26 January that 'Liz and Burton are not just playing Antony and Cleopatra!' Wanger writes, 'I was extremely concerned. Elizabeth is the pivot on which the entire film balances. As the producer, I don't want her involved in any emotional crisis, large or small'.[15] A similar turn from anticipation to consternation is evidenced in correspondence between Fox Publicity Manager Nathan Weiss and Assistant Publicity Manager Jack Brodsky (released in 1963 as *The Cleopatra Papers*). Brodsky writes in late 1961 of his excitement about the couple's chemistry: 'Burton and Taylor will set off sparks and already Fisher is jealous of the lines Burton has'.[16] By 15 February 1962, Brodsky is near frantic, worrying about the picture's exponentially rising costs against the backdrop of its stars' flagrant adultery: 'What we clearly must do is bottle it up as long as we can'.[17]

This seemingly naïve hope nevertheless soon explodes; on 30 March, Weiss writes a telegram from New York, 'PAPERS ARE FILLED TAYLOR BURTON ON TOWN STOP ANGRY LETTERS POURING IN STOP EXECS UPSET BECAUSE AFFAIR NOW PUBLIC STOP THOUGHT YOU SHOULD KNOW'.[18] Energies quickly turn to the practical matter of using Burton and Taylor's scandal strategically, for as *The Cleopatra Papers* reveals, the affair provided the film traction, in large part because Taylor and Burton's life *was* the story. By June 1962, publicity executives are taking cues not from studio executives, but from the paparazzi. Brodsky recounts the ideas of photographer Bert Stern:

> He quickly saw that his story wasn't on the 'set' but beside it. Only the offstage romantic story is commercial, in his opinion, the angle being that it's not what the world thinks, it's full of affection between them and the latter-day parallel of a classic romance. The saving grace of such a layout to be that Mank [director Joseph Mankiewicz] would select from the film script quotes that parallel Stern's pictures, thus linking the affair to the film.[19]

This advice proved fruitful: though Mankiewicz wanted to release *Cleopatra* as two films (the first focusing on Cleopatra and Caesar and the second featuring Cleopatra and Mark Antony) now studio head Darryl Zanuck would have none of it. Instead, the picture was reshaped and reorganized to capitalize on the affair: a planned publicity poster for the film did not even mention the name of the two leads, but rather featured a sketch of a barely clothed Taylor and Burton, dressed as Cleopatra and Antony, lying in each other's arms. According to the creative advertising consultant who recommended the publicity stunt, 'The simple fact is that the campaign could not have been done for any other picture in the history of the business.'[20] (The poster was eventually altered, however, to include Rex Harrison, who played Julius Caesar.)

This publicity campaign nevertheless provides a pivotal indication of the process by which *Cleopatra* transitioned Burton and Taylor from stars to celebrities. Their lives became the central text, eclipsing the film narrative, and giving credence to Taylor's eventual claim that 'I am my own industry. I am my own commodity.'[21] If Taylor's star image once balanced real-life events with film appearances, subsequent to her affair with Burton this equilibrium shifted unalterably, such that the couple's flamboyant, peripatetic and tumultuous lifestyle – and their willingness to commodify it – catapulted them into the realm of global celebrity. If anything, in fact, the vitriol directed against them for their misdeeds only increased their notoriety. This elevation in stature was especially helpful for Burton, who saw his marque value rise as he took on increasingly more commanding screen roles. Parsing out the meaning of 'star-as-celebrity', Christine Geraghty offers that 'the term celebrity indicates someone whose fame happens outside the sphere of their work and who is famous for having a lifestyle.'[22] In such a realm, the film text takes a clear backseat to the life: Geraghty adds, 'In the celebrity mode the films are relatively unimportant.'[23] As revealed by the relative insignificance of *Cleopatra* as a film itself, the crucial aspect of Taylor and Burton's fame was instead the controversy they courted, their hypervisibility, and finally, their status as a 'self-contained media event.'[24]

To return finally to the notion of the 'celebrity nightmare', such a designation is a certain and far cry from the sort of glamourous Hollywood star that rose to prominence during the studio system. While reappraisals of Taylor's life in the wake of her death tended to downplay this latter aspect of her notoriety, its lingering effects can nevertheless be felt in what seemed an all too fitting moment of intertextual resonance. *Lifetime*'s made-for-television movie about the couple stars the controversy-laden Lindsay Lohan as Taylor; similarly a likeable and charismatic child and teen star, Lohan turned into young addict, an actor whose offences now include drugs, public intoxication and a shoddy work ethic. As they were for Taylor, the economic consequences of a tarnished reputation have been visited on Lohan, who was countersued by clothing company DNAM Apparel Industries over her failed clothing label, 6126. In the countersuit, DNAM alleged that Lohan's 'drug-addled image' destroyed her brand's reputation and rendered it impossible to sell the items in her collection. Lohan's casting in *Liz and Dick*, in this respect, adds another level of meaning to Taylor's lasting celebrity, reminding audiences again of how 'real-life' personalities (and their failings) tend to trump professional outputs.

The dawn of paparazzi and the new tabloid system

Shortly after Taylor and Burton begin their steamy affair in the diegeis of Lifetime's *Liz and Dick*, they go out for dinner, seeking what Taylor calls 'somewhere quiet'. Instead, the pair are mobbed as they exit their hired car, greeted with popping flashbulbs, and the headline 'Arrivederci Eddie' appears in the next morning's papers. In the scene that follows, a hapless Fox publicist tries to explain to an exasperated and furious Darryl Zanuck that the pictures were taken by 'paparazzi', a term that describes 'little buzzing insects' and coined by Federico Fellini.[25] Though the publicist comments that they are 'just kids on motor scooters', Taylor and Burton soon clarify the photographers' monumental place in the history of celebrity journalism, explaining that the press would never report such stories before.

Liz and Dick's insistence on Taylor and Burton's central role vis a vis new developments in the history of tabloid journalism has been verified by media scholars and historians. About the famous and steamy paparazzi picture, taken in Italy, where a reclining Taylor lies on a boat, ready to accept a kiss (if not more) from her adulterous lover, Ellis Cashmore writes:

> Once it was possible for Hollywood stars to divide themselves, presenting a public persona to their adoring audience while reserving a space for their private selves. … Even compelling newsworthy figures, like Taylor, were able to keep their distance: there might have been curiosity about her private life, but her audience knew only as much as she and her advisors thought appropriate.[26]

Cashmore suggests that this picture of Taylor and Burton, and the scandal it implied, 'signaled the change',[27] and credits their affair with inaugurating a period where stars were now fair game for the press. Though careful to acknowledge that the outing of the Taylor–Burton liaison did not start the trend per se, Cashmore nevertheless asserts that 'it was the single most important episode in the transition to a culture in which everything we knew arrived via the media'.[28] I want to acknowledge the truth of Cashmore's point that Burton and Taylor's affair served as a harbinger of change, but also press on it a bit to discuss their agency in creating the attributions that would be central to their lasting designation as epic lovers.

Much like the transition from star to celebrity bespeaks fundamental shifts in the notion of a reputation economy, the story of Taylor and Burton's scandal is often deployed to confirm film studios' lessening vice grip in the face of their stars' cult of personality. After being told by Burton that he would have to end the affair because of pressure from his wife, Taylor allegedly attempted suicide in February 1962 – an ordeal attended by hordes of paparazzi who waited outside the hospital. Mann observes, 'How different from the days at MGM, where studio publicity chief Harold Strickling would never have allowed such scandalous news to leak to the press. And stars and publicists had not yet mastered the art of using scandal to their own advantage – although they were learning fast'.[29] What Mann observes as a weakening, however, can also be ascertained as a democratizing and humanizing modification in the cultural function of celebrity gossip: as critic P. David Marshall describes it, celebrity discourse privileges the 'interpersonal dimension – what was often defined in newspaper coverage as the human feature – of the organisation of our culture'.[30] Taylor and Burton's affair coincided with these transitions, a confluence that worked to position their relationship as a natural outgrowth of unstoppable passion, one that defied stodgy convention. In other words, the attribution of their affair as an act of 'emotional emancipation'[31] from a controlling studio and a disapproving public capitalized beautifully on the notion that they were fighting an unfair and unbending system, as well as borrowed from a romantic (and quite American) mythology which held that the chains of propriety and tradition must be thrown over in favour of the needs of the individual, or in this case, the couple.

This mythology not only benefitted Taylor and Burton, but also symbolically empowered audiences to make their own estimations of the couple's intentions, and to feel as if they were doing so without the mediating intervention of studio-hired publicists. As Marshall asserts, 'gossip circulated around celebrities as an explanation of personality that went beyond their on-screen personae and moved them into a public "community" of recognisable figures who revealed at least part of their private experiences to heighten the affective connection to an audience.'[32] This audience connection, in turn, has been central to the couple's casting as great lovers. Many twenty-first-century texts on Taylor and Burton note, for instance, that they were famously open and honest despite their transgressions, an attribution that has fed into the idea that their love was all encompassing enough so as to not be beholden to any other strictures. This sense of devil-may-care towards privacy, however, likely only made the pair more likeable. Reprinting Taylor's famous statement that she refused to get a 'heart attack' over the bad publicity surrounding the affair, and her knowledge that she was regarded as a 'scarlet woman', Mann writes, 'To a new way of thinking, a celebrity who eschewed spin and studio trickery was worth the veneration. She was a heroine indeed. ... For a star to speak so plainly was unprecedented.'[33] This sense of Taylor and Burton's 'authenticity' is, likewise, one that would later align with popular forms like reality television where participants are rewarded for their transparency. (Among other attributions, Taylor and Burton are routinely called the first 'reality stars.')

Taylor and Burton's elaborate dance with the press, which they both courted and scorned, was instrumental, I argue, in the construction of what was a decidedly neoliberal vision of the triumph of individualized love. Their heavily reported and widely emphasized attempts to evade the press – claiming to crave solace from the burden of intrusion – deftly situated them as 'normal' people who merely want to love one another in peace. Describing the period of time when *Cleopatra* was filming, the authors of *Furious Love* recount that

> their happiest moments were when they managed to escape for a few days, hiding out in a pink stucco villa they secretly rented in Porto Santo Stefano. She always relished those occasions when she could pretend to be an ordinary woman: 'We'd spend weekends there. I'd barbecue. There was a crummy old shower and the sheets were always damp. We loved it – absolutely adored it.'[34]

Positioning the couple against the spectre of invasive publicity, such rhetoric paints a picture of a pair who hungers for the sort of quotidian pleasures that non-celebrities routinely access, as well as rather disingenuously suggests their willingness to sacrifice creature comforts in the name of passion. This attribution also sets up some of the couple's hyperbolic excesses (such as living

Figure 13.1 Lindsay Lohan, playing Elizabeth Taylor in *Liz and Dick* (Lifetime Channel, 2012), moments before gesturing to the hordes of paparazzi. Screen grab.

on a 130-foot yacht with their children and a crew of eight as they sailed around the Mediterranean) as a herculean effort to be 'alone'.

Such apocryphal images have, importantly, also become a cornerstone of their celebrity. In an early scene from *Liz and Dick* that appears quite indebted to Taylor's characterization of the stucco villa, Burton and Taylor enjoy a lazy, sex-filled sojourn in what they describe as a mouldy house with no electricity, until they are caught skinny dipping by hordes of photographers (see Figure 13.1). Initially indignant, Taylor yells: 'you call yourselves journalists? Why the hell do you want more photographs of us?' Yet in the next breath, Taylor proclaims: 'Screw it. They want a show, let's give them a show.' This about-face from shying away from to seeking publicity casts the couple as inhabiting their celebrity according to twenty-first edicts, and offers an explanatory rationale for the current tendency to regard them as shedding light on more contemporary modes of celebrity.

Mediatized love is, of course, routinely manufactured by creating obstacles to its realization: in this case, the paparazzi is yet another hurdle to be symbolically overcome with (not incidentally) the couple's considerable fortune. Likewise, as I have argued elsewhere, Taylor and Burton's relationship was perennially circumscribed by reports of their difficulties, namely, Burton's philandering, drinking and jealousy over her career; Taylor's histrionic behaviours, materialism and vanity; and their shared quick tempers and recklessness with money.[35] Their insistent proclamations of the persistence of their relationship in the face of considerably bad odds assisted in manufacturing the appearance of unstoppable love, despite the fact that the couple in fact split up twice, divorcing in 1973, then remarrying again in 1975 and divorcing for the final time nine months later. Their relationship to the press, and their significance to the history of tabloid culture, nevertheless helped to manufacture the attributions of extreme emotionality and devotion for which the couple is still remembered.

Conclusion: Burton and Taylor as celebrity origin text

In its introductory pages, *Furious Love* asserts that Taylor and Burton's love story 'brought us the modern accoutrements of celebrity: the relentless paparazzi, the continuous press exposure, the public airing of private grief. In short it brought us "Liz and Dick," a tabloid shorthand that they hated but that stood for everything extravagant and over-the-top about their all-too-public lives.'[36] This statement succinctly presages (and likely influenced) *Liz and Dick*, a production that serves as an exposé of the pressures of negotiating fame, public life and private turmoil. Reviewing *Liz and Dick*, the online magazine *Slate* comes to a similar conclusion about the couple's enduring appeal:

> The couple retains fascination 50 years after their initial coupling because they managed to be so many things at once: paparazzi-magnet stars and serious actors; epically gluttonous homewreckers who were devoted to their children and, in Taylor's case, charity; the ultimate symbols of old-fashioned glamour who defied Hollywood's rules and all arbiters of propriety (including the pope!) by living exactly as they wished, controversy be damned.[37]

Such useful diagrams of Taylor and Burton's fame trajectory echo this article's emphasis on how celebrity became a central tenet in their lasting relevance. Their status as an origin text likewise stems, we might speculate, from the pair's association with 'extreme' states – namely, emotionality, consumption and sensuality – attributions as equally reflected in their film roles as in their lives.

Though such exaggerations border on the parodic, the couple was undeniably scandal-ridden, hyperconsumptive, hypercombustible and hypersexual, as well as spendthrift and extravagant, qualities crystallized in tangible markers of their coupledom such as the 33-carot Krupp diamond that Burton purchased for Taylor in 1968. A confirmation of what sociologist Eva Illouz has called the 'romantic utopia', Taylor and Burton's lasting attribution as great lovers underlines the extent to which true love is indexed by experiences of consumer capitalism, and ritualized by purchasable quantities such as jewellery and luxury travel.[38] It is no accident, as well, that the contemporary couple most directly aligned with Burton and Taylor is Angelina Jolie and Brad Pitt, a duo whose scandal-ridden beginning has been largely soothed by their globetrotting commitment to the world's children, and whose beauty, devotion to their family and opulent lifestyle has continued to ensure their wide appeal. In both cases, a focus on consumption as glamourous and sexy enterprise assures these couples' functioning as celebrity paragons.

Finally, Taylor and Burton's status as an origin text for celebrity coupling must be said to have benefitted enormously from the fact that all their appearances, be they on film, television or the stage, centralized and focalized on their real life. Even the well-respected *Who's Afraid of Virginia Woolf* (1966), in which the couple plays a duelling long-married pair who generate thrills through lies, illusions and put-downs, reverberated with their real-life status as a couple whose fights were incendiary. This incessant interplay, where the boundaries between life and art are forever undiscernible, is a point also made poignantly if rather pathetically in the BBC made-for-TV movie *Burton and Taylor*, about their real-life appearance in 1983 in Noel Coward's stage play *Private Lives*. In the movie, a trying-to-stay-sober Burton and a pain-killer and alcohol-addicted Taylor negotiate their waning and painful on-again-off-again attraction, while portraying a divorced couple who fall in love again during their separate honeymoons. (The advertisement for the show that ran in the *New York Times* featured an enormous heart with an arrow through it, and the tagline 'Together Again'.) *Burton and Taylor* makes clear that audience interest in the show was driven predominantly by the tantalizing prospect of watching the actors qua themselves; when Taylor cancels a performance as an act of retaliation after being insulted by Burton, half of the audience exits rather than viewing the play with an understudy, and the theatre goes dark the next night. Similarly, audiences gleefully eat up Taylor's hamming it up on stage – winking at them literally and figuratively, she playfully acknowledges that she is portraying herself. The TV movie is nevertheless overlaid with a profound sense of nostalgia, since this professional pairing on the stage represented the last time the couple saw each other before Burton's sudden death of a cerebral haemorrhage in 1984 at the age of fifty-eight. (Also of note is the fact that in this production Taylor is played by the oftentimes offbeat Helena Bonham Carter. Known for her eclectic roles, unconventional pairing with director Tim Burton, and peculiar appearance, Bonham Carter's casting seems calculated to echo Taylor's designation in her later years as a slightly outlandish eccentric.)

In a telling statement, director Joseph Mankiewicz once claimed that for Taylor, 'living life was a kind of acting'.[39] The same could and should be said of Taylor and Burton, consummate performers whose over-the-top lifestyle and persistent commitment to fame work in their so-called real lives added lustre to their professional work and catapulted them into the annals of great loves. The fact that their life is, in the twenty-first century, still such a tantalizing tale that it is retold in myriad forms, including being reproduced in art about the couple, wherein actors (who, as I have argued, bring their own chain of associations and meanings) now play *them*, adds yet another level of intertextuality to a story that was already replete with a palimpsest of notable associations. Such additions further complicate a tale where the distinction between theatricality and authenticity was already impossible to disentangle, yet provide perhaps the most fitting tribute possible to a couple whose celebrity lives on in the same fashion as their love. Forever uber-present, yet not quite accessible, Taylor and Burton's famed coupledom persists through recollections, analysis and metacommentary on their adventures, addictions, sorrows, and most importantly, storied passions.

Notes

1 Sam Kashner and Nancy Schoenberger, *Furious Love: Elizabeth Taylor, Richard Burton, and the Marriage of the Century* (New York: Harper Collins, 2010).

2 William Mann, *How to Be a Movie Star: Elizabeth Taylor in Hollywood* (New York: Houghton Mifflin, 2009); Richard Burton, *The Richard Burton Diaries*, ed. Chris Williams (New Haven, CT: Yale University Press, 2013).

3 Peter Bart, 'When Superstars Came with Super Baggage', *Variety*, 21–27 June 2010, 2.

4 Bart, 2.

5 'Liz, Burton Sued by Fox: $50 Million', AP, *The Los Angeles Herald Examiner*, 22 April 1964.

6 'Liz, Burton Sued by Fox: $50 Million'.

7 Aida Hozić, 'Hollywood Goes on Sale; or, What Do the Violet Eyes of Elizabeth Taylor Have to Do with the Cinema of Attractions?', in *Hollywood Goes Shopping*, ed. David Desser and Gareth S. Jowett (Minneapolis: University of Minnesota Press, 2000), 205–06.

8 See Joshua Gamson, 'The Assembly Line of Greatness: Celebrity in Twentieth Century America', *Critical Studies in Mass Communication* 9 (1992): 1–24 for an overview of the fact that stars were considered studio owned-and-operated commodities until the 1950s.

9 Gamson, 8.

10 Richard Corliss, 'Elizabeth Taylor', *Time*, Vol. 177, Issue 13, 4 April 2011.

11 Alex Tresniowski et al., 'Elizabeth Taylor, 1932-2011', *People*, Vol. 75, Issue 14, 11 April 2011, 62–82.

12 Richard Dyer, *Only Entertainment* (London: Routledge, 1992), 115–16.

13 Susan McLeland, 'Elizabeth Taylor: Hollywood's Last Glamour Girl', in *Swinging Single: Representing Sexuality in the 1960's*, ed. Hillary Radner and Moya Luckett (Minneapolis: University of Minnesota Press, 1999), 248–49.

14 Walter Wanger and Joe Hyams, 'Cleopatra: The Trials and Tribulations of An Epic Film', *Saturday Evening Post*, 1 June 1963, 44.

15 Wanger and Hyams, 44.

16 Jack Brodsky and Nathan Weiss, 'The Cleopatra Papers', *Esquire*, August 1963, 35.

17 Brodsky and Weiss, 35.

18 Brodsky and Weiss, 36.

19 Brodsky and Weiss, 40.

20 'New Brand of Showmanship to Sell "Cleopatra" Via Burton-Taylor Art', *Motion Picture Exhibitor*, 13 February 1963.

21 Quoted in Greil Marcus, *Lipstick Traces: A Secret History of the Twentieth Century* (Cambridge, MA: Harvard University Press, 1989), 106.

22 Christine Geraghty, 'Re-examining Stardom: Questions of Texts, Bodies, and Performance', in *Reinventing Film Studies*, ed. Christine Gledhill and Linda Williams (London: Arnold, 2000), 187.

23 Geraghty, 189.

24 Quoted in Mann, 324.

25 Despite the rather awkward nature of this scene, there is good evidence to indicate that the studio heads were in fact blindsided by Taylor and Burton's affair, and that the paparazzi was fundamental to their gradual understanding of the relationship as more than a passing dalliance.

26 Ellis Cashmore, *Celebrity/Culture* (Abingdon, Oxon: Routledge, 2006), 20.

27 Cashmore, 21.

28 Cashmore, 35.

29 Mann, 27.

30 P. David Marshall, 'The promotion and presentation of the self: celebrity as marker of presentational media', *Celebrity Studies* 1, no. 1 (March 2010): 37.

31 Hozić, 217.

32 Marshall, 37.

33 Mann, 323.

34 Kashner and Schoenberger, 28.

35 See Suzanne Leonard, 'The "True Love" of Elizabeth Taylor and Richard Burton', in *Reclaiming the Archive: Feminism and Film History*, ed. Vicki Callahan (Detroit, MI: Wayne State University Press, 2010), 74–97.

36 Kashner and Schoenberger, viii.

37 Karina Longworth, 'It's the Lifetime Movies that Got Small', *Slate*, 23 November 2012.

38 See Eva Illouz, *Consuming the Romantic Utopia: Love and the Cultural Contradictions of Capitalism* (Berkeley: University of California Press, 1997).

39 Kashner and Schoenberger, 58.

14

'Brad & Angelina: And Now ... Brangelina!': A Sociocultural Analysis of Blended Celebrity Couple Names

Vanessa Díaz

The term *Brangelina* – a name created by blending the first names of the celebrity couple Brad Pitt and Angelina Jolie – made its debut in *People* on 9 May 2005,[1] while I was an intern and reporter for the New York bureau of the magazine. The name was created by former *People* magazine editor Larry Hackett, and fuelled a multipage spread of the couple in the May 9 issue. I remember the mock-ups pasted along the edges of the cubicles on the 30th floor of the Time & Life Building, in Rockerfeller Center. At the time, I did not realize that this *Brangelina* spread would become legendary, would stimulate a continuing trend and would serve as a term I still use to this day as a celebrity reporter.

Brangelina did not just affect celebrity media producers; it popularized a new naming practice among the general public and impacted contemporary meanings of celebrity. With the popularity of *Brangelina*, a new standard was set in which celebrity couples linguistically merged into one, and the term grew to represent several social meanings that I will explore in this chapter. While *Brangelina* was not the first combined celebrity couple name, it led to the practice of combining names becoming commonplace in celebrity media newsrooms and sparked a race between celebrity magazines to come up with the next catchy couple portmanteau. Former *People* magazine reporter Nora Robinson[2] told me, 'The name Brangelina represented a shift in celebrity culture and in celebrity reporting. Saying "Tom Cruise and Katie Holmes," for example, was no longer enough. We needed something short and catchy. The popularity of *Brangelina* reflected our celebrity-focused society. It was not necessarily about them as a couple. It was what they represented – a new level of celebrity.'[3]

Figure 14.1 The Jolie-Pitt family in New Orleans on 24 March 2011. From the left is daughter Zahara, son Pax, son Maddox (only his arm is visible), and daughter Shiloh; behind Shiloh is Jolie, holding twin daughter Vivienne, and Pitt, holding twin son Knox. Photo: Galo Ramírez

The case of *Brangelina* has been analysed from the perspective of film studies, focusing on the couples' star power and character portrayals,[4] but there has yet to be any analysis on the sociocultural implications of the combining of celebrity couples' names and of the name *Brangelina* itself. Not only does *Brangelina* index Brad Pitt and Angelina Jolie (see Figure 14.1), it has also taken on several other meanings in American popular culture; the term is its own cultural entity and it carries with it both symbolic and real capital. In addition, the process of bestowing a nickname on the couple also promotes a sense of intimacy between consumers and celebrities. One of the goals of the celebrity media industry is to promote something that makes people feel invested in, attached to and intimate with celebrities. As I will explore in this chapter, the combining of celebrity couples' names into an informal nickname, the popularity of these nicknames in social circulation and the subsequent practice among the general public of creating our own combined couple names, illustrate the achievement of this goal.

This research is part of a larger ethnographic project on the production of the celebrity weekly magazines – *People, Us Weekly, In Touch, Life & Style, OK!*

and *Star* – that builds on my experience as an intern and freelance reporter for *People* since 2004. My experience working as a celebrity reporter provided me with invaluable access to these cultural producers and knowledge of the entertainment and media industries. My particular interest in the combining of celebrity couples' names stems from my fascination with the media's ability to create the illusion of intimacy by bestowing nicknames upon couples (a practice normally reserved for those intimate with a person) and the unique ways in which consumers have decoded and adopted the practice, as well as the general omission of celebrity couples of colour (like Beyoncé and Jay-Z) and Queer celebrity couples from the practice of combining names.

This chapter explores the celebrity media production practice of combining celebrity couples' names as a way to create a new celebrity entity, and is based on ethnographic fieldwork and interviews conducted with reporters and editors of celebrity weekly magazines in New York and Los Angeles from 2010 to 2014. Robinson recalled the first time *Brangelina* was used in *People* magazine: 'The morphing of the two names described exactly what we do in celebrity journalism. We pair people up together and report on them as one unit.'[5] This is a practice that promotes (imaginary) intimacy between consumers and celebrity couples, thus encouraging the personal interest and investment of individuals in those couples.[6] The combining of celebrity couples' names by media outlets, the social circulation of these names, and the subsequent practice of combining names of non-celebrities is indicative of the power of social circulation of media, the potential impact of current social norms on media-marketing tactics, and the public appetite for fabricated intimacy with celebrities. Through the example of *Brangelina*, I explore these assertions by examining the conditions under which combined celebrity couple names emerged, the social meanings that have been attributed to *Brangelina*, turning it into an adjective rather than just a pronoun representing the couple, and the various social media platforms through which consumers have decoded and adopted the practice of blending the names of two coupled individuals. While anthropologist Grant McCracken suggests that the 'meanings' celebrities come to represent are derived 'from the roles they assume in their television, movie, military, athletic, and other careers',[7] I suggest that these meanings are also derived from the framing of the stars by the celebrity news media industry, including through linguistic marketing tactics such as name combining, which fundamentally shift the identities of individual celebrities. Finally, I argue that the blending of celebrity couples' names is an exclusionary practice that predominantly promotes white heteronormativity.

The history of celebrity couple name blending

Graeme Turner suggests that 'we can map the precise moment a public figure becomes a celebrity. It occurs at the point at which media interest in their activities is transferred from reporting on their public role ... to investigating the details of their private lives.'[8] The name change for couples like *Brangelina* is fully representative of media interest in the personal lives of the celebrities *as a couple*. As a celebrity reporter, I know that the priority in covering celebrities always centres on their love lives – it is a general rule that, in an interview with a celebrity, the more personal information a reporter can get from a celebrity, the better. This is a strategy that has persisted since the popular celebrity gossip columns of Hedda Hopper and Louella Parsons in the first half of the twentieth century.[9] By providing consumers with details about a celebrity's love life, media producers encourage consumers to feel invested in that celebrity. A celebrity in a relationship guarantees additional news – an engagement, a baby, marriage, divorce, cheating or just a break-up – and this news will feed a consumer's already developed appetite. Many consumers become invested in celebrity relationships and take sides as things progress or unravel in any given relationship,[10] as in the case of Jennifer Aniston and Brad Pitt (who left Aniston for Angelina Jolie); this break-up led to the creation of websites, t-shirts and other paraphernalia that allowed individuals to declare themselves members of 'Team Aniston' or 'Team Jolie'.[11] As a couple, Pitt and Aniston missed the blended name trend, but the end of their relationship led to *Brangelina*.

For an individual celebrity, a new relationship provides a space for his or her celebrity to be redefined. Accordingly, it has become increasingly commonplace for popular media outlets to blend the two celebrities' names in order to formally remake them into a new, marketable, celebrity entity.[12]

Celebrity uni-names, bundled names, combined names, name meshing, name blends or celebrity couple portmanteaus[13] – there is no agreed-upon name for this trend, but combining the first or last names of celebrity couples has proven to have sustained momentum in popular media and popular culture in the early twenty-first century. *Brangelina* began as a celebrity magazine's marketing tool and turned into a commonplace newsroom name, a name used by the general public, and a practice the public uses in their everyday lives. But *Brangelina* was not the beginning of the name-blending trend.

As film historian Michael Williams illustrates in this volume, the trend can be traced back to what he believes is the first instance of such a blending in the late1920s, when the fan press referred to John Gilbert and Greta Garbo as *Gilbo*. Referring to their business, rather than their personal life, Desi Arnaz and Lucille Ball gave their production company the name 'Desilu' in 1950.[14] Similarly, John Lennon and Yoko Ono trademarked 'Lenono Music' as the name of their music publishing company in 1980. The name *Billary*, used in reference to Bill and Hillary Clinton, was popular among talk radio in the 1990s during Clinton's first years in the White House, but it never caught on in the mainstream media.[15] In terms of contemporary popular culture, in late 2002 or early 2003, celebrities Jennifer Lopez and Ben Affleck began dating and the term *Bennifer* was coined.[16] *Bennifer* created a media craze until the couple's break-up in early 2004. Scott Huver, a Hollywood-based reporter who has worked for *Us Weekly*, *People* and several other major celebrity-focused media outlets, told me, 'There was a clever bit of inspiration in "Bennifer," the first celeb-couple portmanteau to really hit the zeitgeist hard, and I think it became a fun game for writers, editors, bloggers and their readers to play whenever a new couple surfaced.'[17] *People* magazine last used the term *Bennifer* in 2005.[18] That May, *People* launched *Brangelina*. *TomKat* – a blended name for actors Tom Cruise and Katie Holmes – came shortly thereafter. The trend snowballed from there. More recently, the trend has been applied to younger couples, like Zack Efron and Vanessa Hudgens – *Zanessa*,[19] Robert Pattinson and Kristen Stewart – *Robsten*,[20] Leonardo DiCaprio and Blake Lively – *DiLively*,[21] and reality television stars Spencer Pratt and Heidi Montag – *Speidi*.[22] The newest trending combined name used in mainstream media is *Kimye* – a combination of reality television star Kim Kardashian and music producer and rapper Kanye West.[23]

I have previously explored the new pressure on celebrity weekly magazines to stand out in a newly competitive market at the very time *Brangelina* was first published by *People* magazine.[24] During that time, using new and catchy tactics like combined names was a way to draw and maintain readership. Prior to 2000, the weekly magazine *People*, which launched in 1974, had no direct competition in the magazine market. In 2000, *Us Magazine*, which had existed as a more trade-focused bi-monthly and then monthly publication since 1977, relaunched as a weekly to compete with *People*.[25] Two years later, the magazine *In Touch* began publication. Then in 2004, *Life & Style* entered the market and the tabloid newspaper *Star* was relaunched as a magazine to compete with the other celebrity weeklies. The U.S. version of the British weekly celebrity magazine *OK!* was launched the next year. These new magazines brought about a competition for content that had not previously existed in the industry. The expansion from one celebrity weekly magazine to six in the span of only five years created a market in which the magazines struggled to make their product distinctive. Huver said, 'The celebrity naming trend was fun and familiar-feeling at a time when celebrity gossip was reaching an all-time zenith, and it made for catchy cover blurbs and headlines and actually effectively "branded" some of these celebrity romances for public consumption.'[26] Being the first to publish an issue with a name like *Brangelina* on the cover set *People* apart in an increasingly saturated market.

The effects of blended names on identity and public perception

Whether formal or informal, name changes have effects on identity and public perception of identity and, thus, have powerful social meaning.[27] Turner argues that the 'whole structure of celebrity is built on the construction of the individuated personality'.[28] Along with Turner, Frances Bonner and P. David Marshall see celebrities as 'brand names as well as cultural icons or identities; they operate as marketing tools as well as sites where the agency of the audience is clearly evident; and they represent the achievement of individualism'.[29] Based on the practice of combining celebrity couple names, there is a trend towards the construction of couples, rather than individuals, as icons and marketing tools. As Robinson told me,

> [Blended couple names] add more publicity to them as a couple because it makes for a cuter headline, and it makes for people talking about it. You're in the know if you say *Bennifer* instead of Ben and Jen. It causes more buzz. Any word or phrase that is creative helps promote that thing, be it a film or a couple or a product. It's advertising. It's a hook that people attach onto.[30]

From the media's perspective, there are clear marketing benefits. There are implications for the celebrities who form the couple as well.

They were Brad and Angelina and *now* they're *Brangelina*.[31] Given the significance of names on individual identity, the bestowing of a blended name upon a celebrity couple by the media may feel like a violation to the celebrities it affects. Perhaps this is why Brad Pitt and Angelina Jolie eventually expressed to *People* magazine editors that they would not cooperate on magazine coverage if the name *Brangelina* was used. Former *People* reporter Seth Jameson told me,

Angelina Jolie gave the ultimatum that she would not cooperate with any photos or stories unless we agreed to stop using that combo-name. Clearly having her give the magazine a first look at things like baby photos was more important than a silly name that had been coopted by all of the other celebrity weeklies anyway.[32]

Since Jolie worked almost exclusively with *People*, they obliged her request.

Despite Pitt and Jolie's rejection of the name *Brangelina*, it nonetheless took on a life of its own and its multiple meanings cannot be erased from popular culture. Even though *People* ceased using *Brangelina*, that did not stop other magazines from using the name, nor did it slow the creation of other blended celebrity couples' names. Perhaps most importantly it did not affect the circulation of the name *Brangelina* online by fans and bloggers. Modern celebrity couple name blending is a distinct practice from earlier cases in which the celebrities themselves were exercising their agency, rather than the media. In the cases of *Desilu* and *Lenono* the combined names signified the joint ownership of companies by two celebrities who were partners in both business and marriage. By contrast, modern combined names are bestowed by the media upon pairs of celebrities when they merely begin dating, and signify the media's validation of a pair as an 'official' couple regardless of the way the individuals define their own relationship. This is different to the case of *Gilbo*, in which fans coined the term to express their own agency within the fan magazines (see Chapter 1 by Michael Williams). Although *Gilbo* was bestowed unto the couple by fans who did not know them personally, the practice was later adopted by other celebrities themselves (i.e. the case of *Desilu*) to express their own agency. Today, the practice has returned to the hands of the media and fans.

Anthropologist Richard Alford writes: 'A name change is a constant reminder that an identity change has occurred. ... Most people identify so strongly with their names that a name change almost inevitably affects their sense of self.'[33] While Alford's study of naming practices shows that, in various cultures, names are known to change soon after birth, at marriage or at the death of a relative, they are not known to change at arbitrary points in relationships not marked by marriage or child birth.[34] *Brangelina* and *TomKat* were coined by the media before children were conceived or adopted, and before marriage. In fact, Pitt and Jolie had symbolically become one through the name *Brangelina* nearly a decade prior to becoming one in marriage in 2014 (see Figure 14.2).

Figure 14.2 Just a few months before their wedding, Jolie and Pitt are pictured with daughter Zahara at LAX on 14 June 2014. Photo: Eduardo Pimentel

The Associated Press's breaking news article about the wedding quipped, 'The celebrity press and "Brangelina" fans alike had been consumed with the matrimonial mystery.'[35] However, as former *People* reporter and *New York Times* best-selling author Mark Dagostino told me, it was precisely because of the fact that they were already *Brangelina* that, to celebrity reporters (and presumably fans), 'the wedding seemed like a non-event. They'd long proven themselves to be a real couple.'[36] The use of celebrity couple names is a way for the magazines to suggest who is, in fact, a 'real couple' in a time when committed relationships are not quickly signified by marriage.

In so doing, the magazines further one of their primary goals of making celebrities relatable to the consumer. This goal is evidenced by the first section of every *People* magazine issue, called 'Star Tracks', in which celebrities are shown doing things like picking pumpkins for Halloween with their kids or grocery shopping – things that many American families do. The first section of *Us Weekly* is entitled, 'Stars: They're just like us!' It displays photos similar to 'Star Tracks', reflecting how 'the iconography of celebrity photography has begun to move away from the contrived gloss of "the ideal" towards the more mundane territory of "the real."'[37] The celebrity couple name-blending trend is another way for celebrity magazines to prove that stars are 'just like us' in reflecting the changing trends in marriage and marriage practice. Couples in the USA are increasingly living together without getting married. According to the U.S. Bureau of the Census (2010), the number of 'cohabiting' couples – defined as two unmarried people of opposite sex living together – tripled from 1970 to 1980, nearly doubled from 1980 to 1990, nearly doubled again from 1990 to 2000; and continued to rise from 2000 to 2010.[38] Census Bureau data also confirms that young people are continuing to delay marriage.[39] Considering that *People's* demographic is primarily women aged between eighteen and thirty-four,[40] and that the number of young women delaying marriage is increasing,[41] it is fitting that *People* has worked towards increasing the social acceptability of unmarried couples. Thus, the idea 'Stars: They're just like us!' constructs 'us' as much as it constructs 'them'. The blending of couples' names reflects this new generation that does not necessarily get married or take the man's name in a couple and, by so doing, connects the audience of celebrity magazines to the stars they are observing, idolizing and/or emulating.

Brangelina differs from most nicknames because 'in most societies, many individuals informally receive nicknames from their intimates'.[42] Celebrity couple names are generally not given by the couple's 'intimates' but rather by practical strangers at magazines like *People*, and are then adopted by other media producers, media consumers and fans. Since the use of a nickname is generally demonstrative of a close relationship between the speaker and the subject,[43] the use of celebrity nicknames by the media and public is a concrete example of the imaginary relationships between consumers and celebrities.[44] The celebrity media intentionally cultivates these imaginary relationships. Robinson told me, 'When you put together a name like [Brangelina], we are saying that we are *intimate* with them, that we know them well enough to give them a nickname.'[45] Bonnie Fuller, former managing editor of both *Star* magazine and *Us Weekly* echoed Robinson: '[Media consumers] want to have a nickname for the couples because they feel as if they are part of the stars' extended group of family and friends.'[46] Huver explained how this manufactured intimacy encourages consumers to want to follow the couple further, presumably through the continued purchase of celebrity magazines:

> [Brangelina] made the story of two rich, gorgeous and desirable celebrities feel weirdly intimate to the outside world. And in some ways, I think it also personalized them in a way that downplayed the scandalous nature of their union – despite the notorious circumstances of how they got together, the public seemed to want to root for them to work out as a couple.[47]

The closer and more intimate consumers feel to celebrities, the more likely they are to invest in the magazines, as it aids in the maintenance of these imaginary/para-social relationships. In this way, the combining of a celebrity couple's name is symbolic language capital that can be translated into actual capital for the celebrity industry.

The evolution of *Brangelina*: Meanings and uses

The use of *Brangelina* – first by *People* magazine, then by other media, then by celebrities themselves and the general public – is an example of what linguistic anthropologist Debra Spitulnik describes as social circulation of media discourse. 'Social circulation of media discourse provides a clear and forceful demonstration of how media audiences play an active role in the interpretation and appropriation of media texts and messages.'[48] While *People* may have only intended for *Brangelina* to refer to Brad Pitt and Angelina Jolie – the couple – the term has taken on myriad meanings through a variety of media audiences.

Brangelina refers to a couple: Brad Pitt and Angelina Jolie. It also refers to everything that this couple embodies (e.g. cohabiting, glamour, fame, globe-trotting, etc.). Individual names are bound to certain qualities and ideas,[49] but blended names intensify this binding. *Brangelina* refers to a couple, a family, celebrities and fame. It also refers to marketability, extravagance and beauty. A 13 November 2008, MSNBC segment featured *Us Weekly* editor Albert Lee referring to President Barack Obama and his wife, Michelle, as the 'new Brangelina'. The transcript of this segment of the show is as follows:

> MSNBC ANCHOR: It used to be that if you wanted to sell magazines, you'd put Angelina Jolie and Brad Pitt on the cover.
> US WEEKLY EDITOR: I mean, the Obamas are like the new Brangelina. You know? That's why we keep putting them on the cover, you know, week after week. And we did sell over a million copies with the last issue. Everything else on the newsstands just feels totally irrelevant right now. People want to learn more about this family.[50]

Here, Lee is indexing the celebrity status of the Obamas by equating the marketability of *Brangelina* to the marketability of the Obamas. He is not referring to *Brangelina* in the sense of an extravagant, unwed couple adopting and having babies, rather he is referencing the celebrity status and public importance of *Brangelina* and relating that aspect of the couple to the Obamas.

Even other celebrities are using these new terms to create new forms and meanings for use in everyday interactions. In a *People.com* article on the wedding anniversary of actors Jerry O'Connell and Rebecca Romijn, O'Connell says: 'I wish I had something sexy and all *Brangelina* to tell you where we're going to go flying. But it's really just going to be my in-laws crowding us.'[51] Here, not only has the celebrity used the term to represent another couple of celebrities, but he has also indexed it with a new meaning. Since *Brangelina* are known for their jet-setting travel,[52] O'Connell has taken *Brangelina* to mean extravagant travelling, spontaneity or something 'sexy'. Spitulnik writes that the 'public accessibility' of adopted media terms is 'vital for the production of shared meaning.'[53] Now that O'Connell has used *Brangelina* with a new meaning, it becomes shared via media, which leads to a new, shared meaning of the term, adding a dimension to the indexicality of the name. *Brangelina* has come to index glamour, fame, extravagant travel and sexiness, and it has done so explicitly through the portmanteau of the celebrity couple rather than the individual names Brad Pitt and Angelina Jolie. This challenges the prevailing celebrity studies scholarship that argues celebrity is the apotheosis of neoliberal individualism.[54] *Brangelina* shows that meanings of celebrity are now also being defined through constructions of couples as celebrity entities in their own right, with unique names that develop their own meanings.

An important aspect of the implications of *Brangelina* is the way the media consumer has not only used the name, but also how the practice of celebrity couple name making has impacted the consumer on a more personal level. Chris Rojek writes: 'Fame can be understood to be the "glue" that holds the cultural centre together and which offers the alienated and anomic forms of para-social relations ... a part of a material culture that they can invest in and which "invests" in them.'[55] Investment in consumers was demonstrated through a *People.com* poll that asked website visitors to vote on their favourite combined celebrity couple name; through the poll, *People* could learn which couples to focus on in order to please the consumers.[56] Similarly, *USA Today*'s 'Celebrity Couple Name Maker' database that accompanies an online article on celebrity couple names gives consumers something in return for reading and visiting the site.[57] If they are interested in *Brangelina* and other celebrity couples, they can become a part of the naming practice themselves; thus, the consumer feels rewarded for consumption. As anthropologist Kelly Askew notes, 'Emphasis has shifted from the power of the producers to the power of the consumers.'[58] It is also significant that the user-generated 'How To' site, wikiHow, has a page on 'How to Make Your Celebrity Couple Names'.[59] Separate from the *USA Today* database, *consumers* have created instructions on how to develop their own celebrity couple names. *Brangelina* was fed to media consumers by *People* as simply a combination of the names Brad Pitt and Angelina Jolie to index their relationship. The consumer, from other media producers to celebrities to the general public, has owned the term *Brangelina* and redefined it in several ways. The creation of the wikiHow page shows the completion of the cycle of media production agency to media consumer agency.

Where are *Pellen, Mennifer* and *Jayoncé*?: The marginalization of celebrity couples of colour and LGBTQ celebrity couples

It is important to consider how media producers decide which celebrity couples get their names combined. As I examine in this section, non-white and LGBTQ celebrities are largely left out of the name combining. When exploring this issue in my ethnographic research, I encountered numerous justifications for this, including the aesthetics of the sound and appearance of a blended name, and assumptions about which celebrity couples evoke emotion in readers. Brian Coolidge, a freelance reporter for *People* said, 'The ones that do land seem to be those that have a frenetic amount of attention surrounding their personal lives alongside their tremendous fame, and I think the name combo also simply needs to be fun to say or put in print.'[60]

But, to take one example, Lindsay Lohan and Samantha Ronson were not given a name when they were a couple, despite the media's constant interest in Lohan during these years and the potential catchiness of *Lohnson*. The October 13, 2008, issue of *OK!* magazine featured a cover story and four-page spread about Lohan and Ronson next to a shorter *Brangelina*-focused article, but no attempt was made to combine *their* names.[61] The article proclaimed that Lohan and Ronson had been together for months, which is more than could be said of Pitt and Jolie at the time the phrase *Brangelina* was coined. It is difficult not to interpret the magazine's clear interest yet tangible difference in its attempt to market the couple as connected to their Queerness. From my perspective as someone who works in the industry, this practice has become one that reinforces wider social hierarchies even in the celebrity world. Portia de Rossi and Ellen DeGeneres were featured on the cover of *People* for their 2008 wedding,[62] but they were never given a combined name – *Pellen*, perhaps?

One same-sex couple name that has gained traction among consumers is *Larry Stylinson*, the name One Direction fans have given to the fictional romance fans have dreamt up between group members Louis Tomlinson and Harry Styles. This is the most widely used example of a combined name for a gay couple and not only is it a fake couple, but it is sometimes used by fans as a way to demean the boy band members. Thus the phenomenon of the celebrity heterosexual couple name has been most widely applied to a (imagined) same-sex couple in a way that further ostracizes same-sex relationships.

Like Queer celebrity couples, celebrity couples of colour are noticeably less present in the name-combining trend. Michelle and Barack Obama may have been called the next *Brangelina*, but they have not been given a combined name by the press. Beyoncé and Jay-Z are, and Jennifer Lopez and Marc Anthony were, examples of couples that based on their popularity alone seem natural choices for a blended name. When Jennifer Lopez was with Ben Affleck, it was *Bennifer*. But when she was with Marc Anthony, it was never *Mennifer*. Still, Ben Affleck with Jennifer Garner became *Bennifer 2.0* and then *Garfleck*. When Lopez was in a couple with a white man, she was marketed with a combined name, but when she was with another Latino, they were never given a combined name, even though her former partner was given one immediately. This fact exemplifies structural prejudice within the celebrity media industry and celebrity culture. The difference cannot be attributed to the celebrity status of the individual members of the couples, since Marc Anthony, Jay-Z and Beyonce, for example, are long-time A-List celebrities in the US and are arguably *as famous*, if not more so, as Ben Affleck, Jennifer Garner and Katie Holmes (especially Garner pre-*Garfleck* and Holmes pre-*TomKat*).

Perhaps the most prominent recent case of the blended celebrity couple name is *Kimye*. This is the only combined name commonly used in mainstream celebrity press that includes an African American. Previously the only people of colour included in a highly publicized name were two women – Jennifer Lopez and Vanessa Hudgens; no men of colour were part of the combined names before *Kimye* (and the much lesser used *Khlomar* – for Khloe Kardashian and Lamar Odom). In the case of the Kardashians – especially Kim who launched her entire family's entertainment career from an (allegedly) accidentally leaked sex tape – their entire celebrity is built around access (or the illusion of access) to the intimate moments of their everyday lives. As Alice Leppert explores in this collection, the Kardashian family has reaped profits as a result of the promotion of their romantic relationships; thus, perhaps they are invested in the circulation of the intimacy implicit in blended names in a way that is not true for Brad Pitt, Angelina Jolie and other celebrity couples referenced here.[63] While the inclusion of people of colour in blended celebrity couple names is significant regardless of the circumstances, the structure of the name itself is also significant; perhaps not coincidentally, *Kimye* and *Khlomar* are two of very few combined names anchored in the women's names. *Garfleck* and *Spederline* (the combined name for Brittany Spears and Kevin Federline) are the only other two such names, and neither of those two gained the same degree of widespread usage as names anchored in the man's name, such as *Brangelina* and *TomKat*. There has yet to be a popularized blended name for a couple where both individuals are minorities.

Throughout my ethnographic research other reporters and editors in the celebrity media industry have had reasonable disagreements with my suggestions that celebrity name combining is an exclusionary practice promoting white heteronormativity (or interracial heteronormativity so long as one partner, preferably the male, is white – maintaining the acceptable trope of the available minority woman to the white man).[64] Those in disagreement with my proposal have suggested that perhaps the couples I am pointing out simply do not have good *sounding* possibilities for combined names; after all, marketability has to do with catchiness. However, based on my experience in the industry and my observations of how decisions are made in celebrity media production, I do not believe the many examples I provide to be a mere coincidence, nor do I see it adequate to attribute it to the pleasant *sound* of some of the combined names that have been heavily promoted. My suggestion of *Mennifer*, for example, is *exactly* the same as *Bennifer*, with the exception of one consonant. *Pellen*, *Mirack* or *Jayoncé*, seem to flow better than *Garfleck*, for example, or the recent trendy combined name *Robsten*.

Coolidge admitted, 'Honestly, it only now registered to me that, as a celebrity super-couple, Beyoncé and Jay-Z never landed a portmanteau. There seem to be plenty of fun combos to experiment with. They certainly fit the bill of both being uber-famous.'[65] I attribute this discrepancy in representation not to the aesthetics of the potentially combined name or the level of fame of the individuals, but to conservative decisions made by celebrity media producers (reporters and editors alike) based on what they think will sell to the imagined consumer, which they generally presume will be white 'mainstream' couples. Perhaps this presumption is not surprising, given the lack of diversity in celebrity media newsrooms. *People*, for example, has only had a single African-American Senior Editor in its existence, and she recently filed a lawsuit against the magazine alleging racial discrimination.[66]

In 1950, Anthropologist Hortense Powdermaker wrote: 'Hollywood people live more or less *normal* family lives, and it is the current studio policy to do everything possible to publicize this. Publicity and fan magazines have been concentrating on pictures of "normal" family life.'[67] Note the emphasis on the word 'normal' – a word that, when combined with family life, tends to reference the status quo white American nuclear family. In my experience, not much has changed since Powdermaker's research; the only difference is that the magazines seek this angle out on their own, without the aid of studios, and this can explain the restriction of combined names to largely white celebrities and heteronormative couples. As Halle Berry expressed in her 2002 Academy Award acceptance speech for Best Actress, women of colour have remained 'nameless'[68]; so too, literally, have celebrity couples of colour.

Conclusion

This chapter examines the sociocultural significance of *Brangelina* and the practice of celebrity name combining. This practice encourages consumers to relate to the celebrity, while the producer is also looking for ways to make celebrities relatable to consumers. Still, in trying to promote the image of mainstream white, heteronormative America by focusing on combining the names of white, heteronormative celebrity couples, the producers of celebrity media inevitably eliminate the relatability some consumers might have not just to *Brangelina*, but to the practice of combining couples' names.

The use of the term *Brangelina* began with *People* magazine, but did not end with *People*. Instead, a broad range of media consumers have transformed *Brangelina* into much more than *People* editors ever intended or imagined.

Brangelina first represented the informal, even speculated, union of two people – Brad Pitt and Angelina Jolie. Now it represents the 'blending' of all things that have come to be associated with those two people *as* a couple. Consumers are at once consuming *Brangelina* and producing their own meanings of *Brangelina*; and producers, for example Albert Lee of *Us Weekly*, are producing media based on their own consumption and understanding of *Brangelina*. The '24 hour global [media] clock' is on *Brangelina* and the media depictions that result from *Brangelina*'s surveillance provide the fodder leading to the ever-evolving meanings that *Brangelina* embodies. Thus, this phenomenon represents the dynamic relationship between media and consumer – the media provides images and meanings of *Brangelina* for the consumer, and the consumer creates, moulds and redefines what those images and meanings *are*. This process challenges the assertions of popular culture and celebrity-studies scholars who argue that celebrity is built around individualism. *Brangelina* does not override the individuality of Brad Pitt and Angelina Jolie as celebrities, but is its own entity carrying its own shared meanings and value, thus complicating the ways we understand the construction of celebrity in contemporary culture.

Document Appendix

Table 1.1 Cohabitating couples in the USA:

Year	Total
2010	7,500,000
2000	5,500,000
1990	2,856,000
1980	1,589,000
1970	523,000
1960	439,000

(*Source:* U.S. Bureau of the Census).

Notes

1 Michelle Tauber, Jason Lynch and Chris Strauss, 'Brad & Angelina: And Now ... Brangelina!' *People*, 9 May 2005.

2 The names used throughout this chapter are pseudonyms, in order to protect my collaborators; this is common practice in anthropology. Exceptions are Mark Dagostino and Scott Huver, who requested their names be used.

3 Nora Robinson (pseudonym), Interview with the author, March 2012.

4 Linda Ruth Williams, 'Brangelina: Celebrity, Credibility and the Composite Uberstar', in *Shining in Shadows: Movie Stars of the 2000s*, ed. Murray Pomerance (New Brunswick, NJ: Rutgers University Press, 2012).

5 Nora Robinson (pseudonym), Interview with the author, September 2014.

6 John Caughey, 'Gina As Steven: The Social and Cultural Dimensions of a Media Relationship', *Visual Anthropology Review* 10, no. 1 (1994): 126–35.

7 Grant David McCracken, *Culture and Consumption II: Markets, Meaning, and Brand Management* (Bloomington: Indiana University Press, 2005).

8 Graeme Turner, *Understanding Celebrity* (London: Sage, 2004), 8.

9 Samantha Barbas, *The First Lady of Hollywood a Biography of Louella Parsons* (Berkeley: University of California Press, 2005); Hedda Hopper, *The Whole Truth and Nothing but* (Garden City, NY: Doubleday, 1963).

10 For more on celebrity fans' investment, see Joshua Gamson, *Claims to Fame Celebrity in Contemporary America* (Berkeley: University of California Press, 1994).

11 Stephanie Goldberg, '"Team Aniston," "Team Jolie" or "Team Over It"?' CNN.com, 15 August 2012, http://www.cnn.com/2012/08/14/showbiz/celebrity-news-gossip/jennifer-aniston-angelina-jolie/, accessed 20 September 2014.

12 Denham and Lobeck define blends ('also called portmanteaus') as words 'made from putting parts of two words together' (2009: 197). See complete citation below.

13 Kristin Dehnam and Anne Lobeck, *Linguistics for Everyone: An Introduction* (Boston, MA: Wadsworth/ Cengage Learning, 2010).

14 Michael Park, 'Blame Bennifer: Celeb Uni-Names Multiply', *FoxNews.com*, 13 June 2005, http://www.foxnews.com/story/0,2933,159302,00.html, accessed 1 December 2008.

15 Ibid.

16 Ibid.

17 Scott Huver, Interview with the author, September 2014.

18 'Separate Peace: Bennifer One Year Later', *People*, 17 January 2005.

19 'Zanessa on the Red Carpet: Charlie St. Cloud Premiere Pics', *HollywoodGossip. com*, July 2010, http://www.thehollywoodgossip.com/2010/07/zanessa-on-the-red-carpet-charlie-st-cloud-premiere-pics/, accessed 1 August 2010.

20 Brittany Talarico, 'Rob & Kristen Catch a Concert As a Couple', *OK!*, July 2010, http://www.okmagazine.com/2010/07/rob-kristen-catch-a-concert-as-a-couple/, accessed 1 August 2010.

21 'Scoop: Blake Lively and Leo DiCaprio Heating Up in Europe', *People*, 13 June 2011.

22 Stephen Silverman, 'Speidi: The Next TomKat and Brangelina?' *People.com*, 9 May 2008, http://tvwatch.people.com/2008/05/09/speidi-the-next-tomkat-branjelina/, accessed 1 December 2008.

23 Jennifer Garcia, 'Inside Kim Kardashian and Kanye West's Newlywed Life', *People. com*, 30 July 2014, http://www.people.com/article/kim-kardashian-kanye-west-married-life, accessed 30 July 2014.

24 Vanessa Díaz, 'Latinos at the Margins of Celebrity Culture: Image Sales and the Politics of Paparazzi', in *Contemporary Latina/o Media: Production, Circulation, Politics*, ed. Arlene Dávila and Yeidy Rivero (New York: New York University Press, 2014), 125–48.

25 Alex Kuczynski, 'Striking Back at the Empire; Wenner Media Takes on the Mighty Time Inc. In Transforming Us to a Monthly Magazine', *The New York Times*, 27 September 1999.

26 Huver, Interview, 2014.

27 Richard Alford, *Naming and Identity: A Cross-cultural Study of Personal Naming Practices* (New Haven, CT: HRAF Press, 1988).

28 Graeme Turner, 'The Economy of Celebrity', in *Stardom and Celebrity: A Reader*, ed. Sean Redmond and Su Holmes (London: Sage, 2007), 193–205.

29 Frances Bonner, P. D. Marshall and Graeme Turner, 'The Meaning and Significance of Celebrity', in *The Tabloid Culture Reader*, ed. Anita Biressi and Heather Nunn (Maidenhead: McGraw-Hill/Open University Press, 2008), 141–48.

30 Robinson, Interview, 2012.

31 Tauber, Lynch and Strauss, 'Brad & Angelina', 56.

32 Seth Jameson (pseudonym), Interview with the author, September 2010.

33 Alford, *Naming and Identity*, 85–86.

34 Ibid., 18–19.

35 Jake Coyle, 'Jolie, Pitt wed privately at chateau in France', *Associated Press*, 28 August 2014.

36 Mark Dagostino, Interview with the author, September 2014.

37 Adrienne Lai, 'Glitter and Grain: Aura and Authenticity in the Celebrity Photographs of Juergen Teller', in *Framing Celebrity: New Directions in Celebrity Culture*, ed. Su Holmes and Sean Redmond (London: Routledge, 2006), 215–30.

38 See Table 1.1; Rose Kreider, *Housing and Household Economic Statistics Division Working Paper* (Washington, DC: U.S. Bureau of the Census, 2010).

39 Anthony DeBarros and Sharon Jayson, 'Young Adults Delaying Marriage', *USA Today*, 12 September 2007, http://usatoday30.usatoday.com/news/nation/2007-09-12-census-marriage_N.htm, accessed 1 December 2008.

40 'Online Media Kit', *People.com*, Media kit for People magazine and People.com 2008. http://www.people.com/people/static/onlinemediakit/main.html, accessed 1 December 2008.

41 From 2006 to 2010 women married for the first time at older ages than in previous years; Casey Copen et al., *National Health Statistics Report First Marriages in the United States: Data From the 2006–2010* (National Survey of Family Growth, National Center for Health Statistics, 2012).

42 Alford, *Naming and Identity*, 18.

43 Edward Sapir, 'Language', in *Selected Writings in Language, Culture and Personality*, ed. David G. Mendelbaum (Berkeley: University of California Press, 1949), 15–16.

44 Caughey, 'Gena as Steven'.

45 Robinson, Interview, 2014.

46 Damien Cave, '2005: In a Word; Scalito', *New York Times*, 25 December 2005.

47 Huver, Interview, 2014.

48 Debra Spitulnik, 'The Social Circulation of Media Discourse and the Mediation of Communities', *Journal of Linguistic Anthropology* 6, no. 2 (1996): 165.

49 McCracken, *Culture and Consumption*.

50 Ben Smith, 'The New Brangelina', *Politico.com*, 13 November 2008, http://www.politico.com/blogs/bensmith/1108/The_new_Brangelina.html, accessed 14 November 2008.

51 Monica Rizzo, 'Jerry O'Connell: Anniversary to Be with In-Laws', *People.com*, 15 July 2008, http://www.people.com/people/article/ 0,,20212628,00.html, accessed 1 December 2008.

52 'Brangelina Take Berlin: The Globe-Trotting Couple Takes Their Family to Germany for Their Latest Adventure', *OK!*, 13 October 2008.

53 Spitulnik, 'The Social Circulation of Media Discourse', 162.

54 Bonner, Marshall and Turner, 'The Meaning and Significance of Celebrity', 144; Turner, *The Economy of Celebrity*, 195.

55 Sean Redmond, 'Intimate Fame Everywhere', in *Framing Celebrity: New Directions in Celebrity Culture*, ed. Su Holmes and Sean Redmond (London; New York: Routledge, 2006), 35.

56 'Celebrity Name Game: Brangelina? TomKat?' *People.com*, 23 November 2005, http://www.people.com/people/ article/0,,1133516,00.Html, accessed 1 December 2008.

57 Rod Coddington, Allison Maxwell and Chad Palmer, 'Celebrity Couple Name Maker', *USA Today*, 5 April 2007, http://usatoday30.usatoday.com/life/people/2007-04-05-celeb-nicknames_N.htm, accessed 1 December 2008.

58 Kelly Askew, 'Striking Samburu and a Mad Cow: Adventures in Anthropollywood', in *Off Stage/On Display: Intimacy and Ethnography in the Age of Public Culture*, ed. Andrew Shryock (Stanford, CA: Stanford University Press, 2004), 8.

59 wikiHow, 'How to Make Your Celebrity Couple Names', http://www.wikihow.com/Make-Your-Celebrity-Couple-Names, accessed 1 December 2008.

60 Brian Coolidge (pseudonym), Interview with author, September 2014.

61 Meaghan Murphy, 'Cover Story: Lindsay & Samantha: Inside Their Romance', *OK!*, 13 October 2008; 'Brangelina Take Berlin', *OK!*

62 Julie Jordan, 'Ellen & Portia's Wedding!' *People*, 1 September 2008.

63 When the name *Speidi* was first used, it was suspected by media producers (including myself) that reality television stars Heidi and Spencer Pratt coined this name and suggested that friends who worked at the weekly magazines began using it. It is possible that Kris Jenner ('momager' of the Kardashian sisters) did the same with the names *Khlomar* and *Kimye*. If this is the case, then reality television stars are, in fact, taking the agency back into the hands of the celebrities, as was the case with *Desilu* and *Lenono*.

64 Mary Beltrán and Camilla Fojas, *Mixed Race Hollywood* (New York: New York University Press, 2008); Gina Marchetti, *Romance and the 'Yellow Peril': Race, Sex, and Discursive Strategies in Hollywood Fiction* (Berkeley: University of California Press, 1993).

65 Coolidge, Interview, 2014.

66 Dareh Gregorian, 'Fired Black Editor of People Sues Magazine Over Alleged Discrimination Against African-Americans', *New York Daily News*, 20 August 2014, http://www.nydailynews.com/new-york/ex-black-editor-sues-people-discrimination-claims-article-1.1911165, accessed 20 September 2014.

67 Hortense Powdermaker, *Hollywood: The Dream Factory: An Anthropologist Looks at the Movie-Makers* (Boston: Little, Brown, 1950), 23.

68 Redmond, 'Intimate Fame Everywhere', 31.

15

Jane Fonda, Power Nuptials and the Project of Ageing

Linda Ruth Williams

This chapter investigates the movie star Jane Fonda, the ways her three marriages inform her public profile and the phases of her career, and particularly how marriage to the media magnate Ted Turner and its aftermath saw a developing project of ageing which continues to characterize Fonda's late-life celebrity. The Fonda name was a movie dynasty brand even before she first 'owned' it in the 1960s: daughter of Hollywood star Henry Fonda, she first acted at the tail end of the studio system, became a feted performer in the 1960s and 1970s (with two Oscars to her name), and is still working well into her 70s. She fostered a parallel career as a fitness guru, and has been prominent in left-liberal politics. Her recent autobiographical writings (which are a key source for me) suggest that she feels, or felt, overshadowed by her husbands, yet her partner-choices also coordinate each life-work stage. Married first to French filmmaker Roger Vadim, who directed her in *Barbarella* among other films, from 1965 to 1973, she was then paired with politician and activist Tom Hayden from 1973 to 1990, and to CNN mogul Turner from 1991 to 2001.

It is the Turner liaison which I mostly discuss here. At times Fonda's star wattage imbalanced public representations of the couple, but she also slipped into a 'First Lady' helpmeet role rather at odds with the feisty 'Hanoi Jane' image of previous media representations.[1] Age, or rather ageing, was a key leitmotif in this public coupling, with the romance blossoming when they were both past fifty. The relationship therefore staged two resonantly gendered narratives: a story of competing celebrity between fifty-something megastars in which the woman occasionally shines brighter, and Fonda's individual-developing lifestyle philosophy of gendered ageing, more strongly articulated later and consolidated in her twenty-first century writings. Both ageing stardom and celebrity are currently burgeoning areas in visual and cultural studies, and this chapter is positioned at the intersection between these developing fields. Significant recent work has explored celebrity ageing (in particular Deborah Jermyn's 2012 special issue of *Celebrity Studies* on ageing female stars). Below I show Fonda's negotiation of coupling as key to two rebrandings she has fashioned: from younger revered performer/sex-goddess/fitness guru to still-sexualized, still-fit *grande dame*, and – crucially – from star to celebrity.

He said/she said: Vadim and Hayden through the celebrity autobiography

Discussion of ageing stardom has pointed a particular spotlight on the public negotiation of the ageing process by female performers reformulating images of older women on-screen. By the second half of their lives women such as Meryl Streep, Susan Sarandon and Bette Midler are securely established and have defined public voices. By their 50s and 60s, baby boomer celebrity women may have already worked their way through a number of serial liaisons with fellow celebrities or 'civilians',[2] or may have one constant if shadowy non-celebrity partner supporting them from the wings (Streep, Dolly Parton, Julie Christie). As Elaine Showalter emphasizes in her Introduction to Lynne Segal's 2014 *Out of Time: The Pleasures and the Perils of Ageing*, this generation has also come of age in a pioneering feminist moment, and public ageing impacts upon views of sexual freedom.[3] At the intersection of celebrity and ageing studies, I explore here how publicity around partnerships contributes to older women's dissemination. Relationships are commonly central to popular interest in female celebrities, a platform upon which social difference might be established (opulent weddings; multiple partners) or sameness might be claimed (troubled love lives we might all recognize). How does serial coupledom feed into the charismatic cocktail of constructed stardom – elusive yet nearly normal, unattainable yet just like me?

As promotional materials pedalling preferred versions of life events, celebrity autobiographies are a rich resource for discussions of potent coupling, and form key resources in this chapter.[4] Vadim, Hayden and Turner all addressed their relationships with Fonda in their autobiographies; Fonda's remarkably self-analytic 2005 autobiography *My Life So Far* (hereafter *Life*) examines the marriages in forensic detail. It is quite rare to get complimentary or contradictory accounts of the same relationship, and particularly illuminating to compare views of celebrity marriage over fifty. I will turn to the Fonda–Turner liaison (and the writing it generated) below, but I first want to pause on the two previous 'Mr Jane Fondas'.

Life was promoted as the story of Jane's troubled relationship with her powerful yet cold father, developed through her troubled relationships with her husbands. Structurally it delineates her life through three acts, each roughly thirty years, with over 100 pages detailing later life, her so-called 'Third Act' – a personal-political (and husbandless) phase which is also, I will argue, the moment when she shifts from star to celebrity. *Life*'s account of the marriages provides an illuminating contradiction between the introspective (vulnerable, needing male approval, father-fixated) and the feminist-activist campaigning voice of a generation. She even suggests that her marriages instigated self-abnegating identity shifts: 'maybe I simply become whatever the man I am with wants me to be: "sex kitten," [Vadim] "controversial activist," [Hayden] "ladylike wife on the arm of corporate mogul" [Turner]'.[5] I must stress that in the case of this singular performer who has forged a complex identity outside of her relationships (and despite what Fonda herself says), I do not wish to argue that she is primarily identifiable through men. Her film acting speaks for itself, but it is also precisely her ability so self-analytically to meditate on her relationships which distinguishes her, even in promotional works. Nevertheless, her choice of husbands does uncannily reflect her career and life choices – more provocatively, we might even say she 'accessorises' her image-shifts with appropriate men. Fonda was already an established actor before she married, and was directed by, Vadim. Political activism preceded the liaison with Hayden. She converted Turner to her environmental concerns even while she was supposedly just his trophy wife.

Accounts of the Fonda–Vadim relationship are characterized by her youth and inexperience and his Svengali-Teacher role (as he had been in previous major relationships with Brigitte Bardot and Catherine Deneuve). They met through work, and their relationship was threaded through cinema; her developing star profile in the mid-1960s was promoted with reference to this intercontinental marriage. To the American public Vadim gave the established actress a more sexual profile (the marketing of *Circle of Love* [1964], with a huge poster of a naked Fonda in Times Square, did much to establish her sexualized 1960s image); to the French she was Henry Fonda's daughter (despite moving to

France to escape this identity), and now-partnered with Bardot's Pygmalion. But though this continued to identify her in terms of men, Vadim himself publicly referred to her as 'Janefonda', a one-word label which seems closer to a brand than a romantic nickname.

However a curious reversal happens with the second volume of Vadim's autobiography. Entitled *Bardot, Deneuve and Fonda: The Memoirs of Roger Vadim*, the book squarely identifies Vadim through his attachment to famous women. Patricia Bosworth's authoritative (if not authorized) biography of Fonda follows Vadim's approach of making the marriage emblematic of its moment: Hollywood's post-1967 countercultural renaissance; Paris in May 1968; civil rights and anti-Vietnam protests – the star-couple as symbol of the 1960s zeitgeist. Vadim claims he allowed Fonda to end the failing relationship in order to preserve her fragile ego, while ruefully acknowledging 'Henry's phrase that Jane repeated one day: "One never leaves a Fonda"'.[6] Fonda, claims Vadim, 'was not seeking a new love affair. She wasn't leaving me for another man, but for herself. ... The truth is that I much preferred to see her taking off on the chariot of politics, at war against war, to her leaving me for another man.'[7]

This (self-preserving) line on Fonda's politicization renders the marriage a casualty of war. However, in Fonda's preferred version, penned some nineteen years later when she was in her 60s, it is not the Vietnam War but the sex war which instigates her departure. The most difficult element of the relationship with which she struggles in *Life* (and also the most widely reviewed) – Vadim's predilection for open relationships and three-way sex – becomes a platform for feminist self-analysis in Fonda's 2005 writing. Her reading of feminist Robin Morgan's autobiography in 2001 gave her the language to reassess her own history, and the Vadim relationship is rearticulated through feminism, even as the original event was self-abnegating:

> Until then I had not planned on writing about my own experiences. I thought: There are enough people who dislike me, I don't need to give them even more ammunition. But ... [in reading Robin's book] I saw that if the telling of my life's journey was to matter to other women and to girls, I would, like Robin, have to be honest about how far I've come and the meaning of where I've been.[8]

The question she continues to pose through the book, but first here in relation to Vadim and through an avowed feminism, is: 'In my public life, I am a strong, can-do woman. How is it, then, that behind closed doors, in my most intimate relations, I could voluntarily betray myself?'[9] Of course this inability to make the personal political comes ironically at the same time she becomes an icon of second wave feminism. She then identifies herself as a sister-under-the-skin:

> Overlay her silence with a man's sense of entitlement and inability (or unwillingness) to read his partner's subtle body signals, and you have the makings of a very angry woman, who will stuff her anger for the same reasons she silences her sexual voice.[10]

Clearly Fonda's is not unexamined celebrity-life-writing as mere promotional tool (though it also functions as that – she book-toured *Life*, and has profited from it). To read disarming revelations as simple examples of the 'celebrity confessional' which Sean Redmond analyzes[11] would be to strip them of their politics. The temporal structure of *Life* oscillates from late-life reflective feminism worked through in the 2000s via discussion with Morgan and Gloria Steinem, to earlier primal life events; from life long public activism to private self-abnegation. But if she left Vadim for inchoate sexual–political reasons, other silencings were to follow.

Fonda's celebrity-life-writing as consciousness-raising is further developed in the account of her next marriage, to left-wing activist Tom Hayden. Hayden was a huge figure in the counterculture, revered by Fonda who was by 1971 looking for someone who 'could inspire me, teach me, lead me, not be afraid of me. Who better than Tom Hayden?'[12] Their first date is a slide show which Hayden deployed to raise consciousness about Vietnamese culture, containing information about US plastic surgery which 'Americanises' Vietnamese women's bodies. As Hayden acknowledges in his biography, he saw 'Barbarella–Fonda' as underpinning this political message – almost as if the sexual oppression of Vietnamese women were her fault: 'I was talking about the image of superficial sexiness [Fonda] once promoted and was now trying to shake. I looked at her in a new way. Maybe I could love someone like this.'[13] Fonda then embarked on a marriage in which she funded Hayden's political campaigns (the strapline of Gritten's 1982 article is 'Jane Fonda and Tom Hayden are Working to Put Her Money Where His Mouth Is').[14] *Life* reflects on her blindness to his put-downs (instigated by insecurity prompted by her greater fame), and his sexual straying. Fonda continues to ask, 'In spite of my theoretical identification with feminism, I was passive with Tom, still assuming that whatever was wrong was my fault.'[15] Though his autobiography presents a glowing view of their marriage it was written during its demise when, according to Vadim's daughter Nathalie, 'Tom hated, loathed, despised the Workout. ... Now Jane was not only a movie star; she was a one-woman conglomerate, a veritable household word – an icon. She had embedded herself in the middle-class consciousness in a way that she could not have with her films.'[16] Hayden emerges from Fonda's account as both threatened and augmented by his more dazzling wife's fame, aware that on some level she has 'celebritized' him, paranoid that this might compromise both his masculinity and his politics.

Until Fonda began to speak for herself it was perhaps Richard Dyer's case history of her contradictory star iconography which dominated readings, though in the process this discredited her politics (particularly her feminism) through wealth and whiteness: 'Fonda-as-star-as-revolutionary dramatises the problem of what role privileged white people can have in the struggles of under-privileged non-whites.'[17] Nevertheless she was for Tessa Perkins 'the Hollywood star who, in the seventies at least, came closest to being a feminist heroine'.[18] Given these variable political images, coupling with a left-wing spokesman (Hayden) and then a sometime-Republican capitalist (Turner) only compounded her public contradictions. The disarmingly confessional self-scrutiny of this later phase in Fonda's public life as manifest in *Life* began in earnest during her marriage to Turner, though this was arguably her most silenced phase.

Fun with Ted and Jane: Competitive celebrity in public and private

The coupling of Fonda and Turner was publicly articulated through a discourse of ageing, characterized by undertones of rivalry. Ageing is hardly the daunting prospect it is for lower socio-economic groups if one is wealthy enough to afford top-end healthcare, cosmetic aid and near-unlimited lifestyle choices. Nevertheless as a celebrated beauty, Fonda has negotiated physical change in public, and by the time Turner wooed her he was no longer the sailing action figure of his younger profile.

If Fonda autobiographically divides her life into three Ages, Turner's history is framed primarily through the phases of setting up CNN, losing control of it and his latter-day philanthropy. His answer to *My Life So Far* is *Call Me Ted*, a 2008 autobiography which describes the business triumphs of a brilliant maverick briefly punctuated by personal anecdote and stand-alone sidebars from colleagues. Vadim's strategy of foregrounding women's names as a self-title is clearly not Turner's style: *Call Me Ted* is a bland, self-aggrandizing series of reports in which the triumphs are trumpeted, the problems are manfully admitted to before being quickly passed over. Despite some rueful *mea culpa* moments, this efficient reportage is hardly the reflective self-analysis of Fonda's approach. If Fonda dedicates over 100 pages to her personal life post-50, Turner spends around 2 pages summarizing his marriages and long-term relationships, before providing a slightly longer version of his meeting with Fonda – though it still doesn't match her extensive account.[19] From then on the book only mentions his famous wife when she is party to business dinners and negotiations.

This may be appropriate to his target readership. In US celebrity circles, Turner was far better known than Vadim or Hayden – a business star (perhaps only matched by Donald Trump in the 1980s) and one of the most powerful men in the USA. Ken Auletta cites him as, by 2000, 'a bona fide celebrity – Captain Courageous, Mr. CNN, Mr. Billionaire, Mr. Fonda.'[20] In addition to CNN, by the early 1990s he had established Turner Network Television and Cartoon Network among other media enterprises; he also owned a baseball team, the Atlanta Braves and a basketball team, the Atlanta Hawks. Fonda's brother actor Peter Fonda encouraged the liaison on the grounds that 'He's the *real* Captain America. ... Ted won the America's Cup!'.

Turner pursued Fonda the minute he heard (via a news feed at CNN) that her marriage to Tom Hayden had failed.[21] Fonda's account makes age a regular leitmotif; Turner's does not, though she recalls the fifty-year old Turner, just one year younger, raising the question:

> 'I think you're perfect for me,' he said suddenly. 'We care about the same issues, and we're both overachievers, we're both in the entertainment business, and you need someone who is as successful as you – and I'm *more* successful than you, which is good. Those last two movies you did were real dogs – let's face it.' ... 'In fact,' he went on, 'there's only one negative as far as I'm concerned ... your age.' Wow! And here I was under the impression I was looking pretty good.[22]

Fonda had already been warned that Ted went for younger women, so the suspicion of being 'past it' haunts the account: 'That was when we began "going steady," as we described it, which I thought was rather charming for two fifty-somethings.'[23]

Most tellingly the anecdotes suggest that they are negotiating mutual celebrity from the first date. Both report Turner comparing their fame through reams of press clippings:

> 'I don't know much about you, see, so ... ahhh ... I got CNN to do a printout of your archives. ... The stack was about a foot tall. So ... ahh ... then I had them

do a printout of my files and mine is about three foot tall.' Pause. 'Mine's bigger than yours! Pretty cute, huh?'[24]

This is typical of the disarming insecurity and unfiltered speak-from-the-hip style attributed to Turner (not for nothing is he widely nicknamed 'The Mouth of the South'). But he need not have worried: once committed, Fonda moved in to his small flat in Atlanta, worked hard to tackle prejudice about her East–West Coast liberal associations, and dedicated herself to the marriage (suspecting that her other marriages failed because performing took her away from home for too long).[25] Indeed, though Turner emerges from Fonda's story as a megalomaniac womanizer, she nevertheless presents it as a good match because he is 'not intimidated by me'.[26] As we shall see, however much Fonda strives to make herself unthreatening, this is not entirely true.

Still, movies continue to characterize the liaison. Turner had purchased MGM/UA in 1986, citing one of his reasons for wanting the MGM movie library as his love of *Gone with the Wind* (Fleming, 1939) (as well as the need for programming material to service his burgeoning broadcast empire). This classic film comes to frame his profile as icon of the urbanized New South, with Rhett Butler – a dashing opportunist capitalist – as visual model. Addressing the board of MGM soon after the buyout, he announced (as reported in *Call Me Ted* by Roger Mayer, Executive Vice President of Administration for MGM):

'You probably want to know why I bought this company and I'll tell you why. You own my two favourite movies: *The Wizard of Oz* and *Gone With the Wind*' … and then he pointed to his mustache and said, 'Don't you think I look a little like Rhett Butler?'[27]

Indeed, Helen Taylor argues that ownership of the movie title – which meant Turner could air it twice daily, seven days a week – has made CNN part of the *Gone With The Wind*-related Atlanta tourist trade.[28] Fonda and Turner bizarrely refigured as an ageing Scarlett and Rhett are a fitting image for a non-traditional Southerner and the cosmopolitan woman who reinvents herself as a new-Atlantan when she marries him: celebrity story referencing a celebrated fictional couple. Fonda appeared in movies; Turner is deemed 'actually the kind of character that Henry Fonda might have played in a movie'.[29] Scarlet and Rhett are made for each other because they are cut from the same capitalist cloth: Fonda and Turner were presented as both uniquely well-matched and entirely incompatible. Her left-wing friends thought she had sold out in hooking up with a former Republican[30]; Turner's still-Republican colleagues were shocked by a liaison with Hanoi Jane, while his arch-rivals in the Murdoch press used the Fonda marriage to discredit him.[31]

However mutual celebrity overrides political differences. Biographer of the Fondas, Peter Collier is not surprised by the 'power nuptial' liaison: 'She's always "buying at the top" when it comes to men. Who better at this stage of her life than the King of Cable? She, after all, is the Queen of Hollywood.'[32] The public coupling is articulated as that of two extremely rich, charismatic people presented as soulmates despite perceived political differences. Superlatives drip from the ample reception materials: Dolly Parton raised a glass to them at a party in 1992, toasting 'Man of the Year, Woman of the Hour, Couple of the Century' (Parton is referring to Turner being named as *Time* magazine's Man of the Year in 1991).[33] One of many news reports from early in their relationship crystallizes the threads involved in the liaison's public face:

> Though both have flitted around the block a few times (and down the aisle, twice each), together they bill and coo like young lovebirds. 'They're inseparable, very hand-holding,' says talk show host and Turner pal Larry King, whose own power nuptials to businesswoman Julie Alexander just went bust. … Miraculously, as Fonda and Turner travel the world promoting their individual ventures, they seem to have avoided any clashes of ego. '"One doesn't overshadow the other,' observes Julie Alexander King. 'When she has her moments in the sun, he steps aside, and she does the same for him.'[34]

This is exemplary because it touches a number of celebrity media keynotes – luxury, wealth, power – but inflects them with a dream to which all might equally aspire: even in late-middle age one can have a happy beginning ('bill and coo like young lovebirds'). Yet the message of balanced stardom is undercut when Fonda and Turner come to revisit this in their autobiographies (she at great length, he only briefly). Underpinning this particular power-marriage image is a conjunction of insecurities, with ample confusion over who is the bigger celebrity:

> He told me, so generously and frequently, that he loved me, that he thought I was smart and beautiful, the love of his life, that it began to chip away at my low self-esteem: *Ted Turner thinks I'm great and smart and beautiful, and he's no dummy*. What's touching is that while I was feeling this, Ted was feeling: *Wow, if Jane Fonda loves me, I can't be all that bad*.[35]

Funny as this is, it suggests one contradictory but familiar message of celebrity discourse writ large: here are two of the most famous people in the world, but they have insecurities just like us! But it also suggests a life lived in constant awareness of the celebrity other – her validation of herself because he's 'Ted Turner', his validation because he's married to 'Jane Fonda' (recall Vadim's reference to his wife as 'Janefonda'). The ability to cite one's own name as a brand while simultaneously standing back from it in ironic distance is an experience most 'civilians' cannot share. But Fonda wavers between positions, sometimes demoting herself from celebrity to 'civilian' in her own mind:

> Oh my! Walking into the huge glass-domed atrium [of the CNN Centre], looking up at the building rising fourteen floors all around me, CNN and TURNER everywhere, every nation's flag flying, even that of the United Nations, testifying to Ted's commitment to a global network. *My boyfriend made this all happen!*[36]

Though Turner is first seen as Fonda's 'power consort',[37] as soon as she is established in Atlanta she becomes the silenced, diplomatic support-figure. The primary thing she gave up for him, she writes, is her voice.[38]

However, the moments when her star outshines his are perhaps the most interesting, such as an audience with Mikhail Gorbachev at which the Russian focuses entirely on Fonda (Turner laments that he 'spent twenty-eight minutes staring at Gorbachev's back').[39] Though Hayden got used to (and annoyed by) being referred to as Mr Jane Fonda,[40] to my knowledge the only time Turner is called this is by Southern conservatives deriding the liaison.[41] Yet while more internationally recognizable, Fonda suggests she is happier to be 'civilianized' by the relationship; Turner cannot manage it. Annoyance at her global recognition reinforces the idea that the marriage has celebritized him: he may have been famous in business before, but now his personal life is spot-lit, and he is not at its centre. On a CNN-related world tour in 1994,

> at a banquet in the Great Hall in Beijing hosted by the Chinese government, a thousand people approached the Turner table with cameras. Turner stood up to pose when they asked to take a picture and was stunned when he was told, 'No, no. We want Jane.'[42]

In Japan no one would enter a reception with just Turner at the door; Fonda had to greet them. And then when their India-bound plane made an emergency stop and had to be fixed in Canton, Turner reports a bizarre masochistic fantasy – that the plane would crash, and the subsequent headline will run, 'Jane Fonda and others die in plane crash'.[43] These various threats to Turner's fame suggest celebrity coupling as (a rather one-sided) rivalry. One view of the marriage break-up is that Turner was eclipsed by the ultimate rival – Fonda 'bested' him with God when she became a Christian towards the end of the marriage. Though earlier she left acting to devote more time to him, according to Turner's daughter Laura, they grew apart because of 'another male … – Jesus. … It took time away from him.'[44] Fonda and Turner could never synthesize in the portmanteau manner of Brangelina (Fonner? Turnda?), whereby distinct celebrity identities merge into one singular moniker, a unified brand. Turner and Fonda were never subsumed into each other: Fonda is internationally the bigger star, but she is also the one who steps back into the shadows. Her movie career entirely precedes and post-dates the marriage.

Fonda's project of ageing

Since reaching her 60s and divorcing Turner, Fonda has rebranded herself through a project of ageing, turning her hand to writing books which are part autobiography, part self-help manuals for women: *My Life So Far* was followed in 2011 with *Prime Time: Love, Health, Sex, Fitness, Spirit*, a holistic how-to-grow-old handbook peppered with autobiographical anecdotes. The self-analysis of *Prime Time* also segues with her wider promotions of health-giving practices which she markets in workout videos and merchandise. There is also a weekly blog on her website, plus numerous disseminated talks and interviews on women's ageing and her own methods for coping with life post-60. These later materials are predicated on an earlier workout book for older and post-menopausal women, *Women Coming of Age*, published in 1984 when she was forty-six. *Prime Time* suggests that her wider life has become a work-in-progress; self-analysis is developed as a kind of public feminist project (agency for older women; self-knowledge; physical fitness as empowerment). She is of course not alone in making women's Third Act more visible: feminists from Simone de Beauvoir to Germaine Greer to Lynne Segal have done so; Segal's 2014 book provides a useful overview of recent writing as well as feminism's occasional ageism.[45]

Writerly self-analysis thus has several functions. It contributes to an older personal-as-political story, and it promotes a more intimate public image across diverse outlets. Foundational though Dyer's ingenious reading of Fonda was, I want to consolidate Fonda's shift from stardom to celebrity. Richard Schickel's model of celebrity focuses on public knowability: celebrities are 'intimate strangers' (in the title of his book):

> Most of us retain, in most of our private and professional dealings with people we don't actually know, a sense of their otherness, a decent wariness that protects both ourselves and the stranger from intrusion. But that shyness, if the term may be permitted, is not operative when we are dealing with celebrities. Thanks to television and the rest of the media we know them, or think we do.[46]

This then shifts the balance towards intimacy, towards the illusion of knowability. In her recent writing, Fonda addresses her readers as if they were friends, writing more like an intimate and less like a stranger. If, as a star, she could never be the girl next door (the remoteness of stardom was reinforced by her edgy, awkward braininess), as a septuagenarian celebrity she pitches herself somewhere between glamorous granny and guru. Intimate revelations deploy personal damage as a kind of bridge, a link to a life more ordinary. After depression and eating disorders, the Third Act stages self-healing. A plea to 'sameness' between author and reader suggests that Jane has survived troubles the reader might be going through, and her story is 'our story'. The very premise of a self-help book establishes a parity between author and reader, between the healer and the damaged. However this is an image risk: in comparing the self of the writer to the self of the reader the mystique of stardom is lost. This is just one contradiction of the current form of the brand 'Jane Fonda'. In writing popular memoirs which veer into self-help narratives, Fonda has navigated a life-path from old-school studio-branded stardom to twenty-first-century celebrity.

Fonda post-60 is then a self-publicized creature of mass communication, metamorphosing from star to celebrity via her use of old and new media (from authorship to tweeting). Schickel argues that 'the history of celebrity and the history of communications technology over the last century are very closely linked',[47] and Fonda's Third Act is characterized by celebrification in print and more conventional ways of promoting her product (a product intimately bound to a public image of herself) through appearances on *Oprah*, the late night chat shows, magazine interviews and more. More recently she has set up a blog (in 2009), a Facebook page (also 2009), a Twitter feed (2010) and a personal website (2011) to disseminate family events as well as public moments. These new communication avenues have all been deployed since Fonda turned seventy in 2007. Of course most celebrities use all of these outlets, though many celebrity's Facebook pages are either administered by publicity staff or agents, or are false sites set up by fans. This makes their research-worth limited or misleading. Fonda's postings on @Janefonda are supported by the blue tick of official verification, and her Twitter site connects to a Facebook page and a website which are therefore authenticated, so these are useful research tools in understanding her preferred profile (whether or not she tweets herself or delegates it to her PR team). Compare this to Turner's suspicion of digital media. Though CNN was once the cutting edge new media outlet (inventing rolling news and coming of age with its unprecedented ground-level coverage of the Gulf War in 1991), as Turner has aged he has seemed a technological dinosaur, wedded to broadcast and cable and losing business hegemony following the merger of Time Warner with AOL. In *Call Me Ted* he reports that he does not even do email.

Fonda's strengthening embrace of the digital tells a cannier story. One strong lesson celebrities have had to learn is that digitally there is nowhere to hide, so deploying internet publicity outlets is essential to telling a preferred version of one's story or product endorsement. As we have seen, Turner started the liaison in 1990 with hard copies of news stories printed by his staff; long after the marriage a now older Fonda deploys social media as well as books and fitness products. Usually the one thing stars (particularly female stars) want to hide or disavow is ageing, but Fonda follows an opposite strategy: in both tone and message through all these communication outlets, the politics (and the personal experience) of ageing is central to her activist agenda, and it is also saleable. In a TED Talk delivered in December 2011, she asks us to replace the metaphor of the arc as an image of a lifespan (we rise to a zenith followed by an inevitable decline) with a metaphor of the stairs – we ascend forever upwards towards spiritual heightening.[48] Of course for someone in their Third Act this is a preferable end-story, and on some level famous Fonda has no choice – she cannot escape the fact that her 1937 date of birth is public record. The common etymology of 'celebrate' and 'celebrity' is interesting here: the latin '*celebratus*' means 'to attend in great numbers, from *celeber, celebris, celebre*, thronged, frequented, well-known'. The connection between being well known among many, and having the ability to make your product well known, is a long-established adjunct of stardom. Of late, Fonda has 'celebrated' ageing, and marketed commodities specific to older consumers, but this also makes a virtue of necessity: as a celebrity who cannot hide her age she opts to celebrate as well as exploit it. Since as a celebrity Fonda must grow old in public, she markets her celebration of it to 'great numbers'. There are contradictions too in the way she has approached this: as L'Oreal's oldest model (or Spokesmodel, as they are termed), she suggests that anti-wrinkle cream will make us look like her, but has also gone public about succumbing to cosmetic surgery. Dyer focuses Fonda's star contradictions around the ferment of left-wing politics in 1960s USA, but new forms of contradiction have emerged as she has shifted from star to celebrity and grappled further with ageing as a feminist and glamour icon in a context of digital proliferation.

It is probably fair to say that Fonda's star has continued to rise since her divorce from Turner – as well as becoming a writer, she has returned to acting. In celebrity terms the stairs remain her metaphor; the traditional arc might be more appropriate for Turner. There are now new Fonda incarnations. Though she made no films while married to Turner, her movie, TV and theatrical career has picked up since 2001, with a plum role as a tough CEO of a news channel in HBO's *The Newsroom* (2012–) and a Tony Best Actress Nomination for a Broadway performance under her belt (2009). Cinematic roles have emphasized both coupling and ageing: in *Monster-in-Law* (Luketic, 2005) she embraces her older generational position in relation to Jennifer Lopez's central love interest figure. The troubled *Georgia Rule* (Marshall, 2007) revisits *On Golden Pond* with Fonda as the crotchety grandparent figure which her father had played in that 1981 film. In *Peace, Love and Misunderstanding* (Beresford, 2011) she sends up her politically radical identity, and takes much younger lovers. She also crossed the political divide by briefly playing Republican First Lady Nancy Reagan in *The Butler* (Daniels, 2013). Yet Fonda has still to find the serious older roles which Julie Christie fleshed out in *Away From Her* (Polley, 2006) or Streep found in *August: Osage County* (Wells, 2013). If she were seriously to perform her philosophy of this Third Act she would not represent objects of pity or enfeeblement, and she would be sexualized. Her post-Turner life has emphasized the 'project' of her ageing rather than coupledom, but ageing has been on her mind since she was much younger. Indeed, in *Women Coming of Age*, which was published in her forties, Fonda sees middle age as foundational to powerful old age:

> In my mind I've already laid the first brush strokes toward a picture of the woman I would wish myself to be in the twilight of my life. I see an old woman walking briskly, out-of-doors, in every season. She's feisty. She's not afraid of being alone. Her face is lined and full of life. There's a ruddy flush to her cheeks and a bright curious look in her eye because she's still learning. Her husband often walks with her. They laugh a lot.[49]

By the time she has actually reached this stage Fonda has probably fulfilled most of this, projecting an image of a woman still learning, still fit and – according to

My Life So Far – for the first time not afraid of being alone. The only difference is the lack of a husband.

Auletta suggests that in leaving Turner she was also leaving the institution of marriage: 'Fonda, despite her own notoriety as an actor and as a political activist, had lived in the shadow of three dominant husbands. By leaving Turner, she also announced her own liberation.'[50] By contrast, Turner's post-divorce story is less successful; Auletta characterizes the post-AOL-Time-Warner figure as an exile with diminished business authority and net worth.[51] And while Fonda has said that she won't marry again (despite her forty-something image of an older woman striding out with husband 'often' by her side), Turner's devotion to the institution seems almost incontinent: '"If I got divorced," Turner once told *Modern Maturity* magazine, "I'd probably get married again. I'll marry the first person who comes along. My problem is, I love every woman I meet."'[52] Despite this Fonda remains Turner's sole celebrity liaison.

By contrast Jane Fonda 'celebritizes', albeit briefly, everyone she partners, but marriage is not her primary project. When she does write about her lovers, it both is and is not with what we might think of as a septuagenarian's voice. Jermyn laments a 'girling' tone which characterizes Fonda's L'Oreal advert in denial of her age;

> a vibrant Jane Fonda is seen carefully choosing an outfit and delighting in applying her make-up, before peeking through her window where she glimpses a man outside, evidently waiting for her during what we now understand to be her preparation for a date (www.youtube.com 2011). Such 'girling' of older women is both symptomatic of postfeminist culture and indicative of a move to push back the boundaries of ageing; now in her seventies, this ageing woman star is figured as being just as excited – and just as entitled – to be going out on a date as a woman or girl a fraction of her age might be.[53]

However, in Fonda's autobiographies older coupling does not necessarily emulate youth; sexual activity is part of the ageing process. In the context of her relationship with music producer Richard Perry she has said that, in her 70s she is having the best sex of her life:

> The only thing I have never known is true intimacy with a man. ... It has happened with Richard. I feel totally secure with him. ... Often, when we make love, I see him as he was 30 years ago. ... At 74, I have never had such a fulfilling sex life.[54]

This celebrity coupling in vital old age also markets Fonda as an attractive filmic commodity: still sexy, still seeking work, and perhaps once again 'besting' herself. But this is just the next formation of Fonda's celebrity contradiction: her autobiography is hardly a story of exhausting 'besting'. Furthermore, she is careful to place her sexuality in the context of ageing, framing it publicly with the failing/changing body: 'When I had my knee replaced just over two and a half years ago, I found a lover. ... When I moved in with him I was still using crutches; we haven't been apart since.'[55] Jermyn is right to stress that ageing issues should be at the heart of celebrity discussion, quoting Chris Holmlund's argument in the inaugural edition 2010 of *Celebrity Studies* that 'Assessing ageing is one of the key tasks confronting celebrity studies today'.[56] Fonda is a fitting subject for this challenge, placing her age squarely in the frame of her celebrity. Re-establishing her celebrity as a single woman through her continuing public negotiation of identity and sexuality, she is still acting her age, centre stage.

Acknowledgements

Many thanks to Shelley Cobb and Neil Ewen for useful engagement with and editing of this chapter as it was being redrafted.

Notes

1 For an excellent account of the development of Fonda's radical politics in the 1960s and 1970s see Mary Hershberger's *Jane Fonda's War: A Political Biography of an Antiwar Icon* (New York: The New Press, 2005).

2 After Elizabeth Hurley's early use of the term for the non-famous, documented by Judith Woods, 'Liz Hurley: Hurling Herself Into the Spotlight Once More', *Daily Telegraph*, 14 December 2010, http://www.telegraph.co.uk/news/ celebritynews/8199730/Liz-Hurley-Hurling-herself-into-the-spotlight-once-more.html.

3 Elaine Showalter, 'Introduction', in *Out of Time: The Pleasures & Perils of Ageing*, ed. Lynne Segal (London: Verso, 2014), viii.

4 See Katja Lee, 'Reading Celebrity Autobiographies', *Celebrity Studies* 5, no. 1 (March 2014): 87–9, which theorises how we deploy these primary materials. Also interesting is 'From Life Storytelling to Age Autobiography' in Margaret Morganroth Gullette's fascinating analysis of the cultural constructions of ageing, *Aged by Culture* (Oxford: University of Chicago Press, 2004), 141–58.

5   Jane Fonda, *My Life So Far* (London: Random House, 2005), 532.

6   Roger Vadim, *Bardot, Deneuve and Fonda: The Memoirs of Roger Vadim*, trans. Melinda Porter (London: Hodder and Stoughton, 1987), 314.

7   Ibid., 314.

8   Fonda, *Life*, 156.

9   Ibid.

10 Ibid.

11 Sean Redmond, *The Star and Celebrity Confessional* (London: Routledge, 2010).

12 Fonda, *Life*, 282.

13 Tom Hayden, *Reunion: a Memoir* (London: Hamish Hamilton, 1988), 446. This does not stop Fonda herself succumbing to cosmetic surgery (breast implants and eye surgery in the late 1980s) during her relationship with Hayden, and following its demise.

14 David Gritten, 'Political Bedfellows', *People*, 24 May 1982, archived at http://www.people.com/people/archive/article/0,,20082212,00.html.

15 Fonda, *Life*, 402.

16 Patricia Bosworth, *Jane Fonda: The Private Life of a Public Woman* (London: Robson Press, 2011), 483.

17 Richard Dyer, *Stars* (London: BFI, 1979), 78.

18 Ibid., 238.

19 Ted Turner with Bill Burke, *Call Me Ted* (London: Sphere, 2008), 262–64.

20 Ken Auletta, *Media Man: Ted Turner's Improbable Empire* (New York and London: Norton, 2004), 119.

21 Turner, *Ted*, 256; Fonda, *Life*, 468.

22 Fonda, *Life*, 481–82.

23 Ibid., 490.

24 Ibid., 471.

25 Ibid., 495.

26 Ibid., 496.

27 Turner, *Ted*, 242–43.

28 Helen Taylor, *Scarlett's Women: Gone with the Wind and its Female Fans* (London: Virago, 1989), 221.

29 Bosworth, *Jane Fonda*, 511. In a book shot through with Fonda's insecurities about her father's love, it is easy to equate this all-American hero with Henry Fonda's earlier screen version of that persona; referring to the house he builds for Fonda as 'our Golden Pond' (*Life*, 500) is also strangely Oedipal.

30 Ibid., 513.

31 Auletta, *Media Man*, 81.

32 Cheryl Lavin, 'Henry, Jane and Peter Fonda form one of the great American acting families', *Chicago Tribune*, 3 March 1991, archived at http://articles.chicagotribune. com/1991-03-03/features/9101200191_1_jane-fonda-peter-collier-henry-fonda.

33 Bosworth, *Jane Fonda*, 513.

34 *People* magazine, http://www.people.com/people/archive/article/0,,20113742,00. html, 26 November 1990, vol. 34, no. 21.

35 Fonda, *Life*, 493.

36 Ibid., 492. Compare this to Ted's comment that 'those last two movies were dogs'.

37 Peter Collier, *The Fondas: A Hollywood Dynasty* (New York: G.P. Putnam's Sons, 1991), 297.

38 Fonda, *Life*, 504–05.

39 Fonda, *Life*, 507.

40 Collier, *The Fondas*, 293.

41 'Some of Turner's male colleagues were appalled – Southern good ol'boys who drank with him and sailed with him couldn't figure out how this great embodiment of the capitalist system was planning to marry "Hanoi Jane"' (Bosworth, 511).

42 Auletta, *Media Man*, 60.

43 Ibid., 61.

44 Ibid., 94.

45 Segal, *Out of Time*, 1–38.

46 Schickel, *Intimate Strangers: The Culture of Celebrity in America* (New York: Ivan R Dee Inc., 2000), 4.

47 Ibid., 28.

48 See http://www.ted.com/talks/jane_fonda_life_s_third_act.html.

49 Jane Fonda with Mignon McCarthy, *Women Coming of Age* (New York: Simon and Schuster, 1984), 14–15.

50 Auletta, *Media Man*, 95.

51 Ibid., 175.

52 Ibid., 94.

53 Deborah Jermyn, '"Get a life, ladies. Your old one is not coming back": ageing, ageism and the lifespan of female celebrity', *Celebrity Studies* 3, no. 1 (2012): 1.

54 'Jane Fonda Gets Personal: "At 74, I Have Never Had Such a Fulfilling Sex Life"', in *OK!*, 10/07/2012, Archived at http://okmagazine.com/get-scoop/jane-fonda-talks-sex-life-at-74-richard-perry/.

55 Ibid., *OK!*

56 Jermyn, 'Get a life, ladies', 2.

16

The Making, Unmaking and Re-Making of *Robsten*

Diane Negra

The appetite of contemporary media industries for celebrity couples is a notable feature and millennial culture particularly cherishes the hyped formulation of the composite couple whether *Benifer*, *Brangelina*, *Tomkat*, *Kimye* or innumerable others.[1] Yet the immense industrial and ideological power of the celebrity couple is often displaced by the spectacle of its visual vulnerability under paparazzi regimes and that power has not been adequately factored for in media-studies scholarship.

Certainly theorists like Virginia Wright Wexman and Martha Nochimson have offered fruitful avenues of investigation into the screen couples of film and television. Such couples, as Nochimson observes, have a long history of knitting themselves 'into the public imagination as a fundamental part of the cultural capacity to imagine both erotic intimacy and human connection'.[2] There are fewer extant pathways for analysing couples whose on-screen fictions are matched by off-screen 'authenticity'. Yet it is clear that such couples are also subject to fame protocols which we may readily recognize if struggle to articulate.

In any critical effort to anatomize the celebrity couple it seems crucial to consider the social definition of intimacy around which it is formed. I suggest that *Robsten*, the binational couple portmanteau comprised of American Kristen Stewart and British Robert Pattinson, vividly emblematized a fantasy of privacy in the context of the neoliberal notion 'that private life is the real in contrast to collective life'.[3] Their celebrity couplehood largely borrowed its terms of intimacy from the *Twilight* film franchise in which the pair's fame was sourced and it was heightened by their frequent presentation as 'hunted' paparazzi targets.[4] Vampire love in *Twilight* functions as an expression of our contemporary cultural belief that the couple is the privileged and pre-eminent social unit and that the desire for fully merged closeness can never go too far.

Indeed, the *Robsten* celebrity text moved in and out of compliance with the terms of *Twilight*'s paranormal romance notably via the couple's performance of an embattled intimacy under threat from nebulous but predatory external forces. The tremendous public investment in the couple was a function of the desire to retain an image of innocent romance while simultaneously acknowledging how fraught that conception is. As I will argue, the contemporary cultural intimacy environment is shot through with paradoxes that provide the grist for avid public interest in celebrity couplehood (including 'breakup watches' in which we, in effect, root for the couple to fail) and its associated scandals.

The 'chick flick', for better or worse, serves as Hollywood cinema's premiere genre of romantic intimacy and it is customarily deeply devalued if not excoriated. While not wishing to indulge in the reflexive devaluation associated with female-centred genres, it is hard to dispute that in the decade prior to the 2008 release of *Twilight* the films of this category had become increasingly superficial and rote. Some might argue that the intensely promoted couplehood of Stewart and Pattinson generated significant intertextual interest that helps to explain the popularity of a set of rhetorically and narratively clumsy films whose appeal (even given the prior success of the novels on which they were based) is otherwise hard to fathom. What is clear is that *Twilight* was incontestably 'an intergenerational female sensation' in the words of Anne Helen Petersen with much publicity accompanying the release of the first film emphasizing a demographic of midlife women attracted to/moved by the film's spectacle of romantic devotion.[5] It may be reasonable to consider *Twilight* as offering a repository space for remnants of belief in romantic fantasy at a time when more conventional 'chick flicks' had become deeply unpersuasive. In the film *Crazy Stupid Love* (Ficarra and Requa, 2011), Julianne Moore's midlife Emily Weaver, an unhappy woman who has initiated a separation from her husband and one-time high school sweetheart, symbolically laments the lack of offerings for adult female audiences in the film marketplace when she tells her estranged husband 'You know when I told you I had to work late? I really went to go see the new *Twilight* movie by myself and it was so bad!'

The commercially ingenuous character of the heavily hyped relationship between Pattinson and Stewart is particularly evident in hindsight. The romance clearly worked to sustain interest in the franchise across a staggered multi-year release calendar (wherein a *Twilight* film appeared annually from 2008 to 2012).

A marked feature of *Robsten* was the pair's refusal for most of the duration of their relationship to acknowledge that they were in fact a couple off-screen as well as on. Breathless coverage assessing whether they were indeed together at all, when they might have had a spat or a reconciliation, and closely tracking their physical gestures and spoken remarks for proof of intimacy was an incessant feature of *Robsten* discourse. Public interest in the couple was no doubt heightened by the contrastive drama of turbulent, sexualized emotionalism it presented in counterpoint to the early *Twilight* films' heavy emphasis on restraint and the need to discipline one's sexuality (the franchise has frequently been dubbed a form of 'abstinence porn'). The titillating prospect that the couple formation so long deferred across the franchise was an established fact in 'real life' epistemologically justified intense, ongoing scrutiny of Pattinson and Stewart's public appearances (both separately and together) across a four-year interval from 2008 to 2012. Notably, such scrutiny was undertaken by a range of tabloid and quasi-tabloid press outlets on behalf and for the benefit of a particularly conspicuous fan base comprised of zealous so-called 'Twi-hards' and a surging market for paparazzi photos was crucial to the promotion of Pattinson and Stewart in the period of their celebrity coupledom. As Kim McNamara observes, 'as a result of the digitization of images, the quantum increase in the amount of photos being used – both online and in print publications – shows the obvious burgeoning of the paparazzi as an industry'.[6] Noting that paparazzi photos are visualizations of gossip, McNamara charts the incorporation of celebrity gossip into a wider range of internet activity and postulates that developments such as 'the growing popularity of photo-driven blogs mirrors the changing nature of how audiences relate to celebrities', producing a greater sense of intimacy and access.'[7] It is certainly clear that because *Robsten*'s lifespan accorded with the flowering of digital media forms through which fans could ponder the activities of and express their regard for celebrities it might also be assessed in regard to new technologies of fandom though that will not be my purpose here. While Pattinson and Stewart have since broken up, in this chapter I isolate a period in these celebrities' trajectory of renown which I take to be revealing of contemporary fame economies in a variety of ways I'll seek to detail.

It should be noted that the forms and functions of *Robsten* draw upon long-standing tropes of the romance as the *ne plus ultra* of secret intimacy. The adolescent romance of Romeo and Juliet is the standard-bearer here and in various ways *Twilight* calls upon the full panoply of devices for dividing lovers (working class vs. upper class, innocence vs. experience, more innovatively human vs. vampire differences) in order to situate its focal pair in relation to the long legacy of couples who have faced social disapprobation. In this way and many others, the secrecy associated with *Robsten* is rooted in and an extension of the franchise that vaulted Stewart and Pattinson to stardom.

Particularly given its phenomenal popularity across the most acute years of the global recession, it would be a mistake not to acknowledge the *Twilight* franchise's power as a site of socio-economically inflected fantasies of intimacy and exclusion. In periods of ideological uncertainty we are particularly incentivized to cling to familiar social worlds. Like many postfeminist romances, *Twilight* is a narrative of female class rise through romantic partnership, and the franchise deeply values the (supernaturalized) wealth of the Cullen vampire family and the transcendent, 'empowering' maternity of its heroine, Bella Swan. In the films' creepy presentation of family as subculture, Stewart's Bella is ushered into a 'full family' unified not by biology but superiority and specialness whose plenitude vividly contrasts to the relative scarcity of Bella's homelife with her working-class single father, a domestic arrangement the films pretend to value but actually critique as materially inadequate. In a similar fashion the celebrity couple's phatic functions include the naturalization of deeply unequal formulations of superiority and inequality with the privileged couple at their heart.

Operating in an environment of increasingly concentrated material and social capital, celebrities function as crucial platforms for the performance of status, the display and use of luxury commodities, and the flaunting of VIP experiences and access. We should further note that among other things, the contemporary celebrity power couple articulates the rise in endogamous marriage in an increasingly class-stratified society.[8] Thus, I contend that a celebrity couple like *Robsten* cannot be analysed outside of a context in which 'the concentration of marriage among the richest Americans is amplifying the increase in income inequality'.[9]

Illustrating this remarkable shift in the socio-economic terrain of early millennial American culture, new data depict a changing picture of access to marriage, the most socially valorized form of (straight and increasingly gay) coupledom. Reporting that marriage correlates with affluence more and more, Catherine Rampell notes that, 'Rich men are marrying rich women, creating doubly rich households for them and their children. And the poor are staying poor and alone.'[10] Among the privileged elite who are disproportionately the subjects of popular culture visibility, endogamous relations are thus more and more prevalent. As Chrystia Freeland notes, 'In 1979, nearly 8 percent of the 1 percent had spouses the IRS described as doing blue-collar or service sector jobs – governmentspeak for bosses married to their secretaries. That number has been falling ever since. What economists call assortative mating – the tendency to marry someone you resemble – is on the rise.'[11] Against such a backdrop the various forms of likeness that I will show to be rhetorically central to *Robsten* take on a heightened significance.

In this chapter I want to move through the three clear cycles of *Robsten* celebrity: Stewart and Pattinson's initial formation as a 'real-life' couple heightening and extending the authenticity of *Twilight*'s romance, their rupture through scandal and their tentative reconciliation on schedule in 2012 with the release of the fifth and final franchise film *Breaking Dawn Part 2*. Along the way, I also want to address the fervour of their (multigenerational) fandom, their display of fame discomfort, and their extraordinary overexposure. It is a hallmark of their mega-celebrity that they are covered in all media outlets, up and down the 'quality' spectrum.

Making *Robsten*

The pairing of the starlet and what would have once been called the juvenile is not a prevalent formation of celebrity coupledom. While we can think of exceptions (the studio-orchestrated faux romance of Mickey Rooney and Judy Garland in the 1930s, the ingenuous-seeming pairings of Sean Penn and Elizabeth McGovern in the 1980s and Reese Witherspoon and Ryan Phillippe in the 1990s, perhaps even the jejune reality couple Spencer Pratt and Heidi Montag known as *Speidi* during the 2006–7 height of popularity of *The Hills*) there are few precedents for the nearly five-year *Robsten* phenomenon. The kind of celebrity couple represented by Stewart and Pattinson is rare, its longevity even more so.

From the outset, *Robsten*'s physical and behavioural symmetries were invented/highlighted/talked up in media discourse. The couple's extensive shared performative vocabulary for communicating discomfort in the public eye included grimacing, twitching, squinting and stammering (see Figures 16.1 and 16.2). Photo montages visually juxtaposed their thin, hunched, often hooded frames and made much of Stewart's propensity for wearing androgynous clothing. Their togetherness was quickly fortified by the sense that they were jointly at threat from an avid press and public. Pattinson's

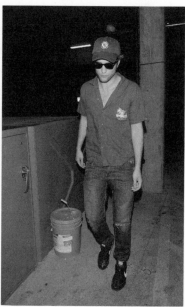

Figures 16.1 and 16.2 Stewart and Pattinson's 'melancholic self-presentation' became a key marker of *Robsten*. Figure 16.1 (Photo: Eduardo Pimentel) Figure 16.2 (Photo: Galo Ramírez)

slightly more mature status and sometimes protective, shielding stance around his co-star symbolically buffered Stewart (still a teenager when the first two *Twilight* films were released) from a voracious mediatized public while lending credence to the belief that the couple were always somewhat in character. (In particular, Pattinson's protection of Stewart almost exactly mimics Edward's protection of Bella and reflects the norms of an earlier turn-of-the-century era inherent in Edward's characterization as a vampire whose human life began in 1901). In these ways early visual representations of *Robsten* communicated the notion that they were together in a deeper, more meaningful way than an average couple.

Another distinctive feature of *Robsten* was that the couple's melancholic self-presentation often seemed to take its affective cues from the gloomy world of the franchise with which they were associated. Stewart in particular refused behavioural compliance with her ingénue role, tending to be reticent, de-energized and vocally monotonous in interviews. As early as 2009, a commentator in *The New York Times* noted that 'everyone from *Access Hollywood* to *The New Zealand Herald* has chewed over her supposedly "moody," "mopey," "melancholy" demeanor'.[12] Pattinson was somewhat less diffident, reaping the benefits of a gendered regime which is far more tolerant of male reserve; additionally his self-presentation was made intelligible by its compliance with the tradition of fidgety, stammering, well-coiffed UK male star imports embodied by Hugh Grant.[13] Stewart, by contrast, was repeatedly rebuked in the press for her putative sullenness as in a 2010 *Mail Online* piece that clustered a set of unflattering paparazzi photographs of the star under the headline 'Cheer Up Kristen You're Dating Robert Pattinson! Stewart Is Usual Scowling Self on Night Out.' In an internet-posted list entitled 'The 13 Most Annoying Stars', Stewart came tops, with a photo caption noting 'it seems that her run as the whiny Bella Swan in *Twilight* has permanently turned her expression to one of sour grapes'.[14]

Stewart's discomfort with fame and tendency to reference it as toxic was an omnipresent element of her star discourse during the period of *Twilight* film releases. She talked about the need to shield herself from public attention by building 'a perimeter of people that are really important to you'[15] and was castigated for having compared press intrusiveness to being raped.[16] More sympathetic accounts took note of the fact that given her early start in the industry as a child actor it was hardly surprising that she was both highly aware and wary of fame. Others characterized Stewart as 'giving off an air in inapproachability' in response to 'suffocating attention'.[17] As I have suggested, some *Robsten* photos seem to work to visually confirm a sheltering, custodial relationship between Pattinson and Stewart, extending the terms of *Twilight* couplehood while implying that there were real-world threats equivalent to vampires from which the ingénue needed protection. Stewart's vulnerability to an excessive, malevolent public was also rhetorically heightened through comparisons between her and her *Panic Room* (Fincher, 2002) co-star Jodie Foster whom she was seen to resemble physically and artistically.[18] A child star like Stewart, Foster, of course, was the famous recipient of the amorous attentions of John Hinkley, Jr who fired shots at President Reagan in an effort to prove his love in what stands as a landmark incident of pathological celebrity worship.

Robsten's long-time unwillingness to confirm their couple status chimed with a clear wariness of both the press and their fans and of course (as I have noted) had the effect of heightening public scrutiny of their behaviour in the search for visual or discursive confirmation that they were indeed together. In a November 2009 article whose title, 'Kristen Stewart On Her Love Life: Bite Me!' sought to reference both the *Twilight* franchise and the star's perceived truculence, it was unclear whether Stewart had the so-called 'Twi-hards' in mind or an intrusive press in quoted remarks that suggested she would have clarified her relationship with Pattinson if 'people hadn't made such a big deal about it. But I'm not going to give the fiending an answer.'[19]

Stewart and Pattinson's professional creative success and fame then, seem never to have registered euphorically for them and, in sharp contrast to other contemporary ingénues like Anne Hathaway or Jennifer Lawrence, Stewart refused to affectively comply with the gendered expectations of fame appreciation. Such consistent rhetoricizing of reluctance by the star may be better understood when we note that a key element in the performance of contemporary higher-order fame is to not appear to be fame-seeking. If lower-order celebrity is defined by the assiduous courting of media interest and financially-incentivized high availability to audiences (as is notably the case with reality celebrities whose craven financialization is often cited as their defining feature), it becomes necessary for stars to find ways to reassert values of artistry and remoteness and the articulation of fame as an unwanted burden accords with this positioning.

A key element of *Robsten*'s couple persona was an ongoing awareness of the vulnerability of being in the public eye, the burdens of overzealous fandom and the pressures of paparizzism. Stewart's quotes in the press sometimes even linked the avidity of public interest to the possibility of her death; in a 2009 account of a mall tour in which she would meet large audiences she noted that the crowds 'could totally assassinate me at any time they wanted.'[20] A few years later she observed that the prevalence of social media forms like Facebook and Twitter made her vulnerable to stalkers: 'I'm going to die because somebody is going to say where I am and somebody is going to kill me.'[21]

What is noteworthy then about this celebrity couple's presentation was that it tempered a traditional conceptualization of the innocence of young love with an ongoing awareness of the couple under threat, notably by a voracious public appetite for the idealizations they represented. Pattinson, and particularly Stewart, inevitably emerge as vulnerable subjects in a contemporary fame environment seen to be injurious/damaging and in which the purity of 'young romance' is always/already imperilled. Going further, we may note that not only did their celebrity couplehood comply with the terms of *Twilight*'s 'undead' romance, *Robsten* embodied the broader ways in which early millennial Hollywood fantasies of a transcendent intimacy and mutuality can skew darker. The popularity of couple formations that blend erotic and thanatotic impulses is apparent also in *Robsten*'s doppelganger and rival binational vampire couple *True Blood*'s Anna Paquin and Stephen Moyer (Sookie and Bill in the series).

Unmaking *Robsten*

By 2012, *Robsten's* saturated and fixed celebrity required some type of innovation as both the industry and its audiences geared up for the final franchise film's release in November. Significantly, the last major widely reported piece of news about Stewart in the summer before major scandal re-positioned the couple was the revelation that she had now become the most highly-paid actress in Hollywood.[22] Given Stewart's frequently critical press treatment throughout her career media outlets were particularly primed for a scandal that would raise the stakes on her problematic self-presentation. July, 2012 paparazzi photos of the star kissing and embracing her *Snow White and the Huntsman* director Rupert Sanders accordingly unleashed global opprobrium, judgement and even devastation. '*Twilight* fans', *Mail Online* reported, had been 'left shocked and confused' by Stewart's affair with the married Sanders.[23] Nearly everyone, it seemed, from devastated 'Twi-hards' weighing in online to 'people on the street' interviewees profiled by news outlets like CNN had an opinion on Stewart's infidelity. The furore over the matter generated commentary by a wide swathe of self-appointed relationship experts that included even the likes of Donald Trump who opined on Twitter that 'Robert Pattinson should not take back Kristen Stewart. She cheated on him like a dog & will do it again – just watch. He can do much better.'[24]

The ongoing conflation of Stewart and Pattinson with their *Twilight* roles was indicated in my favourite headline about the scandal: 'Kristen Stewart Cheats on Vampire Boyfriend with Married Human Father of Two.'[25] Updating an old-fashioned and highly conservative term of moral judgement, the branding of Stewart as a 'trampire' helped to lock the terms of the scandal in place with a potent and novel buzzword while also securing the assumption that it was Stewart who was exclusively responsible for the affair. This gendered discrepancy and the conservative ideological terms on which it rests have been noted by several commentators including Rosemary MacCabe in the *Irish Times* who wrote, 'In the wake of the "scandal" – if the philandering of a married 40-something with an unmarried 20-something can be deemed scandalous instead of sadly inevitable – the least surprising outcome has been the ensuant rush to lay the blame squarely at the feet of Stewart.'[26] For Nico Lang, the frenetic stigmatization of Stewart typifies a 'culture of slut-shaming' that disproportionately penalizes women for their infidelities while leaving male celebrities like Ashton Kutcher unscathed.[27]

The scandal also disrupted two cherished if fragile elements of the *Robsten* celebrity persona. The arc of the *Twilight* romance is to create romantic permanency – recall that Bella wants to be a vampire so that she and Edward will be together forever – and the infidelity scandal indirectly but potently threatened this idea. Adding further to the sense of umbrage over Stewart's affair with her director is that it symbolically displaced the kind of idealized romance that underpins Hollywood's enduring dream factory production of intimacy with its exact opposite and seamier inversion, an adulterous affair between an older male and an ingénue. Stewart's infidelity with her director in other words fits a template for the kinds of relationships the industry can't idealize but which have long been publically associated with the gender asymmetries of Hollywood power.

Also giving grist to the scandal was a cultural backdrop of postfeminist typologization that has fortified the boundaries between valued and devalued femininities. The zealous policing of young women's sexual activity has been a particular tenet of the Republican 'War on Women', and when we bear this in mind, the timeliness of the *Robsten* scandal becomes apparent. The work of the contributors to *Headline Hollywood: A Century of Film Scandal* illuminates how the most high-profile, phenomenal scandals refract up-to-the-minute cultural, moral and ideological dilemmas.[28] While Stewart had been precariously positioned as a valuable body (her characterization as Bella working to reify marital sexuality and motherhood) the revelations of her infidelity raised questions about how this 'misuse' of her sexuality might contaminate her star text. The resulting transformation of Stewart from a beloved subject to a guilty one elicited intense emotions and I don't want to understate the significance and vehemence of public feeling against her during this time – the star's security team for the Los Angeles premiere of *Breaking Dawn Part II* was reportedly doubled after the scandal broke.[29]

Among other things, the unmaking of *Robsten* offers an illustration, as Suzanne Leonard has explored in her work, of the deep cultural violation that female unfaithfulness is seen to constitute.[30] Historically represented as almost unthinkable (except in times when feminist ideas have gained considerable cultural traction), such conduct frequently elicits punishment fantasies from putatively 'liberal' media and remains associated with stock 'bad woman' characterizations and film plots where a good man is emotionally devastated by female infidelity as in the 2012 *Silver Linings Playbook*, a word of mouth hit in exactly the period in which the post-scandal fate of *Robsten* featured heavily in the press.

The visual evidence of Stewart's affair also linked her to earlier historical precedents of female celebrity infidelity involving Ingrid Bergman, Rita Hayworth, Elizabeth Taylor and Meg Ryan. Yet such conduct factors as a heightened transgression in a contemporary era in which famous women routinely disavow their ambition and fetishize their family values. Unfaithfulness that ruptures a cherished celebrity couple is, of course, particularly scandalous – Ryan's long-term marriage to Dennis Quaid ended in the wake of her affair with Russell Crowe and she never had a hit film again (though it is difficult to calculate how much of her career decline can be attributed to the taint of scandal and how much to the perils of ageing in her specialty genre, the romantic comedy, as Ryan turned forty the year after the scandal).

The question of what kinds of infidelities celebrity culture makes visible and how it does so is a complex one. While there is a seeming tolerance for certain kinds of break-up paradigms (low-level serial infidelities that don't rise above the level of rumour, the 'trading in' of a female spouse by a male partner for a younger 'trophy wife') some infidelities are judged inexplicable and/or offensive to public feeling. The infidelity paradigm of the affair of a male star with his family's nanny or housekeeper (Ethan Hawke, Jude Law, Robin Williams, Arnold Schwarzenegger) seems to fall into the latter category as do certainly the incandescent infidelity meltdowns of Tiger Woods, Jesse James and Hugh Grant (in all three cases public outrage seemed closely tied to public approval of the women they cheated on and the fact that the male stars were unfaithful with sex workers or other low-status women). Affairs with women whose domestic or sexual labour undoes family values paradigms strike a particular nerve.

The impermanency of celebrity couples has long been a crucial register for the repressed social realities of American intimacy, most particularly the fact that the US has the highest rates of movement partner-to-partner of any Western nation.[31] The norms of Hollywood relationship durability are such that the separation or break-up of a long-term couple can prompt a degree of public mourning if even only for the short life of a news cycle. Such proved the case in autumn, 2012 for instance with the announcement of the separation of Danny DeVito and Rhea Pearlman. Against the backdrop of customarily quicksilver Hollywood romances and in light of their age and heavy media saturation Stewart and Pattinson, a couple who were (largely) together for five years certainly count as a long-established partnership.

Melissa Gregg has written about the proliferation of what she deems 'adultery technologies', online intimacy surveillance software designed to catch out cheating spouses or partners and most often marketed to women. Drawing upon the work of theorists including Laura Kipnis and Eva Ilouz, she considers how 'the very need for adultery technologies is symptomatic of a moment in which some individuals see few options for intimate support – few visions or practices of community other than the fulfilment to be gained from a dependent partner'.[32] The concordance between Stewart's 'trampire' scandal and the marketing of such technologies is vividly illustrated in the comment trail to a lengthy *Robsten* timeline published on 16 October 2012 by the *Mirror Online* where the first posted comment hawks the services of a company that cracks/hacks email passwords for suspicious partners. The posting reads (in part): 'I think many of you ask yourself, what if i had the password of my friend / girlfriend / boyfriend, associate, life partner, etc ... to know the truth about your near partner, and reassuring that they do not hide you something. You have the right to be reasured! [sic]' When considered in this way, the telephoto lenses of the paparazzi represent only more exaggerated forms of the more banal technologies that work to enact surveillance of the intimacy environment. On either large or small scale such technology-driven surveillance practices mark the critical gap between social realities and the fantasies of transcendent privacy and intimacy fostered by material like *Twilight*.

In an era in which our sense of social belonging is so resolutely tied to couple identity the unravelling of a prominent and beloved couple can elicit strong anxieties, anxieties that are both concretized and caricatured in the image of the excessive fan whose own exclusion from 'correct' intimacies is revealed through their 'dysfunctional' over-involvement in the celebrity sphere. The most prominent representation of this figure in the wake of the *Robsten* split was Emma Clarke, a British *Twilight* 'super-fan' from Kent whose distraught YouTube video lamenting Stewart's infidelity became a phenomenon in itself as it was viewed more than two million times and picked up in numerous media outlets.[33] Clark is comparable in some respects to Chris Crocker, who in his 2007 'Leave Britney Alone' video more or less invented the category of internet celebrity established through the performance of the hysterical, over-identified fan who arbitrates/defends celebrity conduct.[34] Through figures like Clarke and Crocker we trivialize the social emotions of fandom while imposing an affective boundary line between their behaviour and ours.

Re-making *Robsten*

In the wake of an affair in which she was cast as solely blameworthy, Stewart's professional 'comeuppance' was initially staged in the form of reports that she was being written out of the *Snow White* sequel (the film's producer denied this). Interspersed with discourses of hopefulness around the *Robsten* reunion and reports of behavioural modification on Stewart's part that not incidentally drew her closer to models of normative female conduct, were glimmers of a narrative of professional (and personal) retribution towards the star, who, one article noted, had not currently committed to any future projects and about whom the Forbes Bureau Chief is quoted as saying that many in the industry came to perceive Stewart as uncastable and out of control.[35]

With discursive stress placed on the notion of Stewart making restitution through a heightened appreciation of her partner and her public and amid the tentative re-forming of *Robsten*, the weight of commentary increasingly shifted towards more optimistic formulations. MSN.com saw fit to run a piece reminding readers of the numerous reconciled couples to be found in the contemporary celebrity landscape including Kourtney Kardashian and Scott Disick, Pink and Carey Hart, Justin Timberlake and Jessica Biel, and Prince William and Kate Middleton. As media outlets increasingly left behind the initial phase of intense condemnation of Stewart, and gradually transitioned to an acceptance of *Robsten*'s reconciliation Stewart was still sometimes grudgingly reinstated into the idealized fusional couple and often affectively re-positioned as chastened and regretful. For instance, on 16 November 2012 Irish radio station 98FM reported on its 'Showbiz Show' that Stewart understood herself to be on probation with her boyfriend with 'one wrong move and it could all be off again'. In many such accounts the terms of Stewart's relationship with Pattinson were recast so that since their reunion she was described as 'needy' and 'dependent' on him. Predictably she was reported as 'getting broody'.[36] In an extraordinary cover story in its 3 December 2012 issue, *OK!* magazine dramatically upped the ante on such coverage with its feature, 'Kristen & Rob's Baby Joy!' The scant justification for the headline is provided inside where it is reported that 'as long as she stays true to him, he's willing to have a baby with her'. On this basis, *OK!* proceeds to visualize the couple's future nursery. Notably, the piece reports, 'You know the sullen, mopey Kristen you often see in photographs? Well, you wouldn't recognize her now.'[37] Despite such zealous coverage, Pattinson and Stewart broke up for good shortly thereafter.

An emerging element in *Robsten*'s media coverage in this period was the suggestion of the discrepant celebrity capital of the pair. (Stewart's fame trajectory has tended to seem more durable and less random than Pattinson's; while she was locked into the *Twilight* role early on, his casting was more tentative and highly dependent on couple chemistry with her). An article in *The Sunday Times* shrewdly noted that the current representational environment is favourable for Stewart given the vogue for 'kick-ass' young women in franchises from *Batman* to *The Hunger Games* to *Prometheus*.[38]

Overall, then, while there were intermittent suggestions that Stewart was making restitution for the 'offense' experienced jointly by Pattinson and by the public, through demonstrating behaviour in compliance with normative fame and gender protocols, autumn 2012 saw a narrative of couple restoration rather smoothly displacing a narrative of excoriation. Public interest in and desire for ongoing belief in the couple was revealed in the prevalence of the internet meme 'Robsten is Unbroken' which trended on Twitter, flourished on Tumblr and inspired myriad videos uploaded to YouTube.

Conclusion

In nearly all of its guises, the privileged trope of the celebrity couple works to fortify heterosexual coupledom as the premiere form of social intimacy. Moreover, such couples operate as tropes of exclusion (in social class terms among others) though their excluding work is always precarious. I have argued that *Robsten*'s phenomenal coupledom developed in an era in which couple membership itself is increasingly positioned as a marker of privilege. It further accords with the fantasy that is lavishly gratified at the conclusion of *Twilight*: the desire for a private (yet sumptuously affluent) couple-centred world (bolstered at a remove by a network of [inter-species] allies and family members). In films and public appearances playing out over an interval of time marked by acute recessionary exigencies, *Robsten* modelled the rejuvenated norm of the 'power couple' in an era when endogamous relations among the wealthy are surging.

I have suggested that some of the significance of *Robsten* lies in its embodiment of the romantic hyper-mutualization of idealized contemporary coupling. This version of the couple has long been an organizing principle of the 'chick flick' and other female-centred media forms but it has a social status well beyond the representational realm. The embattled intimacy of this heavily publicized celebrity mega-couple overarched the *Twilight* film franchise and their own real-life romance. In an environment of ever more transparent intimacy, audience pleasures are crucially tied to the 'entitlement' of the tabloid press to unrestricted scrutiny of its celebrity subjects (even while those same audiences often decry the press for its actions). In this respect, the mainstreaming of tabloid culture runs in tandem with the fully surveillant state, 'adultery technologies' like spouse monitoring software and the social worlds cultivated by media technologies like Facebook which exercise ever greater powers to see and know more about the intimate conduct of citizens.

Several years on from its demise, *Robsten* remains a significant signifying feature of both Stewart and Pattinson's fame. Yet both stars have lately been widely praised for lowering their profiles and establishing a separation between their creative pursuits and the kind of high-profile, mass-market entertainment associated with hordes of avid, over-identified female consumers. In an account quite typical of the emergent discourse lauding the pair for having superseded the tawdriness of overhyped celebrity coupledom and the female-centred *Twilight* franchise, Donald Clarke has recently praised them as 'fine actors' and predicts that the key to their career longevity will be 'getting in with good powerful directors'.[39] Similarly an Associated Press account alludes to Pattinson 'trying to erase a tabloid persona' and succeeding through a discovery of actorly craft the piece imagines as incompatible with a franchise like *Twilight*.[40] Over time, Robsten may increasingly appear an artifact of a particular developmental stage of the stars' careers. Appearing (separately) at Cannes in 2014, Stewart and Pattinson were celebrated for their ascension to a higher-grade creative position, emphatic separation from the putatively trivial emotional economy of *Twilight* fandom and new association with the right kinds of adulatory publics. The restoration of Stewart and Pattinson to realms of artistic credibility thus would seem to entail making their separate ways both personally and professionally and a repositioning away from low-brow femininities and devalued intimacies.

Acknowledgements

I thank the volume editors, the audience at the Celebrity Couples conference in Southampton and Suzanne Leonard for their useful suggestions in the development of this chapter.

Notes

1   Such formulations distinguish the stratospheric commercial prospects generated by the coming together of two stars whose fame allocations are roughly equivalently proportioned. These sorts of composite couples are hardly a new phenomenon – witness for instance the early Hollywood mega-couple Mary Pickford and Douglas Fairbanks, Jr, the name of whose mansion, Pickfair, anticipated the fusional rhetorical device that would proliferate a century later. Its current ubiquity may suggest something distinctive about contemporary intimacy norms as I go on to explore later in the essay.

2   Martha Nochimson, *Screen Couple Chemistry: The Power of 2* (Austin: University of Texas Press, 2002), 1.

3   Lauren Berlant, 'Intimacy: A Special Issue', in *Intimacy* (Chicago: University of Chicago Press, 2000), 2.

4   The franchise comprises *Twilight* (Hardwicke, 2008), *The Twilight Saga: New Moon* (Weitz, 2009), *The Twilight Saga: Eclipse* (Slade, 2010), *The Twilight Saga: Breaking Dawn – Part 1* (Condon, 2011) and *The Twilight Saga: Breaking Dawn – Part 2* (Condon, 2012).

5   Anne Helen Petersen, 'That Teenage Feeling: *Twilight*, Fantasy and Feminist Readers', *Feminist Media Studies* 1, no. 12 (2012): 53.

6   Kim McNamara, 'The Paparazzi Industry and New Media: The Evolving Production and Consumption of Celebrity News and Gossip Websites', *International Journal of Communication Studies* 14, no. 5 (2011): 526.

7   Ibid., 527.

8   A historically proximate example of the discursive valuing of the high-status celebrity power couple could be found in a high-profile 2012 *Vanity Fair* article about Tom Cruise's reported search for a new partner after his divorce from Nicole Kidman. Going into great detail about an 'auditioning process' for prospective partners supposedly conducted by the Church of Scientology of which Cruise is a member, the article reports 'Tom wanted someone with her own power.' After breaking off relationships with non-celebrity women, Cruise then emerged in a heavily (and at times problematically) hyped new celebrity couple with Katie Holmes. See Maureen Orth, 'What Katie Didn't Know', *Vanity Fair* October, 2012.

9   Catherine Rampell, 'Marriage Is for Rich People', *New York Times*, 6 February 2012.

10 Ibid.

11 Chrystia Freeland, *Plutocrats: The Rise of the New Global Super-Rich and the Fall of Everyone Else* (New York: Penguin, 2012), 87.

12 Brookes Barnes, 'Media Vampires, Beware', *New York Times*, 15 November 2009.

13 The ongoing association between British craft and a discomfort with Hollywood hype was recently exemplified by Damian Lewis who in accepting his 2012 Golden Globe for his role in *Homeland* said from the podium 'I'm one of those pesky Brits – apologies. I don't really believe in judging art but I thought I'd show up just in case. Turned out alright.'

14 'The 13 Most Annoying Stars'. http://celebs.answers.com/lifestyle/the-10-most-annoying-stars.

15 '"I'm Such a Dork," Insists *Twilight* Actress Kristen Stewart As She Lands Her First *Vogue* Cover', *Mail Online*, 19 January 2011, http://www.dailymail.co.uk/tvshowbiz/article-1348357/Kristen-Stewart-claims-shes-dork-new-Vogue-interview.html.

16 The furore over the comment led Stewart to issue an apology. See '"I Made A Big Mistake": *Twilight's* Kristen Stewart Apologises for Rape Remark'. *Mail Online*, 4 June 2010, http://www.dailymail.co.uk/tvshowbiz/article-1284038/Twilights-Kristen-Stewart-apologises-rape-remark.html.

17 Barnes, 'Media Vampires, Beware'.

18 In an August letter to media outlets Foster issued a robust defence of Stewart in a piece that highlighted the trials of fame in the era of social media. She wrote 'If I were a young actor or actress starting my career today in the new era of social media and its sanctioned hunting season, would I survive?'. See Jodie Foster Defends Kristen Stewart, Calls Fame 'Life Lived As A Moving Target', *Huffington Post*, 15 August 2012, http://www.huffingtonpost.com/2012/08/15/jodie-foster-defends-kristen-stewart_n_1778965.html.

19 'Kristen Stewart On Her Love Life: Bite Me!', 4 November 2009. people.com, http://www.people.com/people/package/article/0,,20316279_20317707,00.html.

20 Barnes, 'Media Vampires, Beware'.

21 Paul Thompson, '"Somebody Could Kill Me": Kristen Stewart Fears Fame May Lead to her Death', *Mail Online*, 14 October 2012.

22 See 'Kristen Stewart Knocks Angelina Jolie Off the Top Spot as Hollywood's Highest Paid Actress', *Mail Online*, 19 June 2012, http://www.dailymail.co.uk/tvshowbiz/article-2161801/Kristen-Stewart-knocks-Angelina-Jolie-spot-Hollywoods-highest-paid-actress.html.

23 Fehintola Betiku, 'Twi-hards in Uproar: Kristen Stewart Fans Take to Her Defence on Twitter ... Even After Cheating Star Issues Public Apology', *Mail Online*, 26 July 2012, http://www.dailymail.co.uk/tvshowbiz/article-2178911/Kristen-Stewart-cheated-Robert-Pattinson-Twilight-fans-Twitter-defence.html.

24 'Kristen Stewart, Robert Pattinson Back Together: Actor Wants to Take Things Slow', *Huffington Post*, 1 October 2012, http://www.huffingtonpost.com/2012/10/18/kristen-stewart-robert-pattinson-back-together-take-things-slow_n_1978993.html.

25 Anne Breslaw, 'Kristen Stewart Cheats on Vampire Boyfriend with Married Human Father of Two'. *Jezebel.com*, 25 July 2012, http://jezebel.com/5928865/kristen-stewart-cheats-on-vampire-boyfriend-with-married-human-father-of-two.

26 Rosemary MacCabe, 'Sex, Lies and Scarlet Women', *Irish Times*, 18 August 2012.

27 Nico Lang, '"Trampire": Why the Public Slut Shaming of Kristen Stewart Matters for Young Women', *Huffington Post*, 4 September 2012, http://www.huffingtonpost.com/nico-lang/trampires-why-the-slut-sh_b_1850940.html.

28 Adrienne L. McLean and David A. Cook, eds, *Headline Hollywood: A Century of Scandal* (New Brunswick: Rutgers University Press, 2001).

29 'Robert Pattinson and Kristen Stewart Have "Explosive Row" Before Twilight Premiere', 21 November 2012, http://www.independent.ie/woman/celeb-news/robert-pattinson-and-kristen-stewart-have-explosive-row-before-twilight-premiere-28904075.html.

30 See Suzanne Leonard, '"I Hate My Job, I Hate Everyone Here": Adultery, Boredom, and the "Working Girl" in Twenty-First Century American Cinema', in *Interrogating Postfeminism: Gender and the Politics of Popular Culture*, ed. Yvonne Tasker and Diane Negra (Durham, NC: Duke University Press, 2007), 100–31; and Suzanne Leonard, '"I Really Must Be An Emma Bovary": Female Literacy and Adultery in Feminist Fiction', *Genders* 51 (2010), http://www.genders.org/g51/g51_leonard.html.

31 See Andrew J. Cherlin, *The Marriage-Go-Round: The State of Marriage and the Family Today* (New York: Vintage, 2010).

32 Melissa Gregg, 'Adultery Technologies'. Academia.edu, http://www.academia.edu/1468299/Adultery_Technologies.

33 NuttyMadam, 'HOW COULD YOU DO THIS KRISTEN?!' Youtube video, 4.22. 25 July 2012, https://www.youtube.com/watch?v=V_Qrt1k8qHo.

34 madringking1119, 'Leave Britney Alone (Complete)', Youtube video, 4.17. 11 August 2011, https://www.youtube.com/watch?v=WqSTXuJeTks.

35 Stephanie Theobold, 'Notorious: Has Kristen Stewart Turned Scandal Into Success?' *The Sunday Times*, 11 November 2012.

36 'Kristen Feeling Clucky', *Dublin Metro Herald*, 5 November 2012.

37 Richard Jerome, 'Kristen & Rob's Baby Joy!' *OK! Magazine*, 3 December 2012, 37.

38 Ibid.

39 Donald Clarke, 'R-Pat and Company Rule the Riviera', *Irish Times*, 23 May 2014, http://www.irishtimes.com/culture/film/r-pat-and-company-rule-the-riviera-1.1805512. Clarke has in mind Pattinson's repeat casting in the last few years in films directed by David Cronenberg and Stewart's in a new film by French director Olivier Assayas.

40 Associated Press, 'For Robert Pattinson, Cannes Is a Coming-Out Party', *The New York Times* 20 May 2014.

17

The Good, the Bad and the Broken: Forms and Functions of Neoliberal Celebrity Relationships

Neil Ewen

Certainly one can identify with and fantasize about a fictional entity; the actual existence of celebrities as living humans, the fact that they are somehow now, speaking or kissing or brushing their teeth, gives celebrity fantasy and celebrity identification their power. They require not only pursuing but arriving at a real self. … That self is the destination … both the overall backdrop of authenticity and specific truths are essential to pleasure.

Joshua Gamson[1]

Fantasy is the means by which people hoard idealizing theories and tableaux about how they and the world 'add up to something'. What happens when those fantasies start to fray – depression, disassociation, pragmatism, cynicism, optimism, activism, or an incoherent mash?

Lauren Berlant[2]

As Su Holmes and Sean Redmond point out, 'adulation, identification and emulation are key motifs in the study of celebrity culture'.[3] Blossoming out of the seminal star studies work of, among others, Richard Dyer[4] – which illustrated that the value of film stardom was cultural as well as economic, with stars providing personalities with whom the audience invest emotionally – much recent critical writing on the social and affective functions of celebrity has sought to understand how, in the contemporary world, 'anomic, atomized individuals reach out for idealized stars and celebrities in what might be called a self-directed healing process'.[5]

This process has been viewed in various lights, some more negative than others. Richard Schickel, for instance, writes about the public investment in celebrity as being a form of popular hysteria, underpinned by an 'illusion of intimacy' whereby stars and celebrities provide emotional connections previously maintained through relationships with friends and family.[6] Likewise, but in a different register, Cooper Lawrence suggests that while narcissism often underpins the behaviour of both the famous and those who desire fame, celebrities act as a common currency that reveals the fragility of social bonds in contemporary daily life.[7] Meanwhile, Chris Rojek's influential theoretical work on 'para-social' relationships investigates the aura and charisma of stars, considers the meanings that these stars embody, and (put crudely) argues that celebrity is a kind of replacement for religion in a secular age[8]; while Graeme Turner explains that 'as human relations attenuate and fragment under the pressure of contemporary political and social conditions', leaving an 'affective deficit in modern life', celebrity has the potential to be used 'as a means of constructing a new dimension of community through the media'. One way this happens, Turner suggests, is through gossip and debate about celebrities, which should be understood as intimate spheres in which people find connection.[9]

However – as many of the essays in the present volume point out, and as the volume as a whole has sought to address – the majority of this critical work has, thus far at least, focused on the appeal, meanings and affects of individual celebrities. Accordingly, this chapter considers some of the particular affective functions of celebrity relationships, romantic and familial, in contemporary western media culture, and suggests that if, as much contemporary criticism agrees, the defining cultural symptoms of neoliberalism are anxiety and foreboding arising from globalization, the financialization of capitalism, and the dissolution of institutions that previously structured society,[10] we might also wish to consider that a significant affective function of today's celebrity relationships concerns their potential to alleviate these symptoms, however temporarily, through the generation of comfort and pleasure in their audiences.

Accepting this suggestion, however, requires acknowledgement from the beginning that it is a complex diagnosis. While I agree with Mary Evans' suggestion that neoliberalism endorses 'an every-person-for-themselves view of the world' that has led to 'ideas about "love" inevitably [becoming] confused and confusing', and that '[at] its worst, what individuals think of as love has become another form of consumption', I want to advance and complicate her further suggestion that many ordinary people consider celebrity relationships to be an antidote to the 'emotional barrenness' of neoliberalism.[11] Evans writes that 'many people turn to the artificial cream on the hard neo-liberal cake: the cream of celebrity culture'; that in performances 'often related to consumerist fantasies of transformation', 'these famous, and infamous others, offer a form of comfort, a reassurance that people are still falling in love, still making families and still, simply, having emotional lives'. All of which is true. But, if we go further and recognize that there are different types of famous relationships that generate different types of pleasure (not to mention that there are different types of audiences with varying degrees of awareness about the various processes of celebrity culture[12]), the notion of the celebrity relationship as a fantasy of comfort and escape becomes less straightforward.

As such, the main aim of this chapter is to interrogate and problematize this formulation. In what follows, I suggest that while different types of celebrity relationships all satisfy the economic imperative of generating profit, the media tends to privilege certain types over others. Where each relationship features on the hierarchy, I suggest, rests mainly on conceptions of talent and on how faithfully or not the relationship in question adheres to certain cultural expectations about love, coupledom and marriage, both formally and in terms of morality. 'Good' relationships (for lack of a better term) – the ones that we are repeatedly encouraged to fantasize about – are invariably closed narratives with 'happy ever after' endings, which are elaborated as vehicles of conservative and neo-traditional values, with their participants shown to adhere to notions such as monogamy, 'faithfulness' to each other, and 'settling down' together. Conversely, 'bad' relationships – the ones we are encouraged to sit in judgement over – are those that betray these expectations in that their fragmented narratives, often positioned as occurring because of supposed lapses of morality, or an inability or refusal to act 'properly', resist satisfying the desire for closure.

These judgements are inflected by assumptions about class and status, both in terms of the participants in the relationships and in terms of the means by which they have achieved fame: it is no coincidence, for instance, that a couple such as *The Beckhams* (one of the couples I examine below) are currently closer to being considered 'stars' than their former status as 'celebrities' now that they have been together for a long time, are seen to perform consistently the ideal of a happy family, are now extremely wealthy, and have the ability to manage their reputations in ways that they did not in the past; likewise, it is not a mistake that 'celetoids', such as those reality television contestants so beloved by tabloid culture in part for their constant cycle of on/off relationships, have little scope to mould their personas, and are often described as 'trashy'.[13] As such, in celebrity relationships, the generation and management of 'aura' and 'charisma' are both of central importance and circumscribed by status.

In terms of this last point, we should recognize that revelling in the 'misfortunes' of the on/off celebrity relationship is also a type of pleasure and escape. Meanwhile, we should also recognize the problems inherent in idealizing seemingly perfect celebrity unions by bearing in mind Laura Kipnis' point about how 'the couple form as currently practiced is an ambivalent one' that attempts the impossible process of reconciling a list of seemingly irreconcilable opposites: 'the yearning for intimacy … the desire for autonomy', 'the comfort and security of routine' … 'its soul-deadening predictability'.[14] This I see as useful alongside Lauren Berlant's concept of 'cruel optimism', which she posits as a dynamic that underpins the everyday relations of people attempting to live out fantasies of 'the good life'. Under neoliberalism, as the 'blueprint has faded' and the fantasy becomes 'more fantasmatic, with less and less relation to how people can live',[15] cruel optimism, as a structure of feeling, defines the ranges of affect and emotion that people feel about their 'compromised conditions of possibility' which might include a range of feelings other than, or alongside, optimism, such as pessimism or even despair.[16] In light of this work, then, fantasy can be seen to be a precondition of all celebrity relationships. And, to be sure, the underlying tensions that Kipness and Berlant highlight, are part of the attraction of 'good' celebrity relationships: at any point the fantasy might fragment to reveal the ambivalence that these theorists suggest lies at the heart of all relationships.

To conclude the chapter, I consider the affects of those instances whereby 'good' celebrity relationships disintegrate, explicitly betraying their promise of providing pleasurable fantasies of intimacy and bliss. If 'good' celebrity couples articulate cultural desires for idealized relationships, and 'bad' celebrity couples are examples of how not to live, then it is highly productive and necessary to take into account the 'good' couple turned 'bad': what we might call the 'broken' couple or the 'anti-couple'.[17] While I outline different types of 'anti-couple', I argue that the ways in which the disintegration of these 'good' relationships is narrativized in the media simultaneously provides certain pleasure (in that we revel in the nitty-gritty of the failed couple's exposed private lives), serves to reveal the artifice of all celebrity relationships (in that the processes of their re-narrativization are laid bare), and reinforces dominant conservative discourses (in that the morality of the narrativization becomes explicit).

Fantasies of the future in the era of neoliberalism

Over the last couple of years I have taken to performing a little exercise with my media studies undergraduates in entry-level classes on ideology. I have carried out this activity maybe eight or ten times, and both the process and results are notable for their uncanny consistency. Each time it plays out almost exactly as follows.[18]

I begin by asking for a volunteer willing to share, and be questioned about, their dreams and ambitions for the future in order that we might consider the possibility that the stories we tell ourselves about ourselves, and the fantasies that help structure our lives, are not natural, but rather shaped by external forces such as the mainstream media. Then, in silence, I look around the room as each student does their best to avoid eye contact. I emphasize that the brave participant will not be compelled to divulge any private information, and that simply saying 'pass' will mean that we move on to the next question without hesitation. And then I point out that the volunteer would really be helping me out since my plan for the rest of the class is predicated on the exercise going off smoothly. (This is not strictly true, but it's a strategy that has yet to fail). Following this, a lone female student raises her hand.[19]

After thanking her, I ask the student to imagine her life when she's around about my age – I am 35 – and the exchange begins: 'Are you married?' (YES); 'Do you have kids?' (YES); 'Where do you live?' (SOMEWHERE AFFLUENT); 'Do you own your home?' (YES); 'Do you take vacations regularly?' (YES); 'Where do you holiday?' (ABROAD, SOMEWHERE SUNNY). We then try to work out how she's going to get there. I ask: 'How old are you?' (18/19); 'Have you met the person you will marry yet?' (NO/PROBABLY NOT); 'How old will you be when you have kids?' (HHMMmmmm… NOT SURE, BUT NOT TOO OLD). 'But by my age?' (YES).

Then things begin to get interesting. I inquire about the hesitation over children and a strict set of rules emerges: career, stable relationship and home ownership before marriage; marriage before kids. And then I dig deeper. 'Will your home be nice?' (YES); 'Nicer than average?' (YES). 'OK, so let's say it's a little over the UK's average house price of a quarter of a million pounds?' (OK).[20] 'And you're going to find a partner and buy this house before you get married and before you have children?' (YES).

You might guess where it goes from here. To cut a long story short, I ask them to share their dreams of what Berlant calls the 'good life', and I smash those

fantasies into fragments. I point to the debt the average student will carry as s/
he enters a barren and hostile job market[21]; I point to the fact that wages have
been stagnating for decades and declining in real terms for years[22]; I point to the
huge rise of short-term, temporary and zero-hours contracts that now define the
post-industrial economies of western nations[23]; and I ask them to consider how,
in this economic environment, they will raise the kind of deposit that a bank will
demand to secure a mortgage on their dream home.[24] I itemize this reality not to
be cruel, but in an attempt to expose their fantasies as fantasies and to encourage
them to ponder a number of questions, among them: Why are our dreams so
divorced from reality when many of our parents have fulfilled similar dreams?
From where do these fantasies emerge? And why are these dreams so consistent
and so uniform every time I perform this exercise? One thing that becomes clear
by the time we are done: the ripe old age of thirty-five seems much less far away
to them than it did at the beginning of the class.[25] Indeed, when one student
stated that she wanted to be debt-free before getting a mortgage, we calculated
that she would likely be in her mid-70s by the day of her wedding.

My sense from the repeated performance of this exercise, and the class
discussions that follow, is that, when challenged, these students are largely
aware that their fantasies are unrealizable.[26] How could they not be when they
have spent their entire adolescence immersed in the banal drip-drip of (often
uncritical[27]) news media stories about financial crises, multiple-dip recessions
and the 'need' for austerity? The stories these young adults tell themselves about
their futures, and, perhaps more to the point, the ones they *perform* when
questioned in a public forum, can perhaps be most productively considered as
coping mechanisms[28] employed as a means to deal with the fact that they have
come of age at the very time during which the world they have been trained
to expect to enter has entirely disappeared. Not only do these students lack
any sense of what it was like to live in a pre-9/11 world free from the multiple
anxieties attending the 'War on Terror', they have the added misfortune of being
the first cohort of adults for generations to enter a world utterly at odds with
that of their parents in terms of aspirational life trajectory. Indeed, the typical
meritocratic stories that their parents and teachers would likely have told them as
children about a desirable progression through life – work hard at school, enter
university and gain a degree, get a job, buy a house, get married, have kids – are
now almost entirely redundant as a practical guide. As Richard Sennett (among
many others) has shown, increasingly since the 1970s, alterations to the base
of western economies have had a monumental impact on the organization of

work culture, which, in turn, has profoundly transformed the ways individuals and groups live out, and – crucially – imagine, their lives.[29] Of the post-2008 American context, David Graeber writes:

> There has been a good deal of discussion of late of the erosion of the American middle class, but most of it misses out on the fact that the 'middle class' in the United States has never primarily been an economic category. It has always had everything to do with that feeling of stability and security that comes from being able to simply assume that – whatever one might think about politicians – everyday institutions like the police, education system, health clinics, and even credit providers are basically on your side. ... The growing sense, on the part of Americans, is that the institutional structures that surround them are not really there to help them – even, that they are dark and inimical forces – is a direct consequence of the financialization of capitalism.[30]

Increasingly, the familiar assumptions of prosperity resulting from 'hard work' that defined Anglo-American post-second world war society have dissolved: for the majority of workers, wages have long stagnated and benefits such as pensions have largely disappeared or have been eroded to the point of relative inconsequence, with the result that today's middle-class children cannot reasonably expect to enjoy a higher standard of living than their parents.[31] In this context, as Evans suggests, one of the key points to note about celebrity couples and families is that they enact fantasies that these sociocultural losses can be overcome through emotional connection.

Fantasies as retrenchment

As critical work on postfeminism has shown,[32] this era of neoliberal anxiety is also one of cultural retrenchment. It is also, then, a time during which these good life fantasies demand to be read ideologically and critically. It is no coincidence that at a time of increasing economic stratification and deep social transformation – including anxieties about relatively high rates of divorce,[33] changes to marriage laws,[34] increasing figures of single-occupant households[35] and the emergence of a 'boomerang generation' of adults who have little choice but to remain, or return to, living with parents[36] – that the 'traditional', exclusionary, version of the couple finding love and eventually settling down to middle-class life is the one that remains the most dominant in western media culture. Meanwhile, it should be noted that although alternative versions of this model have become more visible since the mid-1980s, mediated relationships are still overwhelmingly circumscribed by heteronormativity and neo-traditional gender roles.[37]

At the same time as this fantasy is becoming less attainable, it is repeatedly the one that the average person is encouraged to desire through the daily consumption of media and the living of everyday life. Laura Kipnis, provocatively but hardly unreasonably, suggests that romantic coupledom – a key part of this fantasy – constitutes 'omnipresent propaganda beaming into our psyches on an hourly basis: the millions of images of lovestruck couples looming over us from movie screens, televisions, billboards, magazines, incessantly strong-arming us onboard the love train'.[38] Even if one rejects the idea of false consciousness (as I do, with certain reservations), it is clear that this type of story and the morality behind it – considered as part of a much wider trend and underpinning the narratives of fairy tales to action flicks, from news reports to video games – elaborates a logic, a vocabulary, a consciousness, a worldview and a model to which many people aspire, primarily because of its ubiquity, familiarity and repetition.[39]

These discourses are thoroughly ideological; their repeated elaborations, even in their most banal variants, are profoundly political. As Michael Cobb writes, '[Family politics] are not wedge issues but central biopolitical concerns that ferociously animate our present and future politics. Marriage, gay or not, and for that matter most forms of coupledom, are at the heart of this political life'[40] As such, we should bear in mind Jacqueline Rose's contention that 'fantasy … is never only inward-turning; it always contains a historical reference in so far as it involves, alongside the attempt to arrest the present, a journey through the past'.[41] When, for example, in July 2013, the *Daily Mail*'s website *MailOnline* set 'a new global record of 134 million web traffic users … propelled by news stories including the Royal birth [of Prince George]',[42] the subject matter was hardly coincidental.

Coverage of celebrities has been central to the success of *MailOnline*, which has been since 2012 the most visited English-language newspaper website in the world,[43] and it is worth paying particular attention to the ways in which it uses celebrity culture as a vehicle for the reproduction of traditional discourses of coupledom and relationships. Much has made of the so-called 'sidebar of shame', a series of links to stories of 'celebrity misdemeanors', which runs down the right hand side of the screen on every page, and tends to house pictures of young, scantily-clad women, often going to or coming home from nights out, sometimes in 'compromising' situations. Writing about the website's formal properties – similar to those used on other popular websites such as *Buzzfeed* – Jemima Kiss suggests the layout taps into 'an almost primeval instinct [whereby] our brain rewards each tantalizing discovery, keeping us stuck to the screen and scrolling', while Henry Mance suggests that it 'means the next guilty pleasure is never far away'.[44] This focus on what might be considered the more salacious aspects of celebrity culture, and the clear positioning of the viewer as voyeur and judge, is, however, only one example among many of the ways that celebrity culture is presented on the website. On any given day a typical front page comprises celebrations of the British royal family, articles concerning the lifestyles of affluent power couples from Britain's ruling class, as well as picture-heavy pieces about Hollywood superstar couples and their families. But, paying close attention to the website over a longer period also reveals other patterns, and an almost pathological repetition of 'traditional' fantasies featuring 'ordinary' couples and families. Regular visitors to *MailOnline* may begin to notice, for instance, a trend of stories about elderly, long-lasting couples who are presented as having spent entire lifetimes together 'never having a crossed word' (or some such clichéd nonsense) before dying within hours of each other: their fleeting, posthumous celebrity presented as an example to us all (as well as being an ironic award for their long, probably painfully ordinary lives).[45]

MailOnline, then, can be seen as a microcosm of the mainstream media's treatment of celebrity culture juxtaposing the 'immoral' or 'unacceptable' behaviour of 'low class' celebrities with examples of 'higher end' celebrities who largely conform to conservative notions of rectitude. In the discursive frame, this behaviour is inseparable from the wider debates about traditional notions of love, coupledom and families discussed by writers such as Kipnis and Cobb. It becomes clear that celebrity culture is a key vehicle for the discussion of 'traditional' morality and the regulation and judgement of public conduct,[46] in an ostentatious and hypocritical process from which the media profits by exhibiting in intimate detail the very content it purports to abhor (regularly young, under-clothed women, positioned as 'betraying' their femininity).[47]

The celebrity couple hierarchy

Among other things, *MailOnline* highlights the need to acknowledge that the affective function of celebrity relationships are ideological and multifaceted: if they act as fantasies of escape from 'reality', then that escape happens variously across an emotional spectrum from awe to disgust; if some celebrity couples provide aspirational models, others are positioned as abject. Of course, any number of categories, some no doubt more useful than others, might be identified or conjured in an attempt to gain critical and theoretical orientation amid the maelstrom of celebrity alliances. Most obviously, perhaps, we might choose to divide them into binary camps according to a familiar star/celebrity split.[48]

Star couples (such as, say, *Brangelina*) generate pleasure, perhaps primarily, by providing an ideal to which many ordinary people aspire in that they project the appearance of successfully maintaining a happy romantic coupling within a 'traditional' family unit, all the while retaining the capacity to seemingly transcend the drudgery of everyday life. Their ability to manage their privacy and reproduce the intangible 'aura' that is often said to have characterized golden era Hollywood stars symbiotically intensifies with increases in wealth, and endurance as a couple.

Further down the hierarchy we would find *celebrity couples*, for whom the audience finds pleasure not in perceiving the 'finished products of semiotic labour'[49] but in observing the constant cycle of what Diane Negra calls the 'making, unmaking, and re-making' of celebrity relationships, which has emerged and been increasingly emphasized through recent developments in technology, cultural value and audience expectation.[50] This category of celebrity alliance typically involves individuals moving from relationship to relationship, usually, but not always, without those involved ever becoming defined by their association with a single significant other, while audience pleasure in observing these relationships may manifest variously, for example: fascination with the banal, everyday minutia of other people's lives lived out in public; feelings of immersion and/or familiarity in the melodrama of complicated relationships; satisfaction at being positioned as a judge or arbiter; *schadenfreude* in observing bad luck or misery.[51] Alongside outlets like *MailOnline*, certain forms of reality TV are probably the most obvious sites of this type of fame in the contemporary media landscape. As Misha Kavka notes, reality TV has latterly 'disengag[ed] from its documentary roots and [has become] a self-conscious participant in the rituals of self-commodification and self-legitimation that define contemporary celebrity culture'.[52]

The hierarchy of this proposed categorization between the *star couple*/'good' couple, and the *celebrity couple*/'bad' couple, is influenced heavily by a number of different structuring elements. One such element might regard talent and the extent to which their stardom and 'aura' have been 'achieved'. While it may be possible to judge Pitt and Jolie as more individually and collectively talented or superior as a star couple to a pair of inferior contemporary Hollywood actors, the judgement gets complicated if we cross boundaries of, say, time and genre, not to mention, discipline. How do we judge the individual and combined talents and/or aura of *Brangelina* in comparison to *Gilbo*?[53] How might we compare them to Audrey Hollander and Otto Bauer?[54] In other words, we might note that notions of talent in certain spheres are not only somewhat arbitrary and difficult to pin down (especially if we compare acting to something like baseball, a sport in which statistics offer clues as to levels of ability[55]), they are always circumscribed within the boundaries of their own production contexts with specific rules, logics and values. So, while Brad Pitt and Angelina Jolie would likely be considered more worthy of fame – and thus find themselves higher up the hierarchy – than, say, a couple of *Big Brother* contestants whose relationship lasts for a few weeks over the lifetime of the series, this might be the case primarily because Pitt and Jolie's skill at their craft is commonly perceived to be of more value than the self-publicity skills of the average reality television contestant.

Brangelina is useful here in another way, namely as an example of the ways that celebrity couples are brands whose meanings are continually up for contestation and whose construction requires constant attention and management, no matter the levels of talent involved. During their early life together, after meeting on the set of *Mr. & Mrs. Smith* (Liman, 2005), Pitt and Jolie were subjected to widespread censure in the media, and often described as a 'bad' couple. Jolie was the 'other woman' in the disintegration of the 'good' couple comprising Pitt and Jennifer Aniston; and the allegation that Jolie and Pitt had an on-set affair while he was still married to the popular Aniston resulted in the media painting Jolie (already a 'problematic' individual female celebrity, known for her transgressive behaviour)[56] as a marriage-breaking seductress and Pitt as a philanderer who had broken the heart of 'America's Sweetheart'.[57]

So, *Brang*elina's rehabilitation and rebranding as a couple invested in global philanthropy, both through their charity work and the adoption of children from the global south,[58] is evidence of the labour that goes into the production of celebrity couples whose berth on the good/bad hierarchy is always contingent and positional. And, at least in this instance, the labour in becoming a good celebrity couple is more about their maintenance of their happy romantic union and the presentation of their happy family than it is about any value for their on-screen work. In fact, both Pitt and Jolie had been previously lauded for their talent with Oscar nominations and awards long before becoming a couple; theoretically, then, the work of branding themselves as a faithful couple and hands-on parents has done more to highlight their talent than the other way around. As such, this reading of *Brangelina* suggests that morality is at least as important achievement in the positioning of celebrity couples and that there is pre-existing set of cultural expectations to which celebrity couples must comply if they are to attain the aura of superstardom.

The Beckhams and the fantasy of meritocracy

Brangelina's rehabilitation is contained within a romance narrative corroborated by their 'good works', and, at least while it holds, has culminated as them being an extremely prominent example of a traditional, but ultra-modern, happy family.[59] But the rehabilitation process from bad couple to good couple is layered with other issues and meanings depending on the context of the particular couple or family's production. In the case of *The Beckhams*, another high-profile celebrity couple who rode out years of turbulent media treatment to become settled as a fantasy version of a family unit, the key to understanding their appeal is the notion of meritocracy. Although David and Victoria were already established as 'Britain's most famous celebrity couple'[60] for almost a decade before their move to Los Angeles in 2007, their subsequent success in projecting themselves as a mutually supportive, stable couple, successful in both individual and collective endeavours, and who are regularly pictured traversing the globe with kids in tow, has further elevated their status and generated an aura previously unimaginable. At the heart of their appeal (especially from a British perspective) are the ways in which they have risen from humble beginnings to transcend the boundaries of their class and national backgrounds, providing a fantasy that material wealth, emotional happiness and geographical mobility can be earned in an era in which those pathways are disappearing in the real world.

Having enjoyed a distinguished soccer career playing at the highest level while becoming a cultural phenomenon – like no other player before him exploiting English soccer's burgeoning neoliberal economy,[61] challenging notions of traditional English sporting masculinity[62] and becoming the focus of sustained media and academic attention as an icon[63] – David was, on his move to Major League Soccer in 2007, assumed to be easing his way into retirement by heading to a far-off competition of dubious standing, having been disregarded as a player by the England national team. And while Victoria had been one-fifth of The Spice Girls, a girl-band that had enjoyed huge success in the late 1990s, her solo career had long since ground to a halt. By the mid-noughties, she was best known as the 'Queen of the WAGs': WAG being an acronym for 'Wives and Girlfriends', women who are at once visibly supportive of their partners and perfect versions of the postfeminist edict that links independence with hyper-femininity and conspicuous consumption.[64]

From the moment they arrived in LA, however, David and Victoria's image was carefully choreographed by their manager, the former svengali of The Spice Girls, Simon Fuller. David was reinvented as an ambassadorial figure for numerous causes (as a figurehead for MLS, as part of the official delegation that sought to bring the 2012 Olympics to London, as an official 'mentor' to the England players at the 2010 World Cup, and as a part of the London 2012 opening ceremony), while Victoria moved on from being the epitome of neo-traditional postfeminism as 'the Queen of the WAGs' to become a successful, independent and award-winning fashion designer. All the while, their status as a couple and family was constantly referenced and reinforced in the media, and it became clear that their meanings – both individually and collectively – had shifted dramatically. This is implied in the change of title of the second edition of Andrew Morton's biography of the couple.[65] On its first publication in 2000, the book was entitled *Posh & Becks*, gesturing towards an informality and familiarity with a couple whose private lives were, at the time, a daily source of speculation and gossip. In 2007 – upon their arrival in LA – the revised edition was renamed *The Beckhams*, suggesting a distance and even a regality[66] that symbiotically performed and confirmed their flight from the realms of banal celebrity coupledom.

Morton suggests that step was a result of Victoria's coming of age in Los Angeles: 'Her new career as a full-time stylist and trend-maker defined her as a woman with a real flair for fashion', he writes. 'She began to feel truly valued for herself, not for her image.'[67] This intensified over the next few years, as her ability as a fashion designer was recognized internationally. In 2011, the website *stylist. co.uk* took stock when Victoria won a prestigious award for 'Best Emerging Luxury Brand':

This lauded award marks an incredible year for the mum-of-four whose label is said to be on course for a £60million turnover for 2011. Not bad for a label that began in 2008 with a small salon style presentation. There was an initial disdain at the idea of a former Spice Girl turning her hand to luxury fashion but Beckham won the notoriously hard-nosed fashion pack and now has everyone from Jennifer Lopez to Eva Longoria sporting her dresses and bags.[68]

Meanwhile David's reputation had evolved just as dramatically. As Blake Morrison wrote in the *Guardian*:

These days he's the image of mobility – an emissary of intercontinental understanding, equally content to hang out with Sepp Blatter, Nelson Mandela or Tom Cruise. … In 2000, Beckham seemed to symbolise the worst of our culture (narcissism, celebrity worship and ostentatious wealth). In 2010, he stands for hard work, charity, perseverance, family values and global harmony. It's almost a surprise that he didn't attend the climate change conference in Copenhagen. But doubtless he'll be at the next one.[69]

Because of their wealth, status and careers, *The Beckhams* are today perhaps the example *par excellence* of the neoliberal fantasy couple and family. They are mobile, unbound by local concerns, free of worries about finances and unburdened by political conviction or identity. Zygmunt Bauman argues that in today's 'liquid modernity', long-term, stable relationships have lost their relevance for ordinary people because the economy demands a short-term, flexible workforce.[70] However, the genius of *The Beckhams* is that, as they traverse the globe, they manage to successfully position the traditional image of a family unit at the centre of their brand. It is an image that is at once imbued with deep nostalgia and an impossible model for ordinary people. In Bauman's terms, the usual connotations of family with home and stability may seem in contradiction to their liquid modernity, but their symbiosis under the Beckham brand underscores that their collective celebrity far exceeds the sum of its parts.

'Anti-Couples' and the tragic coupling of Oscar and Reeva

While seeking to highlight the constructed nature of all celebrity couples, I have suggested that the notion of 'happy', 'enduring' relationships needs to be deconstructed. I have also suggested that the observation of the daily production of celebrity is one of the pleasures that define lower rank celebrity relationships, while the pleasure in fantasizing about the stable 'happiness' of higher rank stars results, in part, from the protection from intrusion they manage to accrue.

This, though, is a problem for the star couple, because the higher they rise up the hierarchy, the bigger the potential fall. The inherent tension here is clear: the more a relationship creates an aura, the more the audience wants to know the behind-the-scenes details; and the more the audience wants to know, the higher the expectation becomes for a performance of righteousness. *Brangelina* and *The Beckhams*, more than anything else, perhaps, should be recognized not for their respective individual and collective talents, nor for the 'good work' that they do, nor even for the comfort or 'inspiration' that they provide 'ordinary' folks in the era of anxiety: they should be recognized for their mastery of giving their audiences just enough to want more, while keeping private the tensions and existential crises that Kipnis and Berlant illustrate are inherent to all emotional formations.[71] In other words, the production of the 'happy-ever-after', enduring celebrity relationship is a carefully orchestrated process of show and tell: something that is perhaps more difficult to manage successfully compared to an individual celebrity because the couple and/or family is a constant negotiation of different moving parts.

Since we have already examined the 'bad' couple turned 'good', another category that may be of particular critical value is one that covers those relationships defined primarily by breakdown and disintegration; relationships that actively resist being read as having 'happy endings'; relationships that fail and/or refuse to abide by the hegemonic cultural script; relationships whereby the public status of each of the individuals involved becomes subsumed by a new collective identity after their end. From the point of fragmentation onwards, the two (but, potentially, more) individuals comprising the union become imaginatively inseparable as the media weaves them back together in posthumous narratives, and for evermore they become locked together in an uncanny coupling. These alliances are usually, but not necessarily, of a romantic nature; and they may be termed as celebrity 'anti-couple' relationships.[72]

This category, of course, could itself be divided itself into numerous subsections. We might think, for instance, of Romantic and non-Romantic celebrity 'anti-couples'. Romantic celebrity anti-couple narratives of 'making and unmaking' are closely associated with notions of idealism and/or notions of genius, and whose (usually) tragic endings have been written as leaving legacies of unrealized potential. The subsequent process of mythologization suggests that these relationships touch a cultural nerve, and they become seared into the collective memory of western popular culture. Examples include John Lennon and Yoko Ono, Kurt Cobain and Courtney Love, and Tina Turner and Ike Turner.

Of course, break-ups are a regular part of celebrity media culture; but the splitting of these particular couples are markedly more profound. The identifications and affects at play in the narrative processes of their couplings and un-couplings are various and multifaceted: the pleasure in the blossoming of their unions, the pain at their disintegrations, the mixed feelings involved in the ways they are remembered (to simplify greatly these points).[73]

Non-Romantic celebrity anti-couples tend to be associated with transgression of dominant cultural values and/or tragedy of various forms, and might include, for example, the serial killers Fred and Rosemary West, 'the Moors Murderers' Myra Hindley and Ian Brady, the Manson Family, and other cult groupings.[74] As David Schmid suggests in his compelling work on individual serial killers and celebrity,[75] identification with these figures is 'complicated'. It is 'affective as well as intellectual, composed of admiration and resentment, envy and contempt ...' Widening the focus from individual celebrity deviants to consider the politics and affective functions of their unions is certainly an area ripe for research.

In recent years, perhaps the most (in)famous example of a celebrity anti-couple is the South African pairing, Oscar Pistorius and Reeva Steenkamp.[76] Pistorius, whose legs were amputated below the knee in infancy, achieved international stardom by becoming a Paralympic sprint champion, by becoming the first amputee to win an able-bodied world track medal, and by competing at the London 2012 Summer Olympics. His artificial limbs, or blades, earned him the nickname, 'Blade Runner'.[77] Steenkamp was a successful model and television personality in South Africa before her death at Pistorius' hand on the night of Valentine's Day, 2013, at which point the pair had been romantically involved for approximately three months. According to Pistorius, the couple were sleeping in his Pretoria home when he was awoken by a noise; he then shot Steenkamp through the restroom door believing her to be an intruder.[78] After a lengthy court case that attracted global media attention, Pistorius was sentenced to five years in prison for culpable homicide, having been cleared of Steenkamp's murder.

There is obviously much that could be said about Pistorius and Steenkamp as a celebrity anti-couple. In the context of the present discussion, however, the key points I want to emphasize are to do with the production of different types of pleasure, the revelation of artifice, and the discourses of morality that coloured the entire affair. Due to the fact that their relationship was still very young at the time of the tragedy, the South African media was still in the process of establishing the story of their romantic relationship, and up to that point interest was created in ways typical of the production of any new celebrity couple whereby the media and couple engaged in a mutually beneficial relationship. By February 2013, it was yet to be clear what kind of celebrity couple Pistorius and Steenkamp was going to be. As the tragedy broke, however, this trajectory was altered, and the narrative exploded instantaneously into fragments that were then collected and re-narrativized in numerous ways and from multiple points of view. Out of the control of any party (the couple and their publicists, the media, or as is usual at early points of celebrity relationships, a mixture of both) this process performed three main functions.

First, it exposed a hunger for details (about the events of the night, and about the personalities of the actors), and signified a shift in the types of pleasure that the couple had provided thus far, from light entertainment and escapism to horror, disbelief, fascination and any number of other emotions. The familiar injunction to establish the 'truth' was expressed alongside rumour, speculation, and innuendo. Details from officials, such as the police, overlapped with emotional statements from the couple's families and friends, and testimonies of varying relevance of people who claimed to have been in the vicinity of the crime scene at the time of the shooting. In time, the case also came to serve as a touchstone for wider issues, such as the condition of post-apartheid South Africa.[79]

Secondly, the episode revealed explicitly the artifice of celebrity coupledom. The pair's histories – individual and collective – were re-narrativized and revaluated in order to piece together theories about what had happened on the night of Steenkamp's death. Different accounts and new 'revelations' about, for instance, Oscar's alleged previous maltreatment of Reeva, and his love of guns – details that had not characterized his narrative before – were laid bare.[80]

Thirdly, the pre-existing cultural script of celebrity relationships, and the morality that underpins it, became explicit, in that modes of behaviour and character were judged openly in the public sphere, with the more distasteful discourses of celebrity coupledom became exaggerated and revealed as obviously problematic in its elaboration. The British tabloid the *Sun*, for example, felt it appropriate to report the story with a full-length picture of Steenkamp in a bikini on its front page alongside the headline: 'Valentine's Horror: 03.00: 3 Shots. Screams. Silence … 03:10: 3 more shots. Blade Runner Pistorius "Murders

Lover".[81] In 'normal' circumstances, as a model, her body would be her primary
value to tabloid press as the female part of the celebrity couple, something that
would go largely unnoticed and uncommented upon. In light of her death,
though, its value was simultaneously intensified and reduced: in terms of the
former, not only was the image meant to titillate, but it suggested that the fact
that she was beautiful made the crime worse than if it had involved a 'normal'
woman; in terms of the latter it reduced her value to being a good-looking
corpse.[82] In this process of the relationship's disintegration, the misogyny of the
culture simply could not be ignored.

Conclusion

This chapter has covered a lot of ground. In broad strokes, I have attempted to
set up some key categories of celebrity relationships while trying to be mindful
that there are significant overlaps and contradictions within and between them,
and recognizing that there is clearly much, much more to be said about both
the categories and the relationships I have offered as examples. I have attempted
to take into account aspects of the production of celebrity relationships, while
trying to make sense of the multiplicity of meanings and affective power attached
to these relationships. The best I can do at this point is to emphasize that I am
aware of the incompleteness of, for instance, trying to condense a reading of a
case such as Pistorius and Steenkamp into a few pages, and ask that the reader
consider these examples as gestural towards larger trends and the basis for
further examination.

The frame of this analysis has been historically and culturally specific, with
the focus being aimed at western media culture in the neoliberal context.
I have suggested that the discourse of celebrity relationships is structured by
pre-existing cultural assumptions and rules regarding aspects such as talent
and morality, and that some celebrity relationships are valued more than
others because of judgements about a mixture of their abilities and behaviour.
But let's be clear: capitalism at its core desires one thing above all – surplus
profit – and does not discriminate. Put bluntly, the media industries profit
financially from all types of celebrity relationships – good and bad, long and
short, whole and fragmented – and that the discourse underpinning this
culture is structured by judgements about talent and rectitude serves, first
of all, to reproduce the system economically. Star and celebrity relationships

have always been judged in these terms, and have always had the affective potential to stimulate a range of emotions, from sheer joy and awe to sadness and compassion. Perhaps the thing that makes their functions novel in the latest phase of capitalism, however, is that under neoliberalism celebrity relationships serve not only as fantasies of material wealth (which has always set stars apart), but as fantasies of happiness and companionship that conform to a script that is increasingly difficult to follow. In other words, celebrity relationships today act are vehicles of nostalgia not necessarily for a past world, but for a way of imagining the world that feels safe, comforting and appealing. Of course, the life narratives the parents of my students told their children were in the past not always realized, and following this cultural script was in no way a guarantee of economic success and emotional well-being (if counter-cultural history tells us anything, it is of the misery the system from which the script emerged created for untold numbers of marginalized men, women and children, no matter how much the post-war welfare state is romanticized today). However, this narrative of working hard to achieve the good life is now so well established in the collective imagination, through years of repetition in western media culture, that its fragmentation – as a result of the dissolution of institutions, rise of individualist ideology, and changes to the economic base – has engendered an anxiety about loneliness, isolation and broken dreams for the future that the emotional functions of celebrity relationships are well placed to assuage, albeit in myriad ways.

Acknowledgements

Thanks to my former students at Portsmouth, especially those who raised their hands. Thanks to Sean Redmond for planting a seed. And thanks, as ever, to Shelley Cobb.

Notes

1 Joshua Gamson, *Claims to Fame: Celebrity in Contemporary America* (Berkeley and Los Angeles: University of California Press, 1994), 171.

2 Lauren Berlant, *Cruel Optimism* (London and Durham, NC: Duke University Press, 2011), 2.

350 *First Comes Love*

3   Su Holmes and Sean Redmond, *Framing Celebrity: New Directions in Celebrity Culture* (London: Routledge, 2006), 2.

4   Richard Dyer, *Stars*, 2nd ed. (London: BFI, 1998), (orig. ed. 1979); *Heavenly Bodies: Film Stars and Society* (London: BFI/Macmillan, 1986).

5   Holmes and Redmond, *Framing Celebrity*, 3.

6   Richard Schickel, *Intimate Strangers: The Culture of Celebrity in America* (New York: Doubleday, 1985).

7   Cooper Lawrence, *The Cult of Celebrity: What Our Fascination With The Stars Reveals About Us* (Guildford, CT: Skirt!, 2009).

8   Chris Rojek, *Celebrity* (London: Reaktion, 2001); *Fame Attack: The Inflation of Celebrity and its Consequences* (London: Bloomsbury, 2012).

9   Graeme Turner, *Understanding Celebrity*, 2nd ed. (London: Sage, 2014).

10 There is a large and growing body of literature on, variously, the processes and/or affects of neoliberalism. See, for instance, Berlant, *Cruel Optimism*; Paul Mason, *Why It's Still Kicking Off Everywhere* (London: Verso, 2013); Richard Sennett, *The Culture of the New Capitalism* (New Haven: Yale University Press, 2006); David Graeber, *The Democracy Project: A History, a Crisis, a Movement* (London: Allen Lane, 2013); Philip Mirowski, *Never Let a Serious Crisis Go to Waste: How Neoliberalism Survived the Financial Meltdown* (London: Verso, 2014) and Will Davies, *The Limits of Neoliberalism: Authority, Sovereignty and the Logic of Competition* (London: Sage, 2014). A useful article by the Institute of Precarious Consciousness, 'Six Theses on Anxiety', argues that 'Each phase of capitalism has its own dominant reactive affect': 'In the modern era (until the post-war settlement), the dominant affect was *misery*. ... When misery stopped working as a control strategy, capitalism switched to boredom. ... In contemporary capitalism, the dominant reactive affect is *anxiety*.' See 'We Are All Very Anxious', weareplanc. org, http://www.weareplanc.org/we-are-all-very-anxious#f1. Christian Garland and Stephen Harper usefully question the value of the term 'neoliberalism' in media studies, in their article, 'Did Somebody Say Neoliberalism? On the Uses and Limitations of a Critical Concept in Media and Communication Studies', *tripleC* 10, no. 2 (2012): 413–24. While I am sympathetic in some ways to their argument that the term 'neoliberalism' offers little significant advance over the term 'capitalism' I tend to remain of the view that the former remains useful in describing both the period since the mid-1970s, and a logic that constitutes 'the death of the social', in the words of Henry Giroux, who explains: 'Neoliberalism' is a particular political and economic and social project that not only consolidates class power in the hands of the one per cent, but operates off the assumption that economics can divorce itself from social costs, that it doesn't have to deal with matters of ethical

and social responsibility'. See Michael Nevradakis, 'Henry Giroux on the Rise of Neoliberalism', *Truthout*, 19 October 2014, http://www.truth-out.org/opinion/item/26885-henry-giroux-on-the-rise-of-neoliberalism.

11 Mary Evans, 'Love in a time of neo-liberalism', Opendemocracy.net, 6 November 2014, https://www.opendemocracy.net/transformation/mary-evans/love-in-time-of-neo-liberalism.

12 In Gamson's influential formulation, fans were understood as engaging with their subjects across an 'axis of belief and disbelief', from traditional believers to postmodern sceptics. See Joshua Gamson, *Claims to Fame*, 149. See also Gray et al., eds, *Fandom: Identities and Communities in a Mediated World* (New York: New York University Press, 2007). My focus here is on the ways in which these relationships are positioned in the media and their affective functions. Clearly more work needs to be done of the relationships between different (groups of) fans and celebrity couples.

13 Rojek's influential model of 'ascribed', 'achieved' and 'attributed' celebrity is elaborated in *Celebrity*, while he theorises the 'celetoid' in *Fame Attack*.

14 Laura Kipnis, *Against Love: A Polemic* (New York: Vintage, 2004), 34–35.

15 Berlant, *Cruel Optimism*, 11.

16 Ibid., 13.

17 I am indebted here to Sean Redmond, who in his role as reader of this volume's proposal for the publisher suggested that material on what he called 'anti-star couples' would be a useful addition. This chapter forms my first tentative steps at formulating thoughts on this topic, one that is rich with possibility for future work.

18 These exercises were carried out in various lectures and seminars at the University of Portsmouth, UK, between 2012 and 2014. The examples are gestural and are not underpinned by a systematic collection of data.

19 It would be interesting to speculate about reasons for the consistency in the gender of volunteers to share willingly intimate details in this type of public setting. Angela McRobbie has suggested that young women are particularly hailed by postfeminist neoliberalism, in its invitation to 'come forward' and be 'visible' in the new economy by succeeding at school and in family planning, with the view to becoming productive citizens and the 'privileged subjects' of consumerism that is their reward. See Angela McRobbie, *The Aftermath of Feminism: Gender, Culture and Social Changes* (London: Sage, 2009); particularly ch. 3: 'Top Girls? Young Women and the New Sexual Contract'. There are clearly also myriad other factors involved in the dynamics of these classroom interactions that, alas, there is no room to discuss here. Some are clearly more tangible than others, but might include:

background of the students in terms of class, race, sexuality, etc; the tone and delivery of my performance as a teacher, the amount of 'trust' I managed to attain with the students; the 'mood' of the room; etc.

20 In September 2014 the average UK house price was £272,000. See Philip Inman, 'UK house prices hit new record as London average breaks £500,000', theguardian. com, 16 September 2014, http://www.theguardian.com/business/2014/sep/16/ house-prices-record-bubble-interest-rates-uk.

21 Andrew Ross, *Creditocracy: And The Case For Debt Refusal* (New York: OR Books, 2014).

22 David Harvey, *The Enigma of Capital and the Crises of Capitalism* (London: Profile Books, 2010); Paul Mason, *Why It's Still Kicking Off*.

23 Andrew Ross, *Nice Work If You Can Get It: Life and Labor in Precarious Times* (New York: New York University Press, 2009); Richard Sennett, *The Culture of the New Capitalism*.

24 Consumer website *which.co.uk* highlights the levels of savings required to secure a mortgage in the UK. For example: 'The cheapest mortgage deals on the market will typically require you to have a 40% deposit or more, so on a £150,000 property this would mean a deposit of £60,000'. Of course, buyers can get mortgages with smaller deposits, but on a punitive sliding scale in terms of interest on the amount lent. The website also points out that these amounts come before 'extra costs', such as 'legal fees' and 'land registry fees', which add up to many thousands of extra pounds up front. See http://www.which.co.uk/money/mortgages-and-property/guides/ mortgage-deposit-explained/how-much-deposit-do-i-need-for-a-mortgage/.

25 I should add that I attempt to make this process as cheerful as possible by pointing to myself, an adjunct lecturer, as being in the same boat as them, albeit a little further down the river.

26 One of the reasons I feel comfortable carrying out the exercise is precisely because of this awareness. If I thought the students were genuinely innocent to the realities of the world and the struggles that surely await them, I would be much more hesitant to broach the subject. It is precisely this widespread familiarity that makes it so productive as an exercise in that it is something to which almost everyone relates and has direct experience. In the era of media fragmentation and dispersal, there are increasingly fewer texts about which we can say the same.

27 See, for example: Julien Mercille, *The Political Economy and Media Coverage of the European Economic Crisis: The Case of Ireland* (London: Routledge, 2015), esp. ch. 3: 'The Crisis and the Role of the Media'. Mercille writes: 'In sum, the media have provided extensive support for economic and political elites' strategy of austerity. This does not mean that such messages are always absorbed uncritically

by the population, but nevertheless, they contribute to frame the debate in a way favourable to the government and private sector', 29.

28 I borrow the term 'coping mechanisms' and, later, 'drudgery of everyday life' from Melissa Gregg's brilliant essay on contemporary office culture, 'On Friday Night Drinks: Workplace Affects in the Age of the Cubicle', in *The Affect Theory Reader*, ed. Melissa Gregg and Gregory J. Seigworth (Durham, NC and London: Duke University Press, 2010), 250–68.

29 Sennett, *The Culture of the New Capitalism*.

30 Graeber, *The Democracy Project*, xix.

31 See Tom de Castella, 'Have young people never had it so bad?', *bbc.co.uk*, 5 February 2013, http://www.bbc.co.uk/news/magazine-21302065.

32 See, for example: Rosalind Gill, 'Rewriting the Romance: New Femininities in Chick Lit?', *Feminist Media Studies* 6, no. 4 (December 2006): 487–504; Diane Negra, *What a Girl Wants: Fantasizing the Reclamation of Self in Postfeminism* (London: Routledge, 2009).

33 Detailed figures for England and Wales can be found on the website of the Office for National Statistics, ons.gov.uk, http://www.ons.gov.uk/ons/rel/vsob1/divorces-in-england-and-wales/2011/index.html. Detailed figures for the US can be found on the website of the Centers for Disease Control and Prevention, cdc.gov, http://www.cdc.gov/nchs/fastats/marriage-divorce.htm. Both illustrate that the commonly cited figure of one in two marriages ending in divorce are roughly accurate.

34 Shelley Cobb, 'Ellen and Portia's Postfeminist Wedding', this volume.

35 See Eric Klinenberg, *Going Solo: The Extraordinary Rise and Surprising Appeal of Living Alone* (London: Duckworth, 2014).

36 See 'Large increase in 20 to 34-year-olds living with parents since 1996', ons. gov.uk, http://www.ons.gov.uk/ons/rel/family-demography/young-adults-living-with-parents/2013/sty-young-adults.html.

37 Angela McRobbie, 'Postfeminism and Popular Culture: Bridget Jones and the New Gender Regime', *Feminist Media Studies* 4, no. 3 (November 2004): 255–64.

38 Kipnis, *Against Love*, 33–34. See also Eva Illouz, *Cold Intimacies: The Making of Emotional Capitalism* (Cambridge: Polity, 2007).

39 Heteronormative versions of coupled life and the 'traditional' nuclear family have long been the subjects of detailed critiques from a variety of angles, and have animated such thinkers as Marx, Freud, and Deleuze and Guattari. Recent years have seen a growing body of literature that carries on this tradition, often in provocative fashion, including Kipnis' *Against Love* and Michael Cobb, *Single: Arguments for the Uncoupled* (New York: New York University Press, 2012). Cobb writes of the tyranny of 'a world slavishly devoted to the supremacy of the couple', 8.

40 Michael Cobb, *Single: Arguments for the Uncoupled* (New York: New York University Press, 2012), 17–18.

41 Jacqueline Rose, *States of Fantasy* (Oxford: Oxford University Press, 2006), 5.

42 Mark Sweney, 'MailOnline records 134m users in July', 5 August 2013, theguardian. com, http://www.theguardian.com/media/2013/aug/05/mail-online-royal-birth.

43 'MailOnline overtakes NY Times as top online newspaper', 26 January 2012, bbc. co.uk, http://www.bbc.co.uk/news/entertainment-arts-16743645.

44 Jemima Kiss, 'A new medium seeks old skills', *British Journalism Review* 25, no. 3 (2014): 33–38, http://bjr.org.uk/data/2014/no3_kiss; Henry Mance, 'MailOnline and the next page for the "sidebar of shame"', ft.com, 24 September 2014, http://www. ft.com/cms/s/0/cf2e53d2-425e-11e4-a9f4-00144feabdc0.html?siteedition=uk#axzz3 KvhkMmgK.

45 A Google search of 'Daily Mail Couples Die Together' reveals tens of examples from the last couple of years, including stories entitled: '"Close your eyes, I'm coming with you"': Devoted husband's last words to his dying wife – just hours before he died by her side of a broken heart'; 'Brazilian couple dies in the same hospital room just 40 minutes apart after 65 years of marriage'; 'Extraordinary love story of couple married for 72 years who died holding hands just an hour apart – and how wife's heartbeat kept her dead husband's heart monitor going', and 'Couple dies 16 hours apart after 76-year marriage that saw them "flirting until the end"'. To be fair, *MailOnline* is not the only publication in which these types of articles appear, though the extent of their repetition does suggest an obsession with this particular curiosity.

46 See Sofia Johansson, '"Sometimes you wanna hate celebrities": tabloid readers and celebrity coverage', in Holmes and Redmond, *Framing Celebrity*, 343–58. Johansson writes: 'the main reason for the social currency of tabloid celebrity stories is just this: they stimulate debates about fundamental moral and social issues, contributing to create an experience of community', 349.

47 Much feminist scholarship has shown that female celebrities are more closely scrutinized and more harshly criticized than their male counterparts. See, for example: Su Holmes and Diane Negra, eds, *In the Limelight and Under the Microscope: Forms and Functions of Female Celebrity* (New York: Continuum, 2011).

48 The difference between stars and celebrities is much debated in star and celebrity studies. Often, 'stardom' is defined by 'aura' and 'charisma' that eclipses the processes of fabrication that are front and centre in 'celebrity'. See, for example: John Potts, *A History of Charisma* (London: Palgrave Macmillan, 2009); and Ellis Cashmore, *Celebrity Culture*, 2nd ed. (London: Routledge, 2014).

49 Barry King, 'Stardom and symbolic degeneracy: Television and the transformation of the stars as public symbols', *Semiotica* 92, no. 1–2 (1992): 3.

50 Diane Negra, 'The Making, Unmaking and Re-making of *Robsten*', this volume.

51 See Steve Cross and Jo Littler, 'Celebrity and Schadenfreude', *Cultural Studies* 24, no. 3 (2010): 395–417.

52 Misha Kavka, *Reality TV* (Edinburgh: Edinburgh University Press, 2012), 9–10.

53 See Michael Williams, '"Gilbo-Garbage" or "The Champion Lovemakers of Two Nations": Uncoupling Greta Garbo and John Gilbert', in this volume.

54 See Beccy Collings, 'Audrey Hollander and Otto Bauer: The Perfect (Pornographic) Marriage', in this volume.

55 Even basing judgements in sports on empirical data is problematic. See Bill Shaikin, 'Not Everyone in Baseball Bought into "Moneyball"', latimes.com, 11 September 2011, http://articles.latimes.com/2011/sep/11/sports/la-sp-0912-money-ball-20110912.

56 Brooks Barnes, 'Angelina Jolie's Carefully Orchestrated Image', *The New York Times*, 20 November 2008.

57 Leslie Bennetts, 'The Unsinkable Jennifer Aniston', vanityfair.com, http://www.vanityfair.com/culture/features/2005/09/aniston200509.

58 Jo Littler, '"I Feel Your Pain": Cosmopolitan Charity and the Public Fashioning of the Celebrity Soul', *Social Semiotics* 18, no. 2 (2008): 237–51.

59 Diane Negra, 'The Fertile Valley of Celebrity: Brangelina', *The Velvet Light Trap* 65 (2010), http://muse.jhu.edu/journals/the_velvet_light_trap/v065/65.negra.html#fig01.

60 Andrew Morton, *The Beckhams* (London: Michael O'Mara Books, 2007).

61 David Goldblatt, *The Game of Their Lives: The Meaning and Making of English Football* (London: Viking, 2014).

62 Garry Whannel, *Media Sport Stars: Masculinities and Moralities* (London: Routledge, 2002).

63 See, for example: Ellis Cashmore, *Beckham*, 2nd ed. (Cambridge, MA: Polity, 2004).

64 The term 'WAG' originated in the mid-2000s and initially described the wives and girlfriends of sportsmen, usually soccer players, in the UK. It has since exceeded this context and is commonly used to describe 'supportive' women in fields from sports to politics and everything in between. My co-authored conference paper with Shelley Cobb, delivered at the Celebrity Studies 2014 biennial conference, is currently in production as an article. See the abstract: Cobb and Ewen, 'Behind Every Man? The Value of the Celebrity WAG in Western Media Culture', academia.edu, https://www.academia.edu/5377639/Behind_Every_Man_The_Value_of_the_Celebrity_WAG_in_Western_Media_Culture.

65   Andrew Morton, *Posh & Becks* (London: Michael O'Mara, 2000).

66   I use this word advisedly. Victoria had long fashioned, and had fashioned for her, an image based on upward class mobility and royalty: in the Spice Girls, her nickname was 'Posh Spice'; on their wedding day she and David (in)famously sat on thrones and she adorned a crown; and as I have already pointed to, the British media christened her 'Queen of the WAGs'. Morton's involvement in telling their story did this image no harm either: he made his name as a biographer of Diana, Princess of Wales back in the 1990s.

67   Morton, *The Beckhams*, 286.

68   'Victoria Beckham Wins Fashion Award, *stylist.com*, 2011, http://www.stylist.co.uk/ fashion/victoria-beckham-wins-fashion-award.

69   Blake Morrison, 'David Beckham: Icons of the Decade', *Guardian*, 22 December 2009.

70   Zygmunt Bauman, *Liquid Love* (Cambridge, MA: Polity, 2003).

71   Creating an image based on morality is a dangerous game; one that Freudian critics might suggest is bound to fail eventually. Jacqueline Rose writes: 'If moralism backfires, it is not just for reasons of hypocrisy, but because the law, in order to be effective, has to draw on pleasure; the more intense the moral fervour, the greater the sexual charge that is *already there*. It was one of Freud's most valuable insights to stress that moral conscience can only work by drawing on the very energies it is trying to tame (where else could they go?). Which means that morality, not only but especially in the sexual field, has a stunning propensity to defeat itself.' Jacqueline Rose, *States of Fantasy*, 57.

72   Sean Redmond writes about individual celebrity breakdown in terms of 'fame damage' as 'a potent form of identification and an increasingly common way of stars and celebrities to be produced and consumed'. This informs my work here on the fragmentation of celebrity relationships. Sean Redmond, 'Intimate Fame Everywhere', in Holmes and Redmond, *Framing Celebrity*, 27–46.

73   These affects and emotions are also to a large degree subjective, and, of course, highly variable.

74   Work on this would have to take into account Rojek's writing on transgressive celebrity. See Rojek, *Celebrity*.

75   David Schmid, 'Idols of Destruction: Celebrity and the Serial Killer', in Holmes and Redmond, *Framing Celebrity*, 295–310.

76   cf. my earlier comment about celebrity couples as media texts: the Pistorius/ Steenkamp case serves to remind us that behind the mediation of celebrity always lays a real person. As such, I want to acknowledge that while I find this tragedy fascinating in many ways, I remain mindful that a real woman lost her life and

her family and friends suffered a terrible loss. This was something not always acknowledged by the media in discussing it as a 'case' or a 'text': Suzanne Moore, for instance, took to task, among others, her fellow *Guardian* columnist Simon Jenkins for writing an entire commentary without mentioning Reeva Steenkamp's name once, something Moore understood, rightly, as symptomatic of the misogyny in the coverage of the case. Suzanne Moore, 'Reeva Steenkamp was the Victim of Male Violence. That is the Real Story', theguardian.com, 22 October 2014, http://www. theguardian.com/commentisfree/2014/oct/22/discussion-of-reeva-steenkamp-killing-has-sidelined-male-violence. The trending #HerNameWasReeva served the same purpose across social media platforms.

77 'Oscar Pistorius biography', biography.com, 19 December 2014, http://www. biography.com/people/oscar-pistorius-20910935.

78 Sarah Lyall, 'Apologetic and Sobbing, Pistorius Testifies He Killed His Girlfriend By Mistake', NYTimes.com, 7 April 2014, http://nyti.ms/1hSs3Lq.

79 Margie Orford, 'Heart of Oscar's Defence: Imagined Threat of a Black Stranger', *Daily Maverick*, 4 April 2014, http://www.dailymaverick.co.za/article/2014-03-03-heart-of-oscars-defence-imagined-threat-of-a-black-stranger#.Uz8xpCi9x20; Ché Ramsden, 'Oscar Pistorius: The South African Story', opendemocracy.net, 12 September 2014, https://www.opendemocracy.net/5050/ché-ramsden/oscar-pistorius-south-african-story.

80 Amy Davidson, 'Oscar Pistorius's Trigger', *The New Yorker*, 11 April 2014.

81 February 2013.

82 Suzanne Moore called the *Sun*'s front page 'lechery over a corpse'. See Roy Greenslade, 'The Sun's Oscar Pistorius Front Page: "Lechery Over a Corpse"', theguardian.com, 15 February 2013, http://www.theguardian.com/media/greenslade/2013/feb/15/sun-oscar-pistorius.

Index